"I'm reading *Get It On* an[...]
It's my perfect [...]
Josh Wid[...]

"You always know you're going to get a fascinating read from
Spurling, but this is his most vivid book yet – sheer joy! For us old
geezers it's like being miraculously transported back to the 1970s.
And for younger readers I can promise you quite an education."
Patrick Barclay

"It's all here – the swagger, success and excess of '70s football plus
how that tumultuous ten years truly gave birth to the modern era.
This is far more than a brilliant evocation of a game-changing
decade for football – it's also a superb summary of the ch-ch-ch-
changes Britain saw in the '70s – from glam rock to punk,
from Harold Wilson to Margaret Thatcher."
Paul Ross, talkSPORT

"A fascinating, funny and poignant stroll down memory lane of an
era that shaped the modern game. The '70s was the decade when
English football went pop. It exploded. Football went from
black and white to colour."
Henry Winter

"Jon Spurling is a superb navigator through those memories,
recalling the times without hint of rose-coloured spectacles …
Here are original, never-heard-before accounts. It is like the most
poignant literary seance, our lost heroes apparently addressing
us from beyond the grave."
Jim White, *Mail on Sunday*

"Jon Spurling's brilliant, non-judgemental, superbly researched and anecdote-laden book is a wonderful telling of when football and all those involved in it were dragged out of the footballing dark ages of the 1960s and into the money-fuelled and fame-filled combination of excess and success that it has become today."

Guillem Balagué

"Bringing football history to vibrant life is Jon Spurling's gift – and it is also a gift to the reader. He transports us back to a time when the mavericks and marvels challenged convention during the 1970s. It was a fascinating period of old meeting new in the game's evolution and Spurling's storytelling, insights and eye for character and social context shine through."

Amy Lawrence

"*Get It On* is the superbly told story of the decade when football became flash. It has a cast to die for – from Big Mal to Old Big 'Ead, through Bestie, Bowles and the Doc. You can smell the Brut and taste the Watneys Party Seven. A brilliant history of footballers you thought you knew but didn't."

Tim Rich, author of *The Quality of Madness: A Life of Marcelo Bielsa*

"A wonderfully evocative portrait of an incredible decade for English football. It pulls together cultural history seamlessly and brings to life the major characters from the era."

Michael Cox, author of *Zonal Marking: The Making of Modern European Football*

"The big teams, events and personalities, and intriguing new angles on familiar tales … Many of the key figures are no longer with us, but the indefatigable Spurling tracked down many of them and recorded their memories before they left."

David Winner, author of *Brilliant Orange:*
The Neurotic Genius of Dutch Football

"Cracking tales from the terraces amid betrayal in the boardrooms."

Tim Marshall, author of *"Dirty Northern B*st*rds!" and Other Tales*
from the Terraces: The Story of Britain's Football Chants

"Wonderfully nostalgic."

***Choice* magazine**

"Gripping, rich in anecdotes."

11 Freunde

GET IT ON

HOW THE '70s ROCKED FOOTBALL

JON SPURLING

Biteback Publishing

For the Spurls girls xxx

'Have you seen 'em? Prancing round the field like a bunch of male models, kissing and cuddling? In my day when you scored a goal you got a brisk handshake. Now you get covered in love bites.'

RUPERT RIGSBY, *RISING DAMP*

'The air is rancid with beer and onions and belching and worse. The language is a gross purple of obscenity.'

ARTHUR HOPCRAFT ON FOOTBALL GROUNDS
IN *THE FOOTBALL MAN*, 1968

'One time, I had a great night in the casino, cashed in all my chips, shoved my winnings into a paper bag and next morning walked straight to a car showroom where I bought a brand new Jag. In cash. Now that's not a normal thing to do...'

GEORGE BEST, SPEAKING IN 2004

CONTENTS

FOREWORD

How could a tale have been better told?

This is the story of how football's place in life developed and its influence grew, how its players became heroes and the best of them stars of society.

For the older and middle generation there is a myriad of memories on offer; for the younger, who, perhaps, may have been persuaded that football only really began in the early '90s when it reached for the Sky, there is a chance of enlightenment.

The cast list is amazing and the research matches it. The quality of interviewing is exceptional and the stories tumble out into a narrative skilfully guided by the author to show the many big names in a true light, if not always a complimentary one.

Rarely has a book grabbed my attention so quickly – I was immediately back in the unscheduled scrap between ITV and the BBC which I had been a part of on Cup final day at Wembley in 1969, when I worked for the former. Then the story moves on to involve some of my friends, such as John Bromley and Brian Moore, and the ITV World Cup panel.

After four years with ITV, including the 1966 World Cup, the first season of the '70s found me as one of the regular commentators on the BBC's *Match of the Day*. The show broadcast recorded matches but there were no replays. Slow motion was added when the match was edited so we called it as we saw it – changes to this approach were still a long way off.

In *Get It On*, there is much to take in about how commercialism changed the game, how Terry O'Neill's photography played its part and the arrival of new kits. A fascinating chapter sets Sir Alf Ramsey's failure and character in Mexico '70 against the two men vying to be Prime Minister: Harold Wilson and Ted Heath.

There is comparison of the Brian Clough and Peter Taylor axis at Derby with their partnership at Nottingham Forest and the different approaches of Bill Shankly and Bob Paisley at Liverpool. The chapter about George Best is a gem. The joys of the FA Cup upset begin in Hereford and end with Blyth Spartans and a place is found too for the now larger-than-life referees who, at that time, knew their whistle was the law.

With suggestions as to why the most successful club manager Don Revie failed so completely when he took charge of England and then the changing faces on the field and the hooligan problem off it, *Get It On* ends with perhaps '70s football's most dominant personality, Brian Clough, ruling Europe, a reference to the 1979 election and a glimpse of the troubled '80s.

If I may borrow one of the great David Coleman's favoured commentary lines, I found the book 'quite remarkable'.

Barry Davies

INTRODUCTION

Get It On is a book about 1970s football and some of its prime movers and shakers, cult figures and accidental heroes. Several of them were inadvertently sucked into a maelstrom of publicity, breaking new ground and making a name for themselves purely by chance. Others were charismatic, media-savvy, sideburn-clad, cigar-smoking, champagne-swilling, upwardly mobile chat show guests who became household names as the era of colour television began. As well as being about the game itself, this book is also about the politics, the popular culture and the events of the era. These different strands are interconnected, because, as much as football was shaped by that which swirled around it, the national game in the '70s also defined the timbre of the era.

The book doesn't focus specifically on results and seasons and who went up or down. Neither is it a paean to '70s football, which at its best was uplifting, unifying, inventive and touchingly innocent, but which could also be brutal, bullying, thuggish and ugly. I don't hold with the view that the game in the '70s deserves to be labelled as 'the good old days'. But it was certainly far less moneyed, gleaming (or antiseptic, depending on your perspective) and overblown than the top level of the game today, with clubs and stadia planted firmly in local communities. And that, I suppose, is at the root of its ongoing appeal. *Get It On* is also about the texture of football back then, in all its unvarnished, mud-splattered 'glory', told by those who shaped the game, on and off the pitch. Inevitably, it's partly skewed by whom I've spoken to and the fact that, in some cases, I've picked and chosen topics and slants which fit in with my personal interests. So, there's plenty on the FA Cup and TV coverage, the oratory of Clough, Shankly and Paisley and the philosophies lying behind the great teams of the time. Along the way, please also forgive the gratuitous references to obscure '70s football songs, Hugh Johns's and Barry Davies's commentaries and *Porridge*. I haven't always felt constrained to stick to a precise ten-year period as there is a great deal of continuity flowing from the late '60s into the '70s, and several key figures like Jimmy Hill and Sir Alf Ramsey – as is reflected in the text – forged their reputations in the earlier decade. I've deliberately left some stories which straddle the '70s and '80s, including George Best's last hurrah in the North American Soccer League, to an '80s follow-up to this book.

English football in the '70s was a kaleidoscope of drama, innovation, opportunity, controversy, tragedy, melodrama and slapstick. It remains the most cutting edge of all football decades, blazing a trail for what followed, and this is reflected in the burgeoning TV coverage of the time. *Match of the Day* and *The Big Match* drew huge audiences each week during the '70s. TV outlets dispatched their bloodhound news reporters to source the biggest stories of the day, on and off the pitch. Leading managers and players were in demand to appear as guests on TV chat shows and were the subject of documentaries, which meant that viewers were given unprecedented insight into the lives of the superstars of the day, such as Clough, Best, Revie, Shankly, Allison, Docherty and Paisley. It was the first 'modern' football decade, despite often being lampooned and scoffed at, and it set in place much of what is now part and parcel of the game, including sponsorship, TV punditry and football 'personalities'.

Like many areas of '70s TV, fashion and music, not all aspects of football in that era have aged well. Some of the play – by modern standards – appears clunky and cumbersome, the interviews are often cringe-making and insufferable and much of what passed for humour and '70s 'banter' is dated and toe-curling. But the unreconstructed nature of players' and managers' utterings – though jarring when seen or heard fifty years later – are an intrinsic part of the social fabric of the time. There is a danger, as the pre-1992 era recedes into history, that the game in the '70s is reduced to a varnished selection of YouTube clips, a clutch of tales and bon mots handed down via the after-dinner speaking circuit or, worse, written out entirely. I hope that *Get It On* goes some way to redressing the balance.

I've always been fascinated by the history and football of the '70s. As a child, I'd watched the FA Cup finals, the European Cup finals and the 1978 World Cup final (amongst the very few live games broadcast at that time) at the tail end of the decade, and throughout school, university and as a teacher and a football writer, I've spent countless hours thinking, teaching and writing about the period. My twenty-five years of freelancing meant I'd interviewed a large number of figures from the era, so I'd long mooted the possibility of writing a book like this. Jimmy Hill, Tommy Docherty and George Best (especially) were initially wary and asked whom I was working for when I approached them. They visibly relaxed when I told them I was a freelancer with a long-term 1970s book project in mind, and that enabled me to go a little more left of field with some of my questions, although Jack Charlton reckoned I was a 'cheeky bugger' when I pushed things a little too far.

Like several '70s managers, I discovered that the challenge was moulding the individual flair which resonated from my conversations with the likes of Best and Stan Bowles around a coherent and workable structure. A number of random occurrences helped nudge me in the right direction. A few years back, I visited the former '70s referee-turned-artist Gordon Hill in his Exeter studio. The ex-headmaster generously agreed to give me an hour of his time, but, when I arrived, he quite reasonably enquired why I wished to speak to him. I told him that it was for a 1970s football book I was planning. 'You mean you haven't started it yet?' he asked. When I told him that I hadn't really got beyond the pondering stage, he suggested I take a leaf out of his book and apply his artistic philosophy of 'taking a line for a walk' to writing. On days when Hill lacked inspiration, he'd place his pencil on a piece of paper and see which direction it took him in. On the train home, I did just that (with a pen) and started scribbling down phrases and paragraphs which sprang to mind. It worked. And so, very slowly, the plan evolved into a series of semi-connected pieces on the era.

By New Year's Eve 2019, I'd pulled together an overall synopsis for the book which, as it turned out, changed hugely in the intervening period. I sounded out my friend Seb, with whom I'd spent an inordinate amount of time watching and rewatching numerous long-lost VHS football classics at university. Was this book – I asked him as we sipped glasses of Cabernet Sauvignon from Ian Botham's wine range – likely to appeal to football fans? I knew that Seb, given his encyclopaedic knowledge of sport and his ability to repeat decades-old football commentaries verbatim, would give me an honest answer. He answered in the affirmative and even made a few constructive observations about the structure of the book. Or at least I think he did. That Ian Botham wine was quite potent.

Then, on 17 April 2020, I turned fifty and vowed to myself that, having hit the half-tonne, and with lockdown stretching out ahead of me, it was an opportune time to bring my project to fruition.

Television channels had unlocked their archives and were broadcasting hours and hours of retro football in the absence of any live matches. '70s football was all the rage. The time would never be more ripe. First of all, though, I needed to clear some clutter in my study and gather my interviews and cuttings and scribblings together. Whilst sorting out a shelf, I dislodged the hardback copy of Norman Hunter's autobiography and, as it clattered to the floor, the sharp end scraped me right down my shin. The former Leeds United hardman, who'd sadly passed away the day before, still lived up to his 'Bites Yer Legs' nickname. More than that, he'd lacerated the notes I'd made during my interview with George Best back in 2004, lying on the floor below. Taking it as a symbolic event, and one at which both men would no doubt have had a good chortle, I finally got stuck into the writing.

Enjoy the book. I hope it takes you back there.

Jon Spurling
January 2022

1

THE PANEL

'Listen, you're not addressing the House of Lords. Just talk
to Fred and Freda down there in Dorking.'
ITV's head of sport, John Bromley, to ITV's World Cup panel, June 1970

Wembley, May 1969. Perched high up in the stands, BBC match
director Alec Weeks spots the ambush. Disguised in light-blue tracksuits and brandishing microphones, a squadron of ITV reporters
are moving with purpose towards the victorious Manchester City
players, following their victory over Leicester City in the FA Cup
final. They've been sitting incognito behind the manager's dugout
all game, biding their time. The camouflaged ITV matchday team
– wearing the same tracksuits as Manchester City's substitutes –
muscle in on their rivals' turf. 'Move in. Stop these bastards. Use
whatever means possible,' Alec Weeks instructs his crew. A free-
for-all ensues. Punches are thrown. Kicks are aimed. Camera lenses
are smashed. Microphone cords are pulled out. ITV floor manager
David Yallop loses a tooth. Newspaper journalist Ken Jones, working for the BBC that day, receives a torrent of threats when he stops
ITV rivals making a beeline towards City's matchwinner Neil Young.

Prior to what commentator Barry Davies, poised to move from
ITV to BBC, will later call 'the punch-up final', City coach Malcolm

1

Allison, recently signed up by ITV, had craftily smuggled the track-suits into Wembley in a wheelie bin. Jimmy Hill, head of sport at London Weekend Television (LWT), insists, 'We had a non-exclusive contract with both teams.' As it turns out, the BBC's exclusivity extended only to interviewing players *prior* to the match, so ITV were technically within their rights to carry out their covert operations. Noticing how irked the BBC were by the sheer effrontery of their commercial rivals, and with the 1970 Mexico World Cup on the horizon, Hill and LWT controller John Bromley start to hatch a plan that will further up the ante. The result will be the flashy and flamboyant ITV World Cup panel that will transform the public profile of football and footballers for good.

It's a stretch to claim that the television pundit panel was *solely* the brainchild of Hill and Bromley, as has often been claimed. Rather, the pair dragged the concept kicking and screaming into the '70s, making it brasher and edgier than the '60s version, akin to a modish David Bowie mutating into the garish Ziggy Stardust. In 1966, Hill had been part of the BBC's World Cup team, offering insight after England matches. Suited and booted, he appeared alongside established figures, including Manchester City boss Joe Mercer, West Ham coach Ron Greenwood, Billy Wright, recently fired as Arsenal boss, and former referee Ken Aston, whose brainchild – red and yellow cards – would be used for the first time at the Mexico World Cup four years later. Presenter David Coleman oversaw proceedings.

Whilst the other panellists trotted out platitudes and clichés, Hill – with his goatee beard and Brylcreemed hair (in his playing days with Fulham and England he'd been nicknamed the 'Beatnik with a Ball') – got straight to the point. Honing in on Jimmy

Greaves's lacklustre show during England's 2–0 win over Mexico, Hill pre-empted Geoff Hurst's dramatic entry into the team in the quarter-final against Argentina: 'I feel that a Greaves or a Hunt should be a taller man, and very good in the air, because with packed defences this is one of the ways you can get goals against them even if they crowd you.' Hill had an intrinsic skill for delivering the perfect 'soundbite'. He'd perfected the art as chairman of the Professional Footballers' Association (PFA), when, in the white glare of publicity, he successfully campaigned to eradicate the Football League's £20-a-week maximum wage in 1961. Hill, who retired as a player that same year, might have missed out on the rising salaries he helped to secure, but as Coventry City manager he demonstrated an insatiable appetite for innovation and self-publicity, which was making him a wealthy man as he entered his forties. He rebranded the up-and-coming Division Three club, changing their kits from white to sky-blue and introduced the Sky-Blue Express to shuttle Coventry fans to away matches. With Britain's first sports agent, Bagenal Harvey, pulling various strings on Hill's behalf, the former player landed a *News of the World* column and crammed in as many TV appearances, photo opportunities and after-dinner speaking engagements as he could. I interviewed Hill in 2000, a year after he'd moved to Sky to front *Jimmy Hill's Sunday Supplement*. Genial and twinkly eyed, Hill argued, 'Footballers like me who played in the era of the maximum wage were expected to be shrinking violets and speak when spoken to. I never subscribed to that. There was a world of opportunity out there.' After informing me that after a quick measure-up at a recent charity do, Ronnie Corbett had judged that Bruce Forsyth's chin was definitely more protruding than Hill's (I didn't actually ask him), he clapped his hands excitedly and explained how his stint as Coventry boss shaped his thinking on the game, 'Imagination was needed to keep football fresh for the public. We introduced a pop-and-crisps day and autograph-signing days to get the kids to come to Highfield Road. I co-wrote the "Sky Blue Song" with a journalist friend of mine.' Hill even boomed out a few bars with serious gusto:

> Let's all sing together
> Play up sky blues
> While we sing together
> We will never lose.

Touchingly, he welled up at the end of the verse. 'Some people described me as a gimmick merchant. I viewed myself as an innovator.'

After steering Coventry to their inaugural top-flight season in 1967, Hill stepped down and accepted a job at the fledgling London Weekend Television. It was there that he met John Bromley, whom Hill described to me as 'a kindred spirit, a man who had a sixth and seventh sense for what would and wouldn't fly on TV'. Bromley had been a tabloid journalist before making the move into television; he didn't waffle or mince his words and was willing to go with his gut instinct. He was the first editor of ITV's Saturday afternoon *World of Sport*, which went on the air for the first time in January 1965, an experience he later described as 'Blind leading the blind, darling. We had no clue what we were doing.' Yet audiences proved amenable to cliff diving in Acapulco, log rolling and professional wrestling. Hill poached Brian Moore from BBC radio to front LWT's new football highlights show *The Big Match*, and Anglia TV's Bob Cardam to produce it. Hill worked as a match analyst alongside Moore. Broadcast on a Sunday, Keith Mansfield's 'The Young Scene' theme tune, with jazzy trumpets and clattering drums, arrived like a bolt from the blue, and Hill was a revelation. 'In the late '60s and early '70s, there wasn't anyone to touch him when it came to analysis of matches. He knew exactly what to say and how to say it,' explained Barry Davies. John Bromley was highly impressed, particularly with Bob Cardam's ability to persuade the great and the good in London football to be interviewed on the show. Although *The Big Match* wasn't broadcast in all regions, Bromley was keen to pull the best elements of the show into the network's coverage of the 1970 World Cup.

Jimmy Hill claimed that the final decision to run with 'the panel' for the tournament coverage wasn't taken until May 1970, and that the idea took shape following a dinner between himself, Bromley and agent Bagenal Harvey:

> Bagenal predicted that the profile of footballers would grow in the '70s, and that ITV should be at the vanguard of that. Plus we could ruffle a few feathers at the BBC. John Bromley and I looked at each other and nodded. The idea of the World Cup panel now became more obvious, although John only went with it very late in the day.

Harvey's comments touched a nerve with Bromley. After the launch of *World of Sport* in 1965, the BBC's David Coleman had predicted that 'it will be blown out of the water within six months'. As Jimmy Hill recalled, 'We always knew that we'd have to do something different to rival them [the BBC] because they were so established.' It helped Bromley and Hill that, in announcing its team for Mexico in the spring, the BBC had shown its hand slightly early. Out in the broiling heat alongside Coleman would be Leeds manager Don Revie (minus his sheepskin coat), Joe Mercer (still Manchester City boss and without his trilby) and Arsenal supremo Bertie Mee. Studio guests included Coventry boss Noel Cantwell, Liverpool's Ian St John, Arsenal's Bob Wilson, '66 hero Ray Wilson (now sporting a mullet), Fulham hero Johnny Haynes and former Arsenal and Wales defender Wally Barnes. Plus one Brian Clough, whose Derby County side was making a splash in the top flight. 'With Don Revie and Joe Mercer out there with David [Coleman], we thought that was a typical safe BBC move,' explained Hill, 'but their studio mix was more interesting, given the fact that Bob [Wilson] and Ian [St John] were still playing, and that Brian Clough was already gaining a reputation for plain speaking, shall we say. At ITV, we needed to go further.'

The other matter that Bagenal Harvey alluded to was the need to grab the small, but burgeoning, colour TV audience. By 1970, the Hills were one of a privileged 160,000 families to own their own colour TV set, which cost a tidy £362, plus a £10 annual colour TV licence ('a damned fortune back then', Hill complained). There had been a surge in sales shortly before the July '69 moon landings. Another 500,000 colour sets were rented out by Radio Rentals. The majority of the population would therefore be watching the World Cup on an estimated 8.5 million black and white sets, but 'whatever we did needed to be eye-catching', Hill explained.

Commentator Brian Moore was informed that he would anchor ITV's coverage from the London studio. Malcolm Allison – another Bagenal Harvey client – was the first pundit to be snapped up. Seen as the tactical mastermind behind Manchester City's dramatic rise to prominence in the late '60s (City won the League in 1968, the FA Cup in 1969 and both the League Cup and the UEFA Cup Winners' Cup in 1970), Allison was already much sought after by the media for his forthright and lively comments and, as well as penning a couple of newspaper columns, he had also written a cerebral book entitled *Soccer For Thinkers*. 'Malcolm was perfect for TV', explained Jimmy Hill, 'because he knew how to put his point across without waffling on too much. And he liked to stir things up.' Next on board was Derek Dougan, the highly articulate and charismatic Wolves striker. He was hardly averse to courting publicity – he'd handed in a transfer request the day before playing for Blackburn Rovers in the 1960 FA Cup final ('vanity triumphed over common sense', he later admitted) and alienated plenty of teammates at Portsmouth and Wolves with what he insisted was 'constructive criticism' in the dressing room. 'At the core of the panel's strength,' explained Jimmy Hill, 'was the fact that Malcolm and Derek sparked off one another. Malcolm wound up Derek and Derek would always bite. Towards the end of the tournament, I suggested to Mal that he bring a fish hook into the studio and be done with it.'

Dougan and Allison were joined by Manchester United's Pat Crerand, who was as spiky and direct as his midfield play for the Red Devils and, very late in the day, Arsenal full-back Bob McNab, who'd recently flown home from Mexico after Alf Ramsey trimmed his 28-man squad down to twenty-two. Having recently been in Ramsey's circle, McNab provided particular insight when it came to the mindset of the England players. Shortly before the tournament began, Hill and Bromley met with Allison, Crerand, Dougan and McNab and informed them that, rather than operate as individual pundits, they would morph into a 'panel' of experts. 'John Bromley was very clear about his expectations when we met with the four chaps.' recalled Hill.

'Talk to each other like you're football men, not stuffed shirts,' he said. He wanted a contrast with the 'suited and booted' BBC but insisted on sartorial elegance when it came to evening matches. The boys took him at his word. When we aired for the opening match between Mexico and the USSR, I don't think any of us thought the whole thing would fly quite as well as it did.

Over half a century later, it's almost impossible to imagine what it was like to see colour TV for the first time. 'When I first caught sight of myself,' recalled Hill, 'I was quite alarmed. The colours in those days were very garish. I looked like I had terribly high blood pressure. But the "wow" factor of colour was amazing. We wanted our coverage in 1970 to have a carnival feel to it.' ITV's opening credits had the feel of a fiesta, with whistles and bands incorporated into the theme tune. The programme used (perhaps not coincidentally) a new triple-stroke rounded sans-serif font – not unlike the typeface of sportswear manufacturers adidas. Footage showed coloured balloons being released, bands marching and monstrous crowds in the giant Azteca Stadium. For the privileged few, a kaleidoscope of colours poured into their living room from their screens. Whether it was Brazil's golden shirts dazzling, the baize-green pitches blazing or England's white shirts shining, Mexico '70 provided a sensory overload.

Throw in the omnipresent midday heat haze and the fact the satellite link caused the commentators' words to hiss constantly, viewers knew that they were watching football from a long, long way away. From another planet, almost. In the weeks leading up to the World Cup, President Richard Nixon expressed his hope that, by 2050, the USA might have 'sent a man to Mars', and Rupert Murdoch, who'd recently purchased the *News of the World*, predicted that the proliferation of satellites in space would revolutionise TV by the end of the twentieth century. Everyone, it seemed, was looking to the stars, whether in the sky above their heads or on the screen in their living rooms.

In the London Weekend Television studio, the commercial up-starts got their presentation spot on. The wall behind the panel had Aztec style writing on it and the pale-orange backdrop gave the appearance of a Mexican sunset. The panellists' clothes were also eye-catching. Stylists told them to avoid wearing the same colour T-shirts. Bob McNab favoured an orange number, Pat Crerand red and Malcolm Allison City sky-blue. Brian Moore usually wore a suit – often with a yellow shirt – and then there was Jimmy Hill, looking dapper in his custom-made silk neckerchiefs. For the showpiece matches and the England games they were clad in floral kipper ties, bright shirts and loud jackets. 'Malcolm Allison – puffing on his Cuban cigar – looked like a million dollars,' recalled a smiling Brian Moore, when I interviewed him shortly before he travelled to France to commentate on his final World Cup tournament in 1998, 'which was the image he wished to convey, of course.'

Moore had quickly overcome his initial annoyance that he wouldn't be travelling to Mexico to commentate. Exuding almost zen-like calm, which enabled him to keep order in the studio, Moore refereed conversations between the preening peacock panellists before, during the half-time break and after the matches. The 'banter' was as vivid and colourful as the clothing. This might have had something to do with the large amounts of alcohol consumed (mainly by Allison) for the duration of the tournament. The panellists stayed at the iconic Hendon Hall Hotel near Wembley Stadium, where England's 1966 World Cup winners had been holed up four years earlier. The sixteenth-century mansion, with its imposing four-pillared frontage, was beautifully decorated and its well-stocked wine cellar was the envy of oenophiles everywhere. Thanks to Allison's love of holding court there, he racked up a hefty bar bill. ITV happily paid up because, as Hill said, 'The network was so thrilled with the impact the panel had made.'

With its disparate range of nicknamed characters – 'Mal', 'Paddy', 'Doog' and 'Nabbers' – the vibe which emanated from the panel was that of a slimmed-down dressing room. Allison – all Cockney bravado – was the talismanic leader of the pack, with Paddy Crerand snapping like a terrier if the others disagreed with him. Derek Dougan was frequently the butt of Crerand's and Allison's jokes and Bob McNab often appeared to struggle to get a word in edgeways. Jimmy Hill dipped in and out of proceedings as the mild-mannered, pipe-smoking Brian Moore extracted nuggets of sense from what could have been an ill-disciplined rabble. 'It helped that it was commercial TV,' Moore told me, 'because it meant that time was of the essence before we had to cut to adverts. Otherwise, it would have been a free-for-all.' Moore paused for a moment, closed his eyes, inhaled through his nose and smiled, 'The studio reeked of early '70s male ego. There was cigar smoke, the blended scents of Mal's and Derek's exotic aftershaves and the whiff of spirits from Mal. Intoxicating.'

Each member of the panel was paid £500 that summer. The group had a youthful feel. At forty-two, Allison was the oldest and McNab was by some distance, at twenty-six, the youngest. Apart from the lack of swearing, and the absence of any fisticuffs, the way the panel behaved showed the public how footballers actually interacted. Sarcastic and cutting, the panel's alpha males jostled to be top dogs. Allison could be massively patronising when the mood took him. On one occasion, he blew cigar smoke in Derek Dougan's face, saying, 'Doog, you're wearing your Sunday best, but you're stealing all my best lines, baby.' The criticism (particularly of Dougan) could be caustic and swingeing. Towards the end of the tournament, the others rounded on him when he claimed that Brazil forward Jairzinho (who scored in every match) was his player of the tournament. 'For God's sake,' barked an apoplectic Allison. 'Have you never heard of this bloke Pelé?' Pat Crerand later explained that he believed the success of the panel was down to the fact that 'the public identified with it all, because they realised that this was how they and their pals all spoke down the pub on a Saturday night'.

On occasion, the panellists stirred up controversy. Malcolm Allison referred to the Soviet and Romanian players as 'peasants', which saw the ITV switchboard jammed with complaints. As Jimmy Hill recalled, 'Mal would say things like that to get a reaction, but after a few glasses of champagne, the outlandish seems normal.' The panellists also touched upon issues which would soon dominate the media agenda in the 1970s. Jimmy Hill took issue with Alf Ramsey's substitution of Bobby Charlton against West Germany in the quarter-final with England 2–0 up, after which Franz Beckenbauer took a pivotal role as his side fought back to win 3–2 after extra time. 'I think this was early proof that Alf wasn't adept or clever with substitutions,' explained Hill. Pat Crerand insisted that the English game had regressed tactically since Ramsey's men won the World Cup in 1966. But the tone was never mutinous. In the studio, Brian Moore asked the panel whether Ramsey would go on to face more battles in Munich in 1974. For the first time, perhaps, the pundits were slightly evasive. 'He's [Ramsey's] taken it very well,' said Jimmy Hill. Moore raised a concern that Ramsey was seen as a bit of a loner. Allison responded, 'A loner is a man who'll take all the credit and all the flak... he's an independent man... a great man.' Mindful that Bob McNab, still angling for a spot in Ramsey's post-1970 line-up, was being very quiet, Pat Crerand asked him whether Ramsey 'knows the game'. 'I think he does,' McNab responded.

The reaction from the public demonstrated the impact the panellists had on the national consciousness, and ITV was bombarded with correspondence from viewers. 'Some of the content was unbelievable. Many were letters from women describing their love for Malcolm Allison, who was football's James Bond,' explained Brian Moore. 'Others expressed outrage that poor Bob McNab was being "picked on" by the others.' When the quartet went shopping in London during a day off, they were mobbed. Four years before, when Roger Hunt, Nobby Stiles and Bobby Charlton headed back up north after England won the World Cup and stopped off at a service station for a coffee, no one bothered them. Whenever he travelled on the Tube on England business, Alf Ramsey was left alone. But now, after the 1970 World Cup, four young(ish) chaps who were talking about football on television had become national celebrities. As Brian Moore argued,

> The public were seeing a TV persona. Bob [McNab] was incredibly vocal on the pitch for Arsenal and was as combative as they came. And Malcolm could be very quiet and thoughtful without an audience. But get him on TV, after a few drinks in the green room before the show, up went those peacock feathers.

It would be some thirty years before the reality TV era arrived, but ITV realised that the more combative the studio atmosphere, and the more outlandish the comments, the bigger the audience figures became.

Others in the game watched the exploits of the ITV panel with growing interest. On the BBC, the fresh-faced young upstart Brian Clough refused to play ball with the other pundits during the tournament. The Derby boss's outspokenness – which was always out of kilter at the BBC – saw him carve his own niche on Independent Television as the decade progressed. During the World Cup he drew some uncomfortable looks from the Beeb team when, after watching the Brazil goalkeeper Felix make a hash of trying to stop Italy equalising in the final, he lambasted him for being 'an absolute disgrace'. 'He's got more clangers to drop than can ever be imagined,' Clough remarked, as the other guests shifted in their seats uncomfortably. The era of professional outrage had arrived.

For Jack Charlton, who was back home watching the end of the tournament after England's quarter-final defeat, seeing the panel in action was nothing less than a revelation. 'It occurred to me that if you were articulate, willing to put yourself out there and had a gob on you, the world could be your oyster.' By 1974, both Clough and Charlton had joined the ITV World Cup panel, where they linked up with Dougan, Crerand and Allison.

The quartet from the original 1970 panel enjoyed mixed fortunes as the decade progressed. Pat Crerand later joined Manchester United as assistant manager under Tommy Docherty. Bob McNab shot straight back to the Highbury training ground and was a key member of the Arsenal team which won the 1971 double. There was no chance of 'Nabbers' getting all showbizzy with the exacting combination of Don Howe and Bertie Mee overseeing events in N5, although he did appear in 'The Football Match' episode of *On The Buses* in 1973, playing the role of Bob the Busman for the Luxton Lions in a match against the Basildon Bashers.

In his role as chairman of the Professional Footballers' Association from 1970 to 1978, Derek Dougan continued to make waves in the media. As Kettering Town player-manager, he negotiated the first shirt sponsorship deal in English football with Kettering Tyres, although he was later forced to remove it by the football authorities. Dougan also penned a novel entitled *The Footballer*. There was certainly a buzz surrounding Malcolm Allison when he returned to preseason training at Manchester City. He used his extended stay in London during the 1970 World Cup to nurture his 'man about town' image, frequenting the plushest West-End bars and restaurants. His heightened profile meant he'd officially morphed into 'Big Mal'. 'He became addicted to publicity and champagne, and the high life drained him. A great coach but a flawed manager,' was Hill's verdict. At the start of the 1970–71 season, Hill refereed a dispute between Allison and Tottenham star Alan Mullery on *The Big Match*, following Allison's claim that Mullery was a 'good one-paced player but got no acceleration'. 'Malcolm became more critical and unforgiving in his views, which landed him in trouble, but was great for TV ratings,' Hill reflected.

Unquestionably, the main beneficiary of ITV's 1970 World Cup coverage was Jimmy Hill. Three years later – with Bagenal Harvey once again sprinkling his star dust behind the scenes – Hill cashed in on his public persona and the rivalry between the two channels, returning to the BBC to front *Match of the Day* as both presenter and analyst, and doubling his salary to £22,000 a year in the process. Such was the controversy surrounding Hill's renumeration that Arthur Lewis, MP for West Ham North, urged the government to impose a standstill order to prevent the BBC from making good on its offer. His plea fell on deaf ears, and, with the wind in his sails, Hill also set up his own sports consultancy, Jimmy Hill Limited. 'I realised that football was going to become an increasingly global game, and my consultancy business enabled me to explore various avenues abroad in the Middle East and in the United States,' he explained. Speculative and mercantile, Hill was a 'Thatcherite' before the term even existed. He lost none of his love for a photo opportunity, revelling in the resultant publicity when he escorted Hollywood actress Raquel Welch to a Chelsea match at Stamford Bridge in 1972, or for song writing when he penned the lyrics to 'Good Old Arsenal' after Bertie Mee's side reached the 1971 FA Cup final.

ITV used the showpiece match at Wembley to flaunt their technological hardware. Prior to the game, Hill forecast Arsenal's victory by entering data about both sides into a computer named 'Cedric'. 'Sadly, Cedric's metal brain cells were never more accurate than in that '71 Cup final, and it was downhill from there. I don't think he ever made an accurate forecast again,' Hill lamented. On the day after the Cup final, which was broadcast by both BBC and ITV, Moore and Hill were able to trump their BBC rivals again by proving that the Gunners' Eddie Kelly had in fact grabbed Arsenal's equaliser, and not George Graham. A camera behind the goal captured the moment where Graham wafted his foot towards the ball but failed to connect with Kelly's shot as it rolled past Liverpool goalkeeper Ray Clemence. 'A marvellous coup for LWT, thanks to an eagle-eyed video editor,' Hill chuckled.

Hill became one of television's most recognisable and influential characters in the 1970s. As Barry Davies reflected, 'So many in football during that time have every reason to be eternally grateful to Jimmy for raising their profiles.' When I spoke with Hill, it would have been remiss not to have asked him about the subject of how his bearded chin became an essential part of '70s playground parlance. 'I used to get people in the street coming up to me all the time,' he said as he rubbed his now beardless chin, 'saying "Itchy beard" and "Jimmy" and the like. At first I was most baffled. Then I came to regard it as a tremendous honour; a testament to the power of TV.'

The success of the 1970 World Cup panel was a watershed moment, throwing open windows of opportunity for those in the game with the gift of the gab and a penchant for the outlandish. For the likes of Jimmy Hill and Brian Clough, the dawning of a brash and combative new era in English football punditry had arrived.

2

THE ELECTION

'In June, the British [*sic*] football team would be defending its possession of the World Cup in Argentina [*sic*].'
Denis Healey in his memoir, *The Time of My Life*

Downing Street, March 1970. Blinded by popping flashbulbs from the omnipresent paparazzi, the tuxedo-clad George Best, with the ruffles of his shirt only adding to his raffish charm, is nervous as he walks into the Prime Minister's residence. 'The trick is to always look to the side. That way you didn't get blinded and see things in a purple or green haze,' Best later explains. Hugely impressed by Best's remarkable six-goal haul against Northampton Town a few days earlier in Manchester United's 8–2 FA Cup fifth-round victory, Prime Minister Harold Wilson decides that it is time to hold court (once again) with the First Division's most prodigiously gifted star. The Labour leader congratulates Best on his virtuoso performance at the County Ground – a bewitching repertoire of flicks, swerves, feints, dummies and deadly finishing. But once initial pleasantries are over, the conversation takes an unexpected turn. Wilson cuts straight to the chase, asking Best, 'How do you rate England's chances at the World Cup this summer?' 'I thought it was a strange question to ask me – a Northern Ireland international,' the Belfast boy later recalled, 'and I made it pretty clear to him that I didn't really give a shit.' But Wilson most certainly did give a shit. In fact, by the early months of the 1970s, the Prime Minister had become convinced that his political future depended on whether or not England could retain the Jules Rimet Trophy.

━━━

George Best always felt, in his own words, 'slightly uptight' when meeting VIPs 'because I never quite knew what to say to them, or what they were after'. On the face of it, there was plenty for Wilson and Best to discuss. The first commercial jumbo jet had recently landed at Heathrow Airport (something that Best, with his love of travelling to foreign hotspots, would soon use a great deal). There was the protracted break-up of the Beatles, whom, like Best, Wilson had also courted relentlessly throughout the 1960s. In football, Arsenal had just signed Peter Marinello – quickly dubbed 'the next George Best' by the tabloids – from Hibernian. On his debut, Marinello scored at Old Trafford (Best wasn't playing for United that day) and quickly bagged himself a slot presenting prizes on *Top of the Pops*, with Tony Blackburn telling viewers that the player cost the Gunners the 'fantastic fee of £100,000'.

But Wilson was increasingly fixated on the timing of the next general election and whether Sir Alf Ramsey's men could prevail in Mexico that summer. For him, the outcomes of both were intertwined. When Wilson won the 1964 general election, and then the 'snap' election in March 1966, he outlined his vision for a 'New Britain', which called for an increase in many social programmes, such as education and social security, and in civil liberties. Wilson also vowed to 'break down the conventions of the past', blaming the Tories for 'forgetting the everyday common man' during its own time in power. Wilson embraced arts, culture and sport to support his populist programme. Whereas some politicians on both sides thumbed their noses at football and mocked the Beatles' music, Wilson saw Best (labelled the 'Fifth Beatle' by the press) and the Beatles as allies to help build up his political base and appeal to younger voters. With his Gannex raincoat (made in his native Yorkshire), his 'pipe smoker of the year' award in 1965, his love of holidaying in the Isles of Scilly and passion for football, Wilson was keen to present himself as a 'man of the people'. Some felt he tried rather too hard.

Wilson's attempts to charm the Beatles – and the Fifth Beatle – didn't always go smoothly. Despite his intervention to ensure that the Beatles gained MBEs in 1965, John Lennon gave his back in 1969 in protest at the war in Vietnam and the group directly called out both the Prime Minister and the Conservative leader, Edward Heath, in the song 'Taxman' in protest at the 95 per cent supertax, which took away much of their earnings. Shy by nature, George Best was never as abrupt or direct as John Lennon. However, he often simply ignored Harold Wilson's fan letters that he'd send to him on regular occasions. 'He'd congratulate me on my performances and stuff like that, but I rarely responded because I never knew what to say. I couldn't be arsed with it all. And besides which, I never fancied Harold Wilson very much. He wasn't my type,' Best told me.

That said, Wilson and wife Mary received an invitation (courtesy of the *Daily Express*) to Best's housewarming shindig at his £35,000 custom-built house, 'Que Sera', in October 1970, although Wilson declined, writing Best a note, which said, 'Regretfully we can't be there, but to hit the crossbar from 35 yards with five minutes left is a bit much.'

Best always ensured he was at his sartorial best when he did meet Wilson. At the dawning of the 1970s, a conservatively dressed (so to speak) Wilson presented Best with his *Daily Express* Sportsman of the Year award at a Savoy Hotel luncheon in London. Best looked immaculate in his suit and orange shirt-and-tie combination, plucked off the peg of his Manchester boutique.

However, by the start of the '70s, the Fab Four were disintegrating fast and George Best's Manchester United performances were also becoming more erratic. There was perhaps less capital to be gained by hanging out (or trying to) with the icons of the '60s. The cultural sands were shifting under Wilson's feet, but the World Cup, scheduled to start on 31 May, was approaching fast. Wilson wanted to exploit his substantial lead over rival Edward Heath in the opinion polls and hold a summer election. If Ramsey's men happened to be thriving in Mexico as the country went to the polls, so much the better for Wilson, who four years earlier had remarked, 'Have you noticed that England only win the World Cup when Labour is in power?'

For Wilson, there existed – as his Chancellor of the Exchequer Roy Jenkins later described it – a 'mystical symbiosis' between Labour and the England team. In 1966, he'd been at the head of the table for the banquet which took place at the Royal Garden Hotel after Ramsey's men won the World Cup (the players' wives were shoved into an anteroom) and he badgered the BBC – unsuccessfully – to allow him to guest as a pundit at half-time in the World Cup final. Jack Charlton saw the 'mystical symbiosis' slightly differently:

> Harold Wilson loved a bloody photo opportunity more than I loved bloody fishing. After we won in '66, he was there in photos with me and our kid [Bobby] and my mother. Any chance to muscle in and he'd take it, the cheeky bugger. As Prime Minister, he wanted to be associated with England's success. It was good propaganda for him.

And yet, Wilson was indeed a passionate football fan. In April 1981, when he appeared with Bill Shankly as a guest on the Shelley Rohde chat show, he revealed that he still carried a card in his wallet from a newspaper called *Chums* with a picture of the Huddersfield Town team from 1926 on it, the last time the Terriers won the title. When Rohde asked if his support was 'a little out of expediency?', he replied, 'Oh no, it's born loyalties.' Wilson recalled how his mother gave him a bob (5p in decimal money) to get on the tram, buy some food and with the sixpence change buy a standing ticket. His favourite player from the '30s was Alex Jackson. Wilson, using semantics of which Shankly heartily approved, described the game 'as a religion, a way of life'.

Away from the glare of publicity surrounding the England team, Wilson went to matches at Leeds Road as often as his busy schedule would allow. Following Huddersfield's promotion back to the top flight in 1970, former Terriers full-back Trevor Cherry told me that Wilson approached him in the players' lounge after one match:

> He came across as knowledgeable about football tactics and the history of the club. I liked him. He had his pipe on the go – as you'd expect – and he seemed to just like chatting to the players. He was there as a fan, and nothing else. He loved the club, that was clear.

But when Wilson met with his inner circle in April 1970 to determine the date of the general election, he was only thinking about England and the World Cup, much to the annoyance of some of his non-football-loving colleagues. Denis Healey noted that Wilson was fearful that 'if we [England] were defeated just before polling day the government would suffer'. Perhaps if Wilson had retained Labour's high priest of revisionist socialism, Tony Crosland, in his

Cabinet, he may have been lent a sympathetic ear. With his penchant for sporting camel-hair coats, driving fast cars, attending the opera and smoking cheroots, Crosland – author of the highly influential *The Future of Socialism* – seemed the most jarringly incongruous of football fans, but, after being elected MP for Great Grimsby in 1959, he became an altogether more unlikely supporter of Grimsby Town. Political meetings had to be arranged so that Crosland could get to Blundell Park for home matches, and no Saturday evening gathering with Crosland present was complete without *Match of the Day* being available for his full attention. In his biography of Crosland, Kevin Jefferys claimed that he 'sometimes enlisted his step-daughters' help to say that the Prime Minister was on the telephone if he wanted to slip away from guests to watch a match'.

But Crosland was removed from the Labour Party's inner circle in 1970. At Chequers, Wilson and the others agreed to wait for the May local election results before fixing the date for the general election. When they showed a strong swing towards Labour, Wilson plumped for an 18 June election date, when the World Cup was about to reach its business end. Before the tournament kicked off, Wilson became embroiled (from afar) in the infamous 'Bogotá Bracelet' episode, when England skipper Bobby Moore was charged with stealing a bracelet worth £600 from a jewellery store in the Colombian capital. Ramsey's men had travelled to South America in the weeks leading up to the finals to prepare for the competition with a series of friendly matches. Their first match was in Colombia on 20 May and their second in Ecuador four days later. Moore and the rest of the squad touched down in Bogotá two days before their match and after arriving at their hotel the captain visited the gift shop in the foyer with Bobby Charlton, but the two men left empty handed. As both Charlton and Moore chatted with the rest of the squad in the hotel foyer, security guards approached them.

The shop assistant, Clara Padilla, insisted that two footballers had stolen the eighteen-carat bracelet studded with twelve diamonds and twelve emeralds. After giving statements and being searched, Charlton and Moore were released, with Moore playing a starring role as England defeated Colombia 4–0 and Ecuador 2–0.

But with the team now en route to Mexico, the players had a six-hour stop-over in Bogotá and, once again, Moore was stopped by authorities. The owner of the shop was insistent that the England captain was responsible: 'He [Moore] might be the best footballer in the world, the most attractive, distinguished and most highly regarded of anyone, a friend of her British majesty even. But that doesn't mean he's not a kleptomaniac.' Moore was placed under house arrest as the rest of the England squad prepared to fly to Mexico, and the episode threatened to rapidly escalate into a diplomatic incident. Despite Moore's protestations, published in the *Daily Mirror*, the Colombian authorities were initially reluctant to release him.

On 26 May, Wilson cabled FA president Lord Harewood, now in Mexico, assuring him that everything possible was being done to ensure Moore's release. Wilson asked British diplomats in Colombia whether he should contact the Colombian President directly to challenge him about the 'administrative inefficiency' that was delaying Moore's release. British Foreign Secretary Michael Stewart – under orders from Wilson – even left a NATO Council meeting in Rome to oversee proceedings. The British government made it abundantly clear that failure to release Moore with due haste would incur their displeasure. As Stewart later admitted, 'We ensured that the [Colombian] magistrate concerned was privately made aware of the awkward implications of the case for Colombia.' Judge Dorado, who was overseeing the case, was visited in the dead of night by General Leyva, the head of the Colombian secret services, who instructed Dorado to drop proceedings immediately. Dorado told Moore that he hoped he would 'score many goals' as he departed, and Clara Padilla, who initially identified Moore as the 'culprit', retracted her claim, admitting that she was 'confused'. Her 'confusion' increased when, after she repeated her claim that she had seen the England captain shove the bracelet into the pocket of his jacket, Moore pointed out that it had no pockets. Four days before England's opening match in Guadalajara against Romania on 2 June, Moore was released.

Although Ramsey and Moore may have been grateful to Wilson for applying pressure behind the scenes and ensuring he had a full squad for the opening game against Romania, Foreign Office officials were less than impressed by Wilson's involvement in the whole affair. One civil servant complained that 'the Prime Minister took action on Moore's behalf for political reasons during a general election campaign, and I see no reason why we should allow this somewhat dubious intervention to colour our attitude in the future'. In the weeks that followed the incident, the Foreign Office was inundated with pleas from incarcerated British nationals across the globe, keen that their appeals should also be 'fast-tracked' like the England skipper's was.

Success in general elections and World Cups is hugely dependent on timing. If the election had taken place a week earlier (although England had lost 1–0 to Brazil in the second group game, Ramsey's men had proved more than a match for the eventual winners, and there was no disgrace losing in a game memorable for – as well as Jairzinho's winner – Bobby Moore's majestic display and Gordon Banks's miraculous save from Pelé) there would have been little sense of doom and gloom. A week later, and although the England players would be back home, the collective sense of shock at England losing their world crown might well have slightly dissipated.

As it was, voters went to the polls just four days after Ramsey's men were knocked out 3–2 by West Germany. It had all begun so well, with Alan Mullery side-footing home after an excellent pass from Henry Newton and Martin Peters volleying home a cross to give England a 2–0 lead. But then the roof fell in.

In the aftermath, as a bewildered Ramsey attempted to compute how his team had thrown it all away, the England manager shook his head and asked why it had been Gordon Banks, his big-game goalkeeper, who, stricken with a stomach bug (referred to as Montezuma's Revenge in local parlance), was forced to miss the quarter-final. If ever Ramsey needed his number one goalkeeper between the sticks, this was it. Banks's deputy Peter Bonetti appeared nervous and rigid when it counted and timed his dive fractionally wrong when Beckenbauer scored to pull a goal back for West Germany, rocking England back on their heels. The match highlights show a dozen what-ifs for England. Rather than melt away in the Mexican heat, Ramsey's team continued to press forward but missed a litany of chances, with '66 hero Geoff Hurst glancing two headers narrowly wide. Harold Wilson sensed the game was up for England when Ramsey substituted Bobby Charlton with his team still leading 2–1. 'That was the signal to the Germans. All they had to do was pile on the attack,' he commented later. Uwe Seeler's freakish back header floated over a static Bonetti to take the game to extra time, and Gerd Müller volleyed home the winner. It was a defeat of solar plexus-smashing proportions for Ramsey and his men. Wilson also began to have a sinking feeling that the game might be up for Labour's election chances too.

The Prime Minister, who'd written 'good luck' letters to the survivors from the '66 triumph before the 1970 tournament, sent a commiserating telegram to Ramsey, informing him that 'England had done the whole nation proud in Mexico'. With four days to go before polling day, the Labour Party's lead over the Conservatives was already narrowing, and Wilson believed that the lack of a resultant 'feel-good' factor following the defeat might have dealt his party a fatal blow. 'I spoke to some voters who said that after the defeat, they couldn't stand anything now,' he later reflected.

Some key figures held that, given that the quarter-final defeat was meted out by England's old enemy, a small – but significant – section of the electorate associated Wilson and Labour with the loss of the Jules Rimet Trophy. In the years leading up to 1970, more and more nations, once members of Britain's Commonwealth, had declared their independence, and, in 1968, Wilson announced that Britain would permanently withdraw its troops from Suez. The defeat to West Germany in Léon – a direct reversal of the '66 final – seemed to confirm that, in marked contrast to Labour's upbeat election slogan, 'Now Britain's strong – let's make it great to live in', perhaps this was a nation on the cusp of decline. As Tony Benn reflected, 'Tonight England was knocked out of the World Cup which, no doubt, will have another subtle effect on the public.' The morning after the match, Roy Jenkins and Minister for Sport Denis Howell travelled to a meeting in Birmingham. Howell recalled, 'Roy was totally bemused that no question concerned either trade figures or immigration, but solely the football and whether Ramsey or Bonetti was the major culprit ... for the first time I had real doubts and knew the mood was changing fast.'

The veterans from the 1970 World Cup squad never bought into the theory that the loss to West Germany somehow influenced the outcome of the general election. Jack Charlton was clear about what he thought: 'Absolute bollocks. I'm not having that at all. Surely no one's vote in a general election revolves around who won a bloody football match?' Central defender – and Everton captain – Brian Labone was slightly more circumspect, but ultimately rebuffed the theory too:

> I can understand how the mood of a nation can suddenly change because of whether England win or lose in a big match at the World Cup, but to suggest that it affected the outcome of a general election is a bit far-fetched for me. There's way more factors which affect the outcome of elections, the state of the economy being one, and whether or not the voters like the leaders of the parties or not.

Ironically, given that political commentators still struggle to find a clear reason why Edward Heath was able to overhaul Labour's significant lead, and ensure a 4.5 per cent swing to the Tories, Brian Labone's nuanced answer is perhaps the most plausible response. The day after England's defeat, headlines were dominated by a significant balance-of-payments economic deficit. Here, late in the day, Heath and his shadow ministers had concrete evidence of what proved to be Wilson's Achilles heel. The right-wing press had fired off several broadsides at Labour's economic policies over the previous two years, citing rising inflation levels and, in the most recent budget before the 1970 World Cup, a rise in petrol, cigarette and alcohol prices. Wilson had recently announced a bail-out package for Rolls Royce, and steel industry chiefs complained about how the domestic industry was being undercut by cheap foreign imports from the Far East. 'You can't trust Labour with looking after the British economy,' Heath insisted early on his campaign trail. But with the -0.2 per cent balance-of-payments deficit, here was something tangible and timely and Heath immediately went on the offensive, stating, 'As I said, all is not as we'd been led to believe under Labour, and here's the proof.' The news couldn't have been timed better for Heath. On the morning of polling day, one reader named Peter Grosvenor wrote a letter to *The Times*: 'Sir, thinking of strange reversals of fortune: could it be that Harold Wilson is 2–0 up with twenty minutes to play?' As the results began to flood in on the evening of 18 June, it became apparent that Edward Heath had pulled off a miracle. Labour appeared to have been undone less by the national side's misfortune on the pitch and more by their economic record.

Always fond of communicating with the general public through the language of football, Wilson described the 1970 election defeat as a 'relegation'. When he'd become the first Labour Prime Minister in fourteen years, back in 1964, he'd explained his role heading up an inexperienced Cabinet thus: 'I'd take the penalties; I acted as goalkeeper; I went and took the corner kicks, I dashed down the wing.' After Heath gained fewer seats than Wilson in a gruelling 1974 election campaign, but tried to cling to power by forming a coalition with the Liberals, Wilson claimed, 'It's rather as if the referee had blown the whistle and one side has refused to leave the field of play.' And when Heath finally abandoned his coalition plans, leaving his opponent free to begin his second term as Prime Minister, Wilson noted, 'I'm going to be what they used to call a deep-lying centre-half. I can't say I'd be a sweeper, because no one outside football would understand.'

In the years that immediately followed the 1970 general election, Wilson – as leader of the opposition – sought solace in attending a clutch of sportsman dinners, regularly bumping into George Best and Alf Ramsey. 'I thought he [Wilson] looked tired, and I was surprised that he had another go as being Prime Minister,' Best explained, 'although I imagine that he didn't think I looked too chipper either by then.' Wilson could never let go of the lingering feeling that England's defeat in Léon, and the scarring images of Gerd Müller volleying the winner past a flapping Peter Bonetti, had somehow convinced the electorate that all was not as bright in Labour's idyllic rose garden as it seemed. As Wilson informed Bill Shankly years later, 'People get fed up with their government, like supporters get fed up with a team. And that's what happened. When I heard that we'd lost 3–2, I thought there'd be an effect.'

Wilson's critics had claimed he'd run a detached, presidential-style election campaign in 1970 and, following the World Cup in Mexico, the disquiet surrounding Alf Ramsey's public irascibility and aloofness also began to increase in volume.

3

THE STIFF UPPER LIP

'Alf Ramsey was a football man, at home in the company of
his players, but incredibly wary and suspicious of outsiders. He
certainly wasn't what you'd call a "modern" football manager.'

Jack Charlton

Hendon Hall Hotel, March 1970. 'Shall we have a number one?'
asks a stern-faced Alf Ramsey, in his best faux plummy accent.
'You'll have a number one,' replies pop impresario Bill Martin,
who, along with creative partner Phil Coulter, penned cheerful,
singalong hits 'Congratulations' for Cliff Richard and 'Puppet on
a String' for 1967 Eurovision Song Contest winner Sandie Shaw.
Martin arranged to meet Ramsey and his England players during a
spring squad get-together in the lead-up to the 1970 World Cup,
and he had even written the lyrics for a new song for the squad,
entitled 'Back Home'. As the players shuffle their feet on the gravel
outside the hotel, Martin tries to convince Ramsey that the record
will be 'fun' to make. The glaring Ramsey treats the word with the
contempt he thinks it deserves. 'Fun? We don't do *fun* here. We're
here to win.' The manager only agrees to take part after two of his
boys from '66 – Alan Ball and skipper Bobby Moore – point out
that it would be a welcome distraction from the hard work they'll be

putting in. Jack Charlton later asks Ramsey if he will be singing on the disc. 'You must be fuckin' jokin',' snaps the England manager, lapsing back into his Dagenham drawl. On the subject of their tense meeting, Bill Martin later said, 'Alf Ramsey had the stiffest upper lip of any Englishman I ever met.'

━━━━━━

"They were a lovely bunch of chaps,' gushed Bill Martin, who later successfully herded the England players into London's Pye Studios for a one-day recording session. The players teased Martin about Ramsey's hostility towards him, reminding him that the manager couldn't have been more thrilled to meet the fellow Scot and James Bond actor Sean Connery at Pinewood Studios back in '66. 'It's just you he doesn't like, Bill,' Jack Charlton told Martin. In fact, that wasn't true. Ramsey made his general animosity for the Scottish clear. Prior to Home International clashes with the Auld Enemy, Ramsey urged his players to 'get into these Scots fuckers'.

The album was eventually called *The World Beaters Sing The World Beaters*. 'We put big lads like Bobby Moore, Gordon Banks and Jack Charlton at the front, and we tucked wee Alan Ball towards the back. He was a little too high for us,' the colourfully dressed Martin said with a grin, when we met for a morning coffee in London in 2002. The players boomed out a few pub ditties before getting their collective larynxes around 'Back Home'. Martin's insistence that the record would sell 'more than you think' proved to be spot on. Released as a single on 18 April, 'Back Home' spent sixteen weeks in the charts and, by May, it dislodged Norman Greenbaum's 'Spirit in the Sky' from the number one slot. The squad made three appearances on *Top of the Pops* and at its peak the record was selling 100,000 copies per day. 'The song worked because it pulled on the heart strings, describing how even though the team would be "far away" they'll always be thinking of "the folks back home". The simple messages are usually the best, explained Martin. Although *The Observer* described it as 'tacky', suggesting that only George Best had the persona to pull that sort of thing off, the players enjoyed themselves. 'We loved it and sang it on the bus on the way to matches in Mexico,' Alan Ball told me.

The song was not the only attempt made by the players to tap into other forms of revenue. Prior to the 1970 World Cup, the England squad approached George Best's agent Ken Stanley and agreed to pool their earnings from arrangements with a raft of products from frozen-food giant Findus, Ford and Esso, who sported the lion rosette logo and the legend 'Chosen by England' on their branding. This endorsement scheme netted each player around £5,000 (around £68,000 today). It was a huge improvement for the survivors from the 1966 World Cup, who'd looked on helplessly as their lack of stake in commercial activities meant they netted a paltry £1,000 per man for winning the tournament. 'And we bloody well got taxed on that,' laughed Alan Ball.

True to his word, Ramsey – gifted £6,000 by the Football Association in 1966, of which £3,500 found its way into the Treasury's coffers – remained steadfastly detached from anything which had even the faintest whiff of commercialism about it. He described 'Back Home' as 'a bloody racket, like all pop music' to Alan Ball, although it was tame compared to much of what was in the charts at the time. In the same year, American rockers Frijid Pink scored a hit with a psychedelic version of 'The House Of The Rising Sun', and long-haired louts The Move hit the charts with their distinctly heavy sounding 'Brontosaurus'. Bill Martin later reflected, 'I bumped into Alf countless times after 1970, and, despite the success of "Back Home", he always made a point of completely blanking me at social events. He simply did not "do" popular culture.' But Ramsey's crustiness didn't mean he wasn't aware of what was going on. When Esso issued its 1970 coin collection, each silver penny (free

with every gallon of four star, with the mounting board costing
2s 6d) bearing the sculptured head of an England player, Ramsey
teased Jack Charlton that his image made him look 'like a bloody
Roman emperor or something'. Nonetheless, any player who dared
broach the subject of money with Ramsey received short shrift. 'I
mentioned something to Alf about the players' pool,' Brian Labone
told me. 'He literally cut me dead and glared at me. "We're here to
concentrate on football, not outside distractions," he said. He was
totally aloof when it came to anything but the good of the England
team.' Alan Ball received a similarly brusque response when he
burbled to Ramsey about the pay rise he'd received from Everton in
1970. 'That is of no interest to your country whatsoever, Alan,' was
the response. 'Alf made me feel about this big,' said the 5ft 6in. midfielder, leaving a tiny gap between his thumb and his index finger.
'Even smaller than normal.'

Since becoming a manager in his thirties, Ramsey had always been
ruthlessly single-minded and utterly unafraid of breaking with
convention. At Ipswich Town, 'Ramsey's Rustics' – as they were
disparagingly called in the press – won the Second Division title
in 1961 and the league title a year later at the first attempt. Town
played an unusual midfield formation without wide players – an
obvious blueprint for Ramsey's 'wingless wonders' who won the
1966 World Cup. Following Ipswich's title success, the 42-year-old
Ramsey accepted the England job after Walter Winterbottom's
resignation. Shortly after his appointment, the outdated International Selection Committee was scrapped, leaving Ramsey in sole
charge of selecting the team. As the first England manager to have
full control of team affairs, he was free to mould a group according
to his vision and, in doing so, created an indomitable team spirit.

To Ramsey, reputations and status within the game meant nothing. It was all about the team ethic. This was never better illustrated than when he capped the nearly thirty-year-old Jack Charlton for the first time in 1965. Flattered, the Leeds defender asked Ramsey why he'd picked him at such a (relatively) advanced age. 'Well, it's because I select those whom I think will fit best into the team. I don't necessarily pick the best *players*, Jack,' Ramsey told him with the faintest of smirks. Ramsey's attention to detail was forensic, and he lectured the team on diet and sleeping patterns in the build-up to the 1966 World Cup.

Having shorn the England team of wingers, and deployed a more defensive 4–3–3 formation, Ramsey delivered the greatest prize, as he'd predicted before the tournament. Yet, although it earned him huge respect, it didn't make him universally loved by the public. England were functional and highly effective but not expansive or easy on the eye. Ramsey cut a taut figure; almost as strangulated as his vowels. When the final whistle went at Wembley and trainer Harold Shepherdson jumped for joy next to him, Ramsey growled, 'For God's sake, sit down, Harold.' He refused to join the team on its lap of honour. His level of reserve was almost unnatural. Ramsey's aloofness had made him enemies from within the English press corps even during the halcyon days of '66. The *Daily Mirror*'s Ken Jones – one of the few journalists who was on reasonable terms with Ramsey – explained, 'He was incredibly unforgiving of journalists who criticised him, or his team. He knew that many of them mocked that accent of his. Any slight – perceived or real – would be met with an icy stare and a cold silence.' As World Cup winner Alan Ball recalled,

When we were at our training camp, the press converged. Alf would say: 'How long should we give them? Twenty minutes?' And we'd shout: 'Twenty minutes.' At the end of the period, our

trainer Harold Shepherdson would blow the whistle and, whether or not you were in the middle of the interview, that was that.
Alf was in charge.

Out of all of Ramsey's former players whom I spoke to, Ball was
most gushing about the former England boss. I caught up with
the (once) fiery red-haired midfielder after he'd delivered an after-
dinner speech in the early 2000s, which he'd preceded with his
signature line, 'It's nice to be squeaking to you.' Ball's patter was
chock-full of stories about his colourful and sometimes controversial career with Everton, Arsenal, Southampton and England.
At times he could be cutting about his former managers but *never*
about Ramsey, of whom Ball spoke with fondness. Afterwards, he
told me, 'I'd have died for Alf Ramsey, I really would. He was the
most patriotic Englishman I ever met.'

In '66, Ramsey had been on terra firma and, by virtue of the fact
that England won the tournament, journalists, for the time being,
put to one side their reservations about the manager's scratchy
manner. But he rarely helped himself. On the day after England's
victory, Ramsey visited the BBC TV studios where he was met by
his most loyal supporters in the press: Ken Jones, Brian James of
the *Daily Mail* and Clive Toye of the *Daily Express*. After asking
for 'a brief word', Ramsey shut them down, responding, 'Sorry, it's
my day off.' Only after Ramsey's wife Vicky intervened did Ramsey
relent. 'All right, then, but only for a few minutes,' he said reluctant-
ly. 'I looked at him and thought: "Tread carefully, Alf, because this
is probably as good as it will ever get,"' Ken Jones recalled.

On the face of it, England had a stronger squad in 1970 than they'd
had four years earlier, with Manchester City stars Francis Lee and

Colin Bell, Leeds United pair Allan Clarke and Terry Cooper and defender Brian Labone in the frame. The spine of the '66 squad – Banks, Moore, Ball, the Charlton brothers and Hurst – was still present and correct. Whether they were newcomers or not, nearly all fell victim – at one time or another – to Ramsey's tinder-dry put downs. Any player who gave off the air that they were taking their position in the team for granted was snapped back into place. 'Yes, I'll send you a couple of tickets for the game, Geoffrey,' Ramsey responded when, following an England match, Geoff Hurst said, 'See you next time, Alf.' On the plane over to Mexico, Ramsey approached Allan Clarke, who was chatting and laughing with some of his teammates and asked whether he was enjoying himself. When Clarke replied, 'Yes, smashing, Alf,' he received the withering response: 'Well, you're not here to fuckin' well enjoy yourself.' When Ramsey made a technical point about England's opening game against Romania, Brian Labone responded, 'I'll remember that for the next match, Alf.' Quick as a flash, Ramsey snapped, 'Yes, when is Everton's first match of the season, Brian?'

Jack Charlton reckoned that Ramsey reserved his most withering put-downs for him. One day in training, Charlton ballooned a clearance out of play. Ramsey sidled up and asked with a sigh, 'Is there no beginnin' to your talents, Jack?' Charlton always marvelled at Ramsey's propensity to swear simply because the Leeds defender reckoned it 'always sounded so bloody funny. Try as he might, Alf's Dagenham accent would creep in whenever he sounded off.' As the England party arrived in Scotland for an international, Charlton was in the vicinity when a reporter greeted them and said, 'Welcome to Scotland, Mr Ramsey.' 'You must be fuckin' jokin',' was Ramsey's response. Then there was the occasion when, at an official dinner, Ramsey, who'd had a few drinks, informed the waitress, 'No, thank you. I don't want no fuckin' peas.' It's never been proved whether Ramsey – the son of a Dagenham straw dealer – received elocution lessons as he climbed the greasy pole in football management, or whether he simply taught himself to speak 'posh'. But, like Wembley-born Keith Moon, The Who's lunatic drummer, who also liked to affect an upper-class accent in interviews and call everyone 'Dear Boy', Ramsey couldn't quite shake the habit of leavin' his 'h's and his 'n's out of the equation. At a get-together before the 1970 World Cup, Ramsey, who loved Westerns, informed the squad that they were off to the cinema to watch a new Clint Eastwood movie. 'It's called *'Ang 'Hem 'Igh. 'Hang 'Em 'Igh,'* Ramsey stuttered. 'Oh, for Christ's sake, Alf. It's called *Hang 'Em High*. Now, let's get to the cinema, shall we?' suggested Alan Ball.

One of the problems which the reigning champions faced in 1970 was the lingering bad feeling following Ramsey's assertion that in the 1966 World Cup quarter-final Argentina had played like 'animals' during England's 1–0 win. Argentina captain Antonio Rattin infamously refused to leave the pitch after the referee gave him his marching orders, and, at the final whistle, Ramsey intervened to prevent right-back George Cohen from swapping shirts with Alberto Gonzales. The fallout from Ramsey's 'animals' remark could still be felt when England embarked on a South American tour in 1969. Prior to a 'friendly' against Mexico, Ramsey informed the local press, 'There was a band playing outside our hotel until five this morning ... when our players went out to inspect the pitch, they were abused by the crowd. I would have thought the Mexican public would be delighted to welcome England.' Ramsey's comments went down like a lead balloon, and when the England team arrived to defend their trophy a year later the press was baying for blood.

Ramsey provoked fresh outrage in Mexico with his endorsement of frozen-food giant Findus and the news that England would be taking their own provisions with them. The whole episode simply reinforced the view that Ramsey was a xenophobic, petty

Little Englander ('If you are going to throw fruit at the England team, remember to wash it first' was one headline in the Mexican press). Mexican officials later incinerated the team's imported steaks, butter, beef and sausages on the quayside due to fears that Britain was a foot-and-mouth country, leaving the England squad to survive on a diet of fish fingers, ketchup and ready meals for the duration of their trip, plus bottled Malvern water. Prior to England's match against Brazil in Guadalajara, the local press urged the *Tapatíos* and visiting Brazil supporters to 'make a noise'. And so they did – honking their horns and banging drums right outside the Guadalajara Hilton where the England squad was staying. Ramsey seethed.

England eked out two victories in the group stage. Geoff Hurst, the hero of 1966, turned his man smartly to rifle home the winner against Romania in England's opening game, and an Allan Clarke penalty was enough to see off Czechoslovakia in the final Group 3 match, following the loss to Brazil in the second game. 'The wins over Romania and Czechoslovakia weren't memorable. It was a case of getting the job done,' Alan Ball said. The British press was distinctly lukewarm about England's overall showing in those two games, with the word 'functional' bandied around, but more praiseworthy of the showing against Brazil, with most accepting that, for much of the game, England had gone toe-to-toe with the tournament favourites. In the *Daily Mirror*, Ken Jones wrote, 'The difference was in the finishing. Jairzinho emphatically blasted home Brazil's winner, whereas Jeff Astle squandered what was clearly a much easier chance.'

When England were eliminated by West Germany, the Mexican press jumped for joy. 'The Champions are Dead', barked one headline. 'Go Home England', chortled another. The British press was generally sympathetic, with *The Observer*'s Hugh McIlvanney viewing England's defeat as a 'heroic loss'. But not everyone was so forgiving. ITV panellist Malcolm Allison vented his spleen in *The Sun*: 'Ramsey has kept the same pattern since his days at Ipswich, as far back as 1957.' On Radio Four's *PM*, football writer and music critic Hans Keller was incandescent, claiming that England's approach in Mexico was the product of a 'Second Division mind'. As long as England were world champions, Ramsey remained relatively armour-plated. Now, he had to face the music. Perhaps the *News of the World* gauged the prevailing wind most succinctly with its 'Ramsey – A Man Alone' headline.

The white noise, which Ramsey loathed, began as soon as England's plane landed at Heathrow. 'Glad to be home, Alf?' asked one reporter. 'If you ask a stupid question, you'll get a stupid answer,' Ramsey snapped, before he was whisked off to a press conference at a west London hotel. Perhaps it was a combination of lack of sleep, England's defeat and the media scrum, but Ramsey was at his tetchiest in the conference, giving only the briefest of responses. When a reporter suggested that Ramsey wasn't being terribly cooperative, he responded,

I am rude? They stick their faces in front of me, they stick these things [microphones] in front of me and so on and so forth, and I'm being rude? There isn't a word invented that would describe the mannerisms of some of the people I've been confronted with. And yet I'm rude.

Ramsey's unease with the press was also noted in government circles. The British ambassador in Mexico City, in a confidential report entitled 'The World Cup 1970: The Politics of Football', wrote, 'Sir Alf Ramsey is seldom at ease with the press. Although trying hard, he … rarely gives them a felicitous phrase. In the long run, he will show the quality of his defects.' His players remained adamant that Ramsey was the man for the job, with Bobby Charlton arguing, 'Who can

40

replace him?' But on the plane home, the Charlton brothers agreed with Ramsey that it was the opportune moment to call time on their illustrious England careers. One by one, Ramsey's erstwhile lieutenants faded from the scene. His fraught dealings in Mexico with swaggering Chelsea forward Peter Osgood confirmed that a confident new breed of baby-boom footballer was on its way up.

———

'Alf was like something out of an Ealing comedy, with that fake accent of his,' recalled Peter Osgood, as we sat down at a plush King's Road wine bar near Stamford Bridge. Pestered by Chelsea fans for autographs throughout our interview, much of Osgood's chat with them focused on his headed goal in the 1970 FA Cup final replay when the Blues defeated Leeds United at Old Trafford. In case Osgood didn't know it, there hadn't been a Chelsea player since that could match his magnetism and aura, the fans told him. 'I loved entertaining them every week,' the smitten Osgood told me. If Alf Ramsey's persona was seen as a blast from the past by Osgood, then the 'King of Stamford Bridge' was the living embodiment of the new winds blowing through English football.

Blaming Alan Ball (albeit jokingly) for the fact that he was awarded only four caps by Ramsey, Osgood said,

I got my first full cap against Belgium in February 1970. I got on the team coach and Alan Ball started singing, 'Ossie, Ossie, Ossie, Oi! Oi! Oi!' I saw Alf's face. He glared at Alan and Alan shut up. Then he glared at me. I grinned back and said, 'All right, Alf.' I winked at him. He looked at me as if to say, 'I've got your number, Osgood.'

On the King's Road, Chelsea players socialised with a showbiz crowd, including Michael Caine, star of early '70s gangster flick *Get Carter*. Osgood loved Caine's character, the swaggering Jack Carter, and told me that he went to see the film three times in its opening week. He explained what a huge impression the actor had made on him. Caine represented a new generation of upwardly mobile English actors. In 1970, he'd told an interviewer, 'We are here, this is our society, and we are not going away.' Just as Caine – born Maurice Micklewhite and the son of a Billingsgate porter and a charlady – set a new trend in cinema, Osgood was the prototype modern '70s footballer, for whom deference, conformity and privation were things of the past.

'I made no bones about it,' Osgood told me. 'I wanted to make some serious money from the game. There were rewards to be had.' By the early '70s, Osgood was paid around £80 a week for his *Daily Mail* column, received the equivalent amount from Chelsea (before win bonuses), signed a hefty sponsorship deal with sportswear firm Bukta and opened a raft of supermarkets and shops. Osgood reckoned that he was earning around £200 per week at that time, which equates to £1,500 today. 'It was a tidy amount. I wished I earned that much today,' he muttered. Osgood became one of only three sportsmen (boxers Joe Frazier and Muhammad Ali were the others) to be interviewed by journalist Ray Connolly for his influential 'Connolly on Saturday' column in the *London Evening Standard*, in which he wrote, 'I have an agent to earn me money and to get me known as a name. George Best has had it too good up to now. There's been no one to challenge him. I will – although I've got a different image to him.' Osgood confirmed his wish to be 'a married playboy', a 'rich man', and 'never have to worry about money again'. Present and correct at the Connolly interview was Osgood's wife Rose. The couple had married when they were just seventeen, and she sat and knitted as the men talked football. 'Rosemary doesn't like to go out much, she'd rather sit in. She's a quiet type, you know, she likes to do the gardening,' Osgood claimed. Disinterested in football, Mrs O admitted that, sometimes, she'd rather Mr O 'had an ordinary nine-to-five job'. The Osgoods had just sold their house in Windsor and bought a plush £16,000 residence in Tadworth, Surrey, on the edge of Epsom Downs. 'It was beautifully kitted out, with all mod cons in the kitchen,' Osgood told me. 'And a colour telly of course, so I could watch football. Not that I was home much to enjoy it.'

Osgood's impudence and 'man about town' image didn't sit well with Ramsey. 'At Chelsea we prided ourselves on being outspoken and cheeky, but Alf wasn't into that,' Osgood remembered. It wasn't as if Ramsey had never managed cheeky chaps before. In the '60s, Bobby Moore and Jimmy Greaves regularly laughed together about Ramsey's accent and old-school ways. But they did it *quietly*. Osgood had no such filter. On an England get-together before the 1970 World Cup, Ramsey asked Osgood whether he was looking forward to training. 'Not much, Alf,' Osgood responded truthfully, if a little unwisely. Ramsey's eyes narrowed. 'Well, you're going to fuckin' well enjoy it,' came the sledgehammer response. Famously, Osgood likened Ramsey's comeback to seeing 'the Queen kick one of her Corgis up the arse'.

A substitute for the opener against Romania, Osgood was delighted when Bobby Moore told him that he was definitely 'in' against Brazil. In the following day's team meeting, Ramsey confirmed that the players who finished the match would start against Brazil, at which point Moore gave Osgood the thumbs-up sign. Ramsey then quickly apologised and changed tack. 'Sorry – those who *started* the game against Romania will play against Brazil,' he said. In the blink of an eye, Osgood's bubble was burst. Honest error though it was, what Ramsey had done to him – Osgood insisted – was 'worse than breaking my leg'. When Ramsey later knocked on Osgood's hotel bedroom door and attempted to apologise for the error, Osgood yelled at him and told him to 'Go away'. This went down like a lead balloon. Ramsey didn't do histrionics or temper tantrums. Neither was he impressed that Osgood failed to turn up to training that day, after having broken curfew the night before and headed out into town to drown his sorrows in a local bar with a clutch of England fans. Osgood came on from the bench against Czechoslovakia but wasn't amongst the substitutes for the West Germany match. 'Alf never picked me for England again – apart from at the arse-end of his time in charge in 1974 against Italy,' said Osgood.

As Ramsey watched his team training in Mexico, he turned to Ken Jones and said, 'What am I going to do about Osgood?' Right on cue, Osgood began juggling the ball, much to the merriment of his teammates. 'He's a bloody show pony,' Ramsey told Jones. Ramsey's doubts about Osgood encapsulated the growing schism in the '70s between old-school managers and the younger generation of players, for whom tales of the 1930s depression, the war and rationing meant increasingly little. In 1966, Ramsey had coached a group of players to glory whose formative experiences (completing national service and playing under the maximum wage system) were not dissimilar to his own. But after 1970, he needed to assimilate a raft of new players into the team who wanted to play football *their* way, and who were keen to exercise their right to free speech.

Another headline-grabbing player whom Ramsey found hard to fathom was Huddersfield Town striker and Elvis Presley fan Frank Worthington. He explained how Ramsey's conservative attitude extended to include the clothes that the players wore. The Yorkshireman, with his flowing tresses and Zapata moustache, was selected for the touring under-23 side in 1972 and marked his own cards as he arrived at Heathrow airport to meet up with the team. When I met Worthington backstage in Blackpool in the early 2000s – after one of his double-entendre ridden stage shows (his autobiography was called *One Hump Or Two?*) he went through the garments he'd worn to impress Ramsey, counting them off on his fingers as he did so, 'Cowboy boots... a beautiful red silk shirt... black trousers and my crowning glory... a lime green jacket. Now, who could possibly resist me dressed like that?' he asked. As it turned out, Ramsey most certainly could. When he clapped eyes on the forward, he turned to Harold Shepherdson and asked, 'What the fuck have I done?'

The flamboyant, plaid-jacketed Worthington – who'd lost none of his sartorial chutzpah when I met him – was circumspect about his failure to break into the senior squad under Ramsey. 'It wasn't just because of my love of this type of finery,' he said, pointing to his clothes. 'He'd probably also heard something about my nocturnal habits.' Just after Worthington's wardrobe faux pas at Heathrow, his proposed move to Liverpool collapsed because of his high blood pressure. 'Alf's mistrust in me was entirely of my own doing. Sometimes, we have to accept the consequences of the way we live our lives,' Worthington admitted.

In the early '70s, the dogmatic Ramsey eschewed his long-haired lotharios and west London playboys, stayed loyal to his dwindling band of World Cup winners and selected enforcers and tough tacklers like Norman Hunter and Arsenal midfielder Peter Storey – nicknamed 'Snouty' by his Gunners teammates on account of his ability to sniff out trouble, and 'Cold Eyes' by the less than complimentary press corps. On paper, England recovered well from the disappointment of defeat to West Germany at the 1970 World Cup. A very healthy 93,000 crowd turned up at Wembley to watch Ramsey's men defeat East Germany 3–1 in a November 1970 friendly, and England finished above Switzerland, Greece and Malta in their European Championships qualifying group. There was some disquiet about stodgy old tactics, and starchy old Alf, but prior to England's quarter-final clash with West Germany in April 1972 (there was no full finals tournament until four years later), they'd gone ten games unbeaten since losing to Helmut Schön's side in Léon. But now, the wheels were about to come off.

═══════

At Wembley, England lost 3–1, despite being level at 1–1 until the eighty-eighth minute, and were ripped apart by the flaxen-haired Borussia Mönchengladbach midfielder Günter Netzer, who'd barely merited a mention in Ramsey's team talk that night. The West Germans deployed a mind-spinning 1–3–3–3 formation, with Franz Beckenbauer at sweeper and Netzer in midfield. They shifted positions at will, with Netzer dropping deep so that Beckenbauer could surge into and through the midfield. Half a century later, footage of the verve and energy of the green-shirted West Germans still dazzles. Prior to the game, Ramsey was furious when he learnt that, with barely seventy-two hours' notice, Derby County boss Brian Clough had withdrawn centre-back Roy McFarland from the England squad. Forty-eight hours after the England match, McFarland appeared for his club in a crucial Division One match as the Rams closed in on the title. 'This man calls himself a patriot but he has never done anything to help England,' raged an uncharacteristically perturbed Ramsey about Clough. McFarland's absence posed a real problem for Ramsey, who selected Norman Hunter in his place. 'Bobby [Moore] and I never gelled especially well on the pitch,' Hunter admitted. 'He wasn't overly keen on playing the hard-tackling, aerial game which Jack Charlton enjoyed when they were partners for England.' Hunter was mystified that, as the game progressed, Ramsey didn't alter his formation to shackle Netzer. Bobby Moore informed him that 'Alf wouldn't like it' when Hunter suggested that he 'went after' Netzer.

Operating from an advanced-midfield position, Netzer's quick-silver runs and precision passing constantly troubled England's four-man midfield. In contrast to West Germany's dynamism, England relied on hefty diagonal punts in the direction of the largely stationary forward line of Martin Chivers and Geoff Hurst. It was all about sweat and crosses. 'That bloody diagonal aerial ball,' lamented Frank Worthington, 'was the symbol of the crudeness of the English game in that era. England played in the air, whereas the Germans and the Dutch were playing on the floor.' Worthington's parting shot, 'It's a wonder that any English forward from that time has any brain cells left, given how much we headed heavy balls in those days,' is replete with the grimmest of ironies, given that Worthington – like so many players from the '70s – suffered from Alzheimer's disease for many years before he passed away in 2021.

After the match, the newspapers paid homage to the magnificent West Germans. 'They have an infinite variety to their game as they stroke the ball around in a flood of angles on the ground and in the air. It is like light being fed through a prism,' Geoffrey Green wrote in *The Times*. The German tabloid *Bild* coined the phrase '*Ramba-Zamba-Fußball*' to describe Germany's style of play and the interchange between Beckenbauer and Netzer, who'd initially proposed the 1–3–3–3 formation to coach Helmut Schön. Schön apparently responded to the suggestion, 'Do what you like. I don't mind.'

The English press castigated Ramsey and his stultifying 4–4–2 tactics. 'Have the methods of the only man to win the World Cup for England become as dead as a dinosaur?' asked Alan Hoby in the *Sunday Express*. The personal score between Ramsey and Schön was now 3–3, but, tellingly, Schön had prevailed in the past three encounters between the two teams. In the Berlin return a month later, Ramsey played the dogged Peter Storey, who clung to Netzer like a limpet, as England kicked and scraped their way to a grim 0–0 draw on the night. With Norman Hunter also on the pitch, Ramsey fielded the two most feared English tacklers of the era. 'The English team seems to have autographed my right leg,' said Netzer after the game. 'In descending order, I have marks from Summerbee, Hunter, Ball and Storey.'

Unofficially, at least, Ramsey edged 4–3 ahead of Schön in their personal tussle when, two days after Britain formally joined the European Economic Community (EEC) on 1 January 1973, a Wembley crowd of 36,500 watched 'The Three' (comprising the home nations, and fellow Common Market newcomers Ireland and Denmark) face 'The Six' (made up of players from existing EEC nations Belgium, Holland, Luxembourg, Italy, West Germany and France) in an international friendly. Helmut Schön – in charge of 'The Six' – described the match as 'heralding a new era for Europe', whilst Alf Ramsey – managing 'The Three' for the evening – sidestepped the issue of European integration entirely. 'All big Wembley occasions should be cherished,' was his typically clipped response. 'The Three' was laden with stars, including England's Bobbys: Moore and Charlton. For 'The Six', West German and Dutch players were in plentiful supply: Berti Vogts, Horst Blankenburg, Franz Beckenbauer, Johan Neeskens, Jürgen Grabowski, Wim van Hanegem, Gerd Müller and Günter Netzer all appeared. The game was part of the week-long 'Fanfare For Europe' – a European cultural festival. It was certainly better received than Prime Minister Edward Heath's plan to borrow the Bayeux Tapestry and display it in Westminster Hall. The plan was dropped after critics pointed out that images of Saxons being killed by Normans was hardly a symbol of European cooperation.

'The Three' demonstrated a more blue-collar approach to the match but won anyway, thanks to goals from Scotland's Colin Stein and Denmark's Henning Jensen. On a freezing January evening, placard-bearing protesters outside Wembley complained that the 'Fanfare For Europe' festival had cost British taxpayers around £350,000. With the festival over, the English media was free to wring its hands over the intricacies of the common fisheries policy, and the travails of its national football team.

———

The loss to West Germany in the 1972 Euros was a stark reality check. Whereas Schön's side had rebooted themselves after 1966, England had stagnated. There were clear parallels with the state of both countries' economies at the time. In 1970, West German Chancellor Willy Brandt challenged the nation's industrial captains to bring 'fresh ideas forward to invigorate industry' and they responded in kind as the country prospered. In contrast, British industries failed to modernise factories, upskill managers and reform archaic labour practices. Whereas Netzer's and Beckenbauer's creative, blue-sky thinking helped their team win at Wembley, and go on to win the European Championship, Ramsey's England perished as he stuck doggedly to an almost prehistoric formula. 'The West Germans played the game like they were from another planet,' Norman Hunter said. English football, like its industry, was increasingly rooted in the past. The term 'declinism' – the sense that the past was a better place and the future decidedly uncertain – had been bandied about by political commentators since the end of the Second World War. Now, it manifested itself most clearly in both the state of the economy and the fortunes of Ramsey's England, World Cup winners six years earlier.

The tide of opinion was moving against Ramsey. In 1972, FA vice-chairman Sir Harold Thompson wrote a confidential report on the state of the England team, which asserted that 'the wave of euphoria which followed England's World Cup victory nearly six years ago has long since passed'. In October 1972, a few months after the chastening loss to West Germany, two Cambridge University undergraduates – Steve Tongue and Alan Stewart – founded

FOUL, described as 'Football's Alternative Paper!' The first edition was banged out on a typewriter in the students' union, printed for a grand total of £54 and 1,000 copies were distributed to Cambridge retail outlets. A clear parody of magazines such as *GOAL* and *SHOOT!*, it was not only a reaction to much of the superficial pap in many football magazines but also a form of protest against a sport obsessed with a 'win at all costs mentality'. 'The national team had been humiliated by West Germany,' recalled *FOUL* writer Stan Hey, who later wrote scripts for *Auf Wiedersehen, Pet*, 'and teams of that era including Leeds, Arsenal and Liverpool put more emphasis on effort and organisation than on skill and excitement. Despairing at 'Ramseyism', *FOUL* claimed, 'If England should come good [after the West Germany debacle] the result would be disastrous … because it would once again assert Ramsey's values as the ideal.' Ramsey wasn't the only public figure who found himself at the mercy of satirists. At the same time, *Private Eye* was making digs at Prime Minister Edward Heath, placing him in charge of a struggling company called HeathCo. Heath issued outdated, nonsensical instructions as his company disintegrated.

The underlying message was that Heath, as he failed to control inflation, violence in Northern Ireland and the trade unions, and Ramsey, whose tactics and style seemed archaic, no longer had the solutions to the toughest questions the country and its football team was facing. And of course, both men spoke in rather silly, stilted accents that belonged to the past. With an increasingly emboldened media, the criticism would only increase.

4

THE INFLUENCER

'George Best was the player who moved football
from the back pages to the front pages.'

Pat Crerand

Wembley, November 1970. Mesmerising as ever, Manchester United's George Best saunters into the Tottenham half and, spotting the forward to his left, rolls a pass to the England World Cup winner Bobby Charlton. They've perfected this move countless times since the prodigiously gifted Best made his United debut in 1963 as a seventeen-year-old. Charlton holds on to the ball as Best ghosts into space, before he slips it back to the Ulsterman and he thumps in a left-footed shot, which crosses the line despite a sterling effort by the Spurs goalkeeper to keep it out. With the clock running down, Best floats forward once again, feints left, darts to the right and drills home a magnificent shot to give United a breathless 2–1 victory, and in a Wembley final too.

But this is Wembley Arena, not Wembley Stadium, and United have just won the *Daily Express* five-a-side tournament – and £7,500 in prize money. In 1968, Matt Busby's United had thrashed Benfica 4–1 in front of 92,000 fans at the Twin Towers to get their hands on the European Cup. Two years later, with their Dunlop plimsolls squeaking on the wooden floor, Charlton, Best and co. take the *Daily Express* five-a-side trophy on a lap of honour, holding it aloft in front of 10,000 cheering spectators at the indoor venue half a mile down the road. The contrast encapsulates United's increasingly limited horizons as the decade begins.

The five-a-side tournament is damned with faint praise from the stars. 'It's been quite enjoyable,' says a distinctly underwhelmed Bobby Charlton. George Best is even more nonchalant, telling a scrum of journalists, 'I suppose if you've won everything else, you might as well win this,' before disappearing into the London night. Fretting manager Wilf McGuinness, still insisting that Best 'is in his prime', is concerned that the 'Belfast Boy' disappears rather too often these days. The *Daily Express* five-a-side tournament is the last piece of silverware that Best will win and, although his star quality remains undimmed, his on-pitch powers, mirroring United's waning fortunes, are already in terminal decline.

———

Backstage at Southampton's Mayflower Theatre back in February 2004, I was told that I had ten minutes with George Best. Eighteen months after his liver transplant, Best was star guest on the 'Evening with Jimmy Greaves' tour. 'Ten minutes? Is that all?' I asked. A smirk appeared on Best's face. 'Some of my most memorable performances came when I only had ten minutes,' he quipped. The former United star, minus the puffiness around his face, now bore more than a passing resemblance to the handsome athlete who'd blazed a trail across football forty years earlier. He sipped water throughout and was eventually more than generous with his time, although he was a little surprised with my line of questioning, which centred around Harold Wilson, commercialism, nightclubs, the Manchester scene and his career in the United States, rather than his predilection for bedding Miss Worlds. 'Cheers, I enjoyed that. Different questions to normal,' he grinned, before being whisked away.

In any case, there was no need to ask Best about his multiple sexual conquests because, in his half-hour cameo role onstage, he'd been every inch the unreconstructed male. There was the story of how his Edwardia fashion boutique in Manchester was 'just a better way of pulling more birds' and no evening with George would have been complete without the 'George, where did it all go wrong?' anecdote – the line asked by a porter in a five-star hotel after he spotted Mary Stävin (Miss World 1977) sprawled across a king-size bed strewn with cash and a bottle of Dom Pérignon champagne on the side. It is a tale which Stävin has claimed was one of Best's flights of fancy, but he told it with relish nonetheless. As ever, he was playing to the crowd, and an audience of (mainly) forty-somethings lapped up his well-worn anecdotes, repeated often in a raft of biographies and interviews. Later, without a gallery to play to, Best was – for the most part – less boorish and acutely aware of his seismic influence on football. We spoke about the forces which propelled him to superstardom in the '60s and those which dragged him towards ruin in the '70s. 'They were two sides of the same coin,' Best argued. 'What I'd once enjoyed became a drag.'

There's a compelling argument that Manchester – rather than London or Liverpool, buzzing with the Beatles – was at the epicentre of the '60s cultural revolution. At its fulcrum was Granada Television, whose creator Sidney Bernstein wanted to set up an independent franchise away from London's metropolitan influence. Granada set up shop in Quay Street and produced groundbreaking television, including *Coronation Street* and *World in Action*, attracting young talents, including former Fleet Street scribe Michael Parkinson, writers like Jack Rosenthal and Keith Waterhouse and actors including Tom Bell and Tom Courtenay. The city blossomed and a raft of fashionable boutiques, restaurants, nightclubs and salons proliferated. 'Manchester became the "in" place to be,' explained Best. The embodiment of Manchester 'cool' was Best himself. Aged just nineteen, Best was dubbed 'El Beatle' in 1966 after a superlative display in the European Cup helped United destroy Benfica in Estádio de Luz, and by 1968 he was voted European Footballer of the Year when United won the European Cup. 'I'd never seen a footballer like George,' explained teammate Pat Crerand. 'His balance was perfect. He had everything. He was a star in every sense.'

'I wasn't prepared for what happened to me. No one was. I was the first superstar British footballer. The original,' Best said, entirely matter-of-factly. He transcended the game in a mass-media age (even Hollywood icon Bette Davis wanted his autograph) and his fame extended well beyond the parameters of football. He was a non-conformist, the ultimate baby-boom footballer who did things his way in the era after the abolition of national service and the maximum wage. His very presence in the United starting line-up could add an extra 10,000 to the gate at any First Division ground in England. By the late '60s, Best was lending his name to ghost-written newspaper columns and advertising sausages, oranges, razors and aftershave. He was an 'influencer' half a century before such a term even existed. Whatever Best lent his name to sold like hotcakes. By 1970, Stylo had already sold their 250,000th pair of football boots thanks to Best endorsing them and they presented him with a golden pair to mark the occasion. Even when his problems mounted in the early '70s, and he fled, at different times, to Marbella, Majorca and Acapulco, it wasn't just the press pack who followed him to these fashionable hotspots. British travel agents reported that the mere presence of Best in a resort drove up business there by around 20 per cent.

In Matt Busby's opinion, the thriving social scene in Manchester was a matter of grave concern when it came to the wellbeing of his young protégé. The Manchester Rat Pack descended on the Brown Bull pub (Busby could never remember its name, referring to it as the Black Dog and even the Green Parrot when he chastised Best for frequenting the establishment) on Chapel Street in Salford. It may not have looked much from the outside, or been located in the most salubrious of neighbourhoods, but Best's presence, and its proximity to Granada Studios, meant that it attracted celebrities like moths to the flame. Later on, Best would describe Manchester as 'a village' but the cross-fertilisation of ideas within the shabby-chic Brown Bull opened doors to other worlds. It was there that Best socialised with Michael Parkinson, who made the footballer the subject of a *For the Record* Granada show in 1969. The 25-minute segment, in which Best admitted to 'burning the candle at both ends', saw Parkinson conclude with a thinly veiled warning: 'Best could develop into the greatest footballer there's ever been, always provided that he wants it that way.'

When Best was seriously down on his luck in the late '80s, Granada threw him a lifeline by pairing him with former Manchester City legend Rodney Marsh for several bestselling videos about football from the '70s. That quickly led to the creation of the 'Best and Marsh' roadshow, where the pair chatted about what they termed 'the golden era' of football. 'The Best and Marsh act got me back on track,' Best told me. It packed out venues across the country, after the formation of the Premier League in 1992 saw a surge in interest in 'retro' football. Best remained massively in demand for evening appearances right up to his death in 2005. The frisson in the audience just at the mere mention of his name was palpable, but the fact that he was still trotting out the same old tall stories, and deflecting serious questions about his health, showed that he'd never moved on with his life, or come to terms with his situation.

'I gave up booze in 1969. It was the most boring twenty minutes of my life,' was his response to a punter who asked if, given his liver transplant, he'd stopped drinking. Best's riposte was greeted with predictable guffaws. 'It's what the audience expect to hear,' he told me later. 'I get paid to tell stories about booze and birds.'

Best got plenty of both in the Brown Bull. United and City players mixed freely in the pub, and Best struck up a close friendship with City's Mike Summerbee (Best was later Summerbee's best man at his wedding), which led to the pair setting up the Edwardia fashion boutique in Manchester. 'I was able to chat up girls in the Brown Bull and take them back to the flat above the boutique, away from prying eyes,' Best described. On a more cerebral level, he was able to talk architectural design with Frazer Crane, who later designed Best's futuristic Wimslow house (the publicity which surrounded Best's modernist residence led to a mini explosion of 'WowHaus' houses, which spread from Altrincham to Scandinavia) and was approached by German new wave filmmaker Hellmuth Costard, who, after Best gave permission, arranged for eight cameras to follow his every move for the duration of a league match with Coventry City at Old Trafford. The result was the arthouse *Football As Never Before*, which was released in 1971. Best was also friendly with Salford actor Albert Finney. One of Finney's films – the surreal *Charlie Bubbles* – made a particular impression on Best. Having made it big as writer in London, Bubbles returns to his native Manchester, only to discover that his wealth means he no longer has anything in common with those who surround him. At the end, Bubbles disappears in a balloon. 'When things got tough at United in the '70s, I'd imagine I was Charlie Bubbles, floating away,' Best told me.

As early as 1968, Best had an uneasy feeling that things were already going awry. 'I won the European Cup aged just twenty-two and could feel the ambition go out of the club immediately. I never won another bloody thing with United after '68. That was ridiculous for a player with my talents and a club the size of United,' Best reflected. I reminded the former player of that *Daily Express* five-a-side triumph in 1970. 'Yeah, I forgot about that one. It was good fun actually, but knackering because there's no breaks in five-a-side,' he laughed. Best paused for a moment, looked at me with a mischievous smile and said, 'What about United winning third place in the FA Cup in 1970. Another highlight...' He was alluding to the fact that the FA introduced third/fourth place play-off matches in 1969–70, with United beating Watford 2–0 at Highbury in front of 15,105 people on the Friday night before the final. 'As an aperitif for the FA Cup final,' wrote Norman Fox in *The Times* the next day, 'the play-off failed for no more subtle reason than that it was a non-event between two losers.' Following a 1974 FA Cup committee meeting, the play-off was put out of its misery.

On the subject of niche early '70s competitions, Best became the first British player to score in a penalty shoot-out when he netted from the spot against Hull City in the semi-final of the preseason Watney Cup in 1970. The competition – with the sponsorship provided by brewer Watney Mann – tipped the two highest scoring Football League teams in each of the four divisions the previous campaign against each other and ran for four years. Each club received £4,000 for entering and the winners received £1,000. 'It was a two-bit competition, and Watneys Red Barrel was bloody awful beer too,' Best insisted. United – who'd lost to a Halifax Town side clad in orange shirts with numbers on the back and front in 1971 – declined their invitation to enter a year later, choosing to focus on a 'more structured preseason'.

Best then returned to his point:

The United side which won the European Cup was good but not great, and I think that Matt [Busby] needed to start the rebuilding process after '68 because Bobby [Charlton] and Denis [Law] were already getting older. I got pissed off that United had lost its edge. Before that, my socialising and my football were in balance. After that, things got out of control. I felt that everything was on me.

———

The small screen defined Best in the '70s, laying bare his extravagant footballing gifts and his vulnerability. The litany of superlative strikes took the breath away, but Best's celebrations, once exuberant and carefree, had become more muted. 'After a while, it was only when the goal really meant something that I would let myself go,' he explained. In an October 1970 League Cup clash at Old Trafford with Chelsea, after receiving a ball from John Aston, Best galloped forward, rode a scything lunge from Blues skipper Ron 'Chopper' Harris, rounded Peter Bonetti and side-footed the ball home. He collapsed to his knees in front of a delirious Stretford End. 'I loved that goal because I could hear "Chopper" bearing down on me, breathing out of his arse. I had to stay on my feet because the best way to deal with hatchet men in that era was to embarrass them.' Then there was the sublime lobbed goal over the heads of a bamboozled Tottenham defence – and goalkeeper Pat Jennings – at Old Trafford in a 2–1 league win in February 1971. 'Beautiful, absolutely beautiful,' enthused *Match of the Day* commentator Barry Davies. 'I used to room with Pat [Jennings] for Northern Ireland and I thought he was the finest keeper in the country,' Best told me. 'To get anything past him, or over him, meant it had to be something special.'

But some of what Best saw made him, an avid watcher of football on TV, shudder. He didn't care for the 'clockwork soldiers' – as he put it – who began to dominate the game. 'I wouldn't have paid to watch Leeds or Arsenal if I was a spectator,' he said. 'Zonal marking, those long diagonal balls and 4–4–2 never did much for me, although even at United we'd started to play in that way by the end.' Occasionally, he disgusted himself. At Highbury in August 1970, United were hammered 4–0 by Arsenal, and as Best prepared to dance round Gunners goalkeeper Bob Wilson, Wilson grabbed the ball at the last moment. 'It still gives me nightmares now. In fact, I lay awake thinking about that the other night,' Best explained. And what about the May 1971 British Home Championship clash between Northern Ireland and England? Scottish referee Alistair MacKenzie deemed that Best's foot was too high after he'd pinched the ball from Gordon Banks, as he was poised to launch a drop kick into orbit, and headed the ball home. 'Football authorities hated non-conformity and individualism,' Best insisted.

In November 1970, with Fleet Street doyen Hugh McIlvanney providing the solemn commentary, the BBC broadcast *The World of Georgie Best*. The 25-minute programme showed George at his opulent best: pouring bubbly into a tower of champagne glasses at the launch of his third Manchester fashion boutique, zipping off to see how the construction of his £30,000 house in Bramhall was progressing in his brand-new yellow Lotus Europa sportscar and surrounded by gaggles of girls. But there were clear signs of his increasing detachment from events. After popping into Blinkers nightclub (owner Selwyn Demmy revealed that Best was the only member allowed to flaunt the dress code), Best – sporting a natty tie-dyed T-shirt – was filmed sitting by himself, ogling women and sipping a beer before darting off somewhere else. At the tail end of the programme, the footballer stood on the foundations of his unbuilt house, surveying the surrounding countryside. Far from feeling like he was the king of his castle, Best was maudlin. 'Playing football is a very sad sport,' he explained. 'It's the only thing I've been able to do since fifteen and when you get to thirty to thirty-one you know you're on the way out.' McIlvanney argued that Best's

business interests would sustain him in his dotage, but he was assuming that Best would play top-flight football into his thirties and
wouldn't crash and burn in the not-too-distant future.

———

When I interviewed Ken Stanley, Best's former agent, in the late
'90s, he explained, 'By the age of twenty-four, George, more and
more, had that far-away look in his eyes and wasn't really listening
to anyone.' Stanley clearly still retained a huge amount of affec-
tion for Best, but occasionally put his head in his hands when he
spoke of his former client's decline. He wasn't the only one to do
so. Football-wise, Best was at his peak in 1967–68 when he netted
twenty-eight league goals and United won the European Cup,
but, commercially at least, Best appeared to be in his pomp at the
beginning of the 1970s. The George Best fan club had a member-
ship of 17,000 by 1970 and members from such far-flung places as
Moscow, Sydney and Beijing. 'We sold out all initial 20,000 copies
of the George Best annual in just three days. We ended up selling
120,000,' Stanley explained. The agent – a former UK table tennis
champion – often pondered why it went so wrong for Best:

> I think that it's the curse of having an amazing natural talent.
> George was no mere mortal when it came to football. Although
> he trained hard in the early days, he was blessed with a rare gift
> and operated on a different plane from the others. The fame
> which came his way was all consuming. I think it would have
> turned anyone's head.

Three office girls were hired to wade through the deluge of Best
fan mail in Stanley's Huddersfield office, which reached a peak
of 10,000 letters per week in 1970. Most of it was heartfelt and

entirely innocent. Some of it was crude and downright alarming. 'The things which women – and some men – were offering to do to George made the office girls blush,' Stanley remembered.

It got worse over time. I didn't show everything to George, but there were letters which spooked us. One woman asked if George could visit her terminally ill son in hospital and heal him. Another begged George to send her £1,000 or she'd kill herself. I had to report that one to the police. George would shake his head and look at me perplexed. At first, he loved the adulation, but later he found much of it a nightmare.

In November 1971, it was Best's turn to appear on *This Is Your Life*. At times, the long-running TV show could be cringeworthy, wooden and two-dimensional. Yet, amidst all the '70s ephemera of the guests – the kipper ties, the fog of cigarette smoke, the flowing evening dresses and the pastel-coloured synthetic fibres – the two worlds that Best inhabited were laid bare. The player was sprung by host Eamonn Andrews (with his trademark lopsided grin) at a fashion show in London. Throughout the episode, Best appeared shy, articulate and a dutiful son, grandson and brother, delighted to see his family. Some great Best anecdotes featured in the show. For example, the story about how his tonsils were removed after his habit of sucking red wine gums to convince his mother that he had a sore throat and needed to miss school backfired. And how United scout Bob Bishop – who discovered Best – scoffed, 'He was no Goliath,' after seeing the frail Ulsterman play for the first time.

However, there was a darker undercurrent. By 1971, Best's trips home to his native Belfast were becoming rarer, and, like her son, Ann Best was firmly in the grip of alcoholism. She was dead within seven years of *This Is Your Life* going out, unable to cope with the notoriety that her increasingly errant son's antics in England brought on the family. By the time the show aired, the 25-year-old Best had been ordered by United manager Frank O'Farrell to vacate his Cheshire bachelor pad with its sunken bath and snooker room, which he sold for £40,000 before moving back into digs with his former landlady Mary Fullaway.

Although United were flying high at the top of Division One under new manager O'Farrell, trouble was obviously brewing. Eamonn Andrews referred to the 'distraction of London's social scene'. By now, Best and chums were catching the last train from Manchester Piccadilly on a Saturday night, decamping to London and partying the night away at exclusive nightclubs like Tramp. In January 1971, Best – in an episode which became known as his 'lost weekend' – went missing on the eve of an away match against Chelsea and hid at the Islington flat of Irish actress Sinéad Cusack whilst a media frenzy developed outside. 'It was surreal watching TV footage of the outside of the flat I was sitting inside,' Best told me. In 2018, Best's 'lost weekend' was dramatised for the play *Hello Georgie, Goodbye Best*, which opened in Belfast's Strand Arts Centre, with actor and co-writer Robbie Martin describing Best's life as a 'Shakespearean tragedy'.

Frank O'Farrell, appointed manager in July, contented himself with a self-conscious wave to his star player during *This Is Your Life*, allowing Busby to do all the talking, which spoke volumes for the power still wielded by Busby – by this time a director at Old Trafford. Best had received a death threat from the IRA in the run-up to United's game at Newcastle in October after the Best family was wrongly accused of making a £3,000 donation to the Ulster Unionists. He rarely made political statements, though he admitted in *The World of Georgie Best* that, had he remained in Belfast, he might have 'become one of those Protestants who throws stones at Catholics'. As Best told me,

> What they said about the donation to the Unionists was a lie. But in the early '70s it was a lie that could have got me shot. I was scared witless at Newcastle, although I scored the winner and kept running all game because I thought I'd be harder to shoot if I was a moving target. The police told me I was the first British footballer they knew of against whom a credible death threat had been made.

In the wake of the death threat, Best's form, and soon that of United, went into freefall. Unbeknownst to O'Farrell, Best, who'd netted eleven goals in their first fourteen matches of the season, had already enjoyed the last purple patch of his United career. His appearance on *This Is Your Life* was also the last time that the player would be together with his extended family.

———

When Best's Brown Bull buddy Michael Parkinson headed to the BBC in the early '70s and was given his own late-night chat show, it was inevitable that the footballer – a regular house guest at the Parkinsons' – would be near the top of his most-wanted list, along with John Lennon, Orson Welles and Jimmy Cagney. Best appeared on *Parkinson* (regularly watched by audiences of around 14 million) on three occasions in the '70s, laying bare elements of his troubled soul and voicing dissatisfaction about the state of English football and the pressures of fame. In the Barnsley-born Parkinson, Best saw a fellow pioneer. 'Mike was part-journalist, part-chat show host, which was unheard of in Britain. He was a confidant. I was never going to tell him everything. But I told Mike more than I told anyone else,' Best admitted. Parkinson has written and spoken about Best on multiple occasions, insisting there was 'a melancholy' deep within the star's soul. Best was a beguiling interviewee. He told me that he enjoyed completing crossword and Sudoku puzzles in The Phene pub in Chelsea, where I initially approached him for an interview, and that one of his most humbling moments was meeting Dr Jacob Bronowski, the mathematician and TV presenter. Michael Parkinson later described his interview with Bronowski, who narrated the seminal 1973 BBC TV series *The Ascent of Man*, as his most memorable. 'Bronowski signed my book which accompanied the series. Everyone I knew had a copy of it in the '70s. I was quite star struck,' Best gushed.

Parkinson later claimed that his guests appeared on his show because they had something – a book, a play or a film – to plug. So, what exactly, I asked Best, was he selling when he spoke to Parkinson? 'Nothing. I did it simply because Mike was a pal, and I trusted him,' Best responded. It wasn't because of an early '70s attempt to further the Best brand? 'No, I never thought in those terms. I had no concept of the "brand" thing – not that people used such a term in those days anyway.' Best paused before adding, 'Mind you, I showed what was possible for players like Kevin Keegan and David Beckham, whose advisers think in terms of media profiles and portfolios.' On his second *Parkinson* interview, Best appeared shortly after he'd walked out on United in December 1972. With the club in freefall, Best fled to Majorca claiming to be 'finished with football'.

As his relationship with United deteriorated, Best's commercial empire disintegrated. By 1973, his name was scrubbed off the front of his three Manchester boutiques and, in early 1974, the first footballer on these shores to pull in £100,000 a year had no steady income either. No firm bids transpired. 'It's bad enough inheriting the problem,' explained Coventry boss Joe Mercer, 'but imagine buying it for £300,000.' The chairman of a lower-division Norwegian outfit offered Best 'a selection of superb, hand-picked girls' if he played for them. Best declined the offer. 'I must have been very sober that day,' he told me. Stylo terminated their sponsorship deal with the player, announcing that Kevin Keegan would be their star player from now on.

At this juncture, Best diversified. By 1973, with his friend Malcolm Wagner, who ran the Village Barber hairdressers next to Edwardia, the pair invested £3,000 each in a run-down nightclub on Bootle Street called Del Sol and rebranded it Slack Alice, named after a fictional character from camp comedian Larry Grayson's double-entendre strewn act. 'George wrote to Larry, asked permission to use the name Slack Alice and received a telegram saying, "I would be privileged,"' Wagner explained in our telephone interview. Usually referred to as 'Bestie's', it became a hugely popular nightspot amongst star footballers, actors and celebrities, such as Bruce Forsyth and Kenny Lynch.

An ill-fated encounter at Slack Alice and a brief fling with Miss World 1973 – Marjorie Wallace – eventually led to the Texan beauty queen accusing Best of stealing a fur coat and jewellery. The pending court case only collapsed when Wallace's 'steady' boyfriend – motor racing driver Peter Revson – was killed, and Wallace headed back to the US to grieve. But even though Best revelled in his role as part-owner of a nightclub, he harboured regrets. 'My career shouldn't have fallen apart as it did,' he admitted. There was perhaps only one man whose sombre mood matched that of Best: Ken Stanley. 'When I hear the year 1974 mentioned, I shudder,' he told me, blinking furiously. 'George was 75 per cent of my business, and I had a warehouse full of Best merchandise that was now worthless. Along with a few thousand England World Cup '74 bags too. I think most of the stuff ended up on a bloody great bonfire.' The George

Best fan club officially closed in 1975. Symbolically, his waxwork in Madame Tussauds was replaced with that of Dutch superstar Johan Cruyff, the new hero of European football.

As the '70s progressed, the most creative and influential British player of his generation – and perhaps any other – remained in the spotlight, thanks partly to his profile at Slack Alice and the trail he later blazed to the burgeoning North American Soccer League and his renaissance in the Californian sun with Los Angeles Aztecs and San Jose Earthquakes, and in Florida with Fort Lauderdale. There were also cameo roles at footballing outposts, including Stockport County, Dunstable FC and Cork Celtic, with the paparazzi ready and waiting to pounce whenever the former United star stumbled. But before the Bestie roadshow rolled stateside, there was to be one last, doomed resurrection at Old Trafford under Manchester United's brash new manager, Tommy Docherty.

5

THE REFEREE'S A CULT

'Referees should arrive by the back door
and leave by the back door.'
Alan Hardaker, Football League secretary, 1964

Stamford Bridge, September 1970. Chelsea winger Peter Houseman
cuts in from the left and threads a ball to midfielder Alan Hudson,
who lets fly from the edge of the Ipswich Town penalty area. The
ball clatters against the stanchion at the back of the side netting
and rolls back into play. Houseman throws his arms outwards in
frustration and Hudson shakes his head in annoyance at the near
miss. But referee Roy Capey is pointing towards the centre spot,
signalling that the home team have, much to their bemusement,
scored. Chelsea's sheepish stars – mindful of the fact they're on
£30 each per point – laugh and smirk at one another and trot back
into their own half. Furious Ipswich players remonstrate with Capey,
but the phantom goal stands. At the end of injury time, Chelsea's
Ian Hutchinson rounds Ipswich keeper David Best and strokes the
ball into the empty net, but a second before the ball crosses the
line Capey blows the final whistle. 'As far as we know Chelsea
won 2–1,' broadcasts the stadium announcer, reflecting the sense
of bewilderment swirling around Stamford Bridge.

'I was amazed when the Ipswich players queried it. My two linesmen agreed it was a goal,' Capey states after seeing the TV footage of Hudson's 'phantom' goal. The *Daily Mirror* brands Capey's performance 'downright poor'. 'Stanchion-gate' becomes one of a catalogue of refereeing controversies that define the era. Yet, remarkably, an eclectic bunch of amateur referees – including Wolverhampton butcher Jack Taylor, Lancashire headmaster Gordon Hill and Treorchy-born businessman Clive Thomas – transcend the opprobrium and become media personalities in their own right.

━━━━━

In the early part of the 1970s, referees – under fire from all angles – appeared to be an endangered species. Some of English football's most infamous televised flashpoints rendered them helpless as the sport's most notorious gunslingers traded punches, kung fu kicks and X-rated language. 'When things got rough, refs were like by-standers in a saloon shootout,' Jack Charlton told me. Stourbridge referee Eric Jennings adopted a distinctly laissez-faire attitude to his handling of the 1970 FA Cup final – and the notorious replay at Old Trafford between feuding Chelsea and Leeds United players, which was watched by a TV audience of 28 million. After reviewing, in the late '90s, what was arguably English football's most violent ever match, referee David Elleray insisted that he'd have dismissed six players. By 2020, Michael Oliver had increased the number of hypothetical sendings-off to eleven.

Jennings only booked Chelsea's Ian Hutchinson for a foul on Leeds skipper Billy Bremner, ignoring almost everything else. Chelsea skipper Ron Harris recalled his treatment of Leeds' Eddie Gray in the replay when he guested alongside Jimmy Greaves on the after-dinner speaking circuit in 2005.

He was Leeds' danger man, and needed dealing with. It was my job to neutralise him. Prior to the replay at Old Trafford, the teams lined up together in the tunnel, and the phone went. I turned to Eddie and said, 'That's your ambulance driver telling us when he's arriving, Eddie.'

Harris reduced Gray to a virtual passenger early on, with a swift kick to the back of the Scottish winger's knee. Job done by 'Chopper' Harris, although Harris's teammate and the eventual match-winner David Webb had already attempted to remove Gray from the equation with a two-footed lunge after just two minutes. The game descended into chaos from there on in. Webb launched another two-footed lunge on Leeds striker Allan Clarke. Norman Hunter and Eddie McCreadie traded punches. Peter Osgood knocked Jack Charlton to the turf, Charlton jumped to his feet and barged Osgood over. McCreadie's karate kick on Billy Bremner's neck (McCreadie insisted he was going for the ball) could have maimed the Scottish midfielder.

'The ref let everything go, so both sides policed it themselves and kicked seven shades out of one another,' Jack Charlton recalled with a sharp intake of breath. The friction between the two clubs stemmed from a toxic FA Cup semi-final in 1967, where Leeds lost to Tommy Docherty's side, and the 1970 replay gave everyone a chance to settle a few old scores. 'Much was made of the north/south divide,' explained Alan Hudson, 'but it was more about the clash in styles. Chelsea were off the cuff and flamboyant. Leeds were robots. For them, it was win at all costs. That was really what was at the heart of the issue.' In mitigation, several Blues stars, especially the bullet-headed Harris, would stand up for themselves and both sides were capable of mixing brute force with brilliance.

Moments of quality in the replay were few and far between. Mick Jones's finely crafted shot put Leeds ahead and Peter Osgood's beautifully cushioned header levelled the match. Chelsea went on to win 2–1 thanks to a goal from David Webb, which saw the ball cannon off his shoulder in extra time, but the players were perplexed by Jennings's non-intervention in what proved to be his last game before he retired. 'Several times, I thought that he was about to pull out the book, but he never did. Even I was thinking, "Oh, just bloody get on with it will you…"' Norman Hunter described. David Webb likened the match to being 'overseen by a lenient supply teacher, who turns a blind eye, does his crossword at his desk and lets the class kick the shit out of each other'. 'At times, it appeared that Mr Jennings would give a free kick only on production of a death certificate,' Hugh McIlvanney wrote in *The Observer*. When questioned by football writer Brian Glanville as to why he didn't intervene more, Jennings replied, 'It was my last game, and I wasn't going to mar that by sending players to the changing rooms early.'

Boston referee Ray Tinkler's fifteen-year career will for ever be remembered for his controversial decision to allow play to continue at Elland Road in the clash between Leeds and West Bromwich Albion in April 1971. Leeds were trailing 1–0, needing a victory to maintain their lead over Arsenal in the title race, when Tony Brown intercepted a misplaced pass by Norman Hunter and raced clear of the Leeds defence. Albion's Colin Suggett had been standing in an offside position when Brown received the ball and the linesman raised his flag immediately. Tinkler ignored his linesman but he didn't lower his flag and Leeds players wrongly assumed play had stopped. Tinkler was known for playing the advantage (although referees were instructed to halt play when any player was in an offside position in that era), and later argued, 'I was a man who was way ahead of my time.' When Brown surged forward, he slipped the ball to Jeff Astle, who gave Albion a 2–0 lead. All hell broke loose. 'Leeds will go mad. And they've every right to go mad,' cried BBC *Match of the Day* commentator Barry Davies, as Leeds players and even the club secretary surrounded Tinkler. Leeds lost out on the Division One title to Arsenal by a point. Decades later, Tinkler reflected,

> There are some Leeds fans who still bear me a grudge. I was a farmer, and when I was selling potatoes in Yorkshire, one guy used to come and say, 'I'll have some of that bastard referee's potatoes.' I charged him a fiver extra per tonne for calling me that, but I never lose any sleep over what I did.

According to a *Daily Mail* poll carried out in September 1970, seventy-eight out of ninety-two clubs 'condemned referees', with twelve clubs claiming refereeing was 'adequate' and two clubs abstaining, leading the newspaper's Jeff Powell to conclude that 'the vast majority of Football League clubs are dissatisfied with the standard of refereeing'. Roy Darlington of Runcorn stood down after four years as a top-grade official, telling the *Daily Mail* in January 1971, 'It's all about the players' lack of respect for referees, as simple as that.'

In 1970 and 1971, there was much hand wringing in both the media and in government about the escalating level of violence in the UK. Anti-Vietnam War protests got out of hand in Whitehall and violence broke out in Notting Hill between African-Caribbean residents and the police. In Ulster, after the first British soldier was shot dead since British troops moved into Northern Ireland, the number of car bombs and assassinations increased. Far-left militant group the Angry Brigade exploded various devices in and around London. When, following the release of *A Clockwork Orange* in British cinemas, a mob brutally murdered a homeless man in London, copying the actions of Alex and his Droogs in the movie, Stanley Kubrick pulled the film and gave it an X rating.

Referees pondered the rise in aggression on the pitch. 'More and more, I'd see players' tonsils during matches. They hunted in packs, the theory being that referees would only book individual players. Leeds were very vocal, working as a unit. Arsenal were bad too. McLintock, Storey and McNab … Very aggressive,' the granite-jawed Jack Taylor, who'd taken charge of the 1974 World Cup final, told me. Norfolk newsagent Norman Burtenshaw, who refereed the 1971 FA Cup final between Arsenal and Liverpool, explained how financial factors were to blame. 'By the early '70s, teams could miss out on around £50,000 by failing to qualify for Europe. Winning, rather than entertaining, was more crucial. Teams were willing to take short cuts to get what they needed, like going through opponents when they tackled them and stealing yards at free kicks,' he stated in his autobiography.

Help – of sorts – was at hand. In August 1971, Football League referees were sent a memorandum that was short, sharp and simple. The tackle from behind, which was maiming so many players, was outlawed. Any player who handled the ball deliberately to stop another player gaining an advantage would also be booked. Anyone who argued persistently with officials would also be cautioned. 'This will clean up the game, and make referees' lives 100 times easier,' Alan Hardaker said in the press later that week, but it didn't exactly pan out that way.

The main problem was that the season had already started three days earlier, which gave clubs no time to prepare or adjust their style of play to account for the rule changes during the close season. Several managers even denied any knowledge of having received information about the rule changes from the Football League. 'Clubs received communication,' barked Alan Hardaker, 'and those that claim they didn't are lying.' The first flashpoint occurred on 18 August 1971. At a febrile Stamford Bridge, referee Norman Burtenshaw booked Manchester United's Willie Morgan in the forty-first minute after Morgan repeatedly argued that Chelsea's Peter Osgood had fouled a United defender in the build-up to Blues forward

Tommy Baldwin's goal. As Morgan slunk away, George Best approached Burtenshaw, looked him in the eye and said, 'You are a fucking disgrace.' With Morgan now some distance away, Best's insistence that he was talking to Morgan seemed unlikely. Burtenshaw pulled out his book and asked, 'What's your name?' 'Best,' came the response. 'Initial?' the referee enquired. 'George Best,' was the reply. Burtenshaw ordered him off and Best collapsed to the turf, clutching his head in disbelief. In the days following the game, Burtenshaw received death threats, both by telephone and by mail. 'Some of the language used was absolutely revolting and filthy,' he recalled. 'All this for £10.50 per game.'

One referee in particular believed the rule changes placed referees in an invidious position. Headmaster Gordon Hill – famed for his Sergeant Pepper-style moustache and use of industrial language on the football pitch – deployed modernist principles: 'For me, refereeing with words and humour was going to be far more effective than just brandishing the notebook and the pencil. I decided that, more than ever, the progressive approach that I fought for in the schools I ran was going to be key on the pitch.'

There wasn't a more divisive word in early 1970s education circles than 'progressive'. Rather than viewing pupils as meek subjects, drilling them with facts and yelling at them, progressives argued that education should be child-centred, with the use of informality and humour more conducive to producing well-balanced individuals. The press ran stories about furious teachers quitting the profession amidst stories of 'anarchy' in secondary schools. 'To be progressive took planning and a certain type of personality. I refused to have any kind of corporal punishment in my schools. Children were no different from footballers. You had to earn their respect and get them on your side,' Hill told me. However, the permissive Hill wasn't deaf to the terrace chants of the era: 'I first heard the "Who's the bastard in the black?" chant on *Match of the Day*, and before you knew it, every crowd across the country started singing it. Authority was being increasingly challenged.' But Hill stuck doggedly to his belief that a humanist approach worked best.

In his later years, Hill settled in Exeter and became a professional artist. When I visited his gallery, he showed me a painting he called his 'United v. City creation', consisting of ten blue dots, ten red dots and two yellow dots for the goalkeepers. 'And that's me,' Hill said, pointing to a tiny black dot in the centre of the painting. I suggested that the black dot should be a little larger, given his larger-than-life persona. He smiled ruefully. His brand of showmanship irked fellow whistlers. He explained why, by the early '70s, he'd decided to rebel and started unzipping his black referee's top to the sternum, revealing a white T-shirt beneath, thus giving the impression he was sporting an open-collar shirt. 'I saw George Harrison on a US chat show, liked the way he looked and I thought it was about time English referees became more rock 'n' roll. I stuck with the look,' he described. Hill's sartorial sedition didn't go down too well with fellow referee Jack Taylor. 'He told me I needed to smarten up,' Hill explained. But he never listened.

Hill became matey with the coterie of early '70s football characters. The coolest classroom rebel of them all, George Best, loved Hill. In *Best: An Intimate Biography*, the footballer told Michael Parkinson,

> You'd say to Gordon, 'That was a bloody stupid decision,' and he'd say. 'You're not playing too well either.' Next time you keep your mouth shut because he'd take the piss out of you. I rate Gordon Hill. I think he's a fine referee and there's not many I'd say that about.

Hill also got on the wrong side of Liverpool's notoriously combative hard man Tommy Smith, who took him to task after a decision went against the home side at Anfield, telling him, 'That was a fucking shit decision, Gordon.' 'But it wasn't as fucking shit as that shot you had a few minutes ago which ended up in the Kop, was it, Tommy?' Hill retorted. Smith, Hill told me, walked away laughing.

Hill's taste for the limelight didn't always sit comfortably with some players either. 'Bobby Charlton was always curt. I'd have a drink in the players' lounge after games. I felt that if I socialised with the players, we'd have each others' backs on the pitch. Bob used to look at me, as if to say: "You don't belong here,"' Hill described. He wasn't the only referee who stood accused of being a touch ingratiating. In 1975, Manchester City players complained that referee Roger Kirkpatrick 'thought he was the twenty-third player on the pitch', after making penalty-taker Dennis Tueart retake his spot kick twice due to an encroachment on the penalty box. *The Times* later described Kirkpatrick – who once asked a distinctly unimpressed dressing room full of Leeds players whether he'd look better in a toupee – as having a 'chubby frame and glistening pate who finds publicity as readily as Elizabeth Taylor or Vanessa Redgrave'. However, Kirkpatrick, nicknamed 'Mr Pickwick' on account of his bald head and hugely impressive sideburns, possessed a fearsome burst of acceleration across the pitch, which endeared him to crowds across the country. 'I'm only a little bloke with short legs – I have to flippin' run like that,' he told the *Sunday Times* in 1971.

Curiously, at the end of the 1971 FA Cup final, referee Norman Burtenshaw fell to his knees and punched the air in delight, not – as he later explained – because he was an Arsenal fan (they'd just beaten Liverpool), but because he 'couldn't face doing it all again in a Cup final replay'. After the 1978 FA Cup final, referee Derek Nippard, along with linesmen John Lydon (not the Sex Pistols frontman) and Jim Bent, completed a lap of honour after the final whistle. The FA wrote Nippard a letter praising his performance during the game but instructed all referees to refrain from indulging themselves like that in future. Nippard had also refereed the televised match between Derby County and Leeds United at the Baseball Ground in November 1975 where, following an on-going spat between the Rams' Francis Lee and the visitors' Norman Hunter, both men were dismissed. As the pair trudged off the pitch, they traded punches again, which resulted in a free-for-all between both sets of players. Lee's split lip required stitches. He served a four-match ban and was fined £250, but Hunter went unpunished, 'Bloody right too,' laughed Bites Yer Legs in our interview. 'Perhaps after this, referees will be paid danger money,' Nippard said half-jokingly.

═══════

Thanks to their newly acquired TV fame and (minor) celebrity status, Gordon Hill and Norman Burtenshaw spawned '70s football's arguably most niche literary genre – 'ref lit' – when they penned their respective autobiographies *Give a Little Whistle: The Recollections of a Remarkable Referee* (1975) and *Whose Side Are You on Ref? My Life in Soccer* (1973). County Durham referee Pat Partridge added to the list with *Oh, Ref!* in 1979. The biographies are often surprisingly fast-paced, very detailed, delightfully catty and (sometimes) unintentionally hilarious. Prior to the 1971 FA Cup final, Burtenshaw recalled receiving a small parcel from the FA in the referee's room containing a pair of laces and a jockstrap. In a Boxing Day match at Goodison Park, an Everton fan yelled, 'Get back to your fucking pear tree, Partridge,' after a decision went against the home side. In Gordon Hill's book (co-writer Jason Tomas described him as a 'trendy, rebellious personality'), he admitted that his easy-going approach failed to cut much ice with the authorities, and the biggest game he ever took charge of was the 1975 League Cup final. Both Burtenshaw and Partridge took issue with Hill's tendency to swear on the pitch, and Partridge accused him of wanting to 'be the most popular guy with the players'. Hill admitted to me that he was a quintessentially English referee, and that his experience of officiating matches involving foreign teams didn't end well. An Anglo-Italian Cup match between Lazio and Wolves in 1970 Rome ended in riot police entering the field after Hill sent off the Lazio goalkeeper. 'I used to prefer to use words, not the book, and that didn't always work with foreign sides when players couldn't understand what I said to them, or claimed they couldn't...' he wrote in *Give a Little Whistle*.

The whistlers used their autobiographies to air their grievances against a raft of figures in the game. Pat Partridge was surprisingly cutting when it came to England goalkeeper Gordon Banks ('a player who believed in his own publicity') and Manchester United's Bobby Charlton ('one of the biggest moaners I have ever come across'). Norman Burtenshaw described Manchester City forward Francis Lee as a 'flanneller in the box' and claimed Arsenal's Frank McLintock called him 'bent' in the 1971 FA Cup final. Their views on foreigners were either prejudiced and clichéd (Burtenshaw insisted that sneaky fouls 'crept into the English game from the continent long before Britain entered the Common Market') or plain alarming. Pat Partridge appeared impressed with the right-wing military regime in Argentina – which had been heavily criticised for its appalling human rights record – during the 1978 World Cup, where he officiated the Peru v. Poland match. The organisers, he insisted, 'should have received a public apology in all the world's newspapers'. In *Give a Little Whistle*, even the good-natured Hill couldn't resist delivering a sweeping broadside at his polar opposite, Clive Thomas: 'I referee with my mouth, whereas Clive's talking is done with a whistle; he sees the game in purely black and white terms.' Some thirty years after he put those thoughts to paper, I asked Hill if he regretted the passage, given the unwritten rule that referees don't criticise one another. Hill was adamant. 'No, I don't. I wanted to be part of the show in my refereeing career, but Clive wanted to hog the limelight,' he said.

━━━━━

Decades after hanging up his whistle for the last time, former ref Clive Thomas is still being talked about. In April 2020, as the BBC delved into its extensive football archives during the Covid-19 lockdown, highlights were shown of the controversial 1977 Liverpool v. Everton FA Cup semi-final at Maine Road. With the scores tied at 2–2, Thomas overruled his linesman, disallowing Bryan Hamilton's perfectly good-looking goal in the eighty-fifth minute, which may well have sent the Toffees to Wembley. Judging from the fact that Thomas's name trended on Twitter for days, it's still a decision that rankles with Evertonians. After the match, Thomas refused to clarify his reasoning, stating only that 'there was an infringement of the rules of association football'.

In his entertaining autobiography *By the Book* he claimed that he blew up because Hamilton was offside, even though the Liverpool players accepted that he clearly wasn't. When the BBC first aired the popular *Match of the 1970s* series in the mid-1990s, and it came to the 1976–77 season, Liverpool skipper Emlyn Hughes claimed, 'I met Clive on holiday last year, and he admitted, "I might have got that wrong."' At the end of the following week's episode, the rider stated, 'In last week's episode it was suggested that Clive Thomas had admitted he made a mistake in the 1977 FA Cup semi-final. We would like to make it clear that Clive Thomas has never made such a claim.' The statement was so blunt and to the point that it could have been written by the man from Treorchy himself.

Only once, it seems, was Thomas silenced. Whilst refereeing a Fourth Division clash between Reading and Tranmere Rovers in

March 1976, he saw at first hand the extravagant skills of striker Robin Friday, the darling of Elm Park, who had a reputation for hell raising off the pitch. By all accounts, as the title of Paul McGuigan and Paolo Hewitt's biography on Friday suggests, he was perhaps the greatest footballer you never saw. In the first half, Friday controlled a loose ball on his chest, spun around and volleyed his rocket shot home from the halfway line. Thomas stood and applauded. After the match, the referee approached Friday, informing him that it was the best goal he'd ever seen. 'Really?' Friday asked. 'You should come down here more often. I do that every week.' Thomas remained open-mouthed.

As an up-and-coming official in the late 1960s, Thomas received a letter signed by Alan Hardaker which pointed out that the rookie league referee:

1. Had allowed far too much rough play.
2. Had hesitation and indecisiveness in control.
3. Didn't inspire confidence in his decisions.

By the '70s, Thomas – by this time nicknamed Clive 'the Book' by the media, thanks to his predilection for using it – had eliminated those elements from his game, but used to look at Hardaker's letter once a year 'in order to keep my feet on the ground'. Although Thomas produced and sold referees' equipment, on the pitch he exuded the air of a Victorian schoolmaster marshalling a bunch of urchins. He was brusque, stand-offish and aloof – the antithesis of Gordon Hill. And yet, at heart, Hill and Thomas – both deemed not good enough to make the cut back in their youth – were frustrated footballers. Refereeing was the next best thing to playing. Thomas's David Brent-esque comment towards the end of his autobiography: 'It is my simple belief that I am an entertainer, a performer who re-fuses to accept that there are on the field only twenty-two players,' chimes with Gordon Hill's: 'I just wanted to be part of football.' Both craved the limelight. But whereas Hill rubbed shoulders with the stars, Thomas sought out no such friendships.

By the mid-1970s, Thomas was becoming renowned for his flamboyant and often controversial decisions. In March 1974, in the midst of a toxic Manchester derby, he ordered both sides off for a ten-minute cooling down period when City's Mike Doyle and United's Lou Macari refused to leave the pitch after Thomas sent them off. He also made an indelible mark on the world stage. In 1976, he took charge of a spectacularly feisty European Championship semi-final between Czechoslovakia and Holland. 'Johan Cruyff was one of the worst. You had to nail him at the very beginning because if he knew he had control of you then you had had it,' the ref noted. Thomas more than made his point in this match, booking Cruyff in the second half.

After dismissing Johan Neeskens in the seventy-sixth minute for a bad foul on Zdenek Nehoda, Thomas also gave Dutch striker Willem van Hanegem his marching orders, who was booked for dissent on the way back to the halfway line after the Czech's second goal and sent off before the game had even kicked off again. 'Thomas said, "Come over here." Normally the referee comes to the player, so I stayed where I was. He said again, "Come here." I stayed where I was,' van Hanegem told *Brilliant Orange* author David Winner. Thomas was insistent that all players should come to him. 'I am not prepared to run around the field to seek out a recalcitrant footballer,' the ref reasoned. At first, van Hanegem refused to leave the field and Thomas was in the process of walking off and abandoning the game when van Hanegem finally shuffled off. With Holland down to nine men, Czechoslovakia scored a third to go through to the final. 'He's just incredibly vain, when you see that little man walk, so pedantic … always saying, "Come here,"' van Hanegem recalled.

Fellow referees noted Thomas's penchant for theatrics on the pitch. Pat Partridge even took issue with the way he started a match: 'I call him Kick-Start. Have you ever watched him start a game? I used to do that to a motorbike and it started but I never thought it would work with a human being.' 'Whenever Clive flung red or yellow cards around, he did so with pomposity and relish,' Gordon Hill recalled. Issuing cards in English league matches was not a luxury afforded to Gordon Hill, as they weren't introduced until 1976, by which time he'd retired from refereeing at the statutory age of forty-five, though he carried on officiating in the North American Soccer League (NASL) when he took up a headship post there in the '70s. Not that Hill approved of referees brandishing cards anyway. 'They just up the ante, making situations more emotive,' he told me.

Clive Thomas is perhaps most infamous for disallowing Zico's late headed winner at the death in Brazil's 1–1 draw with Sweden at the 1978 World Cup, an incident that will inevitably be part of any top ten controversial footballing moments programme. Prior to the tournament, Thomas had declined to sign a contract preventing World Cup referees from speaking to the press. 'You know me,' he told the *Mirror* in May 1978. 'If I've got something to say, I say it.' Having played almost four minutes of injury time at the end of the match, Thomas decided that there was enough time on the clock for Nelinho to deliver a corner. He took an *achingly* long time, placing and replacing the ball several times, but in the seconds that elapsed between the corner being taken and Zico nodding home, Thomas blew the final whistle. He remained unrepentant about his decision: 'To have blown up early would have been dishonest. To have allowed Zico's goal to stand would have been dishonest.' Disappointed that Jack Taylor criticised him on TV for denying Brazil the late winner (Taylor insisted that he should have blown up before the corner was taken), Thomas was sent home by Friedrich Seipelt, a member of FIFA's referee's committee. 'In a literal sense, Clive is absolutely right. Time was up, but for him it was all about the letter of the law, whereas my approach was more about the spirit of the law,' Gordon Hill concluded after looking at footage of the goal once more on his laptop.

However, both Taylor and Thomas had one thing in common: they'd both become VIP whistlers. In 1974, Taylor had entered the field of play before the World Cup final clutching the Telstar ball dramatically above his head. With his jet-black hair, granite-hewn jawline and brooding looks, he stood chuckling with Johan Cruyff and Willem van Hanegem as he delayed the start of the final because there were no corner flags in place. Within a minute of the match starting, he'd awarded Holland a penalty after the marauding Cruyff was brought down. Clive Thomas left the field in the Mar del Plata stadium with a trail of disgruntled Brazilian stars trailing in his wake, yelling obscenities at him, and with a string of controversial headlines already being penned. 'Zico was too late,' Thomas insisted. 'Possibly only four-tenths of a second too late, but too late nevertheless.'

Referees had become headline news. In the '60s, Alan Hardaker claimed that officials 'should arrive by the back door and leave by the back door'. Now, with TV cameras picking up their every nuance and contentious decision, the men in black were an essential part of the footballing theatrics.

6

THE PARKA AND THE PITCH INVASION

'We pulled off something amazing which united the whole city and which still bonds us as a group. Everyone with the slightest interest in football knows about what happened that day.'

Colin Addison, speaking in 2020

Edgar Street, February 1972. 'Get out t'way, lad, leave it to me!' yells Hereford midfielder Ronnie Radford at player-manager Colin Addison in full Yorkshire brogue, as teammate Brian Owen tees him up for a long-range punt at goal. The odds of Radford scoring in this FA Cup third-round replay are stacked against him. On a glue-pot surface, Radford is fully 35 yards out, and later admitted that from distance 'my shots usually end up in the car park behind the stand'. But after the ball sits up on a divot, Radford lets fly with the utmost venom. Newcastle United striker Malcolm Macdonald is way back down the pitch and watches Radford shape to shoot and is in line with the trajectory of the ball. He knows what's coming. 'There's no way you're saving that, pal,' he says to himself, as goalkeeper Willie McFaul flies vainly through the air. Within seconds of Radford's shot tearing into the back of the net, the pitch is awash with delirious parka-clad youngsters, and the bewildered scorer is almost swept away in a tidal wave of joyful celebration. An extra-time Ricky George winner sees Hereford defeat the team that sits four divisions above them in a match that would go down in English footballing history.

———

It's been voted the greatest FA Cup giant killing on scores of occasions. Ronnie Radford has been asked about his goal so many times that, for years, he went into hiding every time FA Cup third-round day approached, after he suffered from a spot of giant-killing fatigue. 'You're lucky you rang in October,' he laughed when I spoke to him on the phone. His insanely struck 35-yard thunderbolt has been screened hundreds of time at the start of televised FA Cup coverage. Before I even engaged in a spot of market research and asked '70s football enthusiasts on Facebook what their favourite match of the decade was, I already knew how the majority would respond. The question remains, why do the sights, sounds and scenes from that Hereford v. Newcastle FA Cup clash (with the 1973 FA Cup final between Leeds and Sunderland a not-too-distant runner-up) remain so indelibly imprinted in the collective minds of football fans from that era, and, indeed, those who weren't even born when the match was played? Why does it transcend so many other memorable FA Cup moments from an era when the competition had an air of mystique surrounding it?

On the face of it, it's a moot point as to whether it was even the greatest non-league FA Cup story of the '70s. In 1975, Southern League Wimbledon travelled to First Division Burnley in the third round and won 1–0, thanks to a goal from Mick Mahon. They then ventured to Elland Road and somehow clung on to a 0–0 draw with Jimmy Armfield's Leeds United, who'd reach the European Cup final that season, thanks to the heroics of goalkeeper Dickie Guy, who even saved a Peter Lorimer penalty in the second half. The

Dons unluckily lost the replay 1–0 thanks to a Dave Bassett own goal. The problem is that no footage exists of Wimbledon's heroics at Turf Moor because Burnley chairman Bob Lord refused to allow cameras into the ground. 'Television will spell the death knell for football, and will drain clubs of its fans,' he insisted. Mahon's goal, alas, was not blessed with the immortality which television footage has afforded Hereford's efforts in 1972.

'Everything that you see on the television coverage is of its time. It's like an artefact. It screams 1972 at you,' former Hereford striker Billy Meadows explained. The match is a cornucopia of early 1970s symbolism: from Newcastle striker Malcolm Macdonald's superlative mutton-chop sideburns, to the muddy morass of a pitch which, in Macdonald's words, 'wasn't really fit to play on, but because of the postponements due to heavy rain, it had to be played, come hell or high water'. From the pale-blue bubble car oddly parked amongst a clutch of Hereford fans, to the fact that, behind both goals, hordes of home fans were held back only by lengths of rope. When the parka posse breached the barricades after both Radford's equaliser and Ricky George's winner there was an explosion of unfettered joy, all overseen by laughing policemen who behaved like over-indulgent parents as the kids entered proceedings. There are peculiarities: an entire absence of ball boys ('because the crowd was so hemmed in, the club thought they'd do the job just as well,' said Billy Meadows) and the proliferation of supporters sitting on crates by the side of the pitch. Some fans were also perched on bales of hay and, following sixty-four separate press requests for seating, photographers sat in rows on crates behind the goal lines.

After the Hereford team had arrived back from Newcastle after drawing the first game 2–2 at St James's Park, Edgar Street was full with locals. As Colin Addison explained in our 2020 telephone interview,

The club was selling batches of tickets to local businesses. By tea-time of the next day, they'd all gone. The vice-chairman came in in a panic and said to the chairman Frank Miles, 'Frank, we've sold out of tickets.' Frank's response was: 'Don't worry. Print some more.' He then looked at the local chief of police who was in there for approval and, after a few seconds' deliberation, the police chief said, 'OK, but not too many...'

The official attendance for the replay is unknown, and the fact that Hereford supporters were perched on the floodlight pylons speaks volumes for the virtual absence of health and safety procedures during this pre-Hillsborough Disaster era.

Despite Edgar Street's proximity to the Welsh border, the sights and sounds on that wintry day were quintessentially English. The photographs taken from behind Willie McFaul's goal after the mud-splattered Ronnie Radford's screaming effort tore past him shows the scorer with his arms splayed outwards, the kids running amok, with packed terraces, leafless trees with fans nestled in the branches and the dreaming spire of Hereford's All Saints Church providing a stark, yet dramatic, backdrop to events on a chilly, foggy, muddy English winter day. Nature is fused with industry and the church. It's Lowry-esque, a composite of what English football once looked and smelt like. Or perhaps an idyll of what many *think* English football was like in the early '70s, with all its quirks and eccentricities.

There were also bizarre coincidences at play in this particular giant killing. In the previous season, Ronnie Radford played for Division Four side Newport County at non-league Barnet in the FA Cup first round proper. Barnet beat Newport 6–1, with Ricky George scoring a hat-trick for the home side. A year later, both players were on the same side, scoring against Newcastle. Then there was Ricky George's and Billy Meadows's prescient conversation with Newcastle legend Jackie Milburn before the game. On the night before the replay, the pair went out to dinner and returned to Hereford's Green Dragon Hotel at about 10.30, where they were met by Newcastle United legend Jackie Milburn. Meadows recalled,

> Milburn seemed none too impressed that Ricky and me were still up and about. 'If I was your manager, I'd have you tucked up in bed by now,' he said. Ricky knew he was sub for the game and – never a shrinking violet – came back at Milburn: 'If I come on to-morrow and score the winning goal, nobody will mind, will they?'

Up at St James's Park, Hereford had given Newcastle an almighty scare, drawing 2–2. With 8,000 fans on specially chartered trains to the north-east to cheer them on, and Hereford players on £100 a man for a draw or a win, Brian Owen, after seventeen seconds, drilled in a 25-yarder so cleanly that it stuck in the stanchion of McFaul's net. Colin Addison hit home another wonder goal from 30 yards to secure the replay. Hereford even had late chances to win the game. As Addison recalled, 'Many forget that the Edgar Street match was the replay. People have talked about the state of our pitch and how it evened up skill levels, but at St James's Park, on First Division turf, we went toe to toe with Newcastle.' The downside is that – in keeping with so many games from the era – no footage exists of the match. 'It's such a shame,' explained Malcolm Macdonald, 'the first match only exists in the memory of those who played in it or who were there.' Macdonald believes Owen's and Addison's strikes at St James's Park 'were every bit as memorable as Ronnie Radford's'. At the final whistle, the home crowd sportingly applauded the Hereford players off the pitch. 'Drawing up there was an astonishing result,' explained Colin Addison. 'The gulf between First Division players and Southern League players was a chasm. Nowadays, plenty of non-league sides are full time, but that was unheard of back then. We were scattered across the country, and I'd only see all the players as a group on matchdays.'

The replay didn't take place for nearly two weeks because of the amount of rain deposited on Hereford in the intervening period. The repeated postponements suited Hereford better than Newcastle. 'We had our day jobs,' recalled Billy Meadows, who was a carpet cleaner, 'and Ricky and I lived in Barnet and Ronnie [Radford], who was a carpenter, lived in Gloucester, so we weren't actually in Hereford to live and breathe the build-up to the match. The replay wasn't foremost in our minds like it was for the Newcastle players.'

The wait became tiresome, even a little unhygienic for the Newcastle team. As Malcolm Macdonald recalled,

> We travelled down to the West Country to stay in Worcester for the game the following night. The game got called off once, then twice. We'd packed overnight bags but after another postponement we found the replay would finally happen on the Saturday. We went to a Cecil Gee shop in Worcester where we bought some pants, shirts and socks as our clothes began to stink and whiled away the time playing hands of cribbage in a lovely medieval style pub called the Dirty Duck in Worcester, minus alcohol, of course.

By now, Macdonald was at the centre of a tabloid storm, which he claimed wasn't his fault. No '70s forward buckled more swash than the swaggering, stocky, confident, sweatband-wearing Macdonald, who, in the late '60s, had turned out as a full-back for Tonbridge in the Southern League, with Billy Meadows one of his opponents. He'd joined Newcastle from Luton for £180,000 in 1971, scored a hat-trick in his first game for the club against Liverpool, had his front teeth knocked out in the same game after colliding with Ray Clemence's knee and already plundered twenty-three goals before the match at Edgar Street. In the lead-up to the replay, the *Daily Mirror* ran a story claiming that Macdonald had boasted he'd score ten goals in the replay, thus eclipsing Ted McDougall's nine-goal haul for Bournemouth in the first round against non-league Margate. 'I never said that I'd beat McDougall's record,' he insisted. 'I had a *Sun* column and the *Mirror* stitched me up. I'd never uttered the comments they attributed to me. It set me up as a bit of a pantomime villain.' Yet, Macdonald was photographed in the *Mirror* holding up all ten of his digits, and Hereford goalkeeper Fred Potter claimed that Macdonald told him prior to the match that he would put ten past him. Whatever the full truth behind the tabloid 'exclusive', Colin Addison pinned the article up in the Hereford dressing room, urging his charges to throw Macdonald's boasts back in his face.

Addison had joined Hereford in October '71 as player-manager after transferring from First Division Sheffield United. His Bramall Lane colleagues tried to get him to change his mind, but, at thirty-one, Addison wasn't a regular starter and he was keen on pursuing a coaching career. After two visits to Edgar Street, he took the plunge. Chairman Frank Miles made it very clear to the former Arsenal and Nottingham Forest midfielder that securing league status for the Southern League side was paramount. 'Hereford were geared up for league football, and luring Colin [Addison] to the club was a masterstroke because as well as being a great player he had the drive and the organisational skills to make it happen,' Billy Meadows explained. Addison trusted his players implicitly: 'Players were doing the right thing at the local clubs they trained with during the week, like Ricky and Billy at Barnet. They never let me down.'

A month or so after Addison arrived, he was thrown full-tilt into the drama of the FA Cup run, and nearly cost his team dear when, in the dying moments of the first-round match against King's Lynn, he lost his man at a corner and only a fantastic one-handed Fred Potter save kept his side in the cup. 'Fred really had a go at me. My lack of concentration almost cost us. It showed that nobody was above anyone else at Hereford, certainly not the player-manager!' The Bulls won the replay and then defeated Northampton Town after two replays. 'Players prefer to play than train, and we were so fired up with the cup run and the Southern League that our sense of momentum never faltered,' Addison explained.

With Newcastle manager Joe Harvey struggling to maintain his cool due to the multiple postponements, the replay finally took place at the third time of asking, with *Match of the Day* cameras present to record events. 'For any team to have *Match of the Day* cameras at their ground back then was a big deal. But at a non-league side? This was a massive badge of honour,' Ronnie Radford explained. Harvey's players, wearing an all-red away strip, acquitted themselves reasonably well in the first half but struggled to create any real chances of note. The closest they came to scoring was when a Mick McLaughlin clearance hit Newcastle's John Tudor, rebounded against the crossbar and Terry Hibbitt clattered the follow-up against Fred Potter's stanchion. In the second half, Hereford's Ken Mallender headed against the Newcastle post, but the Toon still remained confident of gaining a result and their smooth operators Terry Hibbitt and the skilful Scot Tony Green, a £150,000 signing from Blackpool a few months before, continued to press forward menacingly. On eighty-three minutes, Green pushed the ball wide to Viv Busby, whose pinpoint cross was headed home emphatically by Macdonald. 'Bang. Goal. I was relieved rather than elated. I was thinking: "This is it, and we can all go home,"' Macdonald told me. In the commentary box, John Motson, on a three-month trial with the BBC and on his first *Match of the Day* excursion, uttered, 'That's it.' To all intents and purposes, the tie appeared to be over. After

Macdonald's goal, there was even a minor pitch invasion. Two long-haired Newcastle fans huddled the players, who all looked relieved that the win had seemingly been secured.

Hereford players were furious that their hard work might be for nothing. Minutes later, Ronnie Radford's moment arrived. 'The ball sat up just right for me. I hit it on what I call the sweet spot and knew it was going in from the second it left my boot,' he remembered. Watching *Match of the Day* that night, Radford 'couldn't get over how weird I looked when I ran, because I'd never seen myself on the telly before'. In the crowd, his wife Annie sat in between the couple's two young sons. Just before her husband's superlative strike, one of her sons called for his mother's attention and she turned away briefly to see what the matter was. She turned back just in time to see the ball hit the back of the net but had no idea who'd delivered the shot. 'Your Ron,' came the response, after she asked another Hereford wife who had scored.

Then the pitch invasion happened. 'It was the most incredible sight,' recalled Billy Meadows, 'and every time I see it repeated on TV, it moves me to tears.' Hereford fan Chris Richards – then a twelve-year-old schoolboy and club season-ticket holder – recalled,

It was a pent-up explosion of joy. The average age of the kids who ran on was probably about eleven or twelve, and there was a lot of pre-pubescent screaming going on. It was like being at a pop concert. I touched Ronnie Radford's arm, and he seemed a bit bewildered by the sight of us little parka-clad bastards gate-crashing the show. Billy Meadows, who looked like a bruiser with his crooked nose and a couple of missing teeth, told us to scarper. The whole thing lasted only about twenty seconds.

The USAF N3B jacket, as it was officially known, was originally developed for US flight crews stationed in cold areas, long before the design was 'civilianised'. For a generation of school kids, owning a snorkel parka – which when fully zipped up was a disaster waiting to happen if you tried to cross the road – was an essential '70s rite of passage. Now in his early sixties, Richards still keeps his in his loft. He plumped for the green version (or rather his mum did) rather than navy blue or brown. The orange diamond-quilted lining is totally frayed, which is understandable for an article of clothing that is half a century old that the owner wore to death. On the face of it, his parka should have been consigned to the dustbin decades ago, but Richards will never dispose of it. 'It's an artefact; a piece of social history,' he said proudly. And an extremely musty one at that.

With the match in extra time, Macdonald surged forward but missed a good chance to restore Newcastle's lead, before substitute Ricky George controlled a Dudley Tyler pass and netted Hereford's winner in the second period. Cue another pitch invasion. This time, the police didn't bother attempting to stem the parka tide. As former police constable and Hereford fan Grenville Smith reflected, 'We'd been briefed that there were far more fans than there were tickets, so it was inevitable that the terraces were bursting at the seams. When Ricky scored the winner, and then at the final whistle, I didn't bother trying to stop the surge. I joined in with the crowd.'

With Edgar Street in uproar, Joe Harvey shook all the Hereford players by the hand, and his dumbfounded Newcastle players attempted to process what had happened to them. 'We looked at one another as if to say: "What the bloody hell was that?"' recalled Malcolm Macdonald. On the way home, the team bus pulled over to allow Harvey to vomit on the roadside. There was no time for the Hereford players to draw breath because four days after the win over Newcastle they faced First Division West Ham in another titanic encounter at Edgar Street, in which the Bulls drew 0–0 in front of another gargantuan crowd. For the Upton Park replay, the Hereford players asked their respective employers for the day off because it was due to take place on a Monday afternoon at 2.15, due to the Conservative government's emergency power regulations.

Amidst multiple strikes by workers at coking plants across the country, coal had become increasingly scarce. Clubs, under pressure not to waste precious energy, were urged to bring kick-off times forward and avoid using their floodlights. Total electricity blackouts lasting up to nine hours at a time were imposed across the country as the industrial 'three-day week' began in earnest, with a national miners' strike also in full swing and flying pickets blocking the entrances to mines.

When midweek afternoon kick-offs were first mooted, clubs expressed concerns that attendances might plummet, but in February 1972 crowds at FA Cup matches sky-rocketed. At Upton Park, the crowd of 42,271 was only just shy of the ground record. When he visited Highbury a fortnight later to watch Arsenal take on Derby in a fifth-round replay on a midweek afternoon, *Fever Pitch* author Nick Hornby expected 'that the crowd might consist of me, a few other teenage truants and a scattering of pensioners'. Instead, the crowd of 63,077 was Highbury's biggest of the season, leading Hornby to reflect, 'I was disgusted. No wonder the country was going to the dogs!'

Six British Rail trains departed Hereford for the Upton Park replay. A short film was released in West Country cinemas to commemorate the cup run. To the backdrop of local celebrity Danny Lee – famed for balancing full pints of beer on his head during charity runs – crooning 'Hereford United, We All Love You' in the background (he added the lines: 'Look out West Ham / We're coming right at you / We'll win the Southern League / And we're trying to beat you'), footage showed London-bound fans swigging Watneys Party Seven and playing cards. But, by the time the Hereford hordes had alighted at Paddington and reached the ground, hundreds were locked out. West Ham had refused to make the game all-ticket, and an estimated 6,000 supporters couldn't get in. Frustrated Hereford supporters took drastic action and one group found their way onto the roof of a nearby residential tower block. During the half-time break, a team of policemen turfed them off. A Geoff Hurst hat-trick finally eliminated Hereford, and the Hammers' players lined up to give their opponents a guard of honour as they left the pitch.

Fortunately, the Hereford fairy tale still had mileage, and the club was promoted to the Football League at the end of the campaign, despite finishing second in the Southern League. 'The FA Cup run put the city and the club on the map,' explained Ronnie Radford. Barrow made way. Hereford were promoted to Division Three at the end of the 1972–73 season, although a clutch of FA Cup heroes from 1972 had departed once league status was secured. 'Difficult conversations needed to be had,' recalled Colin Addison. 'We needed to upgrade in several areas, and I had to be honest with the players. Ricky George went back to Barnet. The commute was impossible for him once we went full time. Some, like Ronnie Radford, stayed part time even when we went into the football league.' Billy Meadows – a former Arsenal trainee – departed Edgar Street. 'It suited me to be part time because I knew that my football career wouldn't last for ever. And the drive from north London to the West Country before the M25 was built was murderous.'

In the midst of another energy crisis, Hereford knocked West Ham out of the FA Cup on a crisp Wednesday January afternoon at Edgar Street in 1974 in front of a crowd of over 17,000, courtesy of an Alan Jones winner. Although the terracing wasn't as ramshackle as it had been two years before, and young fans stood behind low walls rather than rope, there was still another pitch invasion. And Chris Richards – bunking school like most other youths in Hereford that afternoon – stormed the pitch when Jones scored. Except this time, he was resplendent in a red, yellow and blue striped pullover. 'I'd grown out of the parka, and the club had grown in the two years since '72,' he beamed.

———

Half a century on, Hereford's FA Cup heroics have lost none of their sepia-tinted charm, and some former Newcastle stars haven't entirely got over the defeat. When Colin Addison – returning to St James's Park for the first time in decades in 2002 – bumped into Malcolm Macdonald, the grinning ex-Toon striker took one look at the former Hereford manager and said, 'Fucking hell. Not you again!' As Ronnie Radford explained, 'It was a team effort, and my goal shouldn't overshadow what others contributed. Ricky George scored the winner – not me – and the best player over both games was Dudley Tyler, who barely gets a mention. But the feeling of what we achieved for ourselves and Hereford was indescribable.'

Throughout the decade, pitch invasions were rarely so joyful, nor matchday policemen so jolly. Quagmire pitches sapped both the energy and skill from most matches and rammed terraces were often anything but fun. But at Edgar Street on 5 February 1972, with The New Seekers' 'I'd Like to Teach the World to Sing (In Perfect Harmony)' at number one in the charts, this was arguably 1970s football at its most beguiling and rhapsodic.

7

THE BEAVER

'I was decades ahead of my time. All the razzamatazz you see in the Premier League today – I laid the foundations with Leeds in the '70s.'

Paul 'the Beaver' Trevillion

Elland Road, February 1972. 'Why don't you fuck off back to London?' barks Jack Charlton. The incandescent Leeds United star glances at manager Don Revie. 'Tell him, Don. We don't need his ideas. Tell him to go home.' The target of Charlton's fury is Paul Trevillion – soon to be known to the Leeds players as the Beaver – who has been granted an audience (by Revie) with the squad to pitch his new-fangled ideas on warm-up routines, target balls, sock tags and tracksuits with the players' names on the back. Trevillion wants Revie's men to become known as 'Super Leeds'. But Big Jack isn't buying it. 'His ideas are bullshit,' screams the 6ft 3in. Charlton, now on his feet and jabbing his finger menacingly towards Trevillion. Revie – his brow even more furrowed than normal – looks long and hard at Charlton but says nothing.

Trevillion, concerned that this is his one and only shot at convincing Revie's team that they could benefit from a cosmetic makeover, makes one last gamble to get the players to listen to him. Picking up a football from the floor, he says, 'Don, throw this against the wall as hard as you like. If I don't catch it, I'll go back to London right now.' Ignoring Big Jack's instruction to 'Boot it against the wall as hard as you fucking can, Don,' Revie hurls the ball against the dressing-room wall with all his might. It strikes Trevillion on the side of the mouth, knocking out one of his teeth. But somehow, he clings on to the ball. After calmly placing it, and his dislodged tooth, on the floor, he continues to tell the players how he can 'rebrand' them – in an era when English footballers have never heard the phrase. By now, blood is trickling down his chin. 'I thought he was a bloody lunatic,' reflected Norman Hunter later, 'but he'd passed a kind of initiation test with us. Now we listened.'

Even Big Jack sits down in stony silence and gives Trevillion his full attention. In fact, within a few months, the 1966 World Cup winner will not only shake the Beaver's hand, he'll even present him with a signed Jack Charlton sock tag.

Half a century after his work with Super Leeds, Trevillion (who is still the reigning world speed kissing champion) remains in no doubt as to his impact on English football: 'The ideas I had in the '70s are now part and parcel of everything you see in the game. I started the process of commercialising football.' His unorthodox background explains how he had the presence of mind to hold his nerve in front of the roughest and toughest of crews and convince the Leeds players that he was actually worth listening to.

One day, I took five jars of jam from the back of my parents' grocers shop, smeared the contents on some paper and drew a horse with it. I had a natural gift. I started bunking school, going to White Hart Lane, which we lived close to, and drawing the Tottenham players at the training ground. I'd sell the pictures for money to my school mates, sometimes the players themselves, and received a caning from my teacher when I eventually got back to school.

His experiences at White Hart Lane helped him understand the psyche of footballers. 'In the early '50s, I drew what I believed was a fine picture of Alf Ramsey heading the ball and I presented it to him,' Trevillion recalled.

Alf took one look at it and tore it up. 'No,' he said. 'Never draw me heading a ball. The higher the ball is in the air – the lower the standard of play. You must draw me doing what I'm best at, with the ball at my feet.' I learnt that footballers wanted things done in a certain way.

By the 1960s, Trevillion was dubbed 'The Master of Movement' by the media for his novel approach to the 'Roy of the Rovers' cartoon strip which appeared in *Tiger*. 'My illustrations were examples of comic art realism,' he explained, 'and I got the inspiration for this from Spider-Man cartoon strips in the States.' In the late '60s, Trevillion relocated to Cleveland, Ohio, to work for Mark McCormack, a legendary sports agent and founder of International Management Group serving sports figures and celebrities, including golfers Jack Nicklaus and Gary Player. 'The commercial opportunities which were open to sports stars with a high US profile were light years ahead of those for top English footballers,' said Trevillion.

When he was out there, he went to a Cleveland Indians baseball match. 'It was all about having a fabulous day out,' he explained.

They gave out free hats, biros, programmes, T-shirts and baseball hats to kids. Before the game began, there were fireworks and dancing girls. The pre-game entertainment meant that families turned up early and ate hot dogs and brought picnics along.

There were tailgate parties. It was a world away from English football.

Trevillion discovered that his extrovert personality went down a storm across the Atlantic: 'My time in the States showed me that if you want to be noticed, you can't be ordinary. Americans don't do ordinary. They prefer you if you're bloody mad.' When he returned from the States in early 1972, he approached Tottenham boss Bill Nicholson, sounding him out about the possibility of enhancing the crowd experience at N17.

I thought football would explode in the '70s because of colour TV. The bolder something was, the better. But Bill [Nicholson] was very anti. When I raised the possibility of the team doing extended warm-up routines before games, he shook his head. 'The players aren't dancers or Tiller girls. But Don Revie at Leeds is a good mate of mine, and he might be interested. I'll ask him.'

A meeting was arranged the following week up in Leeds. Trevillion had already met Revie at a PFA dinner and suggested that by adopting some of his ideas he could add an extra few thousand to the Elland Road gate every home game. Trevillion knew Leeds fullback Terry Cooper as he'd worked with him on his *Sunday Times* column. 'So I was confident that I would get a receptive ear,' he explained.

Trevillion ensured that he arrived early for his 9.30 a.m. appointment after Cooper warned that the Leeds boss, as well as having a superstitious fear of ornamental elephants and feathered birds, also despised lateness. He was treated to the sight of the Double-chasing Leeds players being put through their paces by trainer Les Cocker.

I'd seen Tottenham, Chelsea and Arsenal players train, but Leeds were a level above with their fitness. Les Cocker had them vaulting boarding horses, and they could jump ridiculously high with their knees touching their chests. Reaney, Hunter, Charlton... They were giants. Super fit. I then met with Don, and I ran through the ideas I had again. I told him how it would do wonders for Leeds' public image. He listened intently.

Trevillion had struck a chord.

On Yorkshire TV the week before his meeting with Trevillion, Revie bemoaned the club's dour image. 'We don't have George Best types here. I accept that. But I think my players are wonderfully gifted and deserve far more credit than they've received for their performances,' he argued. Revie had taken over at Elland Road in 1961 and built a team that was tough and ultra-professional. By the end of the '60s, they'd begun to accumulate silver pots, capturing both the League Cup and the Inter-City Fairs Cup (the forerunner of the UEFA Cup) in 1968 and the First Division a year later. Leeds had their idiosyncratic way of doing things. 'My lads and I are a family. And we're happy doing our carpet bowls and bingo, whatever the outside world thinks of it,' Revie argued. He personally massaged his naked players with soap on Thursdays prior to games, and was a father figure and confessor to many of his players who'd been at the club since they were teenagers. His dossiers – with their forensic detail on the opposition's individual strengths and weaknesses – were years ahead of their time. Even the Leeds bus driver was instructed by the manager to drive the players to games smoothly, without braking sharply in case any of Revie's boys' nerves were affected. Nothing was left to chance. Revie himself cut an intense, brooding, uptight figure, clad in his 'lucky' blue suit and brown sheepskin coat, peering on anxiously from the dugout. The team, edged out by Chelsea in the 1970 Cup final and pipped at the post by Arsenal in the league in 1971, was accused by critics of being skittish under pressure. When the going got tough, the manager's self-doubt manifested itself in his players.

True, the 1969 league champions had defeated Juventus in the 1971 Fairs Cup final, but as the '70s got into their stride, some felt that in order to win more, Leeds needed to relax and go with the flow. 'In the early days, we wouldn't have come close to the success we had without Don's professionalism, but later on he could have let us off the leash more,' defender Norman Hunter accepted. 'Even in the early '70s, our style of football was quite regimented. It brought us some success, but there were lots of near misses too,' added Peter Lorimer.

I interviewed the former Leeds duo in a cafe near Elland Road in 2004. Warned that they were sticklers for punctuality, I turned up half an hour early. They were already waiting. It was a trait that Don Revie instilled in them from a young age. 'He'd say "early is on time, on time is late and late is bloody unacceptable,"' recalled Norman Hunter, who was charm personified, in marked contrast to his Bites Yer Legs nickname. 'I was always laid back off the pitch,' Hunter insisted, 'but once I crossed that white line, I played to win,' he said, shooting me the kind of look that brought opposition players out in a cold sweat. The duo spoke of the sad state of their debt-ridden former club, which was about to plummet through the relegation trapdoor from the Premier League. 'Don will be turning in his grave,' muttered Lorimer, looking to the ceiling. On the subject of Revie, Lorimer explained, 'There was so much to him that people never saw. He was labelled "Don Readies" – implying he was greedy – but he had his mother-in-law living with him, and saw to it that his two aunts were cared for as well. He'd grown up during the Great Depression, lost his mum at a young age and he knew what real poverty was. I think that drove him to earn what he could, and he saw to it that we were well paid also.' By 1972, the pair reckoned, Revie was increasingly conscious of the fact that Leeds were seen as unfashionable to outsiders. 'He started to encourage us to express ourselves a little more,' Lorimer reflected. Revie was also aware that Elland Road wasn't always packed to the rafters. 'I think that Don realised their image could be improved,' explained Paul Trevillion, 'and that's why he was receptive to me.'

Despite the fortress mentality which Revie promoted at Elland Road, the manager wasn't averse to allowing outsiders into his inner sanctum. Eight months before Trevillion met with Revie's players, two writers from *Club* magazine (sold as being 'for today's man') – David Henshaw and Mick Brown – were given complete access to the Leeds team after giving club secretary Keith Archer £60 in used notes, which is around £750 in modern money. A precursor to lads' mags *Loaded* and *Front*, *Club*, with its focus on men, motors, clothes, football and soft porn, ran a six-page, in-depth piece entitled 'Leeds United – Anatomy Of A Super Team'. Henshaw recalled being summoned to Revie's office and grilled about his intentions. 'What's in it for me?' Revie asked. 'I told him what I'd paid Archer and he said he wanted £60 too. I had to wire down to London to get the money.' Given that Revie knew nothing about either the magazine or the writers, the fact that Henshaw and Brown were given carte blanche to focus on what they pleased is remarkable. The insight was superbly nuanced. Skipper Billy Bremner (with his twenty-a-day cigarette habit) recounted how, when he was involved in a car accident in Scotland some years earlier, he phoned Revie. 'He got straight out of bed, picked me up and brought me back. It's nothing to do with earning his living – he's interested in the players as people,' the captain recounted.

But Trevillion's level of access was on a different level entirely. He was invited to the famous Elland Road clash with Southampton in February 1972, having been told by Revie that he could put his ideas to the players afterwards. The Londoner was spellbound by what he saw, as was the *Match of the Day* audience, with Leeds trouncing Southampton 7–0. In one famous passage of play, Leeds played keep-ball, which commentator Barry Davies described as being 'almost cruel'. From the main stand, Trevillion – whose mother was Spanish – started an 'Olé!' chant each time the ball was passed between the Leeds players, which spread like wildfire and is audible on the footage of the match. 'It had never been heard in English football before,' he insisted. Then it was on to meet the Leeds players. 'I couldn't see how this fella up from London – with his cockney accent – could help us. We were the most professional, united team in England, and proud of it,' recalled Jack Charlton. 'But me and the lads agreed that his suggestions were interesting. And he could bloody talk, too. Too bloody fast, mind.'

I'd spoken to Charlton on the phone shortly before the 2006 World Cup, ostensibly to get his opinion on England's chances for a US soccer magazine. Incidentally, his assertion that they were a bunch of 'over-rated flash Harrys' was pretty accurate. I was initially puzzled by the sound of water lapping in the background. I asked him if he was washing up. 'Bloody hell, no, I'm in the bath,' he said. It put an image in my mind that would not budge. When I suggested that it *might* be better if we spoke later, he told me he was fishing for the day and to ring back about seven. I did as he asked and duly phoned back later in the day, but he seemed crotchety. I asked if he was okay. He berated me that his bloody steak and ale pie was getting cold. In a more receptive mood after finishing his dinner, we talked about England, Alf Ramsey, the two World Cups he played in, Leeds United and the Beaver. Charlton recalled, 'Much of the stuff we did with the Beaver was fun, looking back on it. And he was right about many things. But I still wish he'd spoken a bit bloody slower.' After well over an hour on the phone, Big Jack told me it was time I 'buggered off'. 'OK, Jack, great to speak to you,' I said. 'Good lad. You too,' he said with a chuckle. Just before he hung up, Charlton said, 'You need to speak to Beaver. Ask him about his meetings with us.' It took me fourteen years to do so, but in 2020, I finally followed Big Jack's advice.

One by one, Trevillion, firing his sentences out at machine-gun pace, laid out his ideas to the Leeds players that would inject the team with a little more vim and vigour. First up, player's names on the back of tracksuits. 'I told them that it would add an element of individuality and flair,' he explained. 'Because, as well as being a fine team, they were supremely gifted individuals.' The players murmured their approval. Second, signed sock tags that players would wear for each match.

> After the games, Leeds stars would present them to kids in the crowd. I said to them, 'Imagine kids at school on Monday saying, "I've got a Norman Hunter sock tag. I'll swap it for a John Giles one..." kids will flock to Elland Road to collect them.' From the work I'd done with showbiz acts on TV like Rod Hull and Emu, I knew that for every kid who attended a live show, they would usually bring two adults with them. I thought the same would apply to football matches.

'I liked that idea,' recalled Norman Hunter. 'We were in favour of attracting more families to games, and crowds generally were lower than they'd been in the '60s.' The players nodded in agreement. Third, target balls. Numbered from one to eleven, as the players ran out for the start of the match, they would hoof the target balls into the crowd. 'I got the idea from numbered pool balls,' Trevillion explained, 'and I believed it would be another collector's item for kids. They'd want the full set.' An affirmative from the Leeds players, although Revie suggested this be introduced slightly further down the line.

And finally, the extended warm-up routine. Big Jack was beside himself once more. 'No way, we're not fucking Tiller girls. I'm not prancing around and waving my arms around before the game like a prat,' he yelled. Trevillion argued the toss with Charlton, pointing out that if the warm-up, and with it more interaction with the crowd, became a regular thing at Leeds matches it would bump up the crowds and crank up the atmosphere. And besides, it was part of that all-conquering 'Super Leeds' package that Trevillion was trying to push. Charlton glowered but calmed down a little. His teammates nodded their assent. As Revie and Trevillion left the meeting, Revie warned him, 'This warm-up thing. You'll have to clear it with [trainer] Les Cocker. He takes care of that side of things. It's up to him.' Trevillion sounded out Cocker, who said he was willing to give it a try, adding, 'It would take a lot of hard work. It would need to be choreographed. Something like the red arrows on grass.' Trevillion was delighted. 'I knew that once the players went along with it it would work brilliantly because everyone at Leeds was so damned professional,' he reflected.

It was agreed that that the 'Super Leeds' rebranding process would commence before the team's plum FA Cup quarter-final at home to Tottenham. There was one further idea that Trevillion had. He approached Peter 'Hotshot' Lorimer and asked him if he'd be willing to half-volley three shots from the half-way line into the net at half-time. Lorimer recalled, 'I thought it might be good fun, and I was blessed in having a pretty formidable shot on me, so I thought, "Why not?"' There was just one thing missing. Unlike the Leeds players, Trevillion himself didn't have a moniker. Shortly before the Tottenham match, he and Revie discussed the final details for project 'Super Leeds', and Revie admitted he was impressed with how Trevillion juggled his newspaper illustration work with other commercial projects. 'You work like a beaver,' he said. The nickname stuck. The Leeds players and Revie himself simply referred to him as the Beaver from then on, as did Trevillion himself.

When one first encounters Trevillion, whose long flowing hair and penchant for donning a pointed black leather hat gives him the appearance of a wizened Gandalf, one cannot help but speculate whether some of his claims to fame are idle boasts. Yet, they all check out. As a young artist, Trevillion drew a cartoon of Winston Churchill: 'I told him I believed he was responsible for Britain winning the war. He said, "I was just the roar. It was the lion spirit of the British people that won it." He said that my portrait was one of the few paintings of him which he actually liked.' It sounds like a fanciful claim, but Churchill only gave his signature to the paintings he liked. The original signed painting currently hangs in the boardroom at the Professional Footballers' Association offices in Manchester and is worth an estimated £1 million. His recollection of a conversation that he had with George Best about drawing also seems far-fetched, but Best later confirmed the veracity of the anecdote: 'Bestie asked me to give him some drawing tips. I looked at him and said, "Why do you do what you do on the pitch?" He looked at me and said, "I don't know, I just do it." That was the point, I told him. Both drawing and football is all about instinct.' But what about the speed kissing title?

I was in a club in the States in the late '70s, and the competition was about to start when a couple near us had a barney and a lady was left on her own. I stepped in and we won because I'd kiss for fifteen minutes, then she'd do the same, so we conserved our energy. I defended the title in Birmingham, and it was broadcast by BBC1 on St Valentine's Day, 1987. The American movie star George Segal narrated the programme. I am still the world speed kissing champion and have the trophy to prove it.

When *The Glory Game* author Hunter Davies encountered Trevillion on the eve of the 1972 Leeds v. Tottenham FA Cup quarter-final, he too was bewildered when he saw the Beaver in action. Granted unprecedented access to the Spurs players throughout the 1971–72 campaign, Davies was initially confused when Trevillion referred to himself in the third person: 'The Beaver is onto this, and the Beaver is working on that.' Davies was highly sceptical about Trevillion's claims that the 'Super Leeds' choreography prior to kick-off would 'blow all your minds'. And yet, the whole spectacle went like clockwork, so much so that Davies later wrote in *The Glory Game* that the rapturous reception afforded to the Leeds players in the warm-up was akin to the 'Nuremberg rally'. 'The players ran out thirty minutes before kick-off, and three players headed to each corner of the pitch. Elland Road was packed, with over 43,000 there. Les Cocker had drilled them in advance and they put on an amazing show,' Trevillion recalled. Peter Lorimer cracked home all three of his half-time half-volleys, 'The crowd loved it,' he recalled. The players handed out the signed sock tags to the kids after the match, and on the very rare occasion these collector's items change hands, they do so for hundreds of pounds. More importantly, Leeds beat Tottenham 2–1, which meant that Revie's men were only a semi-final away from the centenary FA Cup final. This gave the Beaver another idea.

I told Don that Leeds needed an FA Cup final song. In his office, he frowned at me and said, 'Beaver, we're not even in the bloody final yet.' I didn't see there was any way that they could lose to Birmingham in the semi, so I urged Don to move on with the song. After a bit of thought, he said, 'OK, but I want [Tom Jones's producer] Les Reed to do it.' Don was a huge Tom Jones fan, but I thought there was no way we'd get Les Reed. But I went to his house, pressed his doorbell and it played 'Delilah'. Les was flattered that Don liked the songs he'd written for Tom and agreed to do it.

Revie was adamant that he wanted a marching song and that the lyric 'Marching on Together' and 'We Love You, Leeds' needed to be sung. 'Otherwise I'm not bloody interested,' he told Trevillion.

The A-side 'Leeds United' was released as a single and was an upbeat eulogy to the Leeds players that reached number ten in the singles chart. The B-side 'Leeds, Leeds, Leeds' became (as it turned out) the better known of the two songs and was also known as 'Marching on Together'. It's still sung by Leeds fans now. When the record was cut, Trevillion took Revie to a record shop near Elland Road and the manager was delighted and nodded his approval once he'd heard both songs. Revie was then persuaded by Trevillion that the song should be played to Leeds fans before the FA Cup semi-final took place. It was remarkable that Revie agreed to Trevillion's suggestion, given his inherent caution, and the fact that he was concerned about the threat of Birmingham forward Gordon Taylor, the future PFA chairman. "'We'll have to watch that little bastard, Beaver," he said. "We can't let him cut in from the wing, or he'll do us some real damage. He's a bloody menace.'" In the event, Taylor was benched for the semi, and his team was swept aside 3–0 by a vibrant Leeds side at Hillsborough. The Blues even attempted to ape the Leeds warm-up routine prior to the game, but 'they couldn't pull it off like Leeds players did. They didn't have the style or finesse,' Trevillion recalled. Their opponents in the final would be the previous year's Double winners, Arsenal, who'd pipped Leeds to the title in May 1971.

The pomp and pageantry surrounding the centenary final at Wembley (the ninety-first final to be played, due to the two world wars) was something to behold. A raft of dignitaries attended, including the Queen and Prince Philip, who were introduced to the teams prior to kick-off. Prime Minister Edward Heath – an Arsenal fan who'd missed the Gunners beating Liverpool at Wembley in 1971 due to his participation in the Admiral's Cup aboard his boat *Morning Cloud* – made it this time. Heath had secured tickets for his mother and stepfather to watch Charlie George's screaming winner a year earlier. In 1972, there was a parade prior to kick-off as school children marched with the flags of all the sides who'd won the competition. Former FA Cup-winning heroes – some pre-dating the First World War – waved to the expectant crowd.

History and tradition oozed from every corner of Wembley. Yet, as skippers Frank McLintock and Billy Bremner led their teams out of the tunnel onto the pitch, both sides' new-fangled branded bling was on show. Revie's men hurled their target balls into the Leeds hordes on either side of the tunnel, and, as the cameras panned outwards, the huge TV audience caught the first glimpse of their personalised tracksuits. Arsenal's most high-profile stars Charlie George and Alan Ball emerged wearing Hummel boots – red in George's case and white in Ball's. The game itself was a damp squib, and a foul on Alan Ball by Allan Clarke within five seconds set the tone. Arsenal's Bob McNab was booked after forty-eight seconds and the Gunners, lacking the mojo they possessed a year earlier, rarely troubled the Leeds defence. Revie's men always looked comfortable but were cautious. The only moment of genuine quality arrived in the second half when Mick Jones crossed the ball and Allan Clarke – momentarily flummoxed by the height of the cross – headed home magnificently past the Gunners' stand-in keeper Geoff Barnett. Super Leeds had won the FA Cup for the first time in their history.

Although the atmosphere in the dressing room was celebratory, Trevillion was less pleased when Don Revie pulled him aside and informed him that he was 'putting a brake' on things. '"It's all gone too much of a sideshow, Beaver." And Don's word was always final,' reflected Trevillion. But, to cheer him up, Revie gave him his FA embossed paper cutter. And a beaming Big Jack – finally an FA Cup winner at the grand old age of thirty-seven – handed over his signed No. 5 sock tag. So, the Beaver's disappointment at Revie's message was somewhat offset by accruing various items of niche early '70s football ephemera.

Super Leeds continued with much of what Trevillion put into place for them until Brian Clough's brief Elland Road sojourn two years later, and the Beaver remained firm friends with many of the Leeds stars of the era. Surely he received a tidy sum for services rendered? 'No. I never took a penny for what I did. I did it all because I was a football fan.' Arguably, his cleverest piece of marketing was to convince Don Revie to replace the owl club badge with the smiley face, which is now an iconic symbol of Leeds in their pomp. 'It was done with no real fuss,' Trevillion recalled. 'Leeds fans still love that badge, and they still sing "Marching on Together" and fans in their sixties pay huge money for sock tags and target balls on eBay. I knew what I was doing, didn't I?'

Due to Revie calling a halt on Trevillion's activities, the Norman Hunter shinpad ('Beaver was obviously taking the piss of my "Bites Yer Legs nickname", Hunter explained to me) never did see the light of day. And the plan to rename the club Leeds Crusaders (with a blue cross on the front of their white shirts) failed to get beyond the drawing board, although perhaps that's no bad thing. Despite their 1972 makeover, the club struggled to shed the 'nasty Leeds' label, and books including David Peace's *The Damned Utd* (focusing on the 44-day Clough era) have – rightly or wrongly – only reinforced the stereotype that Leeds were an unwelcoming crew. Yet, the football they played when they won the league title in 1974 was widely praised – even by those who'd previously criticised Revie's men's grim professionalism and flatline bullying during games. Trevillion remains as active and highly regarded as ever with the sports illustrations he does for various newspapers. His work was featured in the 'Master of Movement' exhibition at London's Strand Gallery in 2014 and he co-founded the Football Walk of Fame at the National Football Museum in Manchester in 2016.

Within a year of meeting the Beaver, Don Revie was once again 'door-stepped' by outsiders from the commercial world and the ripples from that meeting would re-colour the whole palette of 1970s football.

8

THE (MIS)ADVENTURES OF
THE CLAN

'In they strutted, some of the biggest swinging dicks
in the game, like the world was their oyster.'
Terry O'Neill

March 1972, Fleet Street. Celebrity photographer Terry O'Neill has
pretty much seen it all. The Mayfair-based snapper, whose memorable images of Carnaby Street, Twiggy, Jean Shrimpton, the Rolling
Stones and the Beatles helped encapsulate the spirit of the swinging
'60s, has now turned his attention to photographing footballers like
George Best and Bobby Moore and glam rockers like David Bowie
and Marc Bolan.

The man who once spent a week living at Hugh Hefner's Playboy
mansion is used to rubbing shoulders with the super famous, but
even O'Neill is taken aback when some of London's leading football talent – calling themselves 'the Clan' – roll up to a plush London
eaterie on a chilly spring afternoon, talking about modelling contracts and commercial deals. England's most expensive footballer,
Arsenal's Alan Ball, is there, all £220,000 of him, clad in a flashy
polo neck and jacket. So is Queens Park Rangers forward Rodney
Marsh, about to join Malcolm Allison's Manchester City, and his

QPR teammates Terry Mancini and Terry Venables. They're joined by 1966 hat-trick hero Geoff Hurst plus Chelsea duo David Webb and Alan Hudson. *Godfather*-style, they pose, complete with champagne and cigars, grinning into the camera. 'Footballers need to be more astute and realise there are a wealth of possibilities out there. We hope to exploit this potential.' Terry Venables explains. At the click of O'Neill's shutter, the gang have the commercial world at their feet. At least, that's the plan...

‖ ilm stars were often a bit dismissive and world weary,' Terry O'Neill told me when we met in 2012, 'but footballers saw photo shoots as an adventure.' It was a dramatic sea change for O'Neill, who'd dined out with Audrey Hepburn and Frank Sinatra and later married actress Faye Dunaway, but he'd always enjoyed mixing with footballers: 'We shared similar backgrounds. I was from the East End. We were working-class boys made good. Our time had come.' O'Neill, who passed away in 2019, was splendid company, and brought along some of his work with footballers to show me. I told him I loved his pictures. He grabbed my arm. 'Can you make sure you don't refer to them as "*pictures*"? Paparazzi take pictures. I'm a photographer, and these [he gestured towards the photographs] are called *portraits*.' When I'd nodded in agreement, he let go of my arm and we resumed our conversation. O'Neill liked footballers and musicians wearing their hair longer and sporting feather cuts and sideburns, arguing that it made them 'more appealing and raffish ... less prudish'.

In 1973, the year that glam acts The Sweet, Slade and Wizzard all had number-one hits, Arsenal's Charlie George, whose shoulder-length mane was perhaps the most talked about hairdo of all London footballers, was approached with the idea of making a one-off, novelty glam record. Under the none-too-subtle pseudonym

'Charlie Gorgeous', *Mirror* photographer Monte Fresco snapped him in silver moon boots, velvet zip-up costume and bright make-up. Sadly, the record 'A Love Song for My Lady' was never released, and the hero of the North Bank was forced take the Tube home in full warpaint after the make-up girl forgot to bring any cleanser. Terry O'Neill's profile meant he was ideally placed to see at first hand the cross-fertilisation between football and music during that era. '[Marc] Bolan told me he wanted his hair to look like George Best's, but his was too curly, I'm afraid. Bowie wasn't a football man, but liked Peter Osgood's swagger,' the photographer explained. When O'Neill, a Chelsea fan, saw his team face newly promoted Queens Park Rangers at Stamford Bridge in 1974, he recalled the entire travelling contingent copying the Glitter Band's anthem and singing, 'Hello, Hello, Rangers are back, Rangers are back' throughout the pulsating 3–3 draw. With their camera-hogging ostentatiousness and vainglorious public images, glam rockers and the new generation of footballers had much in common. When Slade appeared on *Top of the Pops* and performed 'Merry Xmas Everybody' at Christmas in 1973, audience members held Slade scarves above their heads, swaying from side to side in the way football fans did on the big occasions.

His 1972 snap of Bobby Moore and wife Tina in Epping Forest, like so many of O'Neill's images, remains a portal to a pivotal moment of social history. Bobby, in polo neck and slacks, bears a fleeting resemblance to Hollywood star Steve McQueen. But Tina, clad in black leather boots, stole the show due to the revealing length of the white England shirt she is wearing. This was the original WAG photograph, taken just six years after England players' partners were barred from attending the 1966 victory banquet and made to eat in another room. 'Just as the husbands were starting to cash in on their fame and secure endorsements, the wives began to cultivate profiles too,' O'Neill explained. Football's modish golden couple were also snapped by O'Neill with their children outside their plush detached Chigwell home. The image is a testament to the increasing social mobility for the top players of the day, with Moore's spotlessly clean white Jaguar tucked neatly under an urbane carport.

O'Neill photographed George Best – whom he described as 'wonderfully camera-friendly, once he overcame his shyness' – on several occasions from the mid '60s onwards. On film (as well as off it), Best gravitated from being a self-effacing mop-top teenager to a full-blown city socialite, with fashion models and champagne flutes usually in shot. 'George was football's first metrosexual player, in an era when the term hadn't even been invented,' O'Neill argued. He had a bad feeling about the 'next George Best' – new Arsenal signing Peter Marinello – as soon as he clapped eyes on him at Highbury. Following a £100,000 move from Hibernian, Marinello failed to dislodge winger George Armstrong from the Gunners line-up, and his career went off the rails after an initial splurge of publicity shots for modelling catalogues. In the 1971 *Fab 208* annual, Marinello explained his love for the band Spooky Tooth and 'Donegal tweed suits, massive kipper ties and maxi-raincoats'. Unlike his fashion sense, his performances rarely caught the eye. 'I took portraits of Marinello early in his Arsenal career. He was a boy in a man's world, surrounded by hangers-on who disappeared when it went wrong for him. I felt terribly sorry him,' O'Neill recalled.

The Clan photograph captures the increasing self-assurance and swank of '70s players. Given the heady atmosphere which surrounded the shoot and the larger-than-life personalities involved, it's hardly surprising that some of the precise details about how it even came about remain open to conjecture. In *The Mavericks*, journalist Rob Steen wrote, 'In the mid-1970s, Alan Ball and a business acquaintance conceived the bright idea of forming the Clan … the syndicate comprised the league's more notorious attractions, the aim to generate extra income from various promotional ventures.' Yet, the picture was taken in 1972, it was O'Neill's idea for it to be taken and Alan Ball denied that he was the driving force behind the scheme. 'I think the suggestion might have come from Terry Venables, who was always very business-minded,' Ball told me. Both Venables and Alan Hudson insisted that the gathering happened at a restaurant just off the King's Road (O'Neill's favoured haunt), but the photograph was taken at the Terrazza Est, just off Fleet Street. 'After the shoot, I literally ran to get the photo developed and then ran even quicker to *The Sun*'s office in order that they could get it in the paper the next day. I missed out on a good drink,' O'Neill recalled. It's fortunate that the photographer remained clear-headed and detached because everyone else's versions of events were hilariously foggy and conflicting.

'It's hazy,' Alan Ball admitted, 'but I recall seeing Terry Mancini puffing away on some enormous Cuban cigars.' That's not entirely true; in the photo Mancini poses with a cigar in his mouth, but he said, 'I've never actually smoked one in my life. I'm not a cigar fan.' And as for Rob Steen's claim that Chelsea star Peter Osgood was a founding member of the Clan, Ball insisted, 'Ossie never turned up for a shoot and had no involvement in it.' The players' motivations for appearing in the shoot also varied. Alan Ball hoped to 'make a few bob out of it'. Rodney Marsh, on the other hand, said he did it purely 'as a favour to Terry O'Neill', who was well connected with top London footballers.

Intriguingly, O'Neill said that the initial seed for the photograph was planted by Malcolm Allison, who'd long considered himself an aesthete. During breaks in filming for the 1970 World Cup, when he wasn't supping wine at Hendon Hall, the ITV panellist slipped away from the throng in a taxi and visited a raft of art galleries across the capital. One night, he met O'Neill at the Ad Lib Club, where the capital's movers and shakers hung out. 'Mal knew a lot about art and sculpture. He was interested in nudes, particularly female ones,' O'Neill recalled with a smirk and a roll of his eyes.

He believed that the '70s would be an era when a footballer's image would be all important. Mal was the most out-of-the-box thinker I ever met in football, and he suggested a photo shoot which reflected footballers' growing profile and affluence. Hence the Clan shoots. Mal was the ringmaster behind the whole show.

A few weeks after the London shoot took place, O'Neill invited Allison to a plush Manchester restaurant, where he was joined by Hurst, Webb, Mancini, Marsh (now at Allison's City), City's Francis Lee and United's Martin Buchan. The picture of the Manchester Clan was published in the *Daily Express* and the star of the show was Allison, puffing away on a big cigar in the middle. 'Mal was at his grandiose best,' recalled O'Neill, 'saying we'd set up a Scouse Clan, a Geordie Clan, a Glasgow Clan. Then we'd go abroad to Milan, to Madrid. We'd be revolutionaries at the vanguard of change. You could almost believe it was possible, except there was absolutely no business plan underpinning it all.'

Both the London and the Manchester Clan failed to make any money. 'It generated nothing for any of us,' recalled Alan Hudson. 'It remains a great photo – a significant photo, but it needed Ossie and Bestie to be involved. The thing was they didn't need the Clan.' Conventional wisdom held that the Clan attempted to (unsuccessfully) cling on to George Best's commercial coat-tails, but Best was famously disinterested in commercial opportunities, saying, 'These people sit there and say I've got a quarter and you've got a quarter. And I used to sit there and think, "They're talking about me like I'm a piece of cake."' In stark contrast to the reluctance of Best, the flamboyant Chelsea team of the late '60s and early '70s eagerly devoured any publicity opportunities that presented themselves. Terry O'Neill and writer and broadcaster Greg Tesser – who'd helped launch the careers of Eric Clapton and Georgie Fame in the '60s – met at Stamford Bridge, dined out regularly on the King's Road and dreamed up the idea of a *Borsalino*-themed photo shoot for Osgood in 1970, months after the gangster movie was released starring Alain Delon. *Borsalino* was set in Marseilles in the 1930s. 'It went down a storm in west London with the in-crowd,' explained O'Neill. 'Anything with subtitles got lapped up in that part of London.' Tesser acquired a Borsalino suit in pure silk from Simpsons of Piccadilly, a fedora, a purple silk shirt and gleaming white loafers. *The Sun* paid a fortune to run the pictures in a major feature. 'Ossie was articulate and Greg was very clever in dubbing Peter as "London's George Best", explained Alan Hudson.

Two years later, Osgood met Hollywood actress Raquel Welch after Terry O'Neill persuaded her to wear a Chelsea kit for a photo-shoot/kickabout in Arizona on the set of the film *Hannie Caulder*. The actress knew little knew about football, but came to Stamford Bridge with Jimmy Hill in February 1972, as Chelsea prepared to take on Leicester City. 'She gave me a lovely wave and shouted to get my attention, "Wooeeee, Ossie, bye-bye, Ossie" and all that. It opened a few doors for me – I received invitations to film premieres and got paid to give my views on the latest Hollywood movies,' Osgood said in our interview. Local boy Alan Hudson, another Chelsea youth team product, and brought up in a prefab a stone's throw away from Stamford Bridge, argued that the King's Road was the catalyst for the high profile the club enjoyed in the media. 'It was unquestionably the place to be at that time.' Hudson told me. 'There were the great restaurants and bars and boutiques, and the music playing in the shops and pubs. At Chelsea, we were part of the scene, eating pasta in restaurants, drinking there after home matches to get everything off our chest and mixing with fans.' The rich and famous gravitated towards Stamford Bridge. Richard Attenborough was already a director at the club, and he was a magnet for the likes of Sean Connery, Michael Caine and Michael Crawford who would come to the matches and hang around and socialise afterwards.

Greg Tesser acted as an agent for winger Charlie Cooke and Peter Osgood. 'Without Greg, the whole showbiz element to Chelsea would never have happened. He opened doors which would have seemed impossible a few years before,' explained Hudson. In 1971, Tesser arranged for Charlie Cooke to pen a *Vogue* article in which Cooke described the tense atmosphere in the dressing room prior to a match: 'The air smelling hot and linimenty, and everyone milling around like nervous bulls. It's different below in the dressing room before a match. There's no cool beer or King's Road dollies.'

Although the Clan itself flopped, Hudson himself developed some lucrative sidelines, with agent Ken Adam pulling the strings. 'I did modelling shots and personal appearances all around London. I have no idea if I could have made more out of it, but I enjoyed it. For me, it was more about the show and the buzz than the cash. I never saw myself as a businessman,' he reflected. However, Hudson was wary of describing the early 1970s as a 'golden era' for football:

Even at Chelsea, the wages were good but not stratospheric. I was on a basic wage of £75 (around £1,080 in modern money) per week. It took hard work and good fortune to stay at the top. In 1970, I'd already suffered a bad ankle injury and I was never the same player again. You're only ever one bad injury away from disaster. That said, football was far less regulated back then. You could be yourself more on and off the pitch.

For Hudson, a graceful and superbly balanced athlete, turbulent times lay ahead. Two weeks before the gathering at Terrazza Est,

Chelsea lost the 1972 League Cup final to Stoke City, thanks to a goal from veteran star George Eastham. It seemed to be just a blip, but in contrast to the highly successful song 'Blue is the Colour', released in late February and which reached number five in the charts, the club went into almost immediate freefall, eventually crippled by debts incurred from building the new East Stand. At odds with Blues manager Dave Sexton, and England boss Alf Ramsey, the twenty-year-old already faced an uncertain future in '70s football. Hudson had been called into the England squad for the 1971 Home Internationals, and was informed by skipper Bobby Moore that Ramsey had confirmed to him that he'd be playing against Wales. When Hudson discovered that wasn't the case, and that he wouldn't play in the next match either, he walked out of the training camp. Ramsey phoned Hudson to inform him that he was still expected to report for training with the Under-23s. But Hudson refused. 'I've got a baby on the way and want to sort out my house,' he told Ramsey. Ramsey's response was unforgiving: 'Your personal issues are not my concern. Report for duty or face the consequences.' Hudson received a year-long international ban from the Football Association, and never received a full cap from Ramsey, something which he said continued to cause him 'great personal trauma', as he described it in our conversation. Hudson moved to Stoke City in 1974 'to straighten myself out. King's Road wasn't always a healthy influence, in terms of the trappings on offer, shall we say. It's why several Chelsea players of that era got divorced and ended up drinking too much.' The famous street had also changed, as landlords hiked up rents to ridiculous levels, forcing out long-established businesses. Stoke manager Tony Waddington ordered Hudson to live with fellow London Clan member Geoff Hurst, who'd joined Stoke from West Ham in 1972, in order to help him 'focus on football'. Lodging with Hurst appeared to work wonders for Hudson, who played some of the best football of his career for the Potters, although he looked back with regret to an era where pragmatism usually took precedence over flair.

As for Malcolm Allison and Rodney Marsh, 1972 should have been a year of triumph. With Manchester City four points clear in the 1971–72 title race, Allison signed Marsh for £200,000 on 8 March because he wanted a forward who could hold up the ball and bring others into play. 'He's the final piece in the jigsaw,' Allison insisted at the time. Football-wise at least, it proved to be Allison's greatest folly. The City fans embraced Marsh immediately, serenading him with a rendition of 'Oh, Rodney, Rodney, Rodney, Rodney, Rodney, Rodney, Rodney Marsh', based on Chicory Tip's 'Son of my Father' number one hit, and Maine Road attendances boomed after his arrival, but Marsh, speaking via Zoom from his Florida home, didn't mince his words when I spoke to him. 'Tactically, at least, my arrival cost City the title,' he said. 'They missed out by the smallest of margins – a single point – and it was down to me.' Prior to Marsh's arrival, Wyn Davies played at centre-forward, with Francis Lee, who ended the campaign with thirty-five goals, playing off him. When Marsh arrived on the scene, Davies was dropped and Lee moved to the centre-forward position. 'My arrival completely changed the dynamic not just of the team, but the club.'

But what an arrival it was. Keen to escape the attentions of journalists down in London as he prepared to head north to Maine Road, Marsh shot out of his garage in his yellow Lotus Europa sportscar, with the personalised number plate EGO 870J, and crashed straight into a tree. 'Keen to save face, I jumped out and said to them, "OK, what can I do for you fellas?" And I gave them a bit of an exclusive. I had no choice, did I?' Wearing an expensive brown leather coat and a floral shirt, the 6ft 1in. Marsh, with the ink drying on his £400 a week contract (£5,800 per week today) and a Puma boot deal in the offing, strutted into Maine Road looking a million dollars. Yet, his philosophy was at odds with that of a potential title-winning side. 'I wanted the fans to enjoy the Rodney Marsh experience from the off. I played my entire career that way and I make no apologies for being that kind of player. Ultimately, I wasn't a team player,' he said. Quickly, there was some dissension in the ranks. Skipper Mike Doyle was unimpressed with Marsh's showmanship, comparing his ball juggling attributes to those of 'a bloody performing seal'. Doyle later claimed, 'You don't win championships with players like Rodney in the team.' It's a statement which Marsh didn't deny when I spoke to him. Another problem was that the City players who'd undergone intense 'power training' sessions under Allison's watchful gaze were ultra-fit. City training sessions were a shock to Marsh's system and he was physically sick after training. Allison dropped Marsh to allow him time to adapt, but when he reappeared in the first team he did so with characteristic panache.

At Old Trafford in April 1972, Marsh was brought on as a 64th-minute substitute for City. He'd spent the early part of the drizzly second half warming up in his bright-yellow tracksuit – designed by Malcolm Allison of course – and receiving 'Rodney Marsh, superstar, walks like a woman and he wears a bra' cat calls from the United fans. After eighty-five minutes, with City 2–1 up, Mike Summerbee sprinted down the right and crossed for Marsh, who drilled the ball home past Alex Stepney into the bottom corner and put his team out of sight. With just seconds remaining, City played the ball into the corner and Marsh put his foot on it in order to waste some time. As United full-back Tony Dunne hared towards him, determined to leave him in a crumpled heap, Marsh sidestepped him and, as the United man skidded over the touch-line, City's new impresario smiled at the United hordes, tapped an imaginary watch on his wrist and mouthed, 'How long to go?' at them. 'They wanted to bloody kill me,' Marsh said. As Allison was happy that Marsh was fully match fit, the forward was restored to the City line-up for the last game of the season against fellow title rivals Derby. Marsh – finally – ran the show. In the first half, he cut in from the right, darted between McFarland and Robson and smashed the ball past Colin Boulton. After the break, following another surge into the Derby box, Marsh was scythed down by Terry Hennessey and Francis Lee converted the spot kick. 'Now the crowd know what this man is all about,' yelled *Match of the Day* commentator Barry Davies. It was a 55,000 crowd too, and one of the reasons Allison had brought Marsh north was to boost the Maine Road attendances. But ultimately, it was a triumph of style over substance. City failed to scoop the league title.

The fallout was dramatic. General manager Joe Mercer – who'd opposed the signing of Marsh – departed the club and Allison was now manager in his own right. 'The board was split about my signing, and, with hindsight, Joe Mercer was right about the fact that I would disturb the equilibrium,' Marsh explained. Just as Joe Mercer was unsure about Marsh's ability to fit into a settled team, Alf Ramsey harboured similar doubts about his suitability for England. Initially capped against Switzerland in 1971, in which Ramsey urged Marsh to 'run yourself into the ground', Marsh was brought into the fold for both legs of the ill-fated European Championship quarter-final with West Germany in April and May 1972. At Wembley, Marsh replaced Geoff Hurst during England's 3–1 defeat, in what proved to be the latter's final international appearance. Apart from a couple of keepie-uppie juggles, which received a roar from the Wembley crowd, Marsh contributed little. The forward started in Berlin but was unable to make inroads on the well-marshalled West German defence and was replaced midway through the second half.

On both occasions against West Germany, Alf instructed me to play like Geoff Hurst. I was amazed because that clearly wasn't my game. Alf must have known that. In training, he told me to spin off my marker, get to the far post, feint and then get to the near post. Just like Geoff did. I knew at that point I wasn't a Ramsey man.

Ultimately, the England experience left Marsh feeling disillusioned because 'players had to fit around the playing system, rather than the system adapting to the talents of individuals'.

Prior to England's World Cup qualifier with Wales in January 1973, Marsh committed his ultimate faux pas with Alf Ramsey. It was the latest in a catalogue of foot-in-mouth moments that littered Marsh's life during and after football. He'd told new QPR manager Gordon Jago two years before in 1971 that the team was '40 per cent behind you' after Jago took over the reins. Later, in the '70s, as Marsh struggled with mental health issues, a psychiatrist offered the opinion that he might be suffering from sabotage syndrome – a borderline personality disorder in which the sufferer is predisposed to self-destructive and unpredictable actions. Before his side faced the Welsh, Ramsey reminded the team of the work level he expected of them throughout the match. 'Rodney, I will be watching you in particular, and if you don't work hard enough then I will pull you off at half-time,' he warned. Ramsey's tee-up was manna from heaven for a prankster like Marsh. 'Christ, Alf. At City, we normally get a cup of tea and an orange,' he replied. Peter Storey – changing nearby – might have found it hilarious, but Ramsey's chilling silence in the moments that followed showed that regardless of whether he fully understood the euphemism or not, he knew he'd been 'had'. 'I got torn off a strip by Bobby Moore, who told me not to speak that way in front of Alf,' Marsh recounted. The player's crass innuendo marked the end of his England career. Ramsey once again maintained the upper hand in the ongoing clash between pragmatism and flair by casting City's showman aside, as he had Peter Osgood and Alan Hudson.

Marsh rediscovered something like his best form in the 1972–73 season, scoring nineteen goals, but in the wake of stuttering performances, and a shock FA Cup exit to Sunderland, Malcolm Allison resigned as City manager, almost a year to the day after the Manchester Clan photoshoot. If the profile he'd built as a panellist at the 1970 World Cup had established him as a larger-than-life character, his post-City career saw him go into full-on 'Big Mal' mode. In fact, the greater the 'Big Mal' caricature became, the more his footballing powers waned. 'By then, Malcolm thought he was bigger than the game, but no one is,' argued Alan Hudson. In the brief period between Allison departing Maine Road and taking over as Crystal Palace manager, Terry O'Neill captured the essence of Big Mal perfectly in his 1973 portrait, which shows Allison with his shirt completely unbuttoned, wearing an enormous, intricately carved medallion around his neck that wouldn't have looked out of place on one of the Bee Gees. Terry O'Neill memorably described Allison's turbulent three-year spell at Selhurst Park to me as a 'blur of skirt-chasing, fedora-wearing, cigar-chomping, publicity-grabbing ridiculousness'.

With ten matches left, Allison was unable to save Palace from relegation from Division One in 1972–73 and they crashed into Division Three the following season. But his revamp of the homely Glaziers into the more dynamic Eagles carried on regardless. On their famous run to the 1976 FA Cup semi-final, Third Division Palace sported their natty blue and red sash number (designed by Allison) in the fifth round against Chelsea at Stamford Bridge, as two goals from Peter Taylor and one from Nick Chatterton saw the Eagles win 3–2. Up in Chelsea's costly new stand, Allison doffed his fedora, which his girlfriend had bought him for Christmas, at the cameras and revelled in the fact that he'd got Peter Taylor, a left-winger, to wreak havoc on the right. 'If Mal wasn't talking about Kennedy's assassination – he had a few bizarre theories of his own about what really happened – he loved babbling on about Taylor,' recalled Terry O'Neill. 'He delighted in Chelsea players' "geometrical confusion" about how to deal with him.'

And then there was the 'skirt chasing', as O'Neill put it. In August 1973, Allison arranged a football match at Hurlingham Park between a Planet of the Apes XI and a Playboy Bunny XI – all in aid of the World Wildlife Fund. Onlookers noted how taken Allison was with mud-caked Prue from the Bunny XI. With Palace dreaming of Wembley in 1976, Allison stripped off to join X-rated actress Fiona Richmond – muse to Soho porn baron Paul Raymond – in the Palace team bath after she visited Selhurst Park. At the press launch for his 1975 autobiography *Colours Of My Life*, Allison puffed on a Cuban cigar and supped Lanson champagne with a Miss United Kingdom finalist perched on his lap. The title, which sounds like a psychedelic album, and the cover photograph – portraying a shirtless Allison in a pose based on Rodin's sculpture *The Thinker* – spoke volumes for the quasi-intellectual way in which he thought about the game. Art critics have suggested that *The Thinker* represents Dante at the gates of hell looking down to the characters in the *Inferno*. Allison's ghostwriter James Lawton – in his introduction – conceded that Allison's 'loss of status has been dramatic'. Terry O'Neill said that behind the bravado and the bling, 'an unhappiness lay deep within him'. After a poor start to the 1976–77 campaign, Allison departed Selhurst Park. Palace defender Jim Cannon later explained, 'No other man could single-handedly take a club from the First Division to the Third Division and still be regarded as a hero.'

By the time Allison departed Selhurst Park, Rodney Marsh had already taken his leave of English football and headed stateside to the Tampa Bay Rowdies for a cut-price £40,000 fee in April 1976. As City captain, he'd clashed with manager Tony Book. After transfer-listing Marsh and telling him to train with the reserves,

Book gave Marsh one last chance to apologise: 'If you think I'm fucking useless it's not going to work. Do you want to take it back?' With an olive branch in front of him, Marsh self-destructed, responding, 'No chance. In fact, thinking about it more, you're not that good.' When he arrived in Florida, he told journalists that 'football in England has become a grey game, played on grey days by grey people'. Almost half a century later, he stood by his comment. 'The maverick players – the flair players – were side-lined. Some of us headed out to the States for a last hurrah. We lost. But if you look at how the national team struggled, the system certainly didn't win,' he said.

Individually, Manchester Clan member Francis Lee enjoyed considerable success in business. The City star (and future club chairman) became a multi-millionaire from his paper-recycling company after he retired from football. By 1974, with sponsorship and advertising deals, not to mention his burgeoning business interests, his side hustles earned him far more from outside the game than he was earning inside. 'My father instilled in me a strong work ethic,' he explained. 'He told me not to sit around because I wasn't going to play football for ever, so I've always been interested in business.' Terry Venables, who'd issued the initial clarion call for footballers to 'exploit their potential', successfully followed his own advice. Backed by the Billy Amstell Jazz Band, he released a cover version of the song 'What Do You Want to Make Those Eyes at Me For?' – even performing it on LWT's *Russell Harty Show* in front of some of his bemused Queens Park Rangers teammates. Along with co-author Gordon Williams, Venables penned five football-themed novels in the 1970s, the first of which was *They Used to Play on Grass* (1973). Venables quickly used the pseudonym P. B. Yuill after critics questioned the level of

input he'd given to his first book. Once again, Venables collaborat-
ed with Gordon Williams in the co-writing of scripts for *Hazell* –
the story of a fictional private detective. With actor Nicholas Ball
playing the lead, *Hazell* was broadcast on ITV in 1978. Venables, by
this time an aspiring coach at Crystal Palace, insisted, 'Footballers
shouldn't feel they are straitjacketed to just playing the game.'

As the '70s progressed, players – often paid in cash for their
trouble – posed on the bonnets of their flashy new motors in the
tabloids, eagerly showing off brand-new MGs, TR7s, Capris and,
the '70s motoring equivalent of the holy grail, Triumph Stags. In
club programmes, they were snapped at home, backed by flowery
wallpaper, showing state-of-the-art music centres complete with
obligatory ABBA, Electric Light Orchestra, New Seekers and 10CC
vinyls. Spouses with flouncy dresses and Farrah Fawcett hairdos
floated around, looking like extras from *Charlie's Angels*. 'Suddenly,
everyone wanted to photograph us,' recalled Alan Ball. 'The attention we received exploded in the early '70s. My wife Lesley wasn't
always comfortable with the attention, but it came with the lifestyle.'

Terry O'Neill photographed a raft of other footballers in the early
'70s. As ever, his aim was 'to bring out their personality'. One such
snap included Tottenham's Cyril Knowles posing with a model.
The strapline, of course, was 'Nice one Cyril...' The photograph
incurred the wrath of Knowles's manager Bill Nicholson, who suggested that such fripperies were an unwanted distraction from his
player's career. However, it wasn't the only reason for Nicholson's
annoyance. 'The photograph went in one of the tabloids, and Bill
was furious because he thought Cyril's hair was too long,' O'Neill
recalled. Arsenal strikers John Radford and Ray Kennedy were por-
trayed as Butch Cassidy and the Sundance Kid and posed with fake
guns and cowboy hats. 'They were very amenable and laid back.
It was a novelty for them to be on the front pages for a change,'
O'Neill said. Two days later, O'Neill received a hand-written note

from Arsenal boss Bertie Mee thanking him for refraining from including 'any young women in the picture'.

Reflecting on the Clan photo shoots, Terry O'Neill recalled, 'Footballers were just awakening to the possibilities open to them. Critics said it was a classic case of style over substance. Football-wise, they had a point.' Not one member of the London Clan won a single piece of silverware as a player after the iconic photograph was taken. Its brightest glam rockers – Alan Hudson and Rodney Marsh – illuminated the English game all too briefly and ultimately failed to live up to their billing due to a combination of injury (in Hudson's case), their own obstreperousness and the harshness of 'the system'. For top players, football really had become a whole new ball game, but that didn't come with any guarantee of success on the pitch or any long-term financial security off of it.

9

THE DISRUPTOR

'If in future they want a puppet to get up and say something to please everybody in the room, I suggest they invite Basil Brush, instead of asking a football manager to give up his only day off of the week.'

Brian Clough, January 1973

The Baseball Ground, October 1972. With their white shirts dazzling under the floodlights, Derby County tear Benfica apart. On nights like these, as the English champions take on the Portuguese giants in the first leg of the European Cup second round, there isn't a more stirring atmosphere anywhere in the country.

Many of the 38,100 supporters are so close to the pitch that they can practically taste the action, and the high stands behind both goals amplify the deafening noise. After just six minutes, winger Alan Hinton – his white boots glistening – delivers a perfect cross and defender Roy McFarland heads home to give the Rams the lead. Another McFarland header sees Kevin Hector volley home superbly to make it 2–0 and, ten minutes before half-time, the marauding John McGovern takes advantage of lax Benfica defending and drills home a third. Brian Clough's team are almost out of sight.

Benfica's talisman Eusebio – kept quiet thanks to a masterful defensive performance from Colin Todd – is puzzled. Despite clear blue skies over the East Midlands for the past two days, the Benfica players sink into a muddy morass the minute they set foot onto the pitch. 'No rain,' Eusebio says to Clough's assistant Peter Taylor, pointing to the heavens. Taylor shrugs, muttering something about the vagaries of the British weather. Despite Benfica lodging an official complaint with FIFA, convinced the pitch has been sabotaged, an ecstatic Clough boasts, 'Nothing is impossible – the sky is the limit.' For Clough more than for Derby, as it turns out.

═══════

Before he morphed into English football's chief disturber of the peace, Brian Clough was – first and foremost – a firebrand tracksuit manager. Along with assistant Peter Taylor, the thirty-year-old Clough rejuvenated Hartlepools United, whom he'd taken over in 1965, and signed players, painted the stands, drove the team coach and even convinced directors to oust the despotic chairman, Ernest Ord. Clough's bombast and obsession with control stemmed from personal tragedy. A prolific striker in his native north-east, Clough's playing career was ended at twenty-nine when he tore his cruciate ligament whilst playing for Sunderland against Bury. The subject of Clough's career-ending injury was strictly off limits to his players at Hartlepools and at Derby County, whom he took over in 1967 – all except for one. Dave Mackay, Tottenham's Double-winning skipper, had twice recovered from a broken leg and signed for Derby in 1968 to help lead the club out of Division Two. Mackay was Clough's most important signing, giving a club whose only major trophy was winning the FA Cup in 1946 new-found gravitas. He once asked Clough how his injury had affected him psychologically. 'I was the only Derby player who could have got away with asking that,' Mackay told me during our interview.

He stared at me for a while and said, 'I think about it every day,

David. Sometimes all day.' That was the only time we ever mentioned it. The pain caused by the way his playing career ended was his Achilles heel, but it fired the rage and ambition inside him too.

At Derby, Clough and Taylor 'turned a pigsty into a football club', as striker John O'Hare put it, transforming what was an ailing Second Division side into First Division champions within five years. His sledgehammer put-downs, pearls of wisdom and tirades live long in the memory of his players. Midfielder John McGovern, who played under Clough at Hartlepools, Derby, Leeds and Nottingham Forest, captured Clough's nasal whine perfectly when I spoke to him in 2021: 'Stand up straight, push your shoulders back and get your hair cut, you look like a bloody girl,' Clough ordered, when he first met the sixteen-year-old. McGovern protested that George Best had his hair styled in that way. 'Well, when you play like him, you can have your hair like him. Get it bloody cut,' came the order. McGovern, who'd lost his father when he was a boy, was reluctant to describe Clough as a father figure: 'You never knew what mood he was going to be in. There was always a distance between us.' Given the number of seasons he played under Clough, it's hardly surprising that McGovern received his fair share of Clough sand-blastings. He described the first. The weekend after he'd made his debut for Hartlepools, Clough told him, 'Dribble around the corner flag and back with the ball as fast as you can.' McGovern complied. 'Now, do it without the ball.' McGovern did so. 'Were you quicker with or without it?' Clough asked. 'Without,' was McGovern's reply. 'Well, why don't you try bloody passing it on a Saturday, then?' Clough asked. 'It was great coaching,' McGovern explained. 'Clough's belief in pass-and-move football never changed in all those years. "If you see a player closer to the opposition box than you, pass to him. Slowing the play down only enables opposition defenders to regroup," he'd say. That was Clough's mantra. Pass and move. It never changed.'

Nineteen-year-old Roy McFarland – then an up-and-coming defender with Tranmere – was dragged from his bed by his parents when Clough and Taylor arrived at the McFarland household late one Friday night, determined to take him to Derby in 1967. 'I had Brian on one side and Peter on the other, and I asked them if we could think the move over. They said no.' After a three-hour propaganda blitz, McFarland's father said, 'If they want you that badly, I think you should sign for them, son.' 'Listen to your father,' said Taylor, leaping to his feet. McFarland put pen to paper at 2 a.m. after the pair refused to leave the house without a firm decision. 'Peter shoved the papers in front of me. I'm not even sure that it wasn't him that signed my name,' McFarland explained. The duo's approach was different with Tottenham's Double-winning skipper Dave Mackay, as he prepared to leave White Hart Lane. 'Brian always called me David,' Mackay told me, 'and when Peter Taylor explained that they were going to convert me from a midfielder into a central defender, I told them they were bloody mad. But it worked.' Mackay led the team into the promised land of Division One at the end of the 1968–69 campaign. 'Clough and Taylor were visionaries,' Mackay recalled. 'Everything played out the way they said it would.'

Taylor, seven years Clough's senior, had taken the young striker under his wing when the pair were Middlesbrough teammates. Eschewing the card school and evenings in the pub, Clough and Taylor talked football, football and more football. Taylor constantly talked Clough up, encouraging his protégé to challenge authority. Clough obliged, forcibly asking the 'Boro manager Bob Dennison how he could possibly speak to his players about games when he didn't actually travel with the team. Nicknamed the 'Odd Couple' by teammates, Clough and Taylor looked to a future in management, and when Clough took the Hartlepools job, he asked Taylor, boss of Southern League side Burton Albion, to be his assistant. 'We're like brothers,' Taylor said in a 1970 TV documentary. There were brotherly tensions under the surface too – often over money and, as Taylor saw it, the lack of recognition he received for his talent-spotting role. Sunderland's towering manager Alan Brown, who drove through the night from a family holiday in Cornwall to sign Clough from Middlesbrough in 1961, always loomed large in Clough's mind. 'You may have heard people say that I'm a bastard. Well, they're right,' 'Bomber' Brown told Clough when he arrived at Roker Park for training. Clough was always glowing about his ex-boss. 'I'd have been nothing in management without him. He taught me the values of discipline and the need to control exactly what was happening at a club.' There was also the 'Clown Prince of Soccer', Len Shackleton, who famously left a blank page in his autobiography on the subject of 'What directors know about foot-ball'. Once a gifted forward with Sunderland, 'Shack', who became a journalist after retiring as a professional, became a confidant of Clough and Taylor, encouraging them to mistrust 'those bloody people upstairs', as Shackleton described them. The seeds of rebel-lion in Clough were sown, but in order to be listened to he needed success at Derby County.

———

'I'll tell you something once and if I like you I'll even tell you twice, but if I have to tell you a third time you'll be out of this club,' Clough warned his team on the training pitch. He insisted that his players kept the ball on the grass and treat it 'like it's your friend'. He joined in five-a-sides, testing out players, daring them to get stuck into him. McFarland told Clough he didn't feel comfortable tackling his manager. 'Put your bloody foot in and sort me out,' he growled at the man who'd win two titles at the Baseball Ground. Dave Mackay was taken aback by Clough's cussedness. 'There were a lot of "shits" and "fucks". I wasn't used to it under Bill Nicholson at Tottenham,' he reflected. Clough swore at Mackay, the older man by a year, just the once. For perhaps the only time in his entire career, Mackay shanked a ball out of play in training. Clough swooped on the error like a bird of prey. 'On the fucking grass, David, if you please, not in the fucking air,' he said. Players were told to stick to their specific roles. When reserve striker Barry Butlin attempted to take a short corner in training, Clough blasted his whistle three times. 'You're a bloody striker. Get in the box, that's what I pay you for,' he yelled.

Clough was also merciless towards players who picked up injuries. Butlin broke his cheekbone in a training-ground clash and Clough towered over him, screaming at him to get up. After Butlin was eventually taken to hospital, his wife turned up at the training ground, asking Clough about the accident. Clough was furious. 'I'll tell you when there's been a bloody accident,' he snarled at Mrs Butlin. Maximum commitment was required. Taylor and Clough grilled anyone they heard had been out on the town. 'What have you been up to, then?' Clough demanded, and the inquisition could last for hours. As Dave Mackay recalled, 'One time, they grilled this poor kid who hadn't even done anything wrong. "It's good for the young man," Clough said. "Shows him we're onto them."' Clough would phone John McGovern on a Friday night, just to check that the professional was home and not out in the town. 'Nothing got past those two,' McGovern explained. By 1970, such attention to detail was paying handsome dividends.

With Taylor scouring the land for players, Derby now had a potent blend on the pitch. The highly rated Kevin Hector arrived from Fourth Division Bradford Park Avenue, but several of Taylor's recommendations left the Derby directors nonplussed. Left-winger Alan Hinton had a reputation for being inconsistent at neighbours Nottingham Forest. 'He's a lightweight,' a director told Clough. 'Your mate Taylor has got it wrong.' Hinton's ability to cross the ball with either foot was one of Derby's most potent weapons as they rose to prominence. There were also mutterings about Mackay's injury record in the boardroom when he arrived. 'I told the Derby directors to keep their bloody noses out and leave football matters to professionals like myself and Taylor,' Clough explained in his autobiography. Taylor's role appeared too nuanced and subtle for the bean counters in the boardroom to fully fathom. 'You always see things before me,' Clough told him in their heyday. It was Taylor who gave goalkeeper Les Green his marching orders on Boxing Day in 1970 after a shaky performance in a 4–4 draw with Manchester United. Taylor had suggested 'something's wrong upstairs with Greeny' to Clough at half-time. He never played for Derby again. When Green asked Taylor's erstwhile partner to intervene, Clough told him, 'If Pete says you're done, you're fucking done, Greeny.' There was no room for sentimentality. The minutiae mattered. Clough also appeared to have a photographic memory. 'He could remember everything you'd done in the first half and analyse it with you at half-time. It was phenomenal. That was where the attention to detail came in,' explained former defender Alan Durban.

Generally speaking, Clough and Taylor tried to keep things simple with the players because, as John McGovern explained, they 'trusted us to get on with it'. The opposition was rarely, if ever, mentioned in team talks. 'It was all about what we did,' John O'Hare explained. When Taylor sensed tension in the camp, he'd lapse into comedy routines, doing impressions, pulling daft faces and making Clough roar with laughter. But there was no defined 'good and bad cop' scenario. 'They could switch roles in the blink of an eye. Sometimes Brian would be talking and Peter Taylor would be pacing behind him, ready to say his piece. Either could lay into the team. But when we were winning, their confidence was intoxicating,' explained Alan Durban. The Rams lifted their first trophy – the Watney Cup – in the summer of 1970 in front of a near-capacity Baseball Ground. Their 4–1 victory over Manchester United was symbolic. 'We beat an ageing United, and winning silverware is always a good habit to get into,' said Dave Mackay.

In February 1971, Derby bought the highly rated Colin Todd from Sunderland for a British record transfer fee for a defender: £175,000. Having coached Todd during his brief spell as Sunderland youth team coach in the early 1960s, Clough called this one, later commenting that 'Taylor never saw him play before he signed for us'. Both Todd and Clough later admitted that the size of the fee led to some rumbles of discontent in Derby, a town where the Rolls Royce plant was making thousands of workers redundant just as Todd arrived. Clough, who prided himself on his ability to reach out to the working man, assured Derby residents that Todd was worth every penny. With Archie Gemmill also replacing the Swindon-bound Mackay, the side looked set for a strong title challenge in the 1971–72 campaign.

In one of the tightest title races on record, Derby went twelve matches unbeaten at the start of the season. However, as Clough acknowledged, 'Our results against those around us will define whether we win or not.' Title rivals Manchester City were swept away at the beginning of December in a 3–1 win, with the game settled by two superb headers from defender Ron Webster and midfielder Alan Durban. Alan Hinton, frequently lambasted by Clough for his lack of physical edge, provided two delicious crosses. Curiously, given Clough's insistence on the team ethic, he stayed quiet about Hinton's famous white Hummel boots, which accentuated the player's grace and athleticism as he dazzled and danced his way down Derby's left wing. On New Year's Day, Derby squeezed past Chelsea at the Baseball Ground thanks to Archie Gemmill's scampering run from his own half and deflected finish after riding a scything Peter Osgood challenge. Commentating on the match for ATV's *Star Soccer* was Hugh Johns, dubbed the 'voice of Midlands football', who'd lubricate his vocal chords with a packet of cigarettes and a couple of pints of Brains Bitter. 'Gemmill kept his feet. And it's a shot. It's a deflection. It's a goal,' yelled Johns in his staccato sentences when Gemmill scored. YouTube clips of Derby in the '70s invariably have Johns rhapsodising about 'one-nothing Derby' scorelines and exclaiming, 'And there it is,' 'Yes, indeed!' or 'What a beaut' when a Rams goal hit the back of the net. Although Clough presented Johns with a golden microphone for services to football in 2002, one of the commentator's lexical habits irked the manager thirty years earlier, and when Clough approached Johns in the commentator's box prior to a match, the occasion was less than cordial. 'Cloughie made a beeline for me, wagging his finger', Johns told me in our 1999 interview, 'and asked me to refrain from calling Ron Webster "Ronnie" and John McGovern "Johnny". "Mr Johns – you're making my Derby players sound like fucking girls," Cloughie said, "and football is a fucking man's game." I ignored him.' Johns, who regularly called Gerd Müller 'Gertie' during his 1970 World Cup commentaries, could still be heard describing Derby midfielder Bruce Rioch as 'Brucie' during the Rams' 1974–75 title challenge.

Johns, his rich, baritone voice as smoky as ever, talked me through his own matchday routine: 'A plate of eggs and bacon and a flick through my notes. Homework and revision. A beer and maybe a chaser. And a ciggie or two. No different from the players back then. I went with the flow. Cut to the chase,' he laughed. The only time Johns ever lost his rag was when *Private Eye* printed one

of his occasional clangers in its Colemanballs column. His classic
gaffe came in the 1974 World Cup when he uttered the immortal
phrase, 'The crowd urges the referee to look at his whistle and blow
his watch.' On the subject of Clough, Johns was gushing: 'He was
perfect for a small town like Derby, which like so many places was
struggling economically. He was a galvaniser and put some dyna-
mite under the town – in a good way of course. And as for the
Baseball Ground – there was nowhere else like it in football.' Johns
regularly drew attention to the state of Derby's pitch, describing it,
at different times, as 'sticky', a 'glue-pot' and a 'ploughed field'. So
convinced was Clough that the state of the Baseball Ground pitch
was a key reason why the Rams had won the league in 1972 that he'd
offered Bob Smith a First Division championship medal – Smith
had gained his three minutes of TV fame in 1977 when he ran onto
the pitch during Derby's home match against Manchester City
with a pot of white paint after the penalty spot disappeared into
the mud. Clough and Taylor believed that a wet pitch suited them
because their players had the skill and fitness levels to cope and
would visit Smith a day or two before a home match, instructing
him to 'do your stuff'. He would then switch on the sprinklers to
flood the pitch. On occasions, the obliging local fire brigade would
drop in at the dead of night and add a final flourish. Given the
high-water line, and the fact that the pitch sat 4ft below street level,
it's little wonder that the surface resembled a winkle-picker's para-
dise for much of the season. Factor in the high stands behind both
goals blocking out the sun and wind, and the toxic clouds drifting
in from the neighbouring Leys Malleable Castings factory and it
was a miracle any grass grew inside the Baseball Ground at all. The
new £250,000 main stand, built above the East Side terracing in
1969, was called the Ley Stand. Clough took a leading role in its size
and design, relishing his visits to the neighbouring factory, because
he met with, as he put it, 'real people, with real concerns about

putting food on the table'. On more than one occasion, referees conducted late pitch inspections to determine whether to postpone matches on account of the waterlogged pitch. Invariably, when they threw the ball down to test its bounce, it would simply plop into the watery mud. Clough would remind the official that the surface would be no better next time so they might as well allow the game to be played. In any case, as John McGovern once heard Clough tell a referee an hour before kick-off, 'You don't want to rob the working man of his wage.'

The Rams appeared to have the title within their grasp when they defeated Leeds on Easter Monday at a sodden Baseball Ground. In front of 38,611 fans, Derby harried Leeds into several defensive errors. John O'Hare headed home before a Norman Hunter own goal settled the match. Later that month, Clough and Taylor – unbeknown to the Derby fans – 'resigned', following an offer from Coventry City chairman Derrick Robbins to take over at Highfield Road. Essentially, it was a ruse to convince Sam Longson to give the pair a hefty pay rise. The scheme worked and the pair stayed, but it demonstrated that even with the title in Derby's sights, trouble was looming. A John McGovern winner against Liverpool in Derby's final match of the campaign on the first day of May, in front of a feverish home crowd, put Derby a point clear at the top of the table. They suffered an agonising wait as Leeds – with a fixture backlog thanks to the team's FA Cup run – played their final match of the season against Wolves a week later. Don Revie's men suffered a surprising loss, which meant that the Rams were crowned champions for the first time in their history. The outcome would have been different had it not been for Alan Durban's miraculous block in the dying seconds of the Liverpool game, as Kevin Keegan prepared to slam home an equaliser which, as things turned out, would have given Bill Shankly's side the title. It was a curious end to an historic season. Clough travelled to the Scilly Islands for a pre-booked holiday with his family, whilst the team travelled to Majorca for an end-of-season jolly with Peter Taylor. Despite the best efforts of Taylor to get a telephone link for the game from his room, Derby players weren't aware that they were 1972 league champions until a swarm of journalists descended on them the next day. From his hotel on Tresco, the triumphant Clough told journalists that winning the European Cup was now the club's priority. However, by this point, tempers were beginning to fray in the Derby boardroom.

The Rams eased past Željezničar Sarajevo in the first round of the 1972–73 European Cup, and the clash in Benfica was the kind of glamour tie that Clough and Taylor had always craved. Two nights before the home leg, Taylor paid groundsman Bob Smith a visit, instructing him to 'do your stuff'. Smith obliged, flooding the pitch. When the Benfica players inspected the surface the night before, the muddy mess slopped over the top of their shoes. 'Clough and Taylor thought that the Benfica players, used to bone-hard pitches in Portugal, would struggle. The day after we beat them at home, Clough gave me a great smacker on the cheek and a couple of bottles of champagne,' Smith told me. How, I asked, did Derby avoid punishment for the heavy Baseball Ground pitch against Benfica? 'Simple, we showed FIFA that all the drainage pipes under the pitch were cracked. The thing is – that was true.'

However, come the spring, not even a full house and another Baseball Ground quagmire could save the Rams in the second leg of their semi-final against Juventus. Derby had lost 3–1 in Turin, with Clough convinced that Juve had 'bought' the referee. West German referee Gerhard Schulenburg booked Archie Gemmill and Roy McFarland within fifteen minutes of each other for trivial offences that ruled them out of the second leg, which ended in a

0–0 draw. At half-time in Turin, Peter Taylor spotted Juve substitute Helmut Haller visiting the referee's room and when he tried to intervene he was dragged away by security guards. After the match, a furious Clough refused to talk to Italian journalists, dismissing them as 'cheating bastards'. Clough's lack of diplomacy caused ructions in the Derby County boardroom, as did his sanctioning of the £225,000 signing of Leicester City defender David Nish, whilst chairman Sam Longson, who owned a haulage firm in the town, was holidaying in the Caribbean. To some Derby County directors, particularly the increasingly influential Jack Kirkland (or the 'big noise from Belper' as Taylor described him), Clough was an embarrassment to the club and within six months of the Juventus defeat Clough and Taylor would be gone. The directors' unease was fuelled by their manager's public utterances which, by the summer of 1973, were becoming more extreme by the week.

In the early '70s, Clough's voice was rapidly becoming the most ubiquitous in English football. Sitting slightly away from the rest of the team of experts, he was unleashed upon an unsuspecting general public on BBC1's *World Cup Grandstand* in June 1970. As the tournament was about to kick off, Clough was reluctant to offer up his prediction to presenter Frank Bough of which country would win the tournament: 'I don't like this type of thing, Frank, because out of the sixteen sides I know very little about over half of them,' he lamented in what would soon become his trademark whine. No comfortable platitudes from Clough, no following the herd or sticking to the script. What's fascinating about that early footage is the reaction of the others in the studio as he speaks. There were nervous coughs, furtive glances and shifting in chairs from the likes of Joe Mercer, as the young upstart coach, who was still only thirty-five at the time, voiced whatever was on his mind. He often smirked at the camera, delighting in causing mischief and disquiet. The genie was well and truly out of the bottle. With industrial and civil strife rising in the early 1970s, there were dire forecasts that the elected government would fall and that the 'system' had – to all intents and purposes – failed. Social disruptors argued that a new order was desirable if society was to survive and flourish. Clough – football's arch-disruptor – was adamant in his belief that the football establishment needed to be turned on its head and relished taking a verbal wrecking ball to establishment figures and sacred cows within the game.

Throughout the 1972–73 season, and the early stages of 1973–74, Clough fired verbal barbs in various directions. He warmed up by criticising Derby fans, whom he labelled 'a disgraceful lot' following the Rams' 2–1 victory over Liverpool at the Baseball Ground in September 1972. 'They started chanting only near the end when we were a goal in front. I want to hear them when we are losing,' the manager remarked. At the time, chairman Sam Longson distanced himself from Clough's remarks and apologised to the supporters. Later that month, Clough suggested that the FA Cup be suspended for a year to give England the best chance possible at the 1974 World Cup – assuming they qualified, that is. Longson, desperate to cultivate friendships within both the Football League and the Football Association, issued grovelling apologies to his friends in high places, but the Derby chairman was warned that unless Clough toned down his criticisms, his club would face disciplinary action.

In the new year, Clough set his sights on his two main bêtes noires: England manager Alf Ramsey and Leeds United, for whom Clough had initially expressed admiration, but now claimed to 'loathe everything they stand for'. Clough argued that he'd be willing to 'swap jobs' with Ramsey and openly declared his support for Derby defender Colin Todd, who'd been banned for two years from international football after refusing to go on a summer tour with England that summer. Todd, Clough argued, was 'suspended for being honest'. In late January, he was invited to be guest speaker at the Yorksport awards ceremony dinner at the Queens Hotel, Leeds. It was a prestigious prize, voted for by Yorkshire Television viewers. Official opposition leader Harold Wilson was present and correct, as were a huge contingent of Leeds fans. After disappearing for fifteen minutes to 'go for a wee', Clough launched a full-on verbal attack. He described the prize winner, Leeds forward Peter Lorimer, as being a player who 'falls when he hasn't been kicked … and protests when he has nothing to protest about', Leeds skipper Billy Bremner 'a little cheat' and stated that the club itself 'should be deducted ten points and relegated for their cynicism'. Clough was drowned out by booing and cries of 'Get off!' Peter Lorimer had already left the venue and didn't hear Clough's tirade, having been whisked away by taxi to join his Leeds teammates prior to an FA Cup replay with Norwich City.

In February, on the BBC, Clough explained how he wanted to become football's 'supreme dictator', advocated scrapping the Home Internationals, explaining, 'They're a waste of time, and the standard of football at the end of a hard season is dreadful,' and suggested ending the 1973–74 season early to give England a chance to prepare for the World Cup. Then, three weeks before the start of the 1973–74 campaign, a *Sunday Express* article penned by Clough pushed Derby chairman Sam Longson over the edge. In the piece, he criticised the FA's decision to fine Leeds £3,000 for their 'above average misconduct' but suspend the punishment. Leeds, Clough insisted 'should be instantly relegated' for their poor disciplinary record. The FA convened an emergency committee to decide whether Clough should be charged with bringing the game into disrepute. The Derby board issued an ultimatum to Clough, instructing him to 'stop engaging in literary work by writing articles in the press and stop entering into commitment with radio and television'.

There was no chance of that happening because Clough had recently joined London Weekend Television on a part-time basis as a pundit on *On the Ball* and *The Big Match*, following Jimmy Hill's move back to the BBC. 'Commercial TV was always going to be more Brian's thing,' Jimmy Hill told me during our 2000 chat. 'He realised very quickly that the more controversial he was, the more media opportunities would come his way.' Now Clough had all the media platforms he needed from which he could wage asymmetrical warfare on all of his pet hates. On 11 October 1973, Longson moved at a Derby board meeting that Clough and Taylor should be sacked. A majority voted against the motion. But less than two weeks later, Clough and Taylor resigned after director Jack Kirkland insisted on Peter Taylor meeting him on the Monday after Derby's 1–0 win at Manchester United to explain precisely what his 'duties' were at the club. Clough, for his part, refused to apologise when Sam Longson accused him of making a two-fingered gesture at Manchester United's Matt Busby and chairman Louis Edwards after the game. Clough was irate that his and Taylor's wives were made to feel unwelcome at Old Trafford, but he vehemently denied flicking the V at the United legends.

Despite insisting that the situation at the Baseball Ground had become 'intolerable', Clough quickly regretted the decision to resign. Whether by accident or design, the Brian Clough media juggernaut was careering out of control.

10

THE FACE-OFFS

'There is some fella in London, England, named some Brian…
Brian Clough. Some soccer player or something… and I want you
to know, whoever you are… you're not a fighter, and you don't
take my job. I'm the talker. Now Clough, I've had enough. Stop it!'

Muhammad Ali, 1973

Wembley Stadium, October 1973. The 'circus clown in gloves' – as
ITV panellist Brian Clough describes him before the game – has
morphed into an acrobat. Poland goalkeeper Jan Tomaszewski is
repelling everything that Alf Ramsey's England side throw at him.
He's hurled himself to his right to tip Colin Bell's shot around the
post, soared through the air to push Mick Channon's header over
the crossbar and then scrambled another Channon effort away with
his feet despite diving the wrong way. The 0–0 half-time score won't
be enough for England, who need to win the World Cup qualifier to
progress to the 1974 finals in Germany. 'Keep calm. Put the kettle
on, mother. Don't worry, the goals are going to come,' Clough tells
viewers at half-time.

Then disaster strikes. After fifty-seven minutes, England defender
Norman Hunter fails to bite his man's legs on the left touchline and
Robert Gadocha scampers away to set up Jan Domarski, whose

low shot squirms under a rigid Peter Shilton. England equalise through an Allan Clarke penalty, lump high balls forward for Clarke and Martin Chivers and throw the kitchen sink at Tomaszewski and his defence. Tony Currie fires two thunderbolts straight at the keeper and Kevin Hector's late header is scrambled off the line, but, in front of a disbelieving Wembley crowd, the Poles hang on for a draw. On the ground where they won the Jules Rimet Trophy seven years before, England are out of the World Cup. Tomaszewski, whom Clough continued to dismiss as 'that clown' after the draw, describes the evening as one that 'Polish people will never forget'. Neither will Brian Clough, who, even by his standards, has had a decidedly turbulent couple of days.

Such was the furore surrounding the joint resignations of Clough and Taylor at Derby, not to mention the 'END OF THE WORLD', as *The Sun* described England's World Cup exit, that stories about the Yom Kippur War and the developing Watergate Scandal were kicked clean off the front pages of tabloids and broadsheets. If Clough and Taylor thought that they could persuade their few remaining allies in the Derby boardroom to oust Sam Longson, they were very much mistaken. On 16 October, Longson announced to a gaggle of journalists that the directors had accepted Clough and Taylor's resignations. Although Longson insisted he'd done so with a 'certain amount of sadness', he didn't appear overly traumatised by the experience. In fact, he came out fighting. 'I must stress that Derby County will always survive and that no individual is bigger than the club,' he stated. The players were pole-axed. 'We knew that things were tense, but we never knew it had got to that stage,' explained John McGovern. Roy McFarland, who also played against Poland the day after Clough's resignation was confirmed, was so traumatised by the events of the previous two days that, following the match at Wembley, he drove directly home to Derby rather than stay on with the rest of the ashen-faced England party.

The Derby players pondered strike action, so determined were they for Clough and Taylor's reinstatement. 'We'd had success and believed that there was much more to come. We were devastated and did our level best to get them back,' McFarland explained. The planned strike action entailed the players flying out to Cala Millor, the Mallorcan resort that the team had visited several times. The plan was abandoned after PFA chairman Cliff Lloyd advised Derby's union representative Terry Hennessy that refusing to play in the upcoming home match against Leicester City would mean that the players had breached their contracts and would potentially face the sack. Nonetheless, to even consider such a course of action was unprecedented in English football history. Candle-lit gatherings took place at players' houses (partly through necessity due to power shortages) and there was a protest at the Baseball Ground during which Alan Hinton placed a tea urn on his head, insisting, 'This is the only piece of silverware we'll win in the future without Clough and Taylor in charge.' Furious supporters formed the Derby County Protest Movement, which director Mike Keeling joined after quitting the board. Spearheading the movement were playwright Don Shaw and local MP Philip Whitehead, for whom Brian Clough had campaigned during the two 1974 general elections.

Swathes of Derby supporters affixed 'Bring Back Clough' (BBC) stickers to the back windows of their cars, and Brian's wife Barbara galvanised the players' wives into attending protest meetings at the city town hall. At one point, the players even staged a sit-in at the Baseball Ground. But despite the petition to the board of directors demanding Clough and Taylor's reinstatement, Sam Longson stood firm, appointing former Rams hero Dave Mackay as the new manager. I interviewed Mackay in 2010, shortly after *The Damned Utd* was released in cinemas. The film version of David Peace's novel, which focuses on Brian Clough's time at Derby, and subsequently at Brighton and Leeds, hadn't sat well with Mackay. 'The film implies that I was still a Derby player when I accepted the manager's job, and that I'd somehow betrayed Brian. I'd left a couple of years before and was actually Forest boss, so I hadn't betrayed anyone,' Mackay told me, his gaze as steely as ever. He sued the filmmakers, winning an undisclosed amount.

Even though he was in his seventies, Mackay, who passed away in 2015, gave the firmest handshake of all '70s footballers I met and still puffed out his chest in the confident way that Clough so admired. On the wall in his lounge hung a Brian West painting showing Mackay collecting the Division Two trophy for Derby at the Baseball Ground. A beaming Peter Taylor pats him on the back and Brian Clough and Mackay stare at one another with mutual admiration and respect. I kept glancing at it. Mackay noticed and grinned, 'Great picture that. Total respect between us all.' After a brief pause, Mackay admitted, 'When I took over at Derby, mind, Cloughie caused me so much grief that I wanted to box his bloody ears.' Mackay's legendary combativeness served him well as he took over at the Baseball Ground:

> I had ex-teammates – friends – ring me, asking me not to take the job because they wanted Brian and Peter back. They were upset, which I could understand. But I was very clear-minded. I told them that Brian and Peter had resigned – they weren't sacked. Brian wasn't coming back, and if I didn't take over, someone else would. In the nicest possible sense, I told them to fuck off.

One of those players was Roy McFarland, who admitted, 'Initially, we were total bastards to Dave, and I don't think anyone else could have possibly fronted it out like he did.' On one occasion, Mackay left the Baseball Ground, walked to his car outside and found it plastered in BBC stickers. 'It cost me a fortune to pay for the damage to the bloody paintwork,' he recalled. Player by player, Mackay pulled them all in and told them, calmly but firmly, that if they weren't prepared to play at Derby under him they could leave. None did, but the Bring Back Clough movement remained active nonetheless.

As Mackay adapted to life in the hotseat at the Baseball Ground, Clough – in between those clandestine meetings with his ex-players – became the country's most high-profile media celebrity. As football writer James Lawton put it in *The Independent*, 'He left surrounded by fascination and great celebrity: abrasive, infuriating, but plugged, immovably, into a vein of the nation.' There wasn't a greasy pole-climbing politician or a publicity-hungry musician who was afforded more column inches or airtime in the twelve months that followed his departure from Derby than Brian Clough. Not even Uri Geller, the Israeli illusionist who became an overnight media sensation in the UK following his spoon-bending shenanigans on David Dimbleby's chat show in 1973. Clough's was the most listened to, imitated, sought-after and occasionally vilified voice in the country. No one had access to more media platforms than Clough. The day after his departure from the Baseball Ground, he took his place alongside fellow panellists Derek Dougan and Jack Charlton inside ITV's wood-panelled studio at Wembley for England's game against Poland. Prior to the match, Clough pulled out a nail from under his desk, looked at the camera and said, 'I've got a nail here in me hand. I want it to go into the Polish coffin, or perhaps it could go in Sir Alf's.'

The feud between Ramsey and Clough, which had begun in the aftermath of England's defeat to West Germany in the European Championship tie in 1972, simmered away. In that year, Clough said, 'The split is between managers like myself who believe in exciting football and managers like Sir Alf Ramsey who want to play like the Russians – clockwork football without rhapsody, music or rhythm. Until someone told me he was from Dagenham, I thought he was Russian.' For once, the normally inscrutable Ramsey responded via the medium of the *TV Times*: 'There's a vast gap between us in terms of our attitude to publicity. Mr Clough would seem to be a man who needs to be in the public eye.' Four months before the fateful Wembley clash and 'clown-gate', England lost 2–0 to Poland in Chorzów in June 1973. Clough took issue with Ramsey's reluctance to utilise his substitute strikers Mick Channon and Malcolm Macdonald when England went 2–0 down in the forty-seventh minute following Bobby Moore's defensive error, which allowed Włodzimierz Lubański to score. Ramsey dithered again at Wembley, citing the fact that, rather symbolically, his watch had stopped as the reason for not subbing Martin Chivers until the eighty-eighth minute and bringing on Kevin Hector, despite Bobby Moore pestering him to make a change far sooner.

Yet, Clough had appeared breezily confident about England's (apparently) inevitable victory at Wembley against Poland, four months after England's away defeat, and was adamant in his belief that Jan Tomaszewski was a catastrophe waiting to happen. Brian Moore, once again tasked with the job of policing the panel, had seen the Poles in training and was convinced that the 1972 Olympic champions were a force to be reckoned with: 'They were great at retaining possession. I felt like they played in a very continental style, despite the fact they were from behind the Iron Curtain.' Moore – by his own admission – 'lost his cool' when Clough repeatedly referred to Tomaszewski as 'that clown' during and after the Wembley clash. 'I felt that Brian was deliberately stirring the pot, and rubbing his hands at the reaction,' Moore told me during our 1998 interview. Clough attempted to (slightly) mitigate his comments by saying, 'Well, would you want him in your team week in, week out?'

Jan Tomasewski's performance was arguably the most eccentric ever seen at the old stadium. 'He hurled himself arms, knees and bumps-a-daisy all over his penalty area like a slackly strung marionette,' wrote Frank Keating in *The Guardian*. One save, in which Tomasewski miraculously charged down Allan Clarke's shot at point-blank range, was truly astounding. As the Polish keeper deflected the ball away, Clarke sunk to his haunches in desperation, looking in sheer disbelief at Tomasewski for what seemed an age. Remarkably, he'd broken five metacarpal bones in his left wrist after an early collision with the Leeds striker but played through the pain for the rest of the match. I interviewed Tomasewski for a US football magazine in 2004, shortly after Brian Clough had died. 'Clough put me on the map by calling me the clown, and I am very grateful to him,' said the man who saved two penalties at the 1974 World Cup, a tournament at which Poland finished in third place. He claimed never to have a watched a rerun of his Wembley heroics: 'I've always said it was my football Oscar, and it will always live in my heart and my head.' The two men met decades later at the BBC. They shook hands, embraced and Clough told Tomasewski that he'd 'broken every Englishman's heart that night'. As the gentlemen of the press wrote their Domesday match reports, Brian Clough headed back to the East Midlands in preparation for another headline-grabbing occasion: an appearance in the audience of impressionist Mike Yarwood's *Talk of the Town* show in Derby the following evening.

During the '70s Yarwood – who'd deployed Partridge-style word play in labelling Clough 'The Great Chatsby' – impersonated Labour politicians Harold Wilson and Denis Healey and *Generation Game* hosts Bruce Forsyth and Larry Grayson, amongst others, but, in October 1973, Yarwood laced his sell-out shows with Clough impressions. 'A fella said to me the other daaaay,' Yarwood said at the start of his *Talk Of The Town* show, drawing out the vowels in classic Clough style, '"do you know any good football jokes?" I said

"Yes, Jimmy Hill." I think he expected me to say Sir Alf, but he's beyond a joke.' Although a serious man, Clough found Yarwood's act hilarious, telling the press, 'I couldn't have put it better myself.' When Ramsey was asked what he thought of Yarwood's routine by a journalist later that week, he tutted and turned away. Satire was never Ramsey's thing. A few weeks earlier, Yarwood appeared on *Parkinson* and, whilst imitating the (still) Derby manager, said the line, 'There's only three things wrong with the England team. Sir. Alf. Ramsey. His biggest mistake is not listening to what I'm telling him.'

Two days after watching Yarwood in Derby, Clough also appeared on *Parkinson*. On the show, Clough, clad in a light-grey suit and lilac shirt-and-tie combo, appeared relaxed despite having a hectic past few days. Initially, he went on the offensive: 'I believe the very sight of them brings the game into disrepute,' he said of football directors. There was some bravado about how he was 'wired into the Derby players' thoughts' but he also displayed a level of honesty about himself that was unprecedented amongst football's leading lights at that time. Clough spoke of how much he missed both his parents – admitting that he hadn't given himself enough time to grieve the death of his mother a year before.

Unsurprisingly, Clough wasn't everyone's cup of tea. 'Our job is difficult enough, without us going around slitting one another's throats,' grumbled Don Revie after being on the receiving end of another Clough broadside that same month. Revie admitted that Clough 'wasn't someone whom I'd like to be stuck with on a desert island, and I'm guessing the feeling is mutual'. Liverpool manager Bill Shankly grumbled that Clough was like 'the rain in Manchester. It never stops.' *FOUL* magazine was unimpressed with what they described in September 1973 as Clough's 'loud-mouthed egotism'. To his detractors, Clough was morphing into a cartoonish version of himself in front of an audience. Brian Moore believed that Clough's media presence 'went beyond saturation point in the months after he left Derby'. The *FOUL* article also suggested that, with his profile on LWT, Clough was as guilty as any TV executive of contributing to the dumbing down of football, where 'the dull bits are edited out, destroying any rhythm a match might have'. *FOUL* urged highlights shows to provide greater analysis of the build-up play rather than purely cramming in as many goals as possible.

Ironically, Clough accepted as much in one of his November 1973 *TV Times* columns. 'These TV people', he wrote, 'can devote so much attention to making it all nice and smooth and flaw-free that they can fall into the trap of making football look easy too.' Clough believed that, rather than drain football of spectators, televised football should showcase the product. 'I'd make both channels put far more into the game than they do now', he explained in April 1974, suggesting a £30,000 fee to be split between both clubs and the Football League for an individual match between leading sides. The manager still reckoned that the televised product was inferior to the real thing, though. Brian Moore told me that Clough pondered long and hard whether to quit football management after departing Derby and move to LWT full time, but that 'ultimately, the call of the game was just too strong. Punditry was always second best.' By November 1973, with Clough still angling to return to Derby, he and Peter Taylor accepted an offer to take over the ailing Third Division side Brighton and Hove Albion.

Clough's nine-month south-coast sojourn demonstrated how, as *FOUL* pointed out, the manager was now indulging in 'self-parodying behaviour'. Jersey-born property developer Mike Bamber had great ambitions for his club, and, by the end of the decade, the Seagulls reached Division One for the first time in their history, albeit not under the tutelage of Clough and Taylor. 'These are First Division wages,' Clough responded when Bamber put the £25,000 joint deal on the table. 'You're First Division managers, and that's where Brighton are headed,' came the response. When he met the expectant Seagulls squad for the first time in a Hove hotel the night before their home match against York City, Clough kept them waiting for more than two hours, immediately launched a verbal tirade against the length of utility player John 'Shirley' Templeman's hair and then asked the chastened squad what they'd like to drink. When one of the squad said that he'd like a lemonade, Clough retorted, 'I mean a proper bloody drink.' 'My first impression was he was a complete head-case,' goalkeeper Brian Powney claimed. Brighton fans who'd scoffed when the *Evening Argus* sports editor speculated a few days beforehand, 'Could the club afford Brian you-know-who?' turned up in their droves at the Goldstone Ground, trebling the previous 5,000 average, which was precisely what chairman Mike Bamber had in mind when he hired the pair.

Clough's indifference was clear from the outset. He was regularly late to training and meetings, leaving the players to sort out tactics for themselves. The sharpness of his tongue intensified. At that first meeting with Brighton players, with the song 'If I Ruled the World' playing in the background, Clough invited any one of the Brighton team to punch him in the face to show that they were 'capable of positive action'. They all politely declined the offer. Betraying his sense of geographical dislocation in Brighton, Clough made Norman Gall captain, insisting that as he was the squad's sole member from the north-east he was the one player he could trust.

Clough frequently went AWOL between Sunday and Thursday, often popping back to Derby to see how the BBC campaign was going. On one occasion, he marched into Dave Mackay's office to see if he could take some Derby reserves on loan at the Goldstone Ground. 'I told him that he had a bloody cheek.' Mackay told me.

Clough flew to New York on the eve of a Brighton match to watch the second instalment of the Muhammad Ali v. Joe Frazier trilogy, leaving an increasingly irked Peter Taylor to oversee the game. The most memorable aspects of Clough's tenure were the leatherings Brighton suffered at the hands of non-league Walton and Hersham in the FA Cup (4–0) and in Division Three against Bristol Rovers (8–2), when his son Nigel sat next to him in the dugout. He admitted on *The Big Match* that the Rovers defeat – during which Brighton fell foul of Eastville's charismatic striking duo Bruce Bannister and Alan Warboys (aka 'Smash 'n' Grab') – was his 'worst day in football'. When Brighton briefly experimented with playing matches on Sunday, Clough objected. With the country still suffering power cuts as a result of the miners' strike, the Football Association agreed to give the go-ahead for early afternoon Sunday matches on an experimental basis for FA Cup third-round ties in January 1974. This was extended to league matches a fortnight later. Under Sunday observance laws, it was illegal to charge admission, so clubs instead charged spectators the normal admission price for the club programme. Although most clubs recorded higher gates than normal, protestors outside grounds held up placards with the following message: 'REMEMBER TO KEEP HOLY THE SABBATH DAY'. Maurice Norvic, Bishop of Norwich, wrote a letter to *The Times* despairing that football on the Sabbath represented the spread 'of the breathless continental and American Sunday' and that Sundays were 'given by God as a day of rest, worship, refreshment and family happiness'. Clough's concerns appeared purely secular. 'Sunday is an Englishman's day off,' he said. On another occasion, he argued that 'Sunday is about being with my wife and bairns.' Yet, he turned up for his *Big Match* slot on Sundays without fail. The exasperated Peter Taylor was once again left to take care of a Brighton team that continued to toil in the nether regions of Division Three.

Through the medium of his *TV Times* column, Clough damned Sir Alf Ramsey with the faintest of praise after the England manager was finally axed in May 1974: 'I actually admired Sir Alf. You've got to hand it to a bloke who can stand by his guns with an almost serene stubbornness. To be stubborn is the essential quality of the football manager.' Ramsey's handshake from the FA was less than golden. His £7,200 a year contract (£70,000 in today's money; his successor Don Revie was paid an estimated £25,000, equivalent to £242,000 today) was settled and he was given a lump sum of £8,000 and an annual pension of £1,200. It was a sad end for the man who steered the national team to its finest hour, but ITV offered Ramsey an opportunity to reinvent himself as a pundit throughout June and July on their 1974 World Cup coverage, which meant that Clough and Ramsey would, briefly, be colleagues. In marked contrast to Clough, who revelled in the heated debates with the three survivors from the 1970 panel, Malcolm Allison, Pat Crerand and Derek Dougan, and new boys Jack Charlton and Bobby Moncur, Ramsey was stilted and stiff. His spikiness still manifested itself. When commentator Hugh Johns asked Ramsey how long he thought the lights would remain off for during a power cut in the stadium during one of the matches, he received the following terse reply, 'I am not an electrician.' Off-air, he claimed that Brian Clough's tournament XI contained 'some right wankers', much to Brian Moore's amusement.

Clough got on famously with the equally outspoken Jack Charlton. One afternoon in the bar, the talk turned to who might be appointed the next England manager, with caretaker boss Joe Mercer temporarily in charge. 'Cloughie and I were adamant that Don [Revie] was the only suitable man for the job, given what he'd achieved,' Charlton told me. This was despite a *Daily Express* poll awarding 30 per cent of the vote share to Clough and 15 per cent to Charlton, whose Middlesbrough team had just been promoted to the top flight. 'So, if Don becomes England manager, who'd become the new Leeds boss?' Charlton asked Clough. 'Not me! There would be a bloody civil war up there,' Clough responded. Both panellists laughed long and hard into their pint glasses.

━━━━━

Quite how the Leeds directors, or the man himself, ever believed that Clough's appointment could work is a mystery, but after a meeting in Hove's Courtlands Hotel, with Peter Taylor and Mike Bamber also present, Brian Clough was announced as the new Leeds United manager on 1 July 1974. 'I saw what went on when you left Derby. I want the kind of manager whose players are prepared to go on strike for him,' Leeds chairman Manny Cussins told Clough, although he was perturbed that Peter Taylor decided to stay on the south coast out of loyalty to Mike Bamber. The Leeds players were stunned at Clough's appointment. 'There were lots of confused faces when we heard that Cloughie was coming, given what he'd said about us,' Peter Lorimer told me in his distinctive Yorkshire/Scottish accent. 'Not outright rebellion though – despite what might have been said and written recently.' The former Scotland international was referring to *The Damned Utd*, in which Revie's ex-players were presented as mutinous and surly from the outset towards Clough. 'We were – how shall I put it – sceptical,' explained Norman Hunter. 'Not simply because of what he'd said about us, but because straight after he was appointed he shot back to Mallorca on holiday with his family at the start of preseason training. It felt wrong.' Officially, Clough was in charge at Elland Road for fifty-four days, but ten of those were spent basking in the Mediterranean sun.

He had no time to grasp how quickly Leeds, known for its clothing and engineering industries, was changing. As the old factories disappeared, plush new office blocks and hotels sprung up, including the posh new Dragonara Hotel (now the Hilton), where Clough stayed during his brief tenure. With the new M1 and M62 motorways connecting Leeds to other major northern cities, the metropolis was dubbed the 'Motorway City of the '70s' on all franked envelopes sent from the city. Yet, for Clough, it remained grim, unforgiving and suspicious of outsiders. 'Cloughie should have broken the ice with us quicker,' Peter Lorimer argued. 'The lack of communication and silence made the whole thing more awkward.' When Clough finally arrived (with young sons Nigel and Simon in tow) to begin work, he said virtually nothing for two days, preferring to observe the players from afar. The very fact that the normally verbose Clough elected to be mute cranked the tension up a few more notches. In training on day two, Peter Lorimer dared to ask Clough a tactical question. 'He put his finger to his lips and walked off,' Lorimer recalled. On day three, Clough called a meeting in the players' room. What followed was the most extraordinary tirade in English football history.

The precise vocabulary that Clough used differed according to which former Leeds player I spoke to, but the barbed messages were crystal-clear nonetheless. According to Peter Lorimer, Clough began the meeting with the phrase, 'Right, gentlemen,' which is consistent with how he tended to start team gatherings. Whereas Norman Hunter suggested that Clough waded in straight in with, 'Right, you fucking lot.' Clough let loose, telling the players they 'could throw all their cups and medals in the nearest dustbin because you've won them all by bloody cheating'. One by one, he lambasted the entire team. 'You may possess the best passing ability in the game, but God didn't give you six studs to wrap around someone else's knee,' he told Johnny Giles. To Norman Hunter: 'No one in the game likes you and I know you want to be liked.' Clough was hardest on Eddie Gray, who'd been particularly unlucky with injuries over the preceding few years: 'If you were a racehorse, young man, you'd have been shot.' But Clough wasn't addressing a collection of callow kids at Hartlepools or starry-eyed youngsters at Derby keen to make their way in the game and in thrall to their manager. He was talking to the most bemedalled footballers in the country, a collection of wealthy, well-travelled professionals in their branded Leeds gear, who'd (almost) won all there was to win in English football. Rather than the 'pigsty' he'd inherited at Derby, this was a stable full of thoroughbreds who'd won more than Clough ever had.

Instead of staring at the floor as he scolded them, the players stared him out. Then they came straight back at him. 'If I get kicked, I kick them back,' shrugged Johnny Giles. 'I don't give a fuck what other people think of me,' Norman Hunter countered. Eddie Gray's was the most nuanced response. 'Didn't your career end through injury?' he asked Clough. The new Leeds boss answered in the affirmative. 'Then you should know how I feel,' Gray said. Clough's opening gambit had failed spectacularly. There was no plan, no strategy, no offer of reconciliation. As the furious players filed out of the room, and Clough prepared to head to the Yorkshire TV studios, Norman Hunter, within earshot of Clough, said to the others, 'We don't fucking need this.'

It is entirely befitting that, for someone who'd spent an inordinate amount of time on television over the past nine months, Clough's tumultuous 44-day reign at Elland Road was bookended by two appearances on the regional current affairs show *Calendar*, presented by future Labour MP Austin Mitchell. The beginning of Clough's first appearance makes for uncomfortable viewing: on the studio monitor, Clough watches black and white footage of his career-ending injury that he suffered when he collided with Bury keeper Chris Harker at Roker Park. Clough writhes around in agony on the slushy surface like a fish out of water before the stretcher-bearers take the stricken striker away. The new Leeds manager appeared mesmerised by the bleak images, later claiming to have not seen the footage before. 'Welcome to Leeds, Mr Clough', runs the caption.

With the mop-topped Mitchell in the chair, Clough was grilled by *The Sun*'s John Sadler, TV producer Keith Macklin and the *Daily Mirror*'s Peter Cooper. The atmosphere was cordial, but the questions were unforgiving. Clough largely tiptoed around them, and his performance was a blend of blatant denial, bravado and idealism. He insisted that although many players were now in their thirties, a rebuilding process would be completed patiently and, astonishingly, that the meeting with his new players had gone 're-markably well'. He set out his vision of the post-Revie Leeds era, insisting that he 'wants to bring warmth and honesty to the club'. Clough argued that Leeds had 'not been good league champions', and that they'd 'sold themselves short'. He stood by his allegation that the club should have been relegated for their poor disciplinary record and was reluctant to admit that in the 1973–74 campaign Leeds cleaned up their act and played a style of football that was applauded by past critics. Told in advance that Clough would appear on TV that night, the Leeds players tuned into *Calendar*. They were unimpressed. 'Half of what Brian said, he shouldn't have repeated in public – the criticism of us and of Don,' Norman Hunter argued, 'and the other half, about how he wanted to change our style, should have been said to our faces earlier that day.'

Perhaps it was the fact that their mercurial new manager had ordered them to walk around a service station carpark in the August drizzle as the coach made its way south for the Charity Shield clash with Liverpool on 10 August 1974, but the Leeds players positively scowled as they walked out behind their new manager at Wembley. In the tunnel, Clough made small-talk with the recently retired Bill Shankly, whom new Liverpool manager Bob Paisley had asked to lead out the team. Revie declined Clough's offer to do likewise with his former players on the Friday afternoon before the game. The match was an ugly spectacle, with retribution meted out by both sides. Early on, Allan Clarke scythed down Liverpool's Phil Thompson, and the Leeds striker was later stretchered off after biting tackles by Tommy Smith and Alec Lindsay removed him from the equation. Ten minutes into the second half, Johnny Giles punched Kevin Keegan to the floor and was booked. Shortly afterwards, the still-furious Keegan tangled with Billy Bremner. Both players were sent off and threw their shirts down on the hallowed turf as a sign of protest. Brian Clough, whose teams – before and after – always had excellent disciplinary records, was horrified by what he saw. So much for the 'warmth and honesty' that he sought to bring to Leeds. The match ended 1–1, with Liverpool's Ian Callaghan's spot kick winning the penalty shootout for Paisley's Liverpool. The following day, both the FA and Football League criticised the players' behaviour. FA secretary Ted Croker, who'd previously expressed concern that violent behaviour on the pitch might lead to hooliganism off it, argued, 'We are trying to make football more acceptable to a wider range of people. Players must learn they cannot throw punches at each other.' The authorities threw the book at Bremner and Keegan, fining both men £500 and suspending them until the end of September. 'You'll pay the bloody fine out of your own pocket,' a furious Clough told Bremner, who'd miss eleven Leeds matches as a result. 'Don paid our fines,' Bremner countered. 'Don's not here now,' Clough snapped.

Keen to begin his remoulding process quickly, and bring in some friendly faces, Clough turned to the East Midlands for salvation, signing Nottingham Forest striker Duncan McKenzie for £250,000 and Derby pair John McGovern and John O'Hare – who'd slipped out of the first-team picture under Dave Mackay – for a combined £125,000 fee. Due to Bremner's suspension, McGovern, whom

Clough aimed to introduce slowly to the first-team picture, was pitched in almost immediately. It was the lowest point of the midfielder's career. 'The Leeds fans booed me from the off,' McGovern told me. 'They hated me because I'd replaced Bremner, and because I was a Clough man.' McGovern accused his former Leeds teammates of delivering 'hospital passes' to him. 'They'd put too much weight on them to make me look bad, or they'd pull up short so my passes overran them. It was systematically done.' Forward John O'Hare recalled, 'The Leeds players constantly asked John [McGovern] and I about what made Clough tick, whether he was like this at Derby and how he'd ever been successful.' O'Hare pondered buying a house in Leeds but quickly opted against doing so because it was 'obvious to me that Clough – and therefore John McGovern and me – wouldn't be at Leeds for very long.' But even O'Hare was amazed at how quickly things fell apart. The team was hammered 3–0 by Stoke City in the opening league game of the campaign, then, with Bremner's long suspension beginning, lost 1–0 at home to Queens Park Rangers. Leeds briefly rallied to beat Birmingham City 1–0 at Elland Road, before drawing with QPR, losing to Manchester City and drawing to Luton (after which home fans booed Clough as he left the dugout). Clough was convinced that his players were in cahoots with Revie to undermine him, an allegation that Norman Hunter, Trevor Cherry and Peter Lorimer denied. As if to demonstrate how Revie had spooked Clough, the England manager, in his brown sheepskin coat and driving gloves ensemble, was present and correct at Clough's final match in charge, a 1–1 draw with Huddersfield at Leeds Road in the League Cup. Clough praised his team's fighting spirit in levelling after being a goal down, but the end was nigh.

At a meeting in the players' room, convened by director Sam Bolton, the stars were invited to offer their opinions on where things were going wrong. At first, Clough was present and John

McGovern explained that the manager offered an olive branch to the players, suggesting that 'we start over'. It was too late for that. On Johnny Giles's request, Clough was asked to step out of the room in order that the Leeds players could speak freely. McGovern and O'Hare – placed in an invidious position – remained silent, as did Allan Clarke. Paul Reaney whispered to O'Hare 'this is wrong'. The rest said their piece, with the normally taciturn Paul Madeley insisting, 'What the boys are trying to say, Mr Bolton, is that he's no good.' In years to come, the Leeds players' room meeting would be cited as growing evidence that the once-silent footballing serfs had well and truly found their collective voices by the 1970s. This was 'player power', plain and simple. Trevor Cherry disagreed, telling me, 'The meeting was set up by Sam Bolton, not by the players. My feeling was that Bolton heard what he wanted to hear. Every time there was a negative comment about Clough, Bolton looked at Manny Cussins and nodded.' Cussins terminated Clough's employment at the club that evening.

When news filtered through over the wires that Clough had been sacked, the folk at *Calendar* moved hastily to set up a televised showdown between Brian Clough and Don Revie – the equivalent of Arsène Wenger and Alex Ferguson squaring up to one another in a TV studio when the rivalry between Arsenal and Manchester United was at its height. The only similar clash of personalities in '70s chat shows was perhaps the appearance of theatre director Jonathan Miller and Enoch Powell together on *The Dick Cavett Show* to debate issues surrounding UK immigration in May 1971. ITV executives agreed that the face-off was worthy of exposure beyond Yorkshire and it was broadcast directly after *News at Ten*.

With Austin Mitchell once again chairing proceedings, Clough, staring directly into the camera, appeared rather giddy and giggled on more than one occasion during the interview. This was perhaps due to the hefty pay-off he'd received from the Leeds board earlier that day, which eventually amounted to almost £100,000 – the equivalent of over £1 million today. 'I've won the bloody pools!' Clough yelled as he was driven to the studios, drinking champagne en route. Uniquely for a manager in that era, Clough – at thirty-nine – was now financially secure. On arrival at the studio, he was handed an envelope by TV executives containing somewhere in the region of £400 in used notes, as was Don Revie. The contrasting screen styles between the two men still makes for compelling viewing, perhaps because the pair were anything but media-trained robots.

Revie, wearing a light-blue blazer, is serious, unsmiling, thoughtful and takes issue with Clough's previous public criticism of both himself and the Leeds players. He suggested that Clough had made an error of judgement on his first day at Elland Road by not gathering all the staff together and introducing both himself and his philosophy. Revie refuted Clough's suggestions that he was 'a cold man' and that there was 'no warmth at the club', describing the family atmosphere he'd fostered during his thirteen years in charge. But, as Clough, McGovern and O'Hare discovered, the Leeds players weren't always so welcoming to outsiders. Revie largely sidestepped Clough's point that eight player contracts were unsigned and that the Leeds team was ageing. Clough's point about playing styles went entirely over Revie's head. 'I believe in a different concept of football. I want to aim for utopia. I believe in fairies at the bottom of the garden,' Clough said. 'No, no, no. There's no way you could win it [the league title] better,' Revie insisted. The only thing that bonded the two men was their unsatiated desire to win the European Cup, but with Revie now England boss, and Clough unceremoniously given his marching orders by the league champions, the prospect of either manager achieving this footballing holy grail appeared uncertain. By the end of the season, Leeds, now under Jimmy Armfield, reached the European Cup final, where they controversially lost to Bayern Munich. But, as Clough suggested, without major investment in the team to replace Bremner, Giles, Hunter and co., Leeds' heyday was already over. Perhaps, as Clough later suggested, Revie – deep down – knew that his players' biological clocks were ticking, and he got out in the nick of time.

In the great managerial shake up of 1974, with Leeds, Liverpool, Tottenham and England embarking on new eras, Brian Clough was abruptly cast into the wilderness. The huge pay-off he received armour-plated him to some degree, but the controversial nature of his departure from Derby, Brighton and now Leeds – all in the space of nine months – placed huge question marks over his future in management. TV exposure helped turn Clough into Britain's most high-profile celebrity, but it had also played a pivotal role in him losing his job at Derby. On *Calendar*, his embarrassment was laid bare in front of the cameras and he confessed to 'wanting to be sick' following the vote of no confidence that was passed by the Leeds players.

'My biggest fear is that I'll be remembered for only this,' Jamaican reggae singer Carl Douglas admitted after his global hit 'Kung Fu Fighting' entered the charts just as Clough departed Elland Road. The early '70s charts were awash with one-hit wonders, and Clough, with his sole number-one hit at Derby in '72, appeared to be in grave danger of becoming Carl Douglas's football equivalent. 'Who will touch you with a barge pole now?' asked Austin Mitchell, pointedly, at the end of Clough's *Calendar* appearance. It was a fair question. The same could be said of Peter Taylor, who was making little headway down in Brighton. And what of John McGovern and John O'Hare, frozen out of the first-team picture at Leeds and left to rot in the reserves?

Fortunately, barge poles were in plentiful supply in the Nottingham Forest boardroom.

11

THE TRAMLINE AND THE CHOCOLATE KIT

'Admiral prices are always a spectacular mark-up on the price
the kit sold for before the deal. But the clubs don't care.
Why should they?'
FOUL, May/June 1976

Wembley, September 1974. Don Revie's opening match as England manager in the European Championship qualifier against Czechoslovakia has gone swimmingly. The 83,858 crowd, with song sheets in hand, boom out 'Land of Hope and Glory' (a Revie innovation) with gusto prior to kick-off and, on the pitch, Revie's England swat aside their eastern European rivals in the second half. Dave Thomas – the skilful Queens Park Rangers winger who always plays with his socks rolled down without any shinpads – delivers a pinpoint cross which is headed in by Southampton's Mick Channon. Channon then slips through a ball which Manchester City midfielder Colin Bell slides home. Late on, Bell nods in a Channon cross to secure a 3–0 win. But amongst the players, opinions are distinctly mixed on the most eye-catching aspect of the night: England's new Admiral kit, with its red and blue tramlines running down the white arms. Liverpool's Kevin Keegan is a fan: 'It's modern and represents the fact that we have entered a new era for the England team.' Some of the players don't like the texture, with Colin Bell – used to turning out in England's classic pure-white number – insisting it's 'like cardboard on the skin'. After the match, Leicester City's Frank Worthington complains that his nipples hurt with all the chafing from the nylon shirt.

'I've always been aware that any form of publicity – good or bad – is great for business,' shrugs the company's stoic sandy-haired director Bert Patrick. Throughout the '70s, Admiral, whose impact on the game will be debated in the House of Commons, the press and in dressing rooms across the country, create both in equal measure.

───

In late 1970, a *Vogue* headline stated, 'There are no rules in the fashion industry any more'. The accompanying article asserted that due to the proliferation of synthetic fibres, multicolour textures, tie-dyed clothes and floral and ethnic patterns the following decade would be all about 'individualism and inventiveness'. *Vogue*'s clarion call for cutting-edge creativity (and its prediction that rust, copper, burnt orange and pistachio would be the dominant shades in the fashion industry) was echoed in car design. Distinctive wings and wedges dominated much of the decade. As automotive journalist Quentin Wilson explained in 2006, the Austin Princess and Maxi, the Ford Capri, the Citroën SM and the Datsun Z – amongst other models – 'will burn long in the memory, due to their unique appearances'. However, in 1970, this modish approach seemed unlikely to catch on when it came to football shirts.

In 1974, departing Tottenham boss Bill Nicholson was asked what he thought of the designs for Leeds United's flashy new Admiral away kit. Amongst the trilby-hatted managers of the early '70s, Nicholson wasn't alone in believing that a club's shirt was sacrosanct.

'I can see it coming that, within a few years, team shirts will be plastered with all sorts...' a disapproving Nicholson argued. He then spoke proudly of the 'purity of the white top and blue cockerel at Tottenham'. A little further up Seven Sisters Road, Arsenal manager Bertie Mee insisted that the Gunners' shirt 'should be purely about the red, the white and the cannon'. Until the mid-1970s, club shirts were made from cotton, tended to have rounded collars and, aside from the club badge and the player's number on the back, were largely uncluttered. The simplistic shirt designs tended to fit in with the view of the old-school managers that football was all about the football and anything else was a distraction. But the old guard's days were numbered. A revolution in kit design was about to sweep through football whether they liked it or not.

This revolution was spearheaded by former journalist Bert Patrick, who, by 1966, became the owner of underwear manufacturing company Cook & Hurst, whose factory premises were based in Wigston, Leicestershire. The firm, established before the First World War, had a fine reputation for making men's and ladies' cotton and wool underwear. Ironically, given the frenzy of publicity which surrounded the firm's designs in the '70s, Patrick always considered the company's brand name Admiral to be conservative and dull. But it would come to symbolise a fashion revolution. The catalyst for change came when England won the World Cup and demand for football kits began to outstrip supply. Admiral switched its production from underwear to plainly designed football tops, which, in Patrick's words, 'were solely lacking in creativity and innovation'. In early 1970, with the World Cup on the horizon, Patrick gathered his staff and informed them that with the advent of colour TV the '70s would be the era when marketing opportunities in football would go stratospheric. Not everyone shared the company director's enthusiasm. Patrick passed away in early 2021, but when I spoke to the softly spoken manufacturing pioneer in 2020, he explained,

One of the girls in my factory said to me, 'It's all right for you to talk about colour telly, but most of us can't afford it.' I took her point, but I knew that the advent of colour TV would change everything for football kits. I wanted children – and their dads – to collect replica kits in the same way that their fathers had collected cigarette cards.

Although he was convinced that it would be a matter of when, and not if, Patrick knew that if he wanted to break into the football shirt market, he needed to do his homework. Patrick discovered that sports retailer Ron Goodman was hugely influential in both the capital and Manchester, offering clubs a personal service providing Umbro kit and adidas boots. Patrick decided to avoid London and the north-west altogether for the time being and target somewhere more provincial. He headed straight to Yorkshire and Elland Road. Patrick reasoned that Don Revie's strong links with Leicester (it had been his first club as a player) might give him an 'in'. Revie had shown himself to be proactive when it came to kit design, altering Leeds' blue and yellow strip to all-white in the '60s, in order to emulate Real Madrid. Admiral bosses knew that if they could convince Revie to make a change, they'd get their foot in the door and they used a two-pronged attack.

Admiral managing director John Griffin, after being turfed out of a sales pitch by a business directly opposite Leeds United's training ground in 1973, watched Revie's men training for a while in the rain and approached the manager as the mud-caked team completed its session. As the players shuffled by, a brief conversation took place between Revie and Griffin. For around £7,000, Griffin said that Admiral would redesign the Leeds away kit and that, together,

The original 1970 World Cup ITV panel, consisting of (*left to right*) Bob McNab, Pat Crerand, Jimmy Hill, Derek Dougan, Brian Moore and Malcolm Allison, which heralded the dawning of a brash new era of TV punditry and professional outrage.
© ITV/Shutterstock

With the press circling, England manager Sir Alf Ramsey and midfielder Bobby Charlton despair following England's 3–2 quarter-final defeat to West Germany in the 1970 World Cup in Mexico.
© Bob Thomas/Getty Images

Sprung by *This Is Your Life* host Eamonn Andrews during a London fashion shoot, George Best (holding brother Ian) receives the 'red book' treatment in November 1971. The show's bonhomie – and classic '70s decor – disguised the Manchester United star's personal troubles.
© *TV Times* via Getty Images

'In they strutted, some of the biggest swinging dicks in the game,' said photographer Terry O'Neill of the Clan. *Back row, left to right*: David Webb, Geoff Hurst and Terry Venables. *Front row, left to right*: Terry Mancini, Alan Ball, Alan Hudson and Rodney Marsh. © Terry O'Neill/Iconic Images/Getty Images

Artist and designer Paul Trevillion, aka 'the Beaver', who worked with 'Super Leeds' in the early '70s, poses with two of his creations: a Johnny Giles target ball and prototype-only Norman 'Bites Yer Legs' Hunter-themed shinpads.
Courtesy of Paul Trevillion

Hereford United's jubilant Ronnie Radford (*No. 11 shirt*) has just scored arguably the FA Cup's most iconic goal against First Division Newcastle United in February 1972 and is engulfed by a tidal wave of ecstatic Parka-clad supporters.

© Bentley Archive/Popperfoto via Getty Images/Getty Images

Brian Clough (*left*) glares at Don Revie, who has recently been appointed England manager, on ITV current affairs show *Calendar* on the day Leeds United terminated Clough's turbulent 44-day spell in charge.

© David Hickes/ Alamy Stock Photo

Liverpool manager Bill Shankly celebrates Liverpool winning the FA Cup final against Newcastle United in 1974. His resignation a few weeks later sent shockwaves well beyond Anfield.

© Trinity Mirror/Mirrorpix/ Alamy Stock Photo

LEFT The mayhem of a Manchester derby as captured by former referee-turned-impressionist painter Gordon Hill. A 'progressive' whistler in the '70s, Hill included himself in the painting (the circled black dot), and his linesmen on the edges with flags.

Courtesy of Veronica Lake at Studio 36, Exeter

BELOW LEFT Sunderland players, including Dennis Tueart (*back left with guitar*), matchwinner Ian Porterfield (*standing, second right*) and goalkeeper Jimmy Montgomery (*standing, far right*), recorded the obligatory FA Cup final song prior to their shock 1–0 win over Leeds United in 1973.

Courtesy of Dennis Tueart

BELOW On a tortuous night for England against Poland in October 1973, Mick Channon (*left*), Martin Chivers (*centre*) and Roy McFarland (*right*) see another chance go begging. Prostrate Polish keeper Jan Tomaszewski (dubbed a 'clown' by ITV pundit Brian Clough) made several vital saves to deny England qualification for the 1974 World Cup.

© PA Images/Alamy Stock Photo

'Supersub' David Fairclough scores Liverpool's vital third goal at Anfield to edge out French champions Saint-Étienne in their pulsating European Cup quarter-final clash in March 1977.

© Trinity Mirror/Mirrorpix/ Alamy Stock Photo

Manchester United manager Tommy Docherty celebrates winning the FA Cup in 1977, with Stuart Pearson (*left*), Lou Macari (*right*) and Gordon Hill (*far right*), but tabloid scandal will soon engulf the 'Doc'.
© PA Images/Alamy Stock Photo

Blyth Spartans striker Terry Johnson puts the non-league side 1–0 up against Wrexham in the fifth round in the Northern League side's historic FA Cup run in 1978.

Courtesy of Blyth Spirit

New Millwall signings Phil Walker (*left*) and Trevor Lee in October 1975. 'We'd received so much abuse in non-league football that we thought we might as well at least get paid for it,' reflected Walker on the pair's £40,000 signing from non-league Epsom & Ewell.

Courtesy of Jim Standen

ABOVE Arguably the most shocking of all '70s football images: Manchester United fan Peter Brookes is carried out of Anfield with a dart sticking through his nose. 'It took four people to remove it,' he said.

© Ray Bradbury/Alamy Stock Photo

LEFT In a move towards 'earth toning', Coventry City's Ian Wallace poses in his club's now infamous Admiral-designed chocolate-brown away kit.

Courtesy of *Coventry Evening Telegraph*

Top left to bottom right: Tramlines on the new England kit; egg-timer markings on the Wales away strip; retina-scarring orange on Luton Town's shirt; and the famous sash on Crystal Palace's jersey. Admiral changed the palette of 1970s football. © John Devlin/www.truecoloursfootballkits.com

English football's first million-pound footballer Trevor Francis heads home the winner for Brian Clough's Nottingham Forest in the 1979 European Cup final against Malmö in Munich's Olympic Stadium. John Robertson, who delivered the cross, looks on from the byline in the right-hand corner. © PA Images/Alamy Stock Photo

Unveiled in 2010, Andy Edwards's statue of Brian Clough and Peter Taylor holding the 1972 Division One trophy takes pride of place outside Derby County's stadium. By some distance, the pair remain '70s football's most successful managerial double act.
© Russ Hamer, CC BY-SA 3.0 via Wikimedia Commons

both club and company would be at the forefront of the replica kit market. Bert Patrick followed up this initial approach by travelling to Elland Road to meet with Revie. Patrick talked about 'the club, its history and its tradition. Don understood that there was now a market for groundbreaking kit design and replica shirts. He was very switched-on commercially.' Revie listened to Patrick intently and after telling him, 'You're not touching our home shirt,' he gave Patrick carte blanche to do as he pleased with the away kit. For a £10,000 fixed payment, with the money going directly into the Leeds players' pool, Admiral had struck its first major football kit deal. Extra bonuses would be forthcoming if Leeds won silverware and this was offset by a 5 per cent royalty on sales of the club's Admiral clothing or leisurewear.

The new Leeds yellow away strip with blue and white tramlines running down the sleeves and the side of the shorts was an overnight success. 'It was all a bit too fancy for my liking,' Leeds fullback Trevor Cherry recalled, 'but I'm reliably informed that it now has a certain '70s cool.' Patrick ensured that the new Leeds gear was registered under the Design Copyright Act 1968, which meant the kit designs were exclusive to Admiral and could not be pirated. Add in the new Leeds tracksuit – white jacket, blue and yellow rings on the sleeves and yellow trim neck – which Revie's men sported on the 1973 official club Christmas card, and Admiral's intervention was perfectly timed. The Leeds players first wore the shirts in the spring of 1974, as they were about to be crowned league champions. 'Demand for the replica shirts and tracksuits from youngsters went through the roof,' recalled Patrick, 'and it was clear that if we were to continue to develop new kits, we'd need to expand.' Patrick acquired two sites in Wigston and another in Ireland to cater for the demand.

Shortly before Revie left for the England job in 1974, he gave Patrick the green light to redesign the Leeds home strip, in time for the start of the 1974–75 season. The changes were fairly conservative. As well as the distinctive Admiral logo on the shirt, collars were added – although not '70s-style butterfly ones. Patrick delivered brand-new Admiral tracksuits and match balls to Elland Road on the night Jimmy Armfield's Leeds faced Barcelona in the 1975 European Cup semi-final. Although he was given two complimentary tickets for the match by the club, the security guard refused to allow him into the private car park as he didn't have a director's box pass. After a prolonged altercation, Patrick opened his boot, showing the security guard the full Admiral regalia. 'If you don't let me in,' he said, pointing to the match balls, 'this match won't take place.' Over 50,393 packed Elland Road to see Leeds win 2–1 on a memorable night for Leeds and a hugely symbolic one for Admiral.

━━━━

Bert Patrick had already been tipped off by Don Revie that he was poised to take the England job in the summer of 1974 and was asked by the coach to draw up designs for a new kit. Both Patrick and Revie sensed that the Football Association wished to pursue a more commercially progressive approach, and Patrick quickly won over the committee, which included Len Shipman, president of the Football League and Leicester City chairman, and FA secretary Ted Croker with his sales pitch. The committee – delighted that Patrick's was an English company – agreed a deal by which Admiral would pay them £15,000, offset against a commission on retail sales of 5 per cent. 'The FA simply had to get that deal done', recalled Patrick, 'because it would be evidence that they were bringing in a new broom and sweeping away the past.' Revie soon negotiated massively improved rewards for his players: £100 for a draw and £200 for a win on top of a flat-rate £100 appearance fee. He approved a deal with Brooke Bond in which Ray Clemence, Colin Todd, Gerry

Francis and Mick Channon would feature on forty cards for the '40 Ways to Play Better Soccer' series, aimed at helping schoolboys improve their game.

Some of Revie's new charges disapproved of his rebranding. Liverpool defender Emlyn Hughes remarked during our interview, 'For me, an England shirt should be plain white, with the three lions. I didn't think there should be the red and blue stripes down the arms and the side of the shorts, because that was more British, not English. I got used to it eventually, although not Don Revie.' As former Arsenal skipper Alan Ball told me,

> One of the first things that he [Revie] did when he met us as a group for the first time was tell us that our appearance fees were going up, and about the new [Admiral] kit. He was trying to win over players with financial promises and cosmetic changes. When it comes to your country, your pride in the shirt and love of England should have been enough. Keep sponsorship and cash out of it.

Frank Worthington remained concerned about the perilous state of his nipples:

> It was made from polyester and was more synthetic than the old England shirt had been. At half-time, a lot of us put Vaseline on to stop the chafing. It was either that or a T-shirt and that would just make you sweat even more because the polyester did make you sweat.

But the majority of players were happy to go along with the kit change, and the first Admiral England kit lasted until 1980.

Ted Croker poured cold water on the suggestions that Revie personally benefited from the Admiral deal:

It benefited only the FA. It was the first of the deals where somebody provided the kit and paid a premium on the basis of replica
sales. Don was very much on the fringe of things … I have no evidence whatsoever that he got anything out of the Admiral deal.

'All the deals that Admiral did with Leeds and England were strictly above board,' insisted Bert Patrick. 'In fact, when Leeds United
renewed their deal with us in 1975, Don was very upset when he got
to hear that their chairman Manny Cussins decided that the money
from Admiral should go into a fund for transfers, rather than the
players' pool.'

Patrick's next major coup came in 1976 when two recent Admiral converts, Manchester United and Southampton, reached the
FA Cup final. Due to the demand created by the United kit contract, along with the England deal, Admiral factories avoided the
dreaded 'short time' (working fewer than the regular hours per
day), which blighted the textile industry as cheaper foreign imports flooded the market by the mid-1970s. As Patrick explained,
United boss Tommy Docherty was the polar opposite of the studi-
ous Revie: 'After a United home match, we met in the Doc's offices
and wolfed down a huge salver of scampi and chips, usually with a
glass or two of champagne. After a meeting with the United board
– Matt Busby, Bobby Charlton and Les Olive were there – the deal
was struck.' Admiral soon brought in other manufacturers to make
United-themed pyjamas and duvets.

As the 1976 FA Cup final approached, Patrick received a phone
call from the BBC. A spokesman said that because the corporation
did not allow advertising the Admiral logo should be removed
from the front of the tracksuits. 'The irate chap told me that if
we would not comply BBC cameras would not cover the match.
I said we would try to cooperate but could make no promises,'
Patrick recalled. Obligingly, he instructed that the Admiral logo

was removed from the front and put on the back of the tracksuits. Inadvertently, it proved to be a crafty case of product placement, as Patrick explained, 'Both sides coming out of the Wembley tunnel and fanning out on the pitch gave us massive publicity on camera.'

The company branched out in a variety of different directions. Leicester City's Peter Shilton became the first goalkeeper to market his own 'pack' – consisting of white shirt (he became the first English goalkeeper to wear white), shorts and socks – and a raft of NASL clubs sported Admiral kits. Top-flight referees now wore Admiral tracksuits, and Patrick was even invited to Iran to deliver a Manchester United shirt (with Bobby Charlton's No. 8 on the back) to the crown prince. 'The world seemed to be our oyster,' he explained.

As the commercialisation of football kits increased, so did the controversy. On 4 February 1977, Roy Hughes, MP for Newport, raised his concerns in the House of Commons. He alleged that the burgeoning replica kit industry meant

> children are being exploited ... The English football team now has Admiral emblazoned on its tracksuits. The firm of Cook & Hurst says that it has exclusive rights to use the English lion emblem on its products. It relies for that on the Copyright Act 1968 and its predecessors. This is an abuse of those Acts...

Roy Hughes insisted that 'the price of the products is excessive' (a typical shirt and socks cost around £9, which is around £35 in today's money) and that a clutch of Welsh sports dealers had refused to sell the new kit. Hughes added that Admiral was gaining 'thousands of hours of free TV advertising', and that 'colour television comes into the story too. Faced constantly with the sight of heroes in the latest strip, it is not surprising that young Johnny begs his parents to buy him a football jersey in the identical colours.' An Admiral advertisement at the time implored consumers to 'show your team you really care'. The statement contained a certain amount of emotional blackmail, with the underlying message being that if you didn't buy a replica shirt then you weren't a proper fan.

Despite the Under-Secretary of State for Prices and Consumer Protection Robert Maclennan responding in the Commons and referring to 'a sense of unfair exploitation by the firms involved', the government never did launch a formal investigation into the replica shirt industry during the 1970s. Bert Patrick refuted the suggestion that Admiral exploited young supporters:

> Of course, it was evidence that football was becoming more commercial. Admiral attracted controversy because we were the first to spot a gap in the market. It's true that parents were pressurised by their children to buy the kits in the late '70s but the feedback we received was that it brought a lot of pleasure to the lives of fans and still does.

As the '70s whizzed on, the company's static prone 'it-kits' remained as vivid and flamboyant as ever, ranging from the iconic blue and red Crystal Palace sash, to Luton Town's retina-scarring orange and white number. In 1977, the ebullient Lindsay Tucker (now Lindsay Jelley) was hired by Admiral as head designer:

> I'd just finished a three-year design course at Loughborough College of Art. I was very young, and I had absolutely no hesitation in doing something new. It helped that I wasn't a football fan and

wasn't shackled by tradition or the past. The vision of Admiral was to pull football shirts into the fashion of the time. It was all about the cut and the colour. The confidence and the buzz within the company was astonishing.

In her three years at Admiral, she designed a raft of new kits, including the new Tottenham, West Ham United, Crystal Palace and Wales kits; four of the most iconic outfits of the era on her £4,000 per year salary. Now an artist based in Leicestershire, when I spoke to her in 2020, she explained, 'The Tottenham kit was a good example of how we worked on home kits, freshening up their traditional white and blue with the lines down the side and adding the butterfly collars.' The bright red Wales shirt, with its curved 'egg-timer' stripes, wasn't altogether favourably received by Admiral's machinists: 'It was difficult to get the three lines running perfectly parallel with one another. Try drawing a bottle and getting both sides perfectly symmetrical. It's very tricky.' Appearing on *Top of the Pops*, Bob Marley, clad in a Wales tracksuit (his father Norval Marley was rumoured to have hailed from Prestatyn in Wales), gave the Admiral design a welcome blast of publicity. Jelley explained how much of the terminology that is now used to describe kits has been applied retrospectively, 'At the time, I don't think we really spoke of tramlines or yokes, like those that were used on the West Ham shirt.' Like Patrick, she was also adamant that Admiral were not exploitative: 'I actually think fans were crying out for the kits. Before Admiral they could only have a scarf and hat. This was a radical new era.'

'Radical' is certainly one way of describing what proved to be Admiral's most contentious design – Coventry City's chocolate-brown away kit. On the one hand, the revamp adhered to an established pattern: Admiral glammed up the traditional sky-blue home shirt, adding egg-timer white and black stripes down the front of the shirt and shorts, before going to town on the away strip. But brown? 'The concept of the brown shirt was mentioned to me, so I based the design around it. It's a carbon copy of the home strip from that era, except for the brown replacing the sky-blue,' Jelley explained. The initial idea arose from a conversation between Bert Patrick and Coventry's managing director, Jimmy Hill. 'Bert and I agreed that whether supporters loved or loathed the new brown shirt, it would certainly get people talking about the club and generate replica shirt sales. Any publicity is good publicity, and Coventry needed it at that time,' Hill told me in our interview.

It certainly generated a lively debate amongst fans, managers and players. Former Coventry defender Jim Holton described it as 'an affront to both fashion and football', and after his Derby side was defeated 2–0 by Highfield Road's chocolate soldiers in September 1978, Rams boss Tommy Docherty lamented, 'I had hoped that Coventry would melt away in the second half.' But, as Jimmy Hill recalled, the jokes about the brown shirt were not always so savoury, 'I heard it described as the "dog-shit" kit on more than one occasion.'

City's away kit may have been atypical when it came to football shirts, but brown was all the rage in the late 1970s. 'Part of me thinks Admiral must have had a stash of cheap brown fabric in the warehouse, but if you watch any documentary or look at photographs from the era', explained Jelley, 'you're struck by the proliferation of burnt-orange and brown carpets and wallpaper and wood panelling. Brown was in.' DI Jack Regan's Ford Consul GT in *The Sweeney* was brown or, officially, 'copper bronze'. In the United States, the abundance of brown in interior design was termed – somewhat prosaically – as earth toning and reached its height when, in December 1979, President Jimmy Carter, wife Rosalind and daughter Amy (wearing a brown corduroy dress) stood on a brown carpet and posed for photographs alongside their giant brown artificial Christmas tree, with wood panelling in the background. Coventry City's own earth-toning experiment – much like Carter's presidency – was over by the early 1980s, but forty years later brown is back. Sort of. At ex-Coventry City player conventions, chocolate shirt-clad forty-somethings swarm around the likes of former stars Ian Wallace and Steve Hunt, posing for pictures. Coventry's replica brown shirt is one of the biggest sellers on the retro kit market. And if any Coventry fan should happen to have an original shirt from the era tucked away somewhere they now sell for around £500 on eBay.

By the late 1970s, Admiral was borrowing huge sums of money simply to keep pace in an industry that was spiralling ever upwards, but, in 1979, replica shirt sales fell sharply when the first skateboard craze took over. Bigger, more established foreign brands like adidas and Le Coq Sportif soon responded with gusto to Admiral's 'baroque' era by getting seriously creative, upping their game and splashing the cash. 'The market was getting more competitive, and the cheques given to clubs in shirt deals were getting bigger. Admiral was – relatively speaking – only a modest-sized firm,' Bert Patrick explained. The Admiral story wasn't yet over, but as the 1980s dawned, the monster that Patrick had unleashed threatened to devour its creator.

12

THE LOST MESSIAH

'Retirement is the most stupid word I've ever heard in all my life.
It should be stricken from the record. You retire when they put the
coffin lid down with your name on top.'
Bill Shankly, 1973

Wembley, May 1974. With his Liverpool team 2–0 up in the FA
Cup final against Newcastle United and only seconds remaining,
Bill Shankly wants more. Sitting on the bench next to chain-smoking
Newcastle boss Joe Harvey, he uses his hands to conduct battle
operations from the sidelines, urging his team to switch the play
from flank to flank. Shanks's army respond. On the left, Kevin
Keegan, busy and industrious, lofts a beautiful 40-yard pass to
Tommy Smith – the hardman of Anfield. Smith cushions a deliciously volleyed pass to Brian Hall, moves forward for the return and
plays a sublime one–two with Steve Heighway on the edge of the
Newcastle area. Smith cuts in, drives in a low cross and Keegan
nudges it home. 3–0. At the final whistle, as photographers make a
beeline for Keegan, Shankly disappears down the tunnel. He's met
by a couple of Liverpool fans who prostrate themselves at the feet
of their messiah. Shankly laughs, telling them to polish his shoes
whilst they're at it. After asking a steward to bring him a cup of tea

and some meat pies, the exhausted Liverpool manager slumps onto a dressing-room bench, listening to the distant 'Shankly, Shankly' chants reverberating through the Wembley walls. Fifteen years on from taking over what was an ailing Division Two club, and three league titles, two FA Cups and one UEFA Cup later, the manager who breathed fire into Liverpool's soul has reached the end of the road. After months of soul searching, English football's most influential manager is bowing out at the top. It's a decision he will quickly come to regret.

ot even the arresting presence of *Generation Game* host Bruce Forsyth, nattily clad in a pair of claret trousers, running across the Wembley turf, sweeping the ball into an empty net, courting the 100,000 crowd with his catchphrase 'Nice to see you, to see you nice!' and leading the crowd in singing 'Abide With Me' prior to the match could upstage Shanks on FA Cup final day. Not quite, anyway. Shankly's team were majestic that afternoon, with Kevin Keegan thumping them into the lead and Steve Heighway sliding home a second, before Keegan added the final flourish. In the Wembley tunnel after the match, with his jubilant players swigging bottles of milk, the Liverpool boss, literally glowing in his luminous pink shirt, painted his vision of the future to ITV reporter Gerald Sinstadt: 'This team won the league last season, the cup this season. They'll win the league next season, thus emulating my Liverpool team of '64, '65 and '66.'

Yet a few weeks later, the coach walked into new Liverpool chairman John Smith's office and announced that, at sixty, he was finished. Smith, who'd been warned by his co-directors that Shankly often made veiled threats about quitting during the close season, only to make a U-turn a few days later, presumed that another change of mind was imminent. However, this time, Shankly meant it. At least, Shankly thought that Shankly meant it. Despite Smith's attempts to change the manager's mind, on 12 July 1974, in front of a stunned gaggle of journalists and TV crews, a sombre Smith announced, 'It is with great regret that I as chairman of Liverpool Football Club have to inform you that Mr Shankly has intimated that he wishes to retire from active participation in league football. And the board has with extreme reluctance accepted his decision...'

In a room stuffed with '70s ephemera, including ashtrays, brown carpets, a dark brown woodchip table and a lone bowler hat perched on the windowsill, there was a stunned silence. On the grass at Liverpool's Melwood training ground, Shankly walked and talked with one reporter and made a bleak analogy: 'It's like going to the electric chair, but once you've made the decision, there's no going back.' The news travelled around the city like wildfire and journalists were dispatched to gauge opinion from slack-jawed and glazed-eyed Liverpool fans. 'You're having us on,' and 'You're joking with us,' were the two most common responses, preserved for posterity on YouTube vox pops videos. 'He'll be back,' claimed Shankly's skipper Tommy Smith. 'The close season is always too long for Shanks, let alone retirement.' But this time, although the former Liverpool manager did lead out the team at Wembley against league champions Leeds United before the 1974 FA Charity Shield in August, there was no going back.

Film crews and reporters had always flocked to Melwood in feverish anticipation, knowing that Shanks would deliver the killer lines they craved. He could be the joker – horsing around with entertainer Norman Wisdom at Anfield after a players' kids' Christmas party – or the hard taskmaster – instructing his players to 'Get your head down, do your bloody exercise' at Melwood, his Ayrshire bark echoing around the training ground. Sometimes, he was the lyricist, reciting the poetry of Rabbie Burns to emphasise the harshness of his upbringing:

> While crashing ice, borne on the rolling spate,
> Sweeps dams, an' mills, an' brigs, a' to the gate;
> And from Glenbuck, down to the Ratton-key,
> Auld Ayr is just one lengthen'd, tumbling sea.

Like many of his former teammates, Emlyn Hughes remained in awe of the man who signed him from Blackpool for £65,000 in 1967. In our 2002 interview, Hughes was as bubbly and impassioned as he'd been on *Question of Sport* as team captain. On the subject of Shankly he was reverential, occasionally closing his eyes and clasping his hands together as if offering a silent prayer. 'When Shanks spoke, even if it was to say "good morning", he delivered the line as if it were conveying the most important message in the world,' he told me. Liverpool's record appearance holder Ian Callaghan, who broke into the first team just after Shankly's arrival at the club in 1959 and played at Anfield until 1978, explained, 'Bill Shankly was the master of the spoken word. Even if I hear him speak now on TV, I still get goosebumps.' Callaghan, his Scouse accent as strong as ever, remained in awe of both Shankly and successor Bob Paisley. 'To have played under both of those gentlemen means I'm the luckiest person in the world,' he told me during our telephone interview. Forty years after his death, Shankly's most famous quips, sayings and one-liners have been repeated, replayed and rerun relentlessly, but his was the first truly authentic voice in British football. In an era when managers spoke in stilted faux plummy accents, like Alf Ramsey, or said as little as possible to the press, like Tottenham's Bill Nicholson and Arsenal's Bertie Mee, Shankly broke the mould.

He was a philosopher, a wisecracker, a quasi-spiritual leader and, later, a cultural icon.

His accent, hewn in the Scottish mining village of Glenbuck, remains uniquely resonant. His voice was blast-furnaced and quarried. Former charges imitate him with relish and reverence. 'Sign for us. The world will be your oyster, son,' Shankly said to Emlyn Hughes on the first occasion they met. Like all former Liverpool stars, when impersonating Shankly, Hughes puts particular emphasis on the word 'son', like a precious jewel mined from deep underground. 'He'd use the word to emphasise his point,' Hughes explained, 'showing us that he was the father figure.' Shankly's oratory was honed during his childhood. As one of ten siblings, he'd had 'to speak fast and get to the point'. He perfected his delivery by watching Jimmy Cagney and Jack Benny movies. When he was in full flow, there was much of Benny in Shankly, right down to the Gatling-gun delivery of lines, and of Cagney, in his ability to hog both the screen and the microphone. Shankly also loved Prohibition-era gangsters. On away match trips, he would herd his team into the hotel's TV room where they would watch *The Untouchables* and watch Eliot Ness fighting crime in 1930s Chicago. 'Shankly had the swagger of a gangster,' recalled Tommy Smith. 'He loved their fashion sense. Shanks looked good in a well-tailored suit, and when the '70s came along, with all the bright shirts and the floral ties, he cut quite a dashing figure.'

Shankly's roots in Britain's industrial past gave him a clear-eyed understanding of the stark problems facing many Liverpudlians by the early '70s. Factories and businesses were closing. Even the docks, which had provided Liverpool with huge wealth in the past, were in decline as the move to 'containerisation' continued. When Shankly spoke of 'the pain and heartbreak of recession on men and families', he did so from painful first-hand experience. Glenbuck

– the village in which he was born in 1913 – became a virtual ghost-town after the last coal mine closed down in 1931, in the midst of the Great Depression. 'I saw people with no hope, their lives devastated,' he explained to Tommy Smith. 'Liverpool fans' happiness depends on us,' he continued. Much of his socialist–football philosophy was rooted in the tight-knit community of Glenbuck, where miners once depended upon one another for their very survival. 'I believe the only way to live and to be truly successful is by collective effort, with everyone working for each other, everyone helping each other and everyone having a share of the rewards at the end of the day,' he argued. The team ethic was the be all and end all. There was absolutely no room for slackers. Shankly was merciless towards his injured players and would stroll into the treatment room and ask Bob Paisley, 'Who's swinging the lead today?' As Emlyn Hughes recalled, 'I hardly missed any matches under Shankly but got injured towards the end of the 1970–71 campaign. Shankly didn't talk to me for a week. He'd walk straight past me, looking at the wall. As soon as I was fit again, he was "Morning, son," and all smiles again.' Shankly never took a sick day during his time at Liverpool. 'When I die, I'll drag my own corpse to Anfield for games,' he said in 1973.

There was no indication that Shankly was losing his lustre by the early '70s. He'd ruthlessly dismantled his ageing 1966 championship side, in the wake of a shock FA Cup quarter-final defeat to Watford in 1970, and rebuilt his squad, casting aside club heroes, including Ian St John, Ron Yeats and Roger Hunt. Liverpool were crowned First Division champions three years later. The Shankly cult grew in fervour, and he spoke in almost mystical terms about being able 'to transmit my thoughts to my players'. Following Liverpool's 1971 FA Cup final defeat to Arsenal, Shankly informed the masses, 'Chairman Mao himself couldn't have hoped for a better red gathering.' His obsession for football remained undimmed, and he'd turn any comment back to the subject of the game he loved. 'Good morning, boss,' Tommy Smith said to Shanks at the start of preseason training in July 1973. 'It's always a good morning for football, son,' came the response. Shankly's distaste for anything blue was unremitting. When Emlyn Hughes mentioned to Shankly that he was thinking of purchasing a pale-blue Hillman Imp, Shankly chastised him. 'Blue stays at Goodison Park,' he quipped. 'It's pale blue, boss,' Hughes argued. 'Blue is blue is bloody blue,' came the response. Shankly also overruled defender Larry Lloyd's fiancée, who'd wanted the interior of their Liverpool clubhouse painted blue and white. The manager would subject potential new Liverpool signings to a propaganda blitz and lambast those players who rejected him. 'You never could play anyway, son,' he told Huddersfield right-back Bob McNab, after he decided to join Arsenal.

A few short months before he resigned, Shankly was sprung at Euston Station by *This Is Your Life* host Eamonn Andrews. The video recording was destroyed in a fire at the BBC archives some years ago but the Shankly family was presented with a vinyl copy of the show. As well as being joined onstage by several of his siblings (his sister Netta's voice is as wonderfully rhythmic as her brother's) and legends from Shankly's playing days, including Tom Finney, Cilla Black was also there in person and touchingly told the studio audience, 'He [Shankly] is the best thing that's happened to football since goalposts.' A clearly humbled Shankly was taciturn. Yet it was still Shankly who delivered the most prescient line of all. When asked by Eamonn Andrews what he thought of his '£2 million team', he responded, 'They're my living.' The mood towards him in the London theatre was reverential. 'It was like he was a cult leader,' explained goalkeeper Ray Clemence. Despite the fact he was now sixty, the thought of Shankly not being Liverpool manager seemed unthinkable. However, within six months of his big red book treatment, Shankly had announced his retirement from football.

═══════

On the face of it, Shankly's decision to step down was perplexing. Aside from a spot of gardening and cleaning out the oven (he did this on the rare occasions Liverpool lost), there was no hinterland of hobbies for Shankly to withdraw into. Holidays bored him and on the odd occasion he stayed with his family in the Norbreck Hotel in Blackpool the restless Scot could often be found organising matches between waiters and porters on the grass outside the hotel. Shanks, who lived, breathed and talked about football all day every day, was never going to be your average pensioner. 'It's so serious [football] that it's unbelievable. And I wonder what all the rest of the world does,' he once stated. 'It made no sense for him to do what he did,' explained Emlyn Hughes. 'If there was one person who wasn't going to be able to cope outside the football bubble, it was Shankly.'

There are several possible reasons why Shankly threw in the towel. His wife Nessie had been in and out of hospital in the early months of 1974 and had urged her husband to stand down the previous year. On that occasion, Shankly refused. The Scot admitted to feeling guilty that they'd only been out twice together since he arrived in the city in 1959. Nessie, although never as demonstrative as her larger-than-life husband, possessed an equally sharp wit, insisting it was a falsehood to suggest that her husband had once taken her to watch a Tranmere Rovers reserve match on their wedding anniversary. 'Absolute nonsense,' she insisted. 'It was Accrington Stanley...' But Shankly's guilt at spending so much time away from home gnawed away at him during his time in the Liverpool dugout.

Shankly was also concerned about the increasing power wielded by Liverpool directors, with whom he had always had a rather strained relationship. This was perfectly illustrated by the curious case of Liverpool's Admiral kit deal that never was. Shortly before the 1974 FA Cup final, company director Bert Patrick convinced Shankly to allow him to show his players mock-up designs for a new home kit (the classic red had the soon-to-be trademark white Admiral chevrons down the sleeves). Patrick journeyed to Melwood and Steve Heighway was picked by the squad to model the proposed new kit. In the midst of Heighway's catwalk act, Shankly walked in and boomed, 'This is nae a bloody circus, Stevie.' But Shanks also approved of the Admiral design, telling Patrick, 'If the boys like it, they can bloody have it.' With the Admiral solicitor on hand, Shankly signed the contract and, as far as Patrick was concerned, the deal was done. But skipper Tommy Smith, in his *Liverpool Echo* column, let slip to readers that the famous shirt was about to receive a makeover and Patrick was summoned to meet John Smith, the new Liverpool chairman. 'You should not have counter-signed that contract,' he told Patrick. Despite Patrick having Shankly's signature as evidence, Smith insisted, 'Contrary to what the British public think, Bill Shankly does not run this football club.' Dismissed from Smith's office, Patrick's solicitor insisted that the contract was bulletproof, but the Admiral boss opted against pursuing legal action. 'I don't think that he [Smith] appreciated being backed into a corner by Shankly, and Bill told me that the incident left a really sour taste in his mouth,' Patrick recalled. 'At a football club, there is a holy trinity – the players, the manager and the fans. Directors don't come into it. They're only there to sign the cheques,' Shankly famously claimed. But at Liverpool in the early '70s, Smith wanted more of a say.

There were also rumours that Shankly was unhappy with the fact that the bonuses he'd earned on the back of Liverpool's title success of 1973 had been eaten up by tax, and that he was disillusioned by his relatively modest wage and pending club pension. Perhaps Emlyn Hughes interpreted the situation accurately:

> We weren't in the European Cup – which was the only thing he'd never won – so he was looking at another two seasons at the helm, at least, and he found it tougher to keep going every season. Perhaps he felt he couldn't keep going any longer. But I do know that he very quickly regretted the decision to step down.

In early August, and with the Liverpool players back in preseason training under new manager Bob Paisley, Shankly stunned chairman Smith by organising a meeting and asking for his old job back. In his Shankly biography *It's Much More Important Than That*, author Stephen Kelly claimed that Shankly told Smith, 'I've made a mistake. I should have sorted everything out, taken a rest. I was tired. But now I feel ready for the new season.' Shankly made no mention of the incident in his own autobiography, which was released in 1976. Given that Smith had spent several fruitless weeks trying to get Shankly to change his mind a few weeks earlier, he was never going to oust Shankly's former number two Paisley from his new role. In any case, reasoned Smith, Shankly would stand down sooner rather than later anyway. Perhaps the more reserved Paisley was the man who would lead Liverpool to the promised land of winning the European Cup.

If Shankly was crushed by Smith's refusal to give him his job back, he didn't show it. Still fighting fit, and restless at home, the former manager turned up at Liverpool's Melwood training ground and trained with his former players, who still referred to him as 'boss'. Pretty soon, he'd appear every day. Shankly's overpowering presence saw him dominate proceedings, and he started holding court, talking to the players about their next opponents and passing judgement on players' individual performances. Ray Kennedy was more than a little confused about events: 'As the new boy, and as the one player who hadn't been mentored by Bill Shankly, I was more removed from what had gone on, and Shankly being there every day blurred the lines in players' eyes.' Bob Paisley, trying to assert his position as the new boss, and keen to show his players that the Shankly era was over, looked on with a growing sense of unease.

After consulting with John Smith, Paisley – politely but firmly – told Shankly that his presence at Melwood was becoming irksome, even embarrassing. Paisley, perhaps mindful of the problems Sir Matt Busby had caused for his successors at Manchester United, Frank O'Farrell and Wilf McGuinness, when he hadn't immediately departed the scene after 'retiring', had no option but to put his foot down. For Shankly, whose foresight and determination in the early '60s saw Melwood redeveloped, it was the ultimate slap in the face. He always believed that Melwood lay at the heart of the club's success. 'On this turf, Liverpool's champions are honed,' he once said. Now, he was being told in no uncertain terms to stay away.

Paisley attempted to soften the blow by offering his former boss some scouting work, but Shankly declined. Instead, he began to give Liverpool and Paisley a wider berth. 'When I got away [at the start of the next season] too well for him, he became a bit jealous and we didn't see much of him,' Paisley wrote in his autobiography. Shankly was initially surprised that Paisley had accepted the manager's job, and Liverpool ended the first post-Shankly season as runners-up to league champions Derby County. Trophy-wise, Liverpool were empty-handed, but the well-oiled machine that Shanks had put in place hadn't simply spluttered to a halt without him. The transition at Anfield had been almost seamless.

As Paisley emulated and then surpassed his predecessor's achievements, the relationship between Shankly and Liverpool Football Club fractured. He still attended Anfield matches but watched from the stand so as to avoid the club's directors. He was happy to hold court with fans and journalists but began spending more time at rival clubs. Shankly became a regular at Everton's Goodison Park, of all places. It seemed bizarre, given that ever since he'd arrived at Anfield, Shanks had always reserved his most caustic remarks for 'that lot across Stanley Park'. 'There's only two sides in the city, Liverpool and Liverpool reserves,' he'd tell new signings, adding, 'If Everton were playing at the bottom of my garden, I'd draw the curtains.' Nessie once joked that her husband would walk their dog across Everton's training ground and wouldn't leave 'until the dog had done its business on the pitch'. In reality, Everton had always been more than worthy opponents for Liverpool, winning two league titles on Shankly's watch. Nonetheless, it was a jarring sight to see Shankly receive a warm reception at Goodison and help out with their junior teams. Shankly loved it there, and whilst at Everton's Bellefield training ground, a journalist told him how well he looked. Shankly thanked him and responded, 'Yes, I feel well today. As a matter of fact, I wouldn't mind if I dropped dead right now.' The journalist looked at him quizzically. 'Well, just imagine. I'd be in a coffin and they'd walk past and say, "Look at Bill, doesn't he look well today. There lies a fit man,"' Shankly explained.

He also assisted former Liverpool skipper Ron Yeats, who was in the formative stages of his managerial career at cash-strapped Tranmere Rovers, based a few miles outside Liverpool, and who still called his former manager 'boss'. At Tranmere on one occasion, he parked himself on the bench and asked Yeats, 'Who's that slow right-winger?' 'That's Alan Duffy, our PFA representative.' 'Christ, why are you paying him if he's on strike?' asked a distinctly unimpressed Shankly. He trained with the players and suggested revising the players' training and matchday routines. The Yeats–Shankly double act didn't last long at Prenton Park, but Shanks could still spot a gem. Winger Steve Coppell – a local lad who also attended the University of Liverpool as an economics student – was clearly a star in the making. Hurt that Liverpool ignored his advice and opted against nabbing Coppell, Shankly told Manchester United boss Tommy Docherty (whom he'd briefly played alongside at Preston) to 'sign this kid'. The Doc obliged.

Shankly visited many north-west grounds after he retired. As journalist John Keith recalled,

> He'd vacate his seat five minutes before the match ended. It was because he wanted to put himself in place outside the directors' lounge so he could chat to them as they went in. And he knew that they'd invite him in, because of the gravitas he had, and he could have some tea and some sandwiches and talk football.

The philanthropic Shankly would often journey to the nearby St Edwards College to deliver their football training, and his charity work included assisting the Royal Institute of the Blind and Alder Hey Hospital. 'When Bill had spent a day with sick children there, he'd come home and be very quiet. It really upset him', Nessie recalled. He delighted in the company of his grandchildren, who regularly visited him and Nessie. He also popped around to former players' houses for cups of tea. 'Shanks did love a cuppa,' recalled Emlyn Hughes, 'but I felt that he was a bit of a lost soul, killing time.'

When it came to the spoken word, Shankly remained in demand. He was a regular at sportsman dinners, where he loved regaling guests with stories of his childhood, his playing days and his time at Liverpool. At a celebratory lunch for record Everton goal scorer Ralph 'Dixie' Dean, Shankly eulogised, 'His record of goalscoring is the most amazing thing under the sun. He belongs in the company of the supremely great, like Beethoven, Shakespeare and Rembrandt.' Shankly's stirring epitaph to his great friend is now recorded on a plaque in Liverpool's Shankly Hotel. Shankly also accepted a role with Merseyside's commercial radio station, Radio City, in 1975, hosting his own weekly chat show. Insistent that his first guest should be former British Prime Minister Harold Wilson, the pair discussed their respective mining backgrounds, the state of the country, the Common Market, religion, football and socialism. Shankly pointed out that his teams were 'socialist teams', as the players 'acted as a unit'. He enjoyed his stint on the radio, interviewing popstars, including Lulu, and north-west comedians like Freddie Starr and Bernard Manning. The manager was also a sought-after guest on TV chat shows. Appearing on Granada's *Good Afternoon* with Mavis Nicholson in 1976, he spoke once more of his belief that successful football teams depended upon a socialist ideal: 'If everyone helps each other and works as a collective, the team wins, but individual players win honours for themselves also.'

Despite Shankly's depth of knowledge and passion for football, a sense of perspective was occasionally lacking during the interview. His opinion on families coming to matches? 'I don't know if the children are old enough to understand it. Women don't really understand football, in my experience.' On hooliganism, which blighted the English game in the '70s, he insisted, 'If you go to a football match and lose your temper, it's quite natural for men to fight. What the hell's wrong with a fight, as long as it's a fair fight? Let the boys have their little flurry, and ignore them.' And on the reasons for George Best's downfall: 'I feel sorry for George. The girls – they've chased after him.' But not for the first, or last, time Shankly bared his soul on national TV, admitting, 'I put my heart and soul into the game to the extent my family suffered.'

Shankly was a man of contradictions. He was a loner who craved company so that he could talk football, football and more football. He gave out mixed messages about the possibility of becoming a director at his former club. In time, it caused him no little heartache. At the press conference when he announced his retirement, journalists asked him if there was any chance that he might 'move upstairs' at Anfield. 'No chance,' replied Shankly. 'Sitting behind a desk isn't for me, lads.' Yet he let it be known he was disappointed that, unlike with Matt Busby at United, he wasn't offered a seat with his name on it or a role at the club. Not that he would ever ask. Shankly was way too proud and respectful for that. Some directors intimated that they feared the influence Shankly would have over club policy and transfers.

Despite the difficult transition, Shankly and Paisley grew closer again by the time Liverpool finally lifted the European Cup in 1977. Shortly afterwards, when Paisley was the subject of *This Is Your Life*, Shankly warmly embraced his old friend during and after the show. Asked by host Eamonn Andrews if he and Paisley ever argued in their professional working life, Shankly responded, 'No, we never rowed. We were too busy deciding where to put all the cups we won.'

Ironically though, it was Liverpool's success on the European stage that finally ostracised Shankly, not from Paisley or the supporters but from the club. He was incensed when, after Liverpool reached the 1976 UEFA Cup final, which they duly won, he was billeted with the players' wives for the second leg in Bruges. Such was his desire to escape the hotel, he insisted that TV presenter Elton Welsby, who'd arranged for him to be co-commentator for the match on ITV, took him to the stadium by 10.30 in the morning. A year later, as Liverpool faced Borussia Mönchengladbach in the 1977 European Cup final in Rome, no invitation to the match was forthcoming from the club. At least, not initially. The club offered Shankly a ticket only after they discovered that the *Daily Mail*'s Jeff

Powell had secured him a press pass. Shankly accompanied Powell for the trip and held court with supporters and journalists with assorted microphones thrust in his direction. He was thrilled to see the Reds – most of whom were still his boys – finally lift the trophy. Throughout the game, TV cameras picked out Shanks in the crowd looking on anxiously and then jubilantly after Terry McDermott, Tommy Smith and Phil Neal scored. At the final whistle he stood aloft with his red scarf stretched between his hands. 'Do you feel detached from what happened on the pitch?' asked one Danish TV reporter. 'Not at all. I'm very pleased for Bob and the boys,' came the truthful, if rather diplomatic, response. Shankly even celebrated with a rare beer afterwards, but, in reality, he couldn't quite get the idea out of his head that Liverpool had overlooked him for the Rome trip. Emlyn Hughes had an interesting take on the situation: 'No one missed Shanks more than me, but he was a victim of the unsentimental culture he'd introduced at the club. Once you'd outlived your usefulness at Liverpool, you were cast aside.'

Shankly made his final chat show appearance in May 1981. *Granada Reports* host Shelley Rohde recalled him

> turning up hours before the show, downing tea and talking to an awestruck crew about football for hours. When I asked him why he was so early, he said, 'In football, early is on time, on time is late and late is bloody unacceptable.' So I said, 'But you're hours early, Bill.' He thought about that, 'Aye, but good preparation is key for everything in life, Shelley.'

On the show, Rohde asked Shankly whether he regretted the fact that he'd spent so little time at home during his career. 'I regret it very much. My family's suffered. They've been neglected,' a tired-looking Shankly responded. Would he change anything, though? 'I'd possibly do the same thing again.' Of course he would have. For

Shankly, football had consumed his very being since he could walk. It was the only path he would ever take. 'It was football or the coal mine. Football won,' he said.

━━━━━━

When he died from a heart attack in November 1981, conventional wisdom held that Shankly's severance from the club he'd transformed drove him to an early grave. Tommy Smith later claimed, 'He died from a broken heart, because he should never have stood down when he did.' That's a touch melodramatic; two of Shankly's brothers also died from heart attacks. Shankly certainly wasn't the first, nor the last, manager of his era to feel petrified about the prospect of retiring; Tottenham's Bill Nicholson, Arsenal's Bertie Mee and Newcastle's Joe Harvey all expressed similar anxieties about filling the void after leaving football. As Ian Callaghan explained, 'These days, someone as quotable as Shankly would make a fortune as a pundit or an analyst.' In the latter part of the '70s, as he laid bare his soul, the arresting cadence of his rasping Scottish drawl was as potent as ever. 'He used such colourful speech that you'd almost fall under a spell when he talked,' recalled Mavis Nicholson. His later TV appearances helped Shankly remind people, and himself, that he still had something to say. But as much as he enjoyed TV exposure, he missed the day-to-day involvement with football more, and perhaps no former manager has ever found life after football as hollow and ultimately disillusioning as the always charismatic and obsessive Bill Shankly.

13

THE EUROPEAN WAY

'I travelled to France a few years back. The fella at passport control looked at me, then at my passport a couple of times, then he stared at me for a bit. "Ah, Fairclough. Saint-Étienne," he said, quite sternly. He waved me through, though.'

David Fairclough

Anfield, March 1977. Ray Kennedy's delicately lobbed pass in the eighty-third minute lands perfectly for substitute David Fairclough to run on to. Quickly into his loping stride, the twenty-year-old striker, Liverpool born and bred, uses his pace to keep Saint-Étienne defender Christian Lopez to his left in order to gain a clear path to goal and blasts the ball low past goalkeeper Ivan Ćurcović. The guttural roar which explodes around Anfield as Fairclough's shot hits the back of the toilet-roll strewn net is – according to those present – like nothing heard before or since. On what's been a drizzly day in Liverpool, steam rises off the Kop as it surges forward en masse. For the remaining six minutes, Liverpool fans, with their red and white scarves held above their heads, chant, 'We shall not be moved!' and 'Allez les Rouges!' at top volume. After a titanic battle with the French champions, Liverpool finally have their noses in front. The 3–2 aggregate victory in the European Cup quarter-final is a seminal evening in Liverpool's history and remains the ultimate benchmark for European nights at Anfield. A year after guiding his team to victory in the UEFA Cup final, the taciturn Bob Paisley believes his team has the system in place to land the 'big 'un', as he calls the European Cup. Reaching the semi-final wouldn't have been possible at all if not for the late, dramatic intervention of Fairclough – Paisley's No. 12 – nicknamed 'the Whip' by teammates, but who will now for ever be known as 'Supersub'.

Despite the fact that the Liverpool manager spoke in such a strong, at times almost indecipherable, north-eastern vernacular and, as Kevin Keegan said, 'rarely used ten words when one would suffice', a raft of Paisleyisms are treasured by his players like priceless mementos. Entirely lacking the gravitas or portentousness of Shankly's utterings, they remain memorable, often for their sheer obliqueness, unfathomability and comic value. Just weeks after gathering his team and introducing himself as the new Liverpool boss with the distinctly underwhelming line 'Well, I didn't want the job, but we'll see how it goes', Paisley prepared to talk tactics at their Melwood training ground. With Liverpool preparing to face newly promoted Luton Town on the opening day of the 1974–75 campaign, Paisley adopted Shankly's strategy of sitting the players around a table with a green baize cloth laid on top of it and blue figures to mark out tactics. New signing Ray Kennedy, keen to hear Paisley's words of wisdom, listened intently:

> Brian Hall was instructed to 'watch wasisname.' Tommy Smith was told to 'keep an eye on your man', but it was never made clear which man. In the end, Bob got bored with questions, swatted the blue figures onto the floor and said, 'Bollocks to it – just go out and bloody beat them.'

Paisley had a stock of idiosyncratic phrases that his players struggled to decrypt. There were 'Fancy Dans' – Paisley's cutting assessment of mavericks like Stan Bowles and Alan Hudson. Liverpool stars were told to avoid the 'slo-rolo' – a long pass along the ground. So often did Paisley deploy the phrase 'Duggie Doin's' when he couldn't recall a player's name that the team nicknamed him 'Duggie'. If a player was injured, Paisley would ask, 'Have you done a one?' And when Paisley lost his temper, he'd lapse into an apoplectic: 'What the fuck? What the fuck?' – a phrase that was endlessly mimicked. Paisley scoffed at the era's most à la mode football phrases, like 'giving the ball enough grass', and 'flair players', to which he would respond, 'What, aren't they a pair of trousers?' 'Whereas Bill Shankly ended sentences with a flourish, Bob Paisley's sentences tailed off with "'n that…", "you know…" or "wasisname?"' Emlyn Hughes told me. Paisley's strength lay not in the spoken word, but in his eye for a player and applying what he'd learnt from his fifteen years as Bill Shankly's assistant, confidant and occasional hatchet man. With his paunch clearly visible under his tight Gola tracksuit, and his hair obviously Brilliantined, Paisley rarely cut a sophisticated figure. Most of the time, he was as inscrutable as a Sphinx. He was almost an anti-personality; Spot the cat compared with Shankly's Penry the janitor of *Hong Kong Phooey* fame. But when it came to Europe, Paisley's tactical acumen, problem-solving ability and clear-minded grasp of game management proved utterly decisive. Not that Paisley would have approved of such highfalutin jargon, of course.

The Liverpool players first started realising the return leg of the quarter-final against Saint-Étienne would be an occasion to remember when they were tucking into their tea and sandwiches at the city's Adelphi Hotel that afternoon. 'Ronnie Moran burst in and said to us, "I hear it's busy on Anfield Road. There's thousands of people already there. We need to make a move." There was a different sense of nervousness surrounding the match,' David Fairclough recalled. As the team bus nosed its way towards Anfield, the sight that greeted the players astonished even seasoned veterans like Tommy Smith:

> There were hordes of Saint-Étienne supporters on one side of the road with their klaxons and their drums and their whistles, and they had green smoke bombs. We could hear through the windows, '*Allez les Verts. Allez les Verts.*' And Liverpool supporters on the other side had their flags and banners.

Around 8,000 French supporters had made the pilgrimage from the Massif Central region, hoping to right what they saw as the injustice of the previous year when they'd lost to Bayern Munich in the final at Hampden Park. Saint-Étienne players and fans remain convinced that if it weren't for Hampden's square goalposts (*les poteaux carrés*), they'd have beaten the West Germans. Jacques Santini and Dominique Bathenay's efforts both struck the sharp edges of the posts and bounced out and the French believed that had the posts been rounded, the ball would have gone in on both occasions. The goalposts now have pride of place in Saint-Étienne's club museum, with club president Roland Romeyer explaining, 'They helped create an emotional tie between the French people and AS Saint-Étienne.'

With the nation desperate for a French team to become European champions, there was a huge amount of attention on Saint-Étienne, clad in their high-energy green shirts, and their star player Dominique Rocheteau, who looked like a cross between George Best and Marc Bolan. Known as *L'Ange Vert* (the green angel), he was prodigiously gifted, although Emlyn Hughes recalled Paisley describing him prior to the away leg as 'the bloke with the frizzy hair'. Yet in the Stade Geoffroy-Guichard, it was the home side's muscular and skilful midfield, consisting of Jean-Michel Larqué, Christian Synaeghel and, in particular, Dominque Bathenay who caused Liverpool problems in a tight match, and a volley from Bathenay gave the home side a slim 1–0 advantage to take to Anfield. With the return leg starting two minutes early, many supporters weren't in position when Kevin Keegan's cross/shot floated over Ćurcović's head to put Liverpool 1–0 up after just two minutes and level the scores on aggregate. Rocheteau had a goal ruled out for offside and then Clemence made two superb saves to deny *L'Ange Vert* his moment of glory. When Bathenay's magnificent shot from 35 yards out swerved beyond Clemence in the fifty-first minute Liverpool, now needing to score twice, appeared to be heading out of the competition. Ray Kennedy's drilled finish after seventy-three minutes put his team back in the game, but with the home side needing one more, Bob Paisley threw David Fairclough into the mix with seventy-three raucous minutes gone.

Even seasoned first-teamers like Ian Callaghan and Ray Clemence were bowled over by the frenzied atmosphere. 'The only game that came close to matching it was the European Cup semi-final against Inter Milan in 1965,' Ian Callaghan explained, 'and I'd played in plenty of Merseyside derbies and other big European nights. But I couldn't take my eyes off the swaying Kop every time we came even close to scoring. It was stoked by Saint-Étienne's massive away following, and the green flares at the Kemlyn Road end. Unreal.' Ray Clemence described how it was 'impossible to shout instructions to defenders because not only could they not hear me, but I couldn't hear myself speak. Saint-Étienne's effervescent green shirts gave the game extra electricity.' As David Fairclough prepared to enter the fray, Bob Paisley ushered him close and whispered in his ear, 'Get a piece of something. See if you can turn it.' It might not have been especially inspirational, but Paisley had judged the tempo and the mood just right. Saint-Étienne were tiring, and Paisley was convinced that the pacey Fairclough – whom he once called his 'lone star ranger', much to Fairclough's bemusement – could pierce the French backline. Fairclough's moment arrived on eighty-three minutes:

> The ball landed between the full-back and the centre-back, and Lopez put in a strong challenge, which I was able to shrug off. I blasted it close to the goalkeeper because I knew he'd struggle to get down to the shot. The noise was deafening when it hit the back of the net.

As the Kop rocked and reeled, Kevin Keegan screamed in Fair-clough's ear, 'You've done it again, Supersub.' Fairclough had first heard the moniker bandied about at the tail end of the previous season, when his impact from the substitute's bench had swung several matches (and the title race) in Liverpool's favour. But it was Gerald Sinstadt's delirious 'Supersub strikes again!' commentary on ITV that night which really sealed the nickname. As Fairclough explained during our 2020 interview,

> I'm 'the Whip' to teammates from that era, but Supersub to everyone else. It wasn't a nickname I was overly fond of at the time because I wanted to start, obviously, but I'm used to it now. I work with the Walton Centre Charity in Liverpool, and people in their sixties – as old as me – say, 'All right Supersub'. 'Supersub's 'ere,' a lady said the other day when I turned up. I'm rarely called David by anyone.

With the dramatic tie won, and Liverpool now facing FC Zürich in the semi-final, Paisley explained, 'This victory shows how I think we've progressed since four years ago, the last time we were in the European Cup. That was a painful lesson.' But it was one which Liverpool had obviously learnt from.

———

The cacophony of sound which engulfed Anfield at the climax of the Saint-Étienne match was in stark contrast with the stunned silence which descended on the ground after Crvena zvezda (Red Star Belgrade) won 2–1 (4–2 on aggregate) against Bill Shankly's Liverpool in November 1973. Despite going down 2–1 away in Yugoslavia, Shankly was confident that his side could overturn the deficit at home, but Milan Miljanić's side's crisp passing and patient build-up saw Shankly's men chasing shadows for much of the evening at Anfield. Both of Red Star's goals were beautifully struck shots, first by Vojin Lazarević and then, in the dying seconds, by Slobodan Janković. Some thirty years later, in our interview, Ray Clemence, stretching to demonstrate how he tried in vain to stop both goals, recalled, 'There was a hush over Anfield that night. Their goals were so well struck that they literally whistled past me. After the last one went in, it was as if a plug had been pulled. The whole ground literally felt drained.' Red Star's patient build-up play was in marked contrast with Liverpool's increasingly desperate play for much of the match, characterised by centre-back Larry Lloyd's long and aimless punts towards striker John Toshack.

The next day, Shankly convened an emergency meeting with his backroom staff. Unusually, he joined them in the boot room, a shabby 12ft by 12ft bolthole under the main stand. The room was largely off-limits to players and has since acquired almost mythical status. Ray Clemence, who joined the club as a teenager, never set foot in there until he was twenty-six. 'As a youngster, I once knocked on the door to see if I could speak to Ronnie Moran. "Piss off" came the shout. I never knocked again.' In the pre-digital age, Shankly's lieutenants created a comprehensive paper database in the form of A4-sized black diaries, which sat on metal shelves in the boot room. Inside Liverpool's holy scriptures were detailed observations on players' fitness and performance, training routines and opposition players. They dated back years.

When Shankly took over at Anfield in 1959, he quickly dispensed with the majority of his players, but retained the backroom staff. In Barney Ronay's *The Manager*, he compared the boot room boys to a collection of pre-Marvel superheroes, each with their own designated role. Paisley was the tactical mastermind and, trained as a physio, had an unerring eye for detail when it came to injuries. 'Bob would say "hip" or "cartilage" just by glancing at you when you walked slightly differently,' recalled Tommy Smith. There was cheery Joe Fagan – nicknamed 'Smokin' Joe' because he usually had a cigarette on the go – who would soften the blow for out-of-favour players when it came to it. Reuben Bennett – described by Shankly as 'the hardest man in the world' – was a physical training instructor (and capable of bending iron bars, so people said) who honed the team's exercise regime and wore shorts and shirt-sleeves in the bitterest weather. Later, there was former club skipper Ronnie Moran – gruff, cutting and to the point – whose voice reverberated around Melwood as he berated slacking players. These dedicated wise men developed an almost telepathic understanding, and an unerring eye for detail. The symbols and the shorthand they used in the notebooks were like some kind of ancient language – indecipherable to anyone outside the inner sanctum.

In the boot room, perched on upturned crates and with naked girls looking on from the calendars on the flaky walls, the boot room boys formalised their tactical plan to win Europe's biggest prize after the Red Star defeat. 'The top Europeans showed us how to break out of defence effectively. The pace of their movement was dictated by their first pass. We had to learn how to be patient like that and think about the next two or three moves when we had the ball,' Shankly later reflected. In fairness, the coach had always espoused the merits of the passing game. In the previous campaign, Liverpool had won the UEFA Cup (no mean feat in itself), but now, against Europe's crème de la crème, they'd been found wanting. A reboot was required.

This would mean a change in emphasis in Liverpool's training regime, after Shankly retired the following summer, it fell to Bob Paisley to oversee this shift. As Emlyn Hughes recalled,

Training became far more about keeping the ball once Bob took over. Patience, patience, building from the back. If you lost the ball in training or made a sloppy pass, whoever was watching you would give you a right bollocking. It didn't matter if you made 100 passes, you needed to keep the ball. That understated, almost metronomic, style of football suited Bob down to the ground.

In a later interview with journalist Stan Hey, when asked about why Liverpool's style morphed in the mid-1970s, a typically blunt Paisley responded, 'We didn't go round Europe with our eyes shut.'

One of the keys to Liverpool's European Cup success was their knowledge and understanding of their opponents. This approach gathered pace throughout the '70s, and was headed up by former teacher and youth coach Tom Saunders, who – Revie style – began to compile dossiers on forthcoming opponents. As Ray Clemence told me,

At the start of the '70s, when it came to Europe, it was usually a case of Shanks telling us to 'play your own game'. But that began to change because of Tom's dossiers, and the contacts he had across Europe. He even had the inside track on clubs behind the Iron Curtain like Dynamo Dresden and Dynamo Berlin. Bob read the dossiers and came around and gave you little titbits of information. 'So-and-so usually goes to the left with his penalties...' that kind of thing. Liverpool became more scientific.

The intelligence network at Liverpool wasn't dissimilar to that at Red Star Belgrade. Coach Milan Miljanić who, taking advantage of Yugoslavia's comparatively lax travel laws with the West during the Cold War, visited Holland and West Germany in the early '70s to observe the total football played by the national team and leading clubs, including Ajax and Bayern Munich. Red Star's playing style was modelled closely on that of western Europe's leading lights, and now Paisley also started introducing more progressive tactics into Liverpool's style. The process wasn't without the occasional speedbump. After a trophy-less campaign in 1974–75, Liverpool faced Queens Park Rangers at Loftus Road in the opening game of the 1975–76 season, with Paisley fielding Joey Jones at left-back and Phil Neal at right-back. The centre-backs, Phil Thompson and skipper Emlyn Hughes, had a torrid afternoon and the side lost 2–0, partly because Hughes roamed up field whenever he had the chance, leaving Thompson exposed. Paisley favoured the Thompson/ Hughes defensive combination, because they were good passers of the ball, and with Jones and Neal on the flanks, the coach hoped to inject more pace and dynamism into the backline, so that they were a more mobile and offensive unit. But things went badly wrong. At the end of the match, Bob Paisley sought out Hughes and blamed him for the defeat. Paisley then put his foot right in it when he said, 'I got the quicker full-backs you asked for. That's the last time I listen to you.'

A chilling silence immediately fell across the Liverpool dressing room, but Tommy Smith, relegated to the bench after losing his position as right-back, broke it by demanding, 'What did you just say? He asked you to buy new full-backs?' As Paisley stammered a response, Smith looked at Hughes and said, 'I should fucking kill you,' before being restrained by teammate Alec Lindsay. The bad blood between Smith and Hughes had simmered for years after Shankly removed the captaincy from Smith and gave it to Hughes, who was the younger man, on Hughes's suggestion. But this was something else entirely. Smith made a point of never speaking to Hughes again (apart from during matches) and criticised his maligned teammate during his post-playing career as an after-dinner speaker, even after Hughes died from a brain tumour in 2004.

When I interviewed Smith at the turn of the century, he remained effusive about all things Liverpool but was clearly in a great deal of pain from the arthritis which now racked his body. 'The pain in my legs is down to the cortisone shots I received as a player,' he said.

So many players would do anything to play in that era that they pumped us full of the stuff. It's only quite recently they have discovered the huge damage it does to your joints. It basically dissolves them over time. So many of us limp around, or stoop, or fall over. I think I'm the biggest cripple of the lot.

Smith had a hip, both knees and an elbow replaced and recounted how, after taking a penalty for Liverpool at half-time during the 1996 FA Cup final in a veterans' clash with Manchester United in front of the cameras, he'd briefly had his incapacity benefits stopped. 'I only kicked the bloody ball once,' he laughed.

His mood and his expression darkened when I uttered Emlyn Hughes's name. 'What did you go and have to mention *him* for?' he asked me, with more than a trace of annoyance. I suddenly realised why the popular story that Merseyside mothers kept a picture of Smith, the man they called the 'The Anfield Iron', on mantelpieces to keep their kids away from the fire had done the rounds for so long. Smith used various expletives to describe Hughes ('He was a two-faced shit,' was one of his milder comments). 'But... [achingly long pause] we'd always congratulate one another after scoring, and he was a fantastic player,' he confessed with a shrug. Emlyn Hughes refused to be drawn on the subject, dismissing my question with a shake of the head: 'I'm well aware of what Smithy says and thinks of me, and we didn't get on. But we respected and complemented one another as players, and that's really all that counts.'

In Paisley's autobiography, the manager noted, 'It never mattered to me if players got on like a house on fire or if they couldn't stand the sight of each other, as long as they didn't let their personal feelings spill over onto the pitch.' The Liverpool manager's pride that the Smith/Hughes feud was not public knowledge was typical of Paisley's stripped-back management style. Emotion and sentimentality were tiresome distractions. All that mattered was the good of the Liverpool team. In any case, as Hughes wryly acknowledged, 'Bob wouldn't have been much good at sorting it out. It wasn't his thing.' Paisley's skill lay in listening and assimilating ideas and concepts that benefited the team. This was in evidence when the coach had a chance meeting with striker Ray Kennedy's former PE teacher, which proved crucial in the squad's development. The burly Geordie had struggled for form since joining from Arsenal in July 1974, but Paisley discovered that as a schoolboy footballer Kennedy had been a midfielder. After pondering the idea for a few weeks, Paisley informed Kennedy that he'd be changing positions. 'You'll play better facing the ball,' Paisley told him. That was an understatement. The switch was a revelation, with Kennedy adding guile and thoughtfulness to Liverpool's midfield.

In the 1975–76 season, Liverpool were heavily reliant on the forward partnership of Kevin Keegan and John Toshack. Previously called 'Little and Large' (Keegan was 5ft 8in. and Toshack

6ft 1in.), they were also referred to as 'Batman and Robin' following a feature in *SHOOT!* in which Toshack was dressed as Gotham's caped crusader and Keegan as his erstwhile sidekick. Such was the understanding and telepathy between the pair on the pitch, that Granada TV decided to test it out. The duo sat facing each other in the TV studio, each holding a card up so the other could not see the symbol on it. There was general astonishment when they each guessed exactly right, although in reality they could see each other's cards in reflected glass. Toshack even wrote an ode to Keegan:

> He came to Anfield in '71
> Shy, embarrassed, a coal miner's son
> Though his signing was hardly a major event
> The transfer turned out to be money well spent.

On and off the pitch, Keegan embodied Liverpool's industrious approach. As well as inheriting George Best's Stylo boot contract as the face of English football, Keegan also took over Best's ghost-written *Daily Express* column. After Keegan arranged to drive up each week to the paper's offices in Manchester, *Express* sportswriter John Roberts was surprised that, unlike Best, the Liverpool forward actually wanted to contribute to his own column. 'Unlike George, who was naturally gifted, I had to work at everything,' Keegan said. The player's work ethic was boundless and he rarely turned down commercial appearances, eventually becoming the face of Brut, Pirelli slippers and Smith's crisps. Bob Paisley allowed Keegan to build his commercial empire, as it didn't affect his performances on the pitch.

On the title run that season, with Liverpool neck and neck with Queens Park Rangers, the Toshack/Keegan double act proved decisive. With Liverpool needing a win or a 0–0 or 1–1 draw with Wolves at Molineux in their forty-second game of the season, the

home side took the lead through Steve Kindon and were still leading with fourteen minutes remaining. But Keegan scrambled home
an equaliser from close range and Toshack, taking his time, steered
home to put Liverpool in the lead with five minutes to go. A late Ray
Kennedy goal confirmed that Liverpool were First Division champions, and a pitch invasion ensued. David Fairclough's dramatic
emergence in the spring also helped swing the title in Liverpool's
favour. Wearing the No. 10 shirt, he netted a priceless winner in a
tight encounter at Carrow Road against Norwich City and a week
later climbed off the Liverpool bench to sink Burnley with two goals
at Anfield. Fairclough further endeared himself to Liverpool fans
with his decisive contribution in the Merseyside derby at Anfield
on 3 April, moved to lunchtime due to the Grand National taking
place at Aintree later that day. Entering the fray late on, Fairclough
received the ball just inside his own half and slalomed past Everton's
bewildered defence to plunder a last-minute winner. Liverpool secured seventeen points out of a possible eighteen in their final nine
games, holding off the challenge of Queens Park Rangers by a single
point. It was a symbolic victory; Paisley's formulaic approach had
narrowly pipped the more freestyle, Stan Bowles-inspired Rangers
to the biggest prize. 'What is the point of being entertaining if you're
not winning?' Keegan asked rhetorically in an interview after the
match. Liverpool now had the European Cup firmly in their sights
for next season.

———

Following the dramatic victory over Saint-Étienne in March 1977,
the European Cup semi-final against FC Zürich was almost anti-
climactic, with Liverpool running out 6–1 aggregate winners. By
now, the Reds were on course for an unprecedented European Cup,
First Division and FA Cup treble. Paisley's team won the league at

a canter; although they only finished a single point ahead of Manchester City, this was because the side took their foot off the gas in the final four games, drawing three matches and losing to Bristol City in the final game of the season. Paisley quickly regretted his decision to drop midfielder Ian Callaghan for the FA Cup final against Manchester United, opting instead to play forward David Johnson, who had been signed from Ipswich Town at the start of the season, in a more attacking line-up. Paisley's decision was based around the fact that the Football Association had decided that, if the final ended in a draw, the replay wouldn't take place for another three weeks, due to Liverpool's involvement in the European Cup final and the Home International tournament. 'Bob was furious with the FA, and became convinced that the authorities in England were against him,' Emlyn Hughes recalled. But Hughes accepted that 'United deserved their 2–1 win, and that we were a bit sluggish that day'. On the train journey home afterwards, the Liverpool players got stuck into the miniatures and indulged in a sugar-cube fight, which was started by Ray Clemence: 'There was a lot of pent-up frustration, and Bob Paisley allowed us to let off steam that night, which is what we needed. But we had no time to mope, because we had the European Cup final against Borussia Mönchengladbach in Rome four days later.'

As the Liverpool players flew out from Speke airport, somewhere between 25,000 and 30,000 fans made their way to the eternal city. According to legend, jewellery was pawned, kitchen appliances sold and giros cashed to fund this very special pilgrimage. In and around the Trevi Fountain and the Colosseum, Scouse arias were sung with gusto. Liverpool fans were joined by a clutch of green wig-wearing Saint-Étienne supporters, who'd adopted Liverpool as their second team following that epic quarter-final. Apart from the à la mode French champions, Mönchengladbach were Europe's other über-cool side. With a metropolitan population of just 260,000, the West German champions were the 'smallest' European Cup finalists of the 1970s. Gladbach won five Bundesliga titles during the decade to Bayern Munich's four, and played at the compact Bökelberg Stadium, hidden amongst rows of smart houses. In the early '70s, coach Hennes Weisweiler constructed a young team (nicknamed '*Die Fohlen*', 'The Foals'), including Rainer Bonhof and Berti Vogts from the local area. Gladbach became the club of choice for left-of-centre supporters across Germany, who disliked the ultra-professionalism of Bayern Munich. They were a home-spun outfit, and former players, returning to see their old teammates, made a point of popping into the club canteen to feast on the legendary sausages that were served up by the club chef.

Gladbach won the UEFA Cup in 1975, but their previous European Cup adventures had been punctuated by outrageous misfortune and bizarre mishaps. Against the Reds' city rivals Everton in the 1970–71 European Cup, midfielder Howard Kendall, spotting that goalkeeper Wolfgang Kleff was removing a toilet roll from his penalty area, lobbed him from 40 yards. Gladbach later crashed out on penalties. In October 1971, Gladbach destroyed Inter Milan's famed defence (which contained four men who'd played in the World Cup final the previous year) and won 7–1 at home. The result was eventually declared null and void because, after nineteen minutes, a beer can was thrown from the crowd and struck Inter striker Roberto Boninsegna in the throat. He was carried from the pitch, and although reports later claimed he was knocked unconscious, the Red Cross attendants claimed there wasn't a mark to be found on his body. The replayed match was drawn 0–0, and Inter won 4–2 in Milan.

In 1976–77, Gladbach won the Bundesliga under new coach Udo Lattek, but Bob Paisley believed that defensively they had weaknesses, particularly in the air. In the days leading up to the final, Paisley led Lattek to believe that John Toshack would be fit to play, even though he'd not appeared in a Liverpool shirt since the quarter-final with Saint-Étienne six weeks before. In the event, Toshack didn't figure at all and David Fairclough, left out of the squad for the FA Cup final, was on the bench. Letting his players down gently was a job that Paisley found tricky. Prior to the FA Cup final, he'd skulked outside Fairclough's hotel room, then told him curtly, 'You're not playing, but I need you in Rome.' If Fairclough ever challenged Paisley about why he wasn't playing, he'd be met with a terse 'Don't come in here on the bounce'. Tommy Smith also saw the unfeeling side of Paisley later on in his Liverpool career. 'There was no ceremony, no arm around the shoulder. Once you weren't in the team, it was a case of out of sight, out of mind,' he described. But on a sweltering Rome night, Smith, in what was widely predicted to be his last match for the club (it wasn't), was in the side, and the other veteran of Liverpool's 1965 European Cup excursion when they made it to the semi-finals – Ian Callaghan – was also selected, his presence designed to help Liverpool squeeze and harry Gladbach's midfield.

In the dressing room, Paisley reminded the Liverpool players that the last time he'd been in Rome was in a tank at the end of the Second World War. There were no vague instructions from Paisley on this occasion. Ronnie Moran and Joe Fagan had quiet words with the Liverpool defenders, reminding them to stay tight on the potent front trio of Allan Simonsen, Herbert Wimmer and the prolific Jupp Heynckes. The mood was calm and purposeful. When the players strode out onto the pitch, they were greeted by the sight of thousands of chequered red and white flags and the now infamous 12ft long banner, which read, 'JOEY ATE THE FROGS LEGS, MADE THE SWISS ROLL, NOW HE'S MUNCHING GLADBACH.' The homage of Liverpool fans Phil Downey and Jimmy Cummings's to the contribution of right-back Joey Jones to the European Cup run was one of the most memorable sights

on an historic evening. From the off, Paisley's players followed his
instructions to 'choke the space', although Rainer Bonhof almost
gave Gladbach an early lead with a shot that cannoned back off the
post. On twenty-eight minutes, Ian Callaghan won the ball in midfield and passed to Steve Heighway. Heighway cut in from the right
wing and threaded the ball through to Terry McDermott, who'd
ghosted into space. The former Newcastle United man drilled the
ball home from 15 yards. 'That's nice, that's McDermott and that's
a goal,' yelled commentator Barry Davies as the Telstar ball spun
deliciously in the back of the loose netting. In his autobiography,
Paisley argued that the goal was 'a coaching masterpiece' as both
Kevin Keegan and Ian Callaghan had made decoy runs to pull defenders away from McDermott. Seven minutes after half-time, the
5ft 5in. Simonsen, named European Footballer of the Year in 1977,
fired home past Ray Clemence after a defensive error by Jimmy
Case.

For the next ten minutes, Gladbach were utterly dominant, and
only a point-blank save by Clemence from Uli Stielike stopped the
West Germans from taking the lead. 'If that had gone in,' Clemence
told me, 'I'm not sure that we would have won.' On sixty-four minutes, with Liverpool having regained their composure, Steve Heighway prepared to take a corner. The Germans failed to notice Tommy
Smith loitering in the box. 'Steve's corner was delivered at the perfect pace, and it was at the perfect height. I caught it just right and
it flew in. I likened it to a hole in one,' Smith told me. With six minutes remaining, and Gladbach stretched, Kevin Keegan scampered
forward, desperately trying to escape the attentions of Berti Vogts,
who'd stuck to him doggedly all night. As Keegan bustled into the
box, Vogts bundled him over. As Ian Callaghan covered his eyes
with his hands ('I was praying because their goalkeeper was enormous') Phil Neal converted the penalty and Liverpool became only
the second English club to win the European Cup. The spot kick was

expertly taken: Neal placed his shot in the opposite corner to which he'd scored against Zürich in the semi-final because he believed that Gladbach would have had done their homework. An unusually animated Paisley punched the air with delight and later described it as 'the greatest night in the history of Liverpool Football Club'.

During the celebrations afterwards, the two old stagers – Ian Callaghan and Tommy Smith – got stuck into the drinks at the hotel bar with Ronnie Moran and Joe Fagan, whilst Paisley remained stone-cold sober. The Italian newspaper *Il Messagero* heaped praise on Liverpool who, they argued, were 'better organised, knew how to deal with their adversaries and used a strategy to block and disorient them'. There was a pleasing symmetry to the Liverpool goal scorers that night. On either side of Bill Shankly's enforcer Tommy Smith notching the second, Paisley's signings Terry McDermott and Phil Neal had proved decisive. Even the two adversaries Smith and skipper Emlyn Hughes briefly put their differences to one side and exchanged (as Smith put it) 'a handshake, a nod and a half grin'. The talismanic Shankly had set out to 'turn Liverpool into a bastion of invincibility, and build a club that will conquer the bloody world', but it was his phlegmatic successor who'd enabled the club to win the European Cup, thereby achieving the holy grail. Key players would come and go, but Liverpool had entered a period of dominance previously unseen in the English game.

14

THE GLAMS

'The Doc, '70s man incarnate. Put him in a kipper tie, in *Man About the House*, next to a Party Seven or behind the wheel of a Capri – does he not fit perfectly with your mental image?'

Richard Kurt and Chris Nickeas, *The Red Army Years: Manchester United in the 1970s*

Wembley Stadium, May 1977. In sweltering temperatures, Tommy Docherty's fresh-faced Manchester United team lock horns with Bob Paisley's treble-chasing Liverpool in the FA Cup final. After fifty-one minutes of a tightly contested match, United striker Stuart 'Pancho' Pearson, all power and poise, thunders forward, skips beyond Joey Jones and drills past Ray Clemence at his near post. Pearson struts towards the jubilant United supporters, his bandaged right fist clenched and pumping his trademark salute. Within two minutes, Liverpool, already crowned league champions, equalise, after Jimmy Case turns and rifles past Alex Stepney. But United regroup and find themselves in front once more when Lou Macari's deflected shot ('If the ball hadn't hit Jimmy Greenhoff's chest, it would have ended up in the station behind Wembley Stadium,' Macari later quipped) loops over Clemence to put United 2–1 up on fifty-five minutes. That's how it remains. Three years after suffering the ignominy of relegation to Division Two, Tommy Docherty's Red Devils revamp appears complete. But, even as he poses for photographers with the FA Cup's lid perched on his head, the orange-shirted, kipper tie-clad Doc is in torment. Within weeks, he'll be swept away, engulfed by a tidal wave of tabloid scandal.

———

'Let me guess,' laughed Thomas Henderson Docherty, thumping me so hard on my shoulder that my beer spilt everywhere: 'You've heard all that shite before.' Before I could answer in the affirmative, the ebullient Glaswegian disappeared to the bar to buy me a replacement drink, prior to commencing our post-'Evening with the Doc' interview. I spoke with Docherty three times in the early 2000s, still in his pomp as an after-dinner speaker: spinning yarns, telling tall football tales and settling old scores in front of tittering audiences. Docherty was always friendly, amusing, totally indiscreet, occasionally libellous about former acquaintances and, perhaps most endearingly, still incredibly passionate about the game.

His colourful managerial career provided him with a raft of toe-curling anecdotes, which he trotted out without fail. In his first coaching post, Docherty, who had been a midfielder with Preston North End and Arsenal, promoted a youth system at Stamford Bridge which produced future Chelsea stars Peter Osgood and Alan Hudson. After losing the 1967 FA Cup final to Tottenham, Docherty left after, as he put it, 'a difference of opinion with the board', heading to struggling Division Two side Rotherham. It didn't go well. 'I promised I would take Rotherham out of the Second Division – and I did. I took them into the Third,' he described. Docherty left Millmoor after just twelve months, alighting at Aston Villa and staying for thirteen months. 'I left when the club was bottom of Division Two. A few weeks earlier, Mr Ellis told me that he was right behind me. I told him I'd rather he was in front of me where I could keep an eye on him.'

When we spoke, the joviality sometimes faded when the subject turned to his tenure at Old Trafford between December 1972 and June 1977. His version of events occasionally varied between interviews, although the absolute certainty with which he wove his stories never wavered. Docherty had resurrected his management career with the Scotland national team after becoming permanent manager in November 1971, and when he departed to take over at United a year later, the Scots were well on course to qualify for the 1974 World Cup. 'Bill Shankly convinced me to take the job at United, or "the Glams" as Shanks called them. It wasn't a compliment. It implied that United were all style and no substance. In fact, they didn't even have any style any more,' he recalled.

United were rock bottom of Division One, after suffering a chastening 5–0 thrashing by fellow strugglers Crystal Palace on 16 December 1972. The United board approached Docherty after the game at Selhurst Park about taking the job and fired manager Frank O'Farrell three days later. After shaking hands on a £15,000 a year salary, Docherty, tasked with rekindling United's *joie de vivre*, was introduced to the Old Trafford crowd the following weekend, prior to a 1–1 draw with Leeds United. Was the subject of relegation mentioned? I asked the Scot. 'Not openly. It was the elephant in the room,' Docherty responded.

As Docherty assessed the task ahead of him, the media was awash with news about the divisive decisions being made by politicians. In response to pay demands from miners, power workers and binmen, Prime Minister Edward Heath declared a controversial ninety-day freeze on pay, wages and rents in an attempt to curb inflation. Heath's beleaguered government was also struggling to enforce direct rule in Northern Ireland, as warring Unionist and Republican factions violently disagreed over the future of the province. 'There was confrontation everywhere', Docherty recalled, 'and Old Trafford was no different. Henry Kissinger wouldn't have lasted forty-eight hours there.' Hackneyed though it was, his reference to President Richard Nixon's National Security Advisor was telling. In the early '70s, the 'Nixinger' double act deployed realpolitik – politics based on pragmatism, rather than moral or ideological ideals – whilst seeking détente with the Soviet Union and China and an end to the war in Vietnam. Docherty quickly became football's arch-exponent of realpolitik in the '70s:

> I wasn't afraid of making difficult decisions. The team was full of fading European Cup winners, and a few good players like Martin Buchan and Sammy McIlroy. Frank O'Farrell warned me that a lot of the old guard had a back channel to [now director] Matt Busby, whom they'd go whining to if they weren't happy.

In one of our conversations, I referred to these players as 'Busbyites'. 'Aye', grinned Docherty, 'I always felt that I had to get rid of them before they got rid of me.' 'By whatever means?' I asked. 'Whatever it took', nodded Docherty.

He compared the state of United in late 1972 with 'a mouth full of rotten teeth'. First to be pulled were European Cup winners Tony Dunne and David Sadler: 'Great servants, but it was time to go.' Bobby Charlton knocked on Docherty's door early in the new year and announced he'd be retiring at the end of the season. 'Bobby did me a favour, because clearing him out would never have been popular', the coach explained. And then there was the Lawman. In April '73, Docherty informed Scottish legend Denis Law, who'd scored 237 goals in 404 United appearances and won two league titles at Old Trafford, that he was being given a free transfer. After some negotiation, the pair agreed that it wouldn't be announced to the press until the day of his testimonial match at the end of the season. Law, who'd initially recommended Docherty for the job to the United board, and who remains the only Scottish Ballon D'Or winner, was bitterly disappointed, insisting that after arriving at Old Trafford, the Doc – in front of witnesses – promised him a job at the club for life. Nonetheless, Law headed to Scotland to see his family, certain that their confidential agreement would remain 'watertight'. Unfortunately, this was not the case.

In an Aberdeen pub on Saturday lunchtime, with *Grandstand* blaring away in the corner, and Law surrounded by family and friends, it was announced that he'd been freed by United with immediate effect. 'Denis was furious and confronted me, but, to this day,' insisted a rapidly blinking Docherty, 'I have no idea about the source of the leak.' On the second occasion I spoke to the former coach, he admitted to 'maybe letting slip to a journalist from the dailies'. Maintaining a dignified silence, Law headed to Manchester City on a free transfer.

Using his contacts from the national team, Docherty imported a clutch of 'Anglos' – Scottish players who plied their trade south of the border. In came defenders Alex Forsyth, Stewart Houston and Jim Holton, Arsenal midfielder George Graham and pint-sized Celtic forward Lou Macari. Although critics felt that playing the intimidating Holton – with his Desperate Dan jawline – at the back sullied United's stylish reputation, United fans delighted in singing 'six foot two, eyes of blue, big Jim Holton's after you!' at opposition players. United fought, scrapped and kicked their way towards top-flight survival in 1972–73, finishing eighteenth, and Holton embodied the team's attritional approach. But in October 1973, with United once more in dire straits, Busby and Docherty agreed that it was time for what would be the calamitous second coming of George Best.

Best had returned to Old Trafford in the summer of 1973 at Matt Busby's behest, vowing to get himself match fit for a return to the team by the time the clocks went back in autumn. Heavily bearded and paunchier, Best divided his time between Old Trafford and his Slack Alice nightclub. 'Initially, I liked Tommy Docherty's enthusiasm, so I thought it could work. I worked at Slack Alice but didn't go near the place as matchday approached. We had an arrangement whereby if I missed morning training, I'd make up the time later. But I didn't push my luck,' Best told me. The winger returned to the United starting line-up against Birmingham City on 20 October 1973, and played a key role in a 1–0 win, with keeper Alex Stepney scoring the winner from the penalty spot. Ultimately, Best couldn't stop the rot. 'George could still beat players but couldn't leave them for dead any more,' explained Docherty.

The messy end came in 1974. Following a 3–0 defeat to QPR on New Year's Day, which left United twentieth in the table, Best headed back to Slack Alice for a party which went on into the early hours of 2 January, missing training that day, and then appearing at Old Trafford prior to the FA Cup third-round match against Plymouth Argyle on 4 January. In Docherty's words: 'George had a bird in tow, was in no fit state to play football and I told him so.' Best promptly disappeared in a fast car and, although he trained the following week, he never played again for the first team. Best always refuted Docherty's version of events, ranting bitterly about how the manager reneged on his promise to let him catch up on missed training. 'He wanted me gone, and got his way deceitfully,' Best told me. Docherty blinked furiously when I recounted Best's version of events to him. 'I dropped him for the Plymouth game, but George ran away from United. Like always. I never kicked him out,' he responded. In the ensuing decades, Best and Docherty fired verbal barbs at one another through the medium of their after-dinner speaking routines.

Best wasn't at Old Trafford by early May when an instinctive backheeled goal from an emotionless Denis Law won the Manchester derby for City, on a day when results elsewhere finally cast Law's former club United into the abyss. Best was sad to see his old team fall through the relegation trapdoor but 'delighted to see Docherty squirm'. On the subject of Law's winning goal, Docherty shrugged, 'It was karma. Ex-players always come back to haunt you.' The good old days were over. And it was time to rebuild.

Although numbed by the twin effects of relegation to Division Two and Courvoisier (a popular choice with '70s bosses, the Doc told me), the United coach made the long-term decision to deploy a daring 4–2–4 formation, which had made his Chelsea side such an attractive proposition in the '60s. As reserve team manager Frank Blunstone (who'd served at Stamford Bridge on Docherty's watch) pointed out, United had overlapping full-backs Jimmy Nicholl and Arthur Albiston coming through the ranks, who would be able to support the wide men whenever they arrived. Docherty asked Blunstone to start scouting around the lower leagues for potential candidates. He was aware that such an expansive approach flew in the face of '70s convention:

England won the '66 World Cup without wingers, but all the successful club sides had one. Arsenal had Geordie Armstrong, Leeds had Eddie Gray and Derby had Alan Hinton. But no one was playing with two out-and-out wingers. We were Manchester United, and it was time to go on the attack and be bold again.

First though, United had to prove that they had the stomach for jarringly unfamiliar Division Two clashes with the likes of York City, Oxford United and, on the opening day of the 1974–75 campaign, Orient. United fans, clad in oversized rosettes, red and white scarves tied around the wrist and patched-up flared jeans, arrived in their hordes in Leytonstone and smashed the windows of shops, houses and cars. In marked contrast with the carnage wrought by their less-than-angelic fans, Docherty's United, clad in their pristine white away kits, displayed a compelling brand of football which would set the division alight. In the first half, right-winger Willie Morgan latched on to a Brian Greenhoff pass, scuttled forward and drilled the ball confidently home. A second-half Stewart Houston header secured a 2–0 win for United, who fielded new signing Stuart Pearson, a striker who'd joined from Hull City during the close season. By the end of August, United had a 100 per cent record. With the shackles loosened on the pitch, United's travelling hordes wreaked havoc off it. By the season's end, Bristol Rovers imposed a 15p hooligan tax on tickets when United travelled to Eastville, mindful of the carnage which was likely to ensue. Docherty and his players were often placed in an invidious position, publicly castigating the hooligans, whilst also thanking the supporters for turning up in their astronomical numbers to support the Red Devils.

Docherty's critical gaze now fell on club captain, Busby confidant and right-winger Willie Morgan. During the summer, Morgan detached the retina in his right eye playing tennis, and Docherty reckoned the player was never quite the same again. From autumn onwards, Docherty substituted him with alarming regularity. Word reached Morgan that the coach had apparently begun badmouthing him around town, his tongue loosened after a few drinks. Dropped in early November, Morgan returned to the United starting line-up for a League Cup clash with Burnley which United won 3–2 and delivered a very clear message to Docherty. After seizing on a poor clearance 30 yards out, he controlled the ball, took two paces forward and calmly side-footed a beautiful 25-yard shot into the very top corner of the Burnley net. Chewing gum, a smirking Morgan casually strolled away, arms aloft, his eyes lasering in on the United bench. 'Willie Morgan was telling me to stick it up my Glaswegian arse,' Docherty recalled.

With United about to be promoted as Division Two champions, Tranmere Rovers right-winger Steve Coppell arrived for £60,000 on the recommendation of Shankly. 'Stevie was like a young pup. I was always keen to promote youth because you can't teach old dogs new tricks.' Against York City in April, Docherty finally unveiled his prototype 4–2–4 formation, with Coppell on the right, and an unhappy Morgan shunted out on the left. At the end of the season, Docherty approached Morgan, insisting that he wanted to be friends and rather than go on United's summer tour, he should instead take his family on holiday, which Morgan agreed to do. The next day, the tabloids led with the headline: 'MORGAN REFUSES TO GO ON TOUR.' 'The papers were misinformed,' Docherty argued. 'Who by?' I asked. 'No idea,' blinked Docherty. Within a month, a tight-lipped Morgan was gone. Soon, Docherty's assistant manager Pat Crerand – another hero of United's 1968 European Cup winning side, who was increasingly being frozen out by Docherty, also departed, although Crerand also kept his counsel, for now.

———

'Whoah! Whoah! United are back! United are back!' sang 8,000 Red Devils supporters as they descended upon Molineux for the first match of the 1975–76 season. Two late Lou Macari goals gave United a 2–0 win on their return to Division One, and after the game United fans ripped half-bricks and corrugated iron off the ground's dilapidated stands and looted the Wolves club shop. 'I was always concerned that those idiots might see us thrown out of the league,' admitted Docherty. United were the early pacesetters, and, by November, the arrival of Millwall's diminutive left-winger Gordon Hill enabled Docherty to add the finishing touch to his 4–2–4 formation.

'We'll cut you down to size, you flash Cockney bastard,' United chairman Louis Edwards told Hill shortly after he put pen to paper. The reason he'd annoyed Edwards was because, according to Docherty, 'Hill strutted around like he owned the place from the minute he arrived.' The new recruit's lack of interest in defensive duties infuriated skipper Martin Buchan, who once clipped Hill around the ear during a match against Coventry City and told him to 'waken up' when he failed to track back, but Hill received carte blanche from an indulgent Docherty to do as he pleased: 'Gordon Hill was bought with the sole purpose of destroying opposition defences, and I let him get on with that.' But, unlike 'Champagne' Louis Edwards, who was rarely seen in public without a cigar in his mouth or a glass of bubbly in his hand, Hill was anything but flashy away from the limelight. A strict teetotaller, he eschewed Manchester's nightlife and lived in Whaley Bridge in the Peak District. There, he'd take early morning walks and 'enjoy the sunrise'.

When I spoke to him via Facetime from the US, where he is a soccer coach, the ever-buoyant Hill was reverential about United. 'I loved the shirt, the texture of it,' he began, as he rubbed his thumb and index finger together, 'and its pure, deep redness. It was before the era of mass-produced shirts. In those days your scarlet shirt was to be treasured.' Hill also remembered well the team's distinctive redolence:

Our physiotherapist Laurie Brown used to massage us with this Five Oils stuff, which was embrocation, liniment and Deep Heat all rolled into one. The odour was like nothing else. It seeped into everything – shirts, tracksuits, boots. You always had to beware sitting on the toilet in the dressing room. Get any trace of Five Oils on your bits and you felt like you were on fire! But it was like a warning stench to other teams. They could smell United a mile off.

A resurgent United finished in third place in 1975–76, four points behind champions Liverpool. Hill's brand of sorcery gave United added swagger. 'I luxuriated in just being a winger,' he recalled. 'The Doc expected us to attack, attack. We peppered the opposition with crosses, and Tommy instructed us to shoot from the outside of the box when we could. It's how I believed the game should be played. Off the cuff and entertaining.' Hill would loiter on the fringes of the opposition box, waiting to feed on the scraps. In the dying minutes of one of his first United games at Old Trafford in December 1975, with the Red Devils unable to break down an obdurate Wolves defence, Hill latched on to a loose ball, chested it down and scorched home a peach of a shot with his left foot to win the match. The 44,269 crowd almost blew the Old Trafford roof off. Despite falling short in the title race, United stormed their way towards the FA Cup final for the first time in thirteen years. Hill's screaming left-foot 30-yard drive helped see off Peterborough in the fourth round, and midfielder Gerry Daly's prowess and goal-scoring ability also shone through. Like Hill, Steve Coppell and Lou Macari, Daly was a touch on the Lilliputian side ('five foot eight, underweight, Gerry Daly's fucking great' sang United fans), but he played with panache. Belying his scrawny frame, he had a right foot like a jack hammer, illustrated by his emphatic finishes against Leicester City and Wolves in the fifth and sixth rounds of the cup. He was also an idealist. Asked about his professional ambition, Daly told *SHOOT!* that he'd like to see 'a return to attractive and open football'.

Daly was the perfect creative foil for Hill in the memorable semi-final against Derby County at Hillsborough. 'That really was our FA Cup final' Hill explained. Following the Doc's standard pre-match talk, which consisted of, 'Enjoy yourselves, and go and play your natural game,' Manchester United terrorised the reigning league champions. After twelve minutes, Brian Greenhoff dispatched a pinpoint ball to Hill, midway inside the Derby half. In one fluid move, Hill controlled it, flicked the ball to Daly and Daly, sauntering forward, slipped the ball to Hill, now skulking with serious intent on the edge of Derby's box. Hill collected, took two rapid touches and curled home a magnificent 20-yard shot. Halfway through the second half, Hill, so far out that the Derby defence didn't even bother constructing their wall properly, thundered home a deflected 25-yard free kick to make it 2–0 and the red hordes behind the Derby goal on the Leppings Lane terrace were in ferment. Hill scampered away, holding his hands up to the Yorkshire sky in prayer, before being engulfed by teammates. 'And there goes the happiest Londoner who ever went to Manchester,' enthused Barry Davies on *Match of the Day*. 'Barry was bang on with that. It was the best day of my football career,' Hill smiled when I spoke to him. He remained in awe of the symbiosis between United players and supporters that day. 'They inspired us to a perfect pitch that day. The problem was that was our FA Cup final, but it was only the semi.'

With the celebratory 'Tommy, Tommy, Tommy, Tommy Docherty' chants ringing in their ears, the Doc and his boys, having reached Wembley in such an exhilarating manner, took their collective eyes off the ball. 'Our lack of maturity affected us,' Hill admitted as the side geared up to take on Second Division Southampton in the FA Cup final. 'The players' pool was a massive distraction,' recalled Brian Greenhoff. 'There were all these visits to factories and schools, and arguments with journalists who wouldn't pay into the pool after they interviewed us. It was bollocks.' United's league form had stuttered, ending any lingering title hopes. Observers reckoned

Docherty was also rather over-confident about beating Southampton. After delivering United's new kit directly to Docherty's hotel room on the eve of the final, Admiral's Bert Patrick recalled, 'seeing the Doc's hotel room strewn with empty champagne bottles. When I arrived he ordered up another crate via room service.'

Southampton had three players – skipper Peter Rodrigues, midfielder Jim McCalliog and striker Peter Osgood – with FA Cup final experience. United had none. Before the match, there were the pleasantries of the TV build-up. On ITV, a light-hearted pen-portrait piece provided glimpses of life behind the United and Southampton dressing-room doors. Lou Macari introduced viewers to a snooker match between Sammy McIlroy and Gerry Daly, over which Macari said of Daly, 'He eats chips during the week, he smokes, he likes the occasional drink.' Saints striker Mick Channon was indiscretion personified, describing how, after working in a fishmongers, David Peach 'comes in smelling of it' and that 'most lads buy Penthouse or Mayfair, but Paul Gilchrist will go and buy a sports car book. The lads are always laughing at him about that.' The Southampton piece concluded with Channon mucking out his stables with buddy Bobby Stokes, consolidating the view that McMenemy's country bumpkins were about to be annihilated.

But the avalanche of United goals never came, with Southampton cutting off the supply route to Coppell and Hill, who described his own performance that afternoon as 'abysmal'. When his No. 11 went up in the sixty-sixth minute, Hill said to Docherty, 'Does it mean me?' Docherty replied, 'No. The whole fucking team.' With seven minutes remaining, former United star Jim McCalliog, collecting a Channon flick, delivered an inch-perfect pass to Bobby Stokes, whose angled volley crept home past Stepney. It remains a far better, more well-constructed goal, than it's been given credit for. At the final whistle, Brian Greenhoff wept bitter tears of disappointment. 'Southampton thoroughly deserved to win on the day,' Docherty admitted. The following day, the Doc – trying to lift everyone's spirits – informed assembled crowds back in Manchester that United would win the FA Cup next year. 'I was convinced of it,' the Doc told me.

━━━━━

United's Achilles heel was their defence. In the close season, Docherty, looking to replace Alex Stepney in goal, attempted – not for the first time – to sign Peter Shilton from Stoke City, but the board refused to sanction Shilton's wage demands. 'With Shilton in goal, we'd have won the league. Liverpool had [Ray] Clemence at his peak, and we had one goalkeeper who was past his best [Stepney], and another who wasn't top class [Paddy Roche],' Docherty told me. In the 1976–77 season, Docherty signed Stoke City's striker Jimmy Greenhoff (brother of Brian), moved Sammy McIlroy back into midfield and controversially sold Gerry Daly to Derby County. United continued to play bells-and-whistles football, scoring seventy-one league goals and conceding sixty-two. 'People said we couldn't defend, but they never saw us defend. My philosophy was "You score one and we'll score two,"' Docherty recalled. Given their gung-ho approach, it was hardly surprising that United slipped further behind the more savvy Liverpool in the title race, finishing sixth, but their quicksilver brand of football, once again, was ideally suited to the FA Cup. Facing Leeds United in the semi-final at Hillsborough, the two teams lined up in the tunnel and the United players were dwarfed by the eleven yellow-shirted giants from over the Pennines. 'Let's crush these fucking midgets,' yelled Leeds United's ogrish central-defender Gordon McQueen. But Leeds, now shorn of the midfield talents of Johnny Giles and Billy Bremner, had no answer to United's relentless attacking, and volleys from Steve Coppell and Jimmy Greenhoff soon put United 2–0 up, before Allan Clarke scored a late consolation.

'We were underdogs in '77, and that made us more focused,' Docherty said. But the Doc didn't always have his eye on the footballing prize, barging his way into starring in a Gillette GII commercial. Initially, winger Steve Coppell was approached and sought Docherty's permission to take part. After telling the right-winger to 'leave it with me', Coppell discovered that, along with Gordon Hill, he was now demoted to a walk-on part, whereas a smug Docherty delivered the killer line to the camera: 'Gillette G11, the old one–two,' pocketing a tidy fee in the process and ending up with, as Hill recalled, 'a car boot full of razors'. Then there was Docherty's curious new habit of calling Sunday-morning meetings with his backroom staff – including physiotherapist Laurie Brown – but failing to show because, he claimed, he'd been too busy taking telephone calls from journalists. That little mystery aside, United minds turned towards the final.

Save for the cluster of goals just after half-time, the 1977 final was a cagey, cat-and-mouse spectacle. United weren't able to play with the gleeful abandon they were accustomed to, but then Liverpool, who would be playing in the European Cup final four days later, were no ordinary opponents. On this occasion, Docherty instructed his wingers to tuck in if necessary and play more of a 4–4–2 formation. 'I told the players that we needed to be more cautious,' he explained. Unusually, Gordon Hill complied. It took Lou Macari a while to grasp the fact that it was Jimmy Greenhoff who'd got the final touch on United's winning goal, a fact that only dawned on him when he saw Greenhoff disappear down the tunnel clutching the Golden Boot trophy for scoring the winning goal. United had ridden their luck on a couple of occasions, but remained disciplined under pressure in the final quarter of the match and defended their

2–1 lead. Liverpool players had a raft of derisory nicknames for United – 'the Munchkins', 'the Diddy Men' and 'the Glams' to name but three, but, as Liverpool skipper Emlyn Hughes recalled, 'There was always the chance that, on their day, United could jump up and bite us on the arse.' Docherty appeared to revel in the victory, waving the trophy in ITV pundit Jack Charlton's direction, who'd accused the Doc of 'not doing his homework' on Southampton the previous season. The next day, in front of a 250,000 crowd back in Manchester, the manager claimed, 'This could be the start of something big.' But on the night that United won the cup, whilst his players enjoyed their victory banquet at the Royal Lancaster Hotel, Docherty was distant and moody. With the *Sunday People* threatening to break the story, the Doc had decided to come clean to his wife and the United board that he was having an extramarital affair with Mary Brown, the wife of physiotherapist Laurie Brown, who was eighteen years his junior.

Events moved fast after Docherty phoned the chairman's son Martin on the Monday to avail him of his news. 'I told him that Mary and I were going to move in together, and that the story would be in the public domain before too long. I was given assurances that the board would treat it as a private matter,' Docherty recounted. Four weeks after United beat Liverpool, the *Sunday People* ran their story, under the headline, 'THE DOC RUNS OFF WITH THE TEAM WIFE'. In return for a £10,000 fee, the Doc cooperated with the tabloid, explaining, 'We're in love. We've got something special going for us…' The United players, who had no idea about the affair, were stunned. Gordon Hill, enjoying his summer holiday in Spain, bumped into Sammy McIlroy, who warned, 'United is a Catholic club, and they won't take kindly to this. The Doc won't survive.' McIlroy was right.

In June, Docherty was summoned to chairman Louis Edwards's house in Alderley Edge and, after refusing to resign, was fired. Although Docherty insisted that he was the only manager ever fired 'for falling in love', he accepted that multiple factors were in play when I spoke to him: 'I'm seventy-one and I reckon that for every year I've lived, I've heard seventy-one "definitive" versions of why I was sacked. It was a combination of several reasons, I've come to understand.' Theories include the fact that, with a staunchly Catholic board of directors, the powers that be – and their wives – couldn't sit idly by and condone Docherty's affair. Another view held that Matt Busby, who'd voiced concern with the controversial way in which two of his favourites – Willie Morgan and Pat Crerand departed Old Trafford – led a boardroom coup to push the ejector button on Docherty. As United boss, the Doc could have approached things differently, rather than arranging Sunday-morning meetings for his backroom staff, including Laurie Brown, and then skipping them so he could spend time with Mary Brown. It later transpired that a private detective also had evidence that Docherty had allegedly sold clutches of FA Cup final tickets to the 'king' of ticket touts, Stan Flashman. Docherty, after reeling off a list of other leading figures at Old Trafford in that era whom, he alleged, were having affairs – and whom he covered for – concluded, 'Mary and I have been together ever since, and no matter what happened afterwards football wise, she's better than ten Manchester Uniteds.'

Football-wise, what happened next was a cross between a Shakespearean tragedy and a West-End farce. Dave Sexton was appointed Manchester United manager and, despite the litany of dazzling goals from the now moustachioed Gordon Hill, when the darling of the Stretford End refused to comply with Sexton's instructions to track back, he was dropped and sold to Derby County, who were now managed by Tommy Docherty. Despite being reunited with Gerry Daly at the Baseball Ground, the rest of Hill's career was plagued by injuries. 'I cried bitterly when I left Old Trafford,' Hill admitted. 'For me, it was a wonderful three years, and things were never the same afterwards.' Sexton, lambasted by United fans for selling their golden boy, bought Gordon McQueen and Joe Jordan from Leeds to install some height and brawn into the team, but fans were unimpressed with the football they saw. The era of 'Cold Trafford' had arrived.

The Doc's departure from United signalled the beginning of the end of his managerial career. Still, 'The worse the experience, the better the anecdote,' he admitted. After leaving Derby, he was sacked by Queens Park Rangers chairman Jim Gregory, before being reinstated nine days later following a player revolt and then finally dismissed in October 1980. 'He offered me £15,000 as an amicable settlement. I told him he'd have to be more amicable than that,' joked the Doc. When he wound up at Altrincham in 1987 – his final assignment, as it turned out, after posts in Australia and at Wolves – it was his fifteenth managerial post. 'We can safely say that I'd had more clubs than Jack Nicklaus,' laughed Docherty, whacking me on the arm for the second time and spilling my pint once again.

Shortly after Docherty's sacking by United, Bolton Wanderers winger Willie Morgan was invited to appear on Granada TV's Friday night football show *Kick-Off*. Asked by presenter Gerald Sinstadt who the best manager he'd ever played under was, Morgan replied, 'Matt Busby', before stating that Docherty was the worst. In fact, Morgan added, 'Tommy Docherty is the worst manager there's ever been.' A few days later, Morgan received a letter from Granada's solicitors informing him that Docherty intended to sue for libel. The case ended up in the Old Bailey in 1979, some two years after Morgan received the original writ. During that time, Morgan's legal team had busied themselves collecting testimonials from Denis Law and Pat Crerand. The 'Busbyites', whom Docherty so mistrusted at Old Trafford, sharpened their axes, ready to finally give their side of how they were manoeuvred out from

United. Morgan's QC told him, 'I am fully confident that as soon as his team see the evidence we have and the statements we will produce, they'll drop it.' As Docherty prepared to give evidence, chuckling and joking as always, Morgan was instructed to tug his QC's gown every time the Doc lied. After half an hour, Mr Wilpshire told Willie Morgan to stop because his gown was in danger of being pulled off his back. Morgan's QC then spent two hours grilling the Doc, during which time Docherty was reduced to stuttering out monosyllabic responses. After cross-examining him about his contradictory account of his treatment of Denis Law, Mr Wilpshire looked at Docherty and said, 'You told a pack of lies to the jury about this, didn't you?' Chastened and bowed, Docherty shrugged, 'Yes, it turned out this way, yes.' Docherty dropped his libel case. When I spoke to the Doc twenty three-years later, he admitted, 'I wish I'd never issued that bloody libel writ.'

Of course, he fronted it out on the after-dinner speaking circuit. 'Some of those whom I fell out with I've since patched it up with,' he told the crowd in Blackpool in 2002. The audience guffawed, and after shouts of 'Like who?' Docherty fumbled, 'Well, Denis Law and I are now on nodding terms.' Willie Morgan? 'No.' Pat Crerand? Docherty grimaced and shook his head. George Best? There was a sharp intake of breath from those present, 'If I was on fire, George wouldn't piss on me,' was the response. Docherty paused. 'In fact, given his liquid intake, he definitely would.' Cue hoots of laughter around the theatre.

The Doc built an exhilarating young United team, whose brand of football burns brightly in the minds of those who watched them. For many, they were the sole standard bearers of entertaining football in an era of functionality and negativity. But Docherty's realpolitik and deep suspicion of the 'Busbyites' made him a string of powerful enemies, and he will perhaps be remembered more for the scandals that engulfed him than for how he restored Manchester United's long-lost mojo.

15

THE GIANT KILLERS

THE LEATHERHEAD LIP

'The bigger the stage, the more Leatherhead like it.'
Chris Kelly, January 1975

Blink, and the moment is gone. But there, for a nano-second, Leatherhead forward Chris Kelly's name appears on the back page of Norman Stanley Fletcher's copy of *The Sun*. It was a badge of honour for a select group of '70s footballers, but the fact that 'Budgie' – as his Isthmian League contemporaries called him – enjoyed his fleeting moment of *Porridge* fame speaks volumes for the impact the Epsom-born forward made on the nation's consciousness in the early months of 1975 due to the Tanners' remarkable FA Cup run. Thanks to tabloid coverage and full *Match of the Day* exposure, Budgie soon morphed into the 'Leatherhead Lip'.

The Surrey plodders reached the dizzy heights of the Athenian League by the mid-1960s, and reached two FA Amateur Cup semi-finals after floodlights were installed at Fetcham Grove. Despite gaining a reputation as a good cup side, there were always cash-flow problems and, but for a generous chairman, the 1974–75 FA Cup run might never have happened. At the start of the campaign, manager Billy Miller told his dumbfounded group of electricians, plumbers, shopkeepers and – in Chris Kelly's case – upholsterers that there was no money for wages, 'If you don't want to play, you're free to leave.'

At the eleventh hour, chairman Chris Luff dipped into his savings and the wages were sorted. As midfielder Peter McGillicuddy explained during our 2020 telephone interview,

> We played for the love of the game. I'd do a full day working as an electrician in north London, then travel the 27 miles to Leatherhead on the train. Some days I was knackered, and I'd say to Billy Miller, 'Do I have to train today?' He'd retort, 'Pete – if you don't train, you don't get paid.' I think I was on £8 per week from Leatherhead, a decent amount, so I cracked on.

Leatherhead defeated Isthmian League rivals Bishops Stortford in a first-round replay, before Colchester United became the Surrey side's first football league scalp in round two, as a capacity 3,400 crowd at Fetcham Grove (which flooded regularly due to the proximity of the river Mole) saw Leatherhead win 1–0. 'You live for days like that as a non-league player. The clubhouse was overflowing, and it was brilliant to have a few beers with the fans after the game,' the still chirpy Chris Kelly told me during our interview. The Colchester match also revealed that the club had a small but prominent hooligan problem, as around fifty Tanners fans – including Colin Ward, who penned the first hooligan memoir *Steaming In* – fought a running battle with Colchester counterparts behind the Shed End. 'It seems astonishing that such a high police presence is required at games … it is a sad reflection on a minority of our fans,' the *Leatherhead Observer* noted.

After Leatherhead were drawn away at Third Division Brighton in the third round, the tabloids sat up and took notice. Chris Kelly's tendency to shoot from the lip meant that reporters were keen to hear what he had to say. 'Watch us go, I'm about to put Leatherhead on the map,' he told *Mirror* journalist Jack Steggles. With the papers also building up the third heavyweight clash between Joe Frazier and Muhammad Ali (the Thrilla in Manila), and Ali's outlandish predictions of what he was going to do to Frazier, Steggles compared Kelly to the 'Louisville Lip'. Photographer Monty Fresco snapped the Leatherhead Lip jabbing his finger – Ali style – at the camera.

With 2,000 travelling Tanners fans watching their team soak up huge pressure at the Goldstone Ground, Kelly broke forward late in the game and mis-hit the winner. 'I meant to shoot left, but the ball went right. I was slightly lucky.' Brighton manager Peter Taylor was scathing: 'Leatherhead players have full-time jobs and have done a full working week. Whereas my Brighton players are professionals and had all week to prepare. Some of them might not be professionals for much longer,' he told the *Brighton Argus*. The media circus went full swing. Uniquely, the fourth-round draw was made immediately after the third-round games were completed on the Saturday afternoon, and Leatherhead drew First Division Leicester City at home. For financial reasons, Chris Luff made the decision to switch the tie to Filbert Street in Leicester. It was obvious that the Tanners' heroics at Brighton would see them receive top billing on *Match of the Day* come fourth-round day, but directly after the Brighton game, the programme's audience received an early taste of the impudent 'Leatherhead Lip'. As Kelly remembered,

After we'd beaten Brighton, the commentator Alan Weeks came into the pub I was in with the lads and some fans and said that the BBC wanted me to appear on *Match of the Day* that night. I thought: 'Why not?' So I got chauffeured up to London. The problem was, I'd had a few beers and was quite 'lucid', shall we say…

Even presenter Jimmy Hill was taken aback by Kelly's forthright-ness. 'Leicester are rubbish. We'll stuff them in the next round. Moving the tie to Filbert Street makes things easier for us,' Kelly insisted. When Hill asked Kelly how he felt about facing Foxes' England defender Jeff Blockley, Kelly responded, 'He's useless. I hope he's playing.' Looks-wise, Kelly was a hybrid of '70s mavericks Rodney Marsh, Stan Bowles and *Confessions Of…* star Robin Ask-with. All three, like Kelly, loved the limelight. The atmosphere was well and truly stoked.

Not even the rain, the cold and the realisation that they'd be playing in short sleeves (Billy Miller left the long-sleeved shirts in Surrey) could dampen the Leatherhead players' enthusiasm for the Filbert Street clash. Kelly incensed Leicester supporters by blowing kisses at them as he and his teammates walked around the pitch before the match. As Peter McGillicuddy recalled,

'Budgie' was always doing daft things. He was a brilliant mimic and imitated the sound of the referee's whistle perfectly. In one Isthmian League game, the opposition was about to score, and 'Budgie' made his whistle sound. The opposition stopped play-ing, and the confused ref never did work out what happened.

In the first half, Leatherhead – in verdant baize-green shirts – dom-inated. With McGillicuddy, whose long hair and moustache made him look like a member of Crosby, Stills, Nash & Young, pulling the strings, the Tanners poured forward relentlessly and the former Tottenham trainee put Leatherhead 1–0 up. 'I'm now a pub quiz question,' he explained, 'because I was the first outfield player in green to score on *Match of the Day*.' Then Kelly did what he'd promised to do, glancing home a beautifully flighted free kick to put his side 2–0 up after twenty-seven minutes, spinning round in mid-air to watch his effort sail into the net. Jimmy Bloomfield's side was shellshocked. Minutes after half-time, Kelly had a fantastic chance to put Leatherhead 3–0 up. Prior to the game, Kelly spoke of his 'Ali-shuffle' – a stepover manoeuvre that out-foxed opposition defenders. Now, he deployed it. Seizing on a loose ball, he rounded keeper Mark Wallington and did his party piece. 'Can he score? He will if he does his shuffle,' blurted commentator John Motson, but Foxes defender Malcolm Munro scrambled the shot away. Twenty yards away, Peter McGillicuddy screamed in frustration. 'If Budgie had squared it, I'd have had an easy tap in. But that's strikers for you. Leicester's Jon Sammels said if that had gone in, the game would have been over,' he lamented.

As it was, the roof fell in and Leicester scored three times in half an hour to knock the Tanners out. 'Leicester did a professional job in the second half. They put Steve Whitworth on Pete and snuffed him out,' recalled Chris Kelly, now living in France. McGillicuddy, an Arsenal fan, was disappointed that the Tanners missed out on a fifth-round clash with the Gunners at Highbury. As well as denying Leatherhead another huge payday, the players also missed out on a tidy windfall. 'We got a £10 bonus for reaching the fourth round,' McGillicuddy explained, 'and we'd have earned £50 for a draw and £100 for a win.'

'We'll be back next year,' boasted Chris Kelly. But McGillicuddy departed to Enfield and, despite rumoured interest from Arsenal and Nottingham Forest, Kelly left for Third Division Millwall. He didn't enjoy the experience: 'At Millwall, there wasn't the same level of camaraderie or natural love for the game that I was used to in the non-league.' Kelly also claimed that Millwall scuppered his chance of a shot in the North American Soccer league with Tampa Bay Rowdies by withholding his contract when, after eight months, he decided to return to Leatherhead. 'I think I'd have liked the raz-zamatazz of the NASL,' he said.

The Tanners used the profits from the Brighton and Leicester games to revamp the clubhouse and, fittingly, it remains a pictorial shrine to those FA Cup heroics and the 'Leatherhead Lip's' memorable fifteen minutes of football fame.

THE ESSEX AMBUSH

'The most fantastic result you'll ever see.'
The People, 14 February 1971

Since gaining league status in 1950, Colchester United have bounced around the lower divisions for two decades. After taking over as manager at Layer Road in 1968, Dick Graham was collared by a board member and told, 'This club needs a kick up the arse, but there's bugger-all money for transfers.' The former Crystal Palace goalkeeper has set about his job with gusto, steering the Us to sixth place in the Fourth Division in his first season. Then, in 1970–71 the Us embark on a remarkable FA Cup run, putting three goals past Ringmer and Cambridge United in rounds one and two, edging past non-league Barnet in the third round and hammering Rochdale 5–0 in a fourth-round replay. 'Making it to the fifth round was an enormous achievement for a Fourth Division club, but no one outside Colchester really took any notice,' Graham recalled years later. As the fifth-round draw is made on the radio on the Monday lunchtime, the familiar sound of the balls rattling around inside the velvet bag sends a frisson of excitement around the gathered players and local dignitaries, listening intently to the draw on a transistor. Colchester's name is called out first, followed by, 'will play… Leeds United.' A huge cheer erupts. Soon, all eyes will be fixed on this Essex outpost.

———

Some thirty years after the historic clash, Dick Graham was still in no mood to divulge to me the name of the reserve team player whom he'd dispatched to Yorkshire to 'spy' on Don Revie's men as they took on Liverpool the week before the Layer Road clash. Initially, Graham was unimpressed with the spy's feedback. Despite the fact they'd lost to Shankly's Liverpool, Graham's mole described how Leeds were light years ahead of the Essex side in terms of natural ability. 'I already bloody knew that,' Graham laughed. Graham was also informed that Leeds keeper Gary Sprake looked vulnerable on crosses. 'Anyone who watched football knew that too,' Graham said. But there was one more thing. The further Sprake (nicknamed 'Careless Hands' on account of his tendency to drop the occasional clanger in matches) ventured off his line, the shakier his communication became with his backline and the more jittery Leeds looked. Suddenly, Dick Graham was all ears.

The Colchester spy suggested that slinging in crosses 10 yards or more away from Sprake's goal line might pay dividends. He also reckoned the tighter confines of Layer Road might not suit Leeds, who liked playing an expansive game. Graham immediately phoned the club office, instructing them to commandeer all the chairs from the town hall. Secondly, on the Monday, five days before the big match, he took his boys to a blustery Clacton-on-Sea, to draw some lines in the sand and to give his boys a blast of fresh air. On the windswept beach, Graham and a couple of reserves marked out the precise dimensions of the Layer Road pitch and ordered dead-ball specialists Brian Lewis and Dave Simmons to

fire in cross after cross onto the head of veteran striker Ray Crawford. Now thirty-four years old, the former England international
had won the Division One title with Alf Ramsey's Ipswich Town
in 1962, and Graham knew that if anyone had the temperament to
cope with such a huge occasion, it was Crawford. 'Dick Graham
always worked us ultra-hard in training,' he recalled.

> But in the lead-up to the Leeds game we only worked on the
> attacking side. Both Dave [Simmons] and Brian [Lewis] had a
> superb cross on them. Dick told them to aim for the penalty spot,
> where I'd be lurking. Cross after cross. He drilled and drilled us.
> That would be where we'd hit Leeds on Saturday.

After training finished each day, Graham popped back to Layer
Road and, as well as dealing personally with requests from fans
who hadn't been able to get tickets, he arranged for around 200
first-aiders, war veterans and tea ladies to sit pitch-side. 'They'll be
about a yard, if that, from the touch line,' Graham told his men.
'We'll hem Leeds in.'

'Very few gave us a prayer,' Dick Graham told me, 'but I knew that if
we succeeded, it wouldn't be due to a "happy accident". We'd done our
homework.' As Colchester boss, the (then) crew-cut Graham drilled
his troops hard. 'They thought of me as a sergeant major figure, but I
paid for them all to have an ice cream on the day we trained on Clac-
ton beach, just to show what an old softie I really was,' he grinned. His
most inspired move was to snap up Ray Crawford, who ended up at
Colchester after he had rung Layer Road in the summer of 1970 when
he heard that Graham was looking for a striker.

> I was winding down my career with Kettering and planned to
> move to South Africa to play with Durban, but I fancied one last

stab at league football. Dick took me. I cost him £3,000. Because of injuries, Dick also signed Brian Lewis from Oxford and Dave Simmons from Aston Villa. In total, we all cost £14,000. That was big money for Colchester, and there was a lot of experience in the side.

The press labelled Colchester 'Dad's Army' due to the fact that many members of the team were over thirty.

For Crawford, a star of English football's black and white era, his twelve-month stay in Essex was the perfect swan song for an illustrious career in which he scored almost 300 league goals. In the 1970–71 campaign, he'd already plundered twenty-four goals before Leeds hove into view in February. His haul was about to improve. When the players emerged from the tunnel, 16,000 fans – the majority of whom were crammed in on Layer Road's open terraces – greeted them on a crisp Essex afternoon. Following Graham's orders to the letter, Colchester quickly set about Leeds. After eighteen minutes, Brian Lewis drilled in a pin-point free kick from the left, which Crawford headed home emphatically as the Leeds defence froze. A roll of toilet paper, hurled from the Layer Road terraces, zephyred its way past the side-burned striker as he ran off to celebrate, with his right fist punching the air. 'The toilet roll was a sign from the football gods!' laughed Crawford. 'What amazed me was that fact that no one in the Leeds defence shouted "mine". It showed that Gary Sprake didn't always command his penalty area.' Then the sun came out and obligingly shone right in Sprake's face. 'I saw Gary put his cap on to shield his eyes, and that made me further up the ante,' recalled Dick Graham, who urged his men to loft in high crosses, forcing the Leeds keeper to look straight into the fireball.

On twenty-four minutes, Brian Gibbs slung in a cross from the right and the lurking Crawford headed the ball against the back of Paul Madeley's head and crashed to the turf.

For a split second, I lost sight of the ball, but then I heard Jack Charlton shout, 'Sprakey, get the ball.' So I knew it was live. Instinct took over. I simply stuck out a boot when I was on my back and hooked the ball over the line, with Dave Simmons following up to make sure.

As well as venting their spleen at Sprake, the Leeds defenders lost their rag with the eclectic mix of spectators pitch side. 'Every time you ran towards the side of the pitch,' recalled Norman Hunter, 'you were aware of them. There were photographers, first-aid guys, Salvation Army, all of them sipping their bloody flasks of tea. I asked a couple of fellas to move. They ignored me. We'd been had...'

With his team 2–0 up at half-time, Graham told me, 'There wasn't a feeling that we'd been lucky. We deserved our lead. The one thing I said to them was not to concede early in the second half.' It was Colchester who added another goal. Brian Lewis delivered another perfectly executed ball from the right – putting pressure on Sprake to either come and claim it or stay on his line and let Paul Reaney deal with the danger from Dave Simmons. Instead, Sprake dithered and Simmons headed home, ahead of the Welsh goalkeeper's clumsy challenge. 3–0 Colchester. 'The crowd was foaming at the mouth,' said Dick Graham.

However, Leeds fought back. Hunter headed home from a corner in the sixtieth minute, and Johnny Giles fired home after a beautiful interplay of passes on the edge of the Colchester box in the seventy-eighth. Only a brilliant save from Dave Smith prevented a Leeds equaliser, but Colchester clung on to claim a famous 3–2 win. Revie shook every home player by the hand afterwards and his team was out of Layer Road within half an hour, whisked north by private plane. The following weekend, Leeds swatted Wolves aside 3–0, as if the Colchester debacle had never happened.

The Colchester team celebrated in town afterwards, with Graham describing it as the 'best night of my football life'. With fixtures piling up, his team received a 5–0 pasting from Everton at Goodison Park in the quarter-final and narrowly missed out on promotion to the Third Division. Ray Crawford, who ended his final season with thirty-eight goals in all competitions, didn't stick around long enough to see Colchester defeat West Bromwich Albion in the final of the short-lived Watney Cup during the 1971 close season, as he departed to South Africa once the campaign ended. Dick Graham left Layer Road in May 1972, following a disagreement with a share-holder. 'I left part of my heart there too,' he admitted. For Crawford, the events at Layer Road over half a century ago continued to burn brightly. 'It was the day of all days,' said the ebullient former Colchester front man.

THE BLOODY CORNER FLAG

'We are playing for north-east pride in a depressed soccer
area and we won't let anybody down.'
Blyth Spartans manager Brian Slane, February 1978

Blyth Council has run out of salt to grit the town's roads during the bitterly cold early days of 1978; concerned Blyth Valley MP John Ryman says, 'I hope this unhappy situation can be resolved quickly. Blyth's economy and industry has suffered enough over recent years. The town needs a change of fortune.' The main industries which helped the town prosper – shipbuilding and coal mining – have fallen into terminal decline and the town's railway station closed down a decade or so before. Salvation lies with the town's football team, and Blyth Spartans' FA Cup heroics in 1978 will make them heroes well beyond the borders of Northumberland.

———

At thirty-three years of age, Spartans full-back Ron Guthrie – a member of Sunderland's 1973 FA Cup winning team – might have been forgiven for thinking that his career had tailed off. Guthrie is one of a tiny clutch of players to have won in every round of the FA Cup, from the first qualifying round (Blyth beat Shildon, Consett, Crook Town and Bishop Auckland before reaching the first-round proper) back in late summer 1977, to the showpiece match at Wembley in May 1978. The 164-day cup run shot a bolt of much-needed electricity through the whole area. As Guthrie, who supplemented his £10 weekly wage from Blyth with a milk round, explained,

> There were supporters alive at that time who'd seen Sunderland win the FA Cup twice, and Newcastle win it twice too. The competition was engrained up here, and as Blyth's FA Cup run gained momentum in 1977–78, the passion grew. By the time we beat Chesterfield in the second round, we pulled in almost 4,000 to Croft Park. The whole region was getting behind us.

North-east football was at a low ebb, with Sunderland toiling in the second tier and Newcastle United rock bottom of Division One. The Blyth Spartans story was a happy, unifying distraction. Player-manager Brian Slane – a maths teacher in a local comprehensive – dovetailed perfectly with trainer Jackie Marks, a grizzled veteran from the Northern League circuit. 'They were an excellent combination,' recalled Guthrie. 'Brian was thoughtful and reasoned, while Jackie was all passion and guts.' Thanks to average home league attendances of around 800, Spartans had invested in an excellent scouting structure, which saw them secure the services of the finest non-league goalkeeper of his era, Dave Clarke, and nab former Southend striker Terry Johnson.

Anchored in the sixth tier of English football, the Spartans were a tough crew, embodied by their uncompromising forward, Alan Shoulder, a deputy at the nearby Horden Colliery, who was signed from Bishop Auckland for £200 in December 1977. What he lacked in height (he stands 5ft 5in.), he made up for with maximum commitment. 'I always made sure that I did the night shift at the pit [midnight to 8 a.m.], otherwise I wouldn't have been able to play football during the afternoons,' Shoulder explained when I spoke to him in 2020 about Blyth's famous cup run.

I was fortunate that my job kept me fit. When I was at Fishburn Colliery, we still used pit ponies. One time, we were racing them when we shouldn't have been. I cut my head open on a metal girder, and there was blood everywhere. It was my own fault, and I still have the scar to prove it. That aside, the only real injuries I sustained underground was some damage to my fingers, which is par for the course if you're a miner. But those conditions definitely toughen you up.

There was no hiding place in the Northern League in the '70s. Shoulder recalls playing in gale-force fog at Whitley Bay, and at Tow Law 'where the wind was so strong that the ball blew back into our own goal when the goalkeeper punted it out'. Founding club secretary Fred Stoker, who, by choosing the 'Spartans' suffix in 1899, hoped that it would inspire his players to fight in every match, would have been proud of Shoulder's attitude.

Shoulder's FA Cup debut for Blyth Spartans came in the third-round game at Croft Park against an excellent Enfield side who were unbeaten in thirty-two matches, and he recalls 'almost snapping my neck in two' after swivelling 180 degrees to head home the winner. The Spartans were drawn to play Second Division Stoke City in the fourth round at the Victoria Ground. Torrential rain saw the match postponed twice, and the Stoke v. Blyth match was the final fourth-round tie to be played. 'The pity was that many Blyth fans couldn't make it there on the Monday night because of work commitments,' recalled Ron Guthrie. It was a ding-dong battle, with Terry Johnson giving the visitors the lead, Viv Busby and Garth Crooks scoring to put Stoke in front and Steve Carney levelling the scores. At the death, Terry Johnson won the game for the visitors and ran to the travelling fans to celebrate. It prompted Brian Slane to comment, 'I might as well retire now. How can I ever surpass this?'

The publicity machine went into full swing. The next morning, Ladbrokes slashed the Spartans' odds on winning the FA Cup from 20,000:1 to 2,000:1 and revealed that a 'lot of money is being taken' in the Blyth and Ashington branches. Blyth were priced at 11:2 to beat Wrexham (Newcastle fluffed their lines and lost to the Welsh club in the fourth round, destroying the Spartans' dream of a fairy tale local derby) and reach the quarter-finals. Gifts showered down on the team, including a brand-new set of Bukta strips, which they sported at Wrexham's Racehorse Ground, a new pair of boots for every player and £400 worth of free bedroom furniture from a local Blyth company. If that wasn't enough, the press laid siege to the non-leaguers' camp in the build-up to the clash. Much was made of the players taking a sip of trainer Jackie Marks's 'speed oil' prior to matches ('It was whisky,' recalled Alan Shoulder), their team sing song ('Victory Do-Dah') prior to matches and, of course, their eye-catching green and white striped kit. Plus, the fact that they would be the top billing on *Match of the Day*.

The Spartans were the first non-league side to reach the FA Cup fifth round in twenty-nine years, and fellow north-easterner Lawrie McMenemy supplied Brian Slane with a dossier on Wrexham. A frozen surface threatened to see the tie postponed, but the pitch was deemed playable and 7,000 Blyth fans, 'making the type of noise that only fans from the north-east can make', Barry Davies claimed on *Match of the Day*, in the Tech End saw Terry Johnson put the visitors ahead after twelve minutes. Blyth more than held their own for the rest of the match but, with the team running down the clock in the dying seconds, the cruellest of luck befell them. Back in the sixty-seventh minute, referee Alf Grey, noticing that one of the corner flags was falling over, had run over and tried to knock it into the frozen ground. Grey's attempts were unsuccessful and after wrongly awarding Wrexham an 89th-minute corner (the ball came off Bobby Shinton after Blyth skipper John Waterson cleverly played it against him), a bizarre chain of events unfolded.

With the corner flag lying at an angle, Grey again tried to knock it into place. Blyth goalkeeper Dave Clarke punched the in-swinging ball from Les Cartwright out for another corner. Cartwright pushed the flag over to give himself some more room to take the corner and, as Dave Clarke comfortably caught the ball, Grey ordered a retake because the flag wasn't in place. After Cartwright swung the ball over for a second time (with the corner flag back in position), Wrexham's Dixie McNeill headed home to bag a replay for his side. Amidst safety concerns about Croft Park, the replay would be played at St James's Park, with a home clash against Arsenal awaiting the winners in the quarter-finals.

With tickets selling well, a crowd of around 20,000 was expected for the postponed replay, but as the Blyth players reached the outskirts of Newcastle on the day of the match, they got stuck in the mother of all traffic jams. 'We thought there had been an accident, but we were told that we'd need to be escorted to the ground.

The jam was due to the amount of traffic headed to St James's Park. Only then did the magnitude of what we'd done fully sink in.' Ron Guthrie described.

The official 41,187 crowd (thousands more broke into the ground as the game progressed) generated – in Wrexham manager Arfon Griffiths's opinion – 'the most intense atmosphere at a match since Manchester United's first match at Old Trafford after the Munich air crash.' Griffiths's side raced into a 2–0 lead, before Blyth pulled a goal back with seven minutes left. 'The crowd were baying so loud for us to get the equaliser that I thought my ears would burst, but sadly it wasn't to be,' Shoulder remembered. The Spartans' adventure was over, but they gained some revenge over Wrexham in May by defeating them in the two-legged 1978 Debenhams Cup final. The short-lived competition was set up for the two clubs from outside the top two divisions who'd progressed furthest in the FA Cup. Blyth scooped the £7,000 prize and, over forty years later, are still the reigning champions.

Within a year, Alan Shoulder, having put himself in the shop window during those early months of 1978, headed back to St James's Park, this time as a Newcastle player.

Their manager Bill McGarry offered £20,000, which Blyth accepted. On the Monday, I went to one of the Horden Colliery bosses and told him I'd be signing for Newcastle later that week. His reply stunned me: 'I'll be the judge of that, young man. You've signed a contract with the National Coal Board. You have to give three months' notice.' Horden colliery was only three miles from Sunderland, and I was worried that this guy was perhaps a season-ticket holder at Roker Park. Then he smiled, told me he was a Newcastle fan and wished me the best of luck.

Shoulder made his debut against Stoke City, and was warned by

Bill McGarry that he'd face the notoriously tough-tackling Dennis Smith. 'I told McGarry that I'd spent nine hours a day underground and I wasn't scared of Dennis Smith.' His wages jumped from £14 per week at Blyth, plus his colliery wage of £70, to £180 plus bonuses. Shoulder's bustling style made him popular at St James's Park and, a few months later, ex-Blyth teammate Steve Carney joined him there.

The battle-scarred Ron Guthrie looked back with pride on his career when we talked: 'I've got various aches and pains in my legs, and a joint replacement or two. But I wouldn't change a thing. Whenever any of us go back to Croft Park, we're treated like kings. Nothing will ever change that.' 'LET THE NORTH SALUTE THEM' ran the *Daily Mirror* headline after Blyth's defeat by Wrexham. Decades later, those Spartans remain as venerated as ever.

16

THE WEMBLEY HEROES

THE SAVE

'And Lorimer makes it one each... no... astonishing!'
David Coleman

Roker Park, December 1972. As Sunderland's disconsolate team head for the sanctuary of the dressing room, following a 1–0 home defeat to Burnley, a clutch of angry home fans gather near the tunnel to harangue new manager Bob Stokoe. 'Bugger off back to your black and white stripes, Stokoe!' they yell at the former Newcastle defender. A few days earlier, in front of BBC cameras, a beaming Stokoe had strolled across the Roker Park pitch with his new squad – a talented group which included forwards Billy Hughes and Dennis Tueart, midfielder Ian Porterfield and goalkeeper Jim Montgomery. It was all smiles and jokes and bonhomie. But the Burnley defeat is a jarring reality check.

With Sunderland fourth from the bottom of the Second Division and crowds plummeting by the week, Stokoe appears to have inherited a poisoned chalice from previous boss Alan Brown, who'd abruptly resigned in late October. The club's six-year stay in the First Division had come to an end with relegation in May 1970, and the prevailing mood is sombre. A flu epidemic amongst the players sees all the club's Christmas matches postponed, meaning that Sunderland had sunk into the bottom three. 'Things are at a low ebb,' admits Stokoe to local journalist Bob Cass. 'But I fancy us for us a decent FA Cup run.' Within four months, as Stokoe's side blaze a trail to Wembley, Cass and the success-starved Sunderland fans will label Stokoe the 'messiah'.

The enforced Christmas break enabled Stokoe, who had joined Sunderland from Blackpool, to take stock of the dire situation in which the club and the city found itself. Industrial strife was everywhere. There was a strike at North Sands Shipyard, and a dispute at Coles Cranes. Speculation was rife (and correct, as it turned out) that redundancies were imminent at several coal mines in the area, and unemployment was at its highest for a decade. With the majority of Sunderland fans employed in heavy industry, Roker Park attendances were badly affected.

In his low-key way, Stokoe got to work. The £35,000 acquisition of versatile Newcastle defenders Ron Guthrie and Dave Young was bargain-basement at best. The general consensus was that Stokoe had landed a couple of Toon rejects, but Guthrie and Young both shored up Sunderland's previously porous backline. Stokoe also brought in striker Vic Halom – a robust and combative forward – from Luton Town. After reinforcing his squad, Stokoe turned his attention to the clapped-out clock on the Clock Stand, which hadn't ticked a single tock in years. Rather like the club, some said. When the players returned for the games at the start of the new year (in their first game for three weeks, Sunderland walloped Brighton 4–0 in a morale-boosting victory at Roker Park), Stokoe informed them that, from now on, they'd play midweek matches on a Tuesday, not a Wednesday, in order that shipyard workers, who did the late shift on Wednesdays, could get to matches once more. Never one for Churchillian speeches in the dressing room, Stokoe preferred to deploy clever tricks to motivate his men. He'd offer little wagers (£1 maximum) to his strikers challenging them to score, and to defenders for keeping a clean sheet. 'He tapped into a player's psyche about offering us a challenge,' explained Dennis Tueart, when I assisted him with his 2010 autobiography. The last time Sunderland had won anything of note was 1937, when goals from Bobby Gunney, Eddie Burbanks and local hero Raich Carter helped defeat Preston at Wembley. After Stokoe took over, Carter described how, after the victory in 1937, supporters queued ten-deep next to the rail tracks, and tug boats on the Wear tooted with joy. Carter pointed out that if you flipped the digits around 1937 became 1973. It had to be a sign, maybe this could be Sunderland's year.

But at Meadow Lane in the FA Cup third round on 13 January, with Sunderland 1–0 down to Notts County on a mudheap of a pitch, Stokoe's team appeared to be heading for an early exit. After seventy minutes, County striker Les Bradd looked set to double team's lead as he powered a header towards the top corner of Jim Montgomery's net. Montgomery – Sunderland born and bred – pulled off a miraculous save. Stretching backwards, he twisted himself around in mid-air and tipped the ball away for a Notts County corner. As Montgomery crashed to the turf, and the disbelieving Bradd looked to the heavens, the Sunderland players thanked their lucky stars for the 5ft 11in. Montgomery's acrobatics that were the result of his zealous approach to training. In an era before goal-keeping coaches, 'Monty' asked his teammates to repeatedly hurl the ball to either side of him in order to keep his reactions razor-sharp. 'I'd rock myself left or right to catch the ball. I'd then get up using only my legs,' he explained. 'It was incredibly demanding, but it meant that I could keep my hands free which gave me a better chance of getting to the ball.' Montgomery also excelled in one particular repeat exercise that served him well at Meadow Lane: 'The boys would hold the ball on the penalty spot,' he described. 'I'd run off my line, touch the ball and they'd throw it over my head, which made me back-pedal and claw the ball away. Les Bradd's header, for me, was straight from our training ground.' Seconds after Montgomery's heroics, defender Dave Watson grabbed an equaliser to force the replay, which Sunderland won 2–0.

After edging out Reading in the fourth round after two matches, Sunderland faced a showpiece match against Malcolm Allison's Manchester City in the fifth round at Maine Road on 24 February. Following a 2–2 draw in front of *Match of the Day* cameras, where the quicksilver Billy Hughes, his long dark hair flapping in the breeze, caused the star-studded City – with the 'holy trinity' of Francis Lee, Mike Summerbee and Colin Bell all in action – a myriad of problems, Sunderland set up a mouth-watering midweek replay at home. When the Sunderland players got back from Manchester just after midnight on the Saturday, they were greeted by the incredible sight of queuing fans wrapping themselves around the ground twice over. On the coldest night of the year, supporters huddled together like penguins as they queued to buy replay tickets that went on sale at 9 a.m. on Sunday morning. Burger vans worked through the night. Residents in the streets surrounding Roker Park opened their doors to make hot drinks for freezing fans. 'The whole community was behind us,' explained Jim Montgomery. By 11 a.m. on Sunday, all 49,000 of the available tickets had been snapped up.

City swaggered into town on Tuesday 27 February (Big Mal had boasted in the press what City would do to 'little Sunderland'), as a cold North-Sea wind buffeted the Roker End. Tiles were blown off the rooves of nearby houses, dustbins blew over and paper rubbish swirled around in a raging gale. 'It was impossible to hear or think in that din,' recalled defender Ron Guthrie. Sunderland, literally, threw caution to the wind and went straight for City's jugular. Vic Halom's superb 25-yard shot gave Stokoe's men the lead after fifteen minutes and, after a fantastic interchange of passes with skipper Bobby Kerr, Billy Hughes put the home side two goals to the good after thirty-six minutes. Francis Lee pulled a City goal back in the second half, but Billy Hughes slid in a third for Sunderland after Dennis Tueart's shot was parried away. 3–1 to Sunderland. 'CRASH – OUT GO CITY!' ran the *Mirror* headline, and Sunderland's cup odds were cut from 250:1 to 100:1. Big Mal knocked on the home dressing-room door and congratulated each and every one of the Sunderland players, telling them that he'd keep his mouth shut next time. After a routine 2–0 win over Luton, Sunderland's FA Cup odds were slashed to 70:1, and they faced Arsenal in the semi-final at Hillsborough.

There were 21,800 Sunderland fans piled high on the Kop, the huge arc of terracing framed by hills, trees and houses. Sunderland's forwards – the burly Vic Halom in particular – sensed that Arsenal, minus influential skipper Frank McLintock, were nervous. His replacement Jeff Blockley, signed from Birmingham for £200,000, had a disastrous day. After thirty minutes, with Halom snarling and snapping at his heels, Blockley's back pass failed to reach Gunners keeper Bob Wilson, and Halom nipped in to give Sunderland the lead. Arsenal's best chance came from a wickedly deflected George Armstrong pass. Jim Montgomery, already moving to his left, abruptly changed direction, pushing with his legs to dive down to his right and somehow scoop the ball away. 'I always tried to ensure that I was economic with my movement and didn't move too far to one side or the other, in case of deflections,' he said. A Billy Hughes header put Sunderland 2–0 up, and they weathered a late Arsenal push, when Charlie George clawed a goal back. At the final whistle, Bob Stokoe, moved to tears, was granted full icon status by Sunderland fans, who chanted 'Stokoe, Stokoe,

Stokoe'. The elated players, none of whom had played at Wembley before, prepared for an FA Cup final showdown with the mighty Leeds.

In the intervening weeks between the victory over Arsenal and the FA Cup final, the Sunderland players took full advantage of the publicity opportunities that came their way and visited local factories and department stores. 'Some of the locals were shedding tears of joy. It was incredibly humbling,' Dennis Tueart recalled. The team recorded an FA Cup final song, and Tueart, Billy Hughes and Ian Porterfield did some modelling shots for the Lord John fashion boutique on Carnaby Street. The players' pool was swelled by donations from local industry. Wear shipbuilders donated a lump sum of £650 for Sunderland reaching the semi-final, and £1,300 for the final. Absenteeism in the shipyards was at an all-time low because the workforce couldn't wait to get their fill of Sunderland chat.

At their Selsdon Park Hotel on the morning of the final, the Sunderland players were in a relaxed mood. When the BBC's Barry Davies arrived to interview the players, he was somewhat taken aback by the laid-back atmosphere: 'Right in the middle of my interview with the players, Billy Hughes pulled out a laughing policeman toy, and suddenly the room was full of ho-ho-hos.' In contrast with the regimented Leeds players, Bob Stokoe adopted a laissez-faire attitude to his stars' sartorial style. In the pre-match Wembley walkabout, Sunderland players – laughing and joking with one another – sported a range of assorted coloured suits and kipper ties. We called ourselves 'raggedy-arsed Rovers', remembered Dennis Tueart. The Leeds players, with top buttons done up, were tailored to within an inch of their lives. The starkest difference was between the immaculately blazered Leeds boss Don Revie and Bob Stokoe, who was clad in his bright red Sunderland tracksuit.

The teams emerged from the tunnel to a deafening roar, and a tight match pivoted around two key moments. First was Sunderland midfielder Ian Porterfield's unerring finish. Half an hour in, the Scot, often called out by previous boss Alan Brown for his reluctance to use his right foot, flicked the ball up with his left, drove home expertly past Leeds keeper David Harvey with his 'dead leg', as he described it, and promptly disappeared amidst a forest of red and white candy-striped arms.

With Leeds pushing forward for a second-half equaliser, Trevor Cherry's flying header from a lofted cross was parried away by the diving Jim Montgomery. 'The ball was wet, so I pushed it away,' he explained. Following up on the rebound was Peter 'Hotshot' Lorimer, credited with having the most thunderous shot in '70s football. Eight yards out, Lorimer opted to place the ball, rather than put his foot through it. Montgomery rocked himself sideways with his legs 'and instinctively headed for the part of the goal where I knew Lorimer would put it. He wasn't going to blast it at where I'd come from, so I moved to block the rest of the goal.' Montgomery deflected the ball with his right arm and it hit the underside of the bar and bounced down. The still prostrate Cherry attempted to flick the ball home with his right foot before it was cleared. The save was an astonishing piece of athleticism, which happened in the blink of an eye. The blinding speed of his double save was such that both David Coleman (BBC) and Brian Moore (ITV) initially claimed that Leeds had equalised. Montgomery himself had no time to process what had happened as Sunderland had to defend the resultant throw-in.

A few minutes later, Norman Hunter turned to Dennis Tueart, shrugged and said, 'It looks like it's your day, Dennis.' When the final whistle went, the majority of the Sunderland players sank to their knees in celebration, but Bob Stokoe sprang to life and loped across the Wembley turf, heading straight to Jim Montgomery. Even in an era when TV audiences were used to glam-rock bands like Slade performing on *Top of the Pops* in bizarre combinations of mirrored top hats, tartan and platform boots, Stokoe's eclectic mix of garments was startling. His trilby, beige raincoat, red tracksuit trousers and trainers ensemble is now preserved in bronze outside Sunderland's Stadium of Light. Stokoe hugged Montgomery tight, but due to the din inside the ground Montgomery couldn't hear what his manager said to him. Later, Stokoe told Montgomery he'd yelled, 'Thank you for the save at Notts County, from Armstrong in the semi-final and for your save from Lorimer today.' 'We were all on cloud nine afterwards. I suppose the only pity of it was that we weren't able to witness the scenes in the city on the day,' Montgomery recalled. Fortunately, Tyne Tees Television produced a wonderfully evocative documentary called *Meanwhile Back In Sunderland*, which recorded how, from midday onwards, the whole town ground to a halt as everyone (save for one man walking his dog) tuned into the final and the build-up to the game. One group crowded around colour TV sets in the window at Rumbelows. Most enjoyed FA Cup final TV parties in their lounges. Three days after the final, the Sunderland players brought the FA Cup home. As their open-top bus trundled towards Roker Park, where over 50,000 ecstatic fans were waiting, players were greeted by bedridden hospital patients wheeled out onto balconies and hordes of schoolchildren who'd been given the afternoon off to welcome back Stokoe and his men. 'In the fields just outside Sunderland, farmers had even stuck giant red rosettes to their cattle,' Montgomery explained during our 2020 interview.

The Wearside giants didn't make it back to the top flight for three more years, and the celebratory atmosphere from the cup run evaporated after the team made a sluggish start to the 1973–74 season. Dennis Tueart and Dave Watson left for Maine Road. But the bond between the former Sunderland players, who still wax lyrical about those intoxicating few months, remained as strong as ever. 'Because it's a one-club city, we shared something completely unique,' explained Jim Montgomery, whose incredible double save is often regarded as Wembley's finest. 'The cup run still enriches all our lives.'

THE BANNER FINAL

'IPSWICH WILL HAVE ARSENAL BY THE WARK AND BURLEYS'
FA Cup final banner, 1978

The Nou Camp, December 1977. After a succession of European excursions and top-six finishes in the First Division, the wheels appear to be coming off the Ipswich Town bandwagon. The Suffolk side demolished Barcelona at Portman Road in the UEFA Cup third-round first leg at Portman Road, with goals from Eric Gates, Trevor Whymark and Brian Talbot. But Ipswich capitulate in Catalonia, crashing out on penalties after a 3–0 defeat. Ipswich's eccentric chairman John Cobbold, known to everyone at the club as 'Mr John' insists, 'There will never be a crisis at Ipswich Town unless the white wine runs out in the board room.' But with the club sinking like a stone in Division One in 1977–78, Cobbold and manager Bobby Robson have a full-blown crisis on their hands. The team win only five more Division One matches that season after their Barca backlash, avoiding relegation by three points. Come January, Robson insists that the FA Cup could prove to be his club's salvation, encouraging his men 'to become heroes'. Local boy Roger Osborne, a midfielder who'd man-marked Barca's Johan Cruyff out of the Portman Road game, takes heed.

One of twelve siblings, Osborne was born in the Suffolk village of Otley to a cowman, enjoyed the occasional moorhen omelette as a boy and ended up at Ipswich almost by accident. Working for a demolition firm and playing part-time football in his early twenties, Osborne was the only one in his family with a car and drove his brother to train with the youth team. He was approached by Ipswich because they were suffering from an injury crisis in midfield, and 'things quickly went from there', explained Osborne modestly. Tough summers of prising sugar beet out of the ground and lugging huge 18-stone sacks of grain around farmyards meant there was no chance of Osborne, who didn't make his first-team debut until he was twenty-three, taking his football career for granted, especially not on the wages he was offered. With Clerk Demolition, he earned £25 per week. Ipswich offered him £15 per week initially as a part-timer, and £25 with a £2 win bonus as a full-timer. Yet by his mid-twenties, he was facing the world's finest. 'Bobby [Robson] told me to do a job on Johan, and I stuck to him like a limpet. He tried his "Cruyff turn" on me, but the ball ran out of play when he changed direction. Afterwards, we swapped shirts,' he recounted during our 2020 interview.

Throughout the season, Robson's side suffered from a horrendous catalogue of injuries, losing experienced strikers Colin Viljoen and Trevor Whymark for long periods, and centre-back Kevin Beattie – once described by Bobby Robson as 'the most naturally gifted player I ever saw' – played only when his troublesome knees would allow. 'After the Barcelona game at Portman Road,' he explained, 'my knee blew up to the size of a balloon. I got through matches by taking cortisone shots before matches. My knee felt fine during the game, but the next day, I'd be screaming in pain.' I met with Beattie in 2012. One of nine children from a Carlisle council estate, his life hadn't been an easy one. 'I used to truant school sometimes because I didn't have any shoes, and when I met Bobby Robson to sign for Ipswich, I wore my father's shoes, because my parents couldn't stretch to buy me a pair. He sorted me out, did Bobby. Made sure I was properly dressed.' Beattie spoke of his financial struggles and battles with alcohol, depression and his wife Maggie's battle with multiple sclerosis (Beattie was her carer) without a hint of bitterness. 'Life happens,' he said. At thirty-seven, his life nearly ended when he contracted pancreatis and he was even given the last rites. Later, following a testimonial match at Ipswich, the Professional Footballers' Association gave him £50,000, which put him on 'more of an even keel', as he put it. 'Anyway,' he said, throwing his hands in the air, 'enough about all that depressing crap. Let's talk about the cup.'

The FA Cup offered a welcome distraction from Ipswich's league woes. Routine victories over Cardiff City and Hartlepool in rounds three and four afforded Ipswich the opportunity to visit arguably the most shabby of all grounds of that era – Eastville. Bristol Rovers' ramshackle home doubled as a speedway and greyhound racing venue, and around the pitch's oval perimeter was strewn all manner of clutter: dog kennels, motorbike wheels and bits and bobs from old scoreboards. It was the closest English ground to a motorway, and the elevated M32 actually touched the south-east corner of the ground. When the Ipswich team (Robson's men donned a one-off orange away kit, because their blue home shirt and white away top clashed with Rovers' chequered blue and white shirts) headed to the West Country in mid-February, they found Eastville covered in a blanket of snow, which meant the appearance of that most '70s of football props – the orange ball. When a referee produced an orange ball at the start of a game, a frisson of excitement pulsed across the terraces (and living rooms), given that, even in an era of harsh winters and primitive under-soil heating, it was such a novelty. The Bristol and Ipswich players tip-toed around the rock-hard pitch like newborn foals. Only a late Paul Mariner equaliser saved

Ipswich's blushes and forced the Portman Road replay. Ipswich crushed Rovers 3–0 in the replay, setting up a quarter-final against Millwall at the much-feared Lions' Den.

Ipswich fans who journeyed to Cold Blow Lane in south London received a hostile reception, and their coaches were pelted with rocks by Millwall fans upon arrival. Some of the Ipswich players were nervous too. 'My roommate John Wark, who was a young player at the time, needed the toilet several times the night before,' recalled Paul Mariner. Fans inside the Den watched a mock Wild West shootout before the game started – an odd choice for pre-match entertainment by a club which had recently acknowledged that its hooligan problem was worsening. Whatever jitters the Ipswich players may have had, they produced a superlative display. Goals from George Burley and a brace from Paul Mariner put Ipswich 3–0 up, before a pitch invasion saw both sides taken off for fifteen minutes early in the second half. After returning to the fray, John Wark (who later explained how a brick whizzed past his head in the second half) then volleyed home a superb effort from a Mariner header and Ipswich romped to a 6–1 win against the Second Division side. The normally mild-mannered Bobby Robson was so enraged by the actions of Millwall's hooligans, that he insisted he would 'take a flamethrower to them'.

Drawn against Ron Atkinson's emerging West Bromwich Albion side in the semi-final at Highbury, Ipswich produced arguably their most polished performance of the season. Brian Talbot's flying header gave them the lead, but in the act of scoring, the midfielder cut his head open following a clash with Albion skipper John Wile and left the field with concussion and blood pouring down his face. Wile carried on regardless, in his claret-stained yellow and green striped shirt. John Wark's late header, in front of delirious Ipswich fans in the Clock End, secured a 3–1 win. Ipswich were going to Wembley for the first time in their history. One Ipswich banner (an ode to winger Clive Woods) on the Clock End read, 'ALBION GO DOWN TO THE WOODS TODAY'. In the four weeks leading up to the FA Cup final against Arsenal, Ipswich wordsmiths got busy with their felt-tip pens and bedsheets and went to town on writing some more banners.

A week before the FA Cup final, with their top-flight status finally secured, Ipswich lost 6–1 away at Aston Villa. It was hardly the most auspicious performance before their trip to Wembley. To Roger Osborne's alarm, he was left out of the starting line-up against Villa to make room for the returning striker Colin Viljoen.

Having played in all the rounds leading up to the final, I was worried that I'd miss out. Several of the players, including Paul Mariner and Mick Mills, had words with Bobby Robson, who'd shifted the team around to accommodate Colin, and told him in no uncertain terms that I needed to be back in midfield. Bobby complied.

With the rain lashing down in the days leading up to the game – *The Sun* labelled it 'THE WEMBLEY MUDBATH' – both teams had injury worries. Bobby Robson claimed that his side was 'bludgeoned' by concerns, and defenders Mick Mills and Allan Hunter underwent late fitness tests, although Kevin Beattie suggested that Robson exaggerated the problems in order to play up to Ipswich's billing as underdogs. Bookmakers offered odds of 9:4 on an Ipswich win, whilst the Gunners, who were in fine fettle in the league, were evens. The reality was that physically, Arsenal were in far worse shape, with defenders Pat Rice, Sammy Nelson and Willie Young carrying knocks, striker Malcolm Macdonald's knee had been regularly locking up during matches and talisman Liam Brady was suffering from an ankle injury.

Before the game, Robson discussed tactics with his charges

(allowing Kevin Beattie, who'd had three cortisone shots in his knee to enable him to play, and Allan Hunter to sneak off for a cigarette in the toilets) and how he would deploy his secret weapon – young winger Dave Geddis. The teenager played on the right-hand side in order to occupy Gunners left-back Sammy Nelson and prevent him from making overlapping runs to join the Arsenal attack. As kick-off approached, the homemade banners inside Wembley were hoisted high. The Arsenal fans weren't exactly unimaginative, conjuring up 'ADMIRAL NELSON SINKS MARINER, BRADY SELLS MORE DUMMIES THAN MOTHERCARE' and, perhaps most obscurely, 'CLIVE WOOD IF HE COULD BUT HE CAN'T'. As it turned out, Nelson and Brady had poor games, and Clive did because he could. Several Ipswich banners predicted a rough afternoon for Gunners skipper Pat Rice ('MILLS GRINDS RICE', 'WOODS FRIES RICE' and 'WIZARD WOODS EATS RICE' were three examples) and Sammy Nelson ('MARINER SINKS NELSON'). Town striker Paul Mariner's goal-getting abilities were espoused ('MARINER STRIKES MORE THAN BRISH LEYLAND'), and the same applied for midfielder John Wark ('JOHNNY WARKS ALL OVER ARSENAL'). But perhaps the most eye-opening banner read, 'BEATTIE'S FIRE MELTS PLASTIC MAC' – an unsubtle reminder that, a year before the final, Beattie (who described the banner as 'one of the funniest things I ever saw') sustained first-degree burns when a fire in his garden got out of control, causing him to miss the end of the season. Beattie did indeed keep Malcolm Macdonald quiet at Wembley. Ipswich set about Arsenal with gusto. In the first half, Mariner fired his shot against Pat Jennings's crossbar. At half-time, Bobby Robson, convinced that his dominant side would eventually break through, urged his team to stay patient. Ipswich turned the screw in the second half. Two John Wark shots whistled past Pat Jennings, only to crash against the right-hand post, and Jennings made an excellent save from a George Burley header.

On seventy-seven minutes, the moment Ipswich had been waiting for arrived. Geddis twisted past Nelson and drilled the ball low into the Arsenal penalty area. Aware that Paul Mariner was lurking behind him, Willie Young tried to clear the ball, but it fell perfectly for Roger Osborne – with his socks rolled down – who drilled home past Jennings. 'I was very conscious to keep my head over the ball so I didn't blast over the bar,' he recalled. 'Bobby had always been telling me to use my left foot more often. I thought now was the chance to show him that I'd listened.' Osborne pogoed in the air three times before being submerged under a ruck of jubilant teammates. BBC commentator David Coleman often enjoyed a period of silent reflection after describing a dramatic Wembley goal, but he outdid himself in the interlude following his trademark: 'Osborne. 1–0.' It took Coleman twenty-one seconds to gather his thoughts, by which time Osborne had 'a funny turn' – 'the heat, the heavy pitch, the fact I was buried under everybody and the sense of occasion caught up with me, I didn't pass out, as some have said, but I certainly felt unwell,' he recounted. As a result, he was substituted by Mick Lambert. As Coleman explained to viewers, the goalscorer's large family had piled into the specially chartered 'Osborne bus' that morning to go and watch him play at Wembley. Family members later smothered his house in 'IPSWICH' and 'WELL DONE ROGER!' banners. After the game, as a rehydrated Osborne celebrated with his teammates, Kevin Beattie's knees began to hurt. 'I found I couldn't jog around with the rest of the team, so I cadged a cigarette off a steward and walked the lap of honour with the FA Cup lid on my head.' The Ipswich team bus headed back to Suffolk after the game, and after a stop at Chelmsford services for more alcohol, the A12 was lined with jubilant supporters welcoming home their heroes.

The civic reception was a sight to behold, with crowds serenading Beattie with chants of 'Beattie is Back' and chanting 'Roger,

Roger,' at the self-effacing matchwinner. In fact, the final proved to be as good as it got for both players, as Bobby Robson looked to Holland and midfielders Arnold Mühren and Frans Thijssen to upgrade a squad that had faltered so badly in Division One, and play in a more 'continental' style. After a summer cartilage operation, Osborne soon faded from the first-team scene. 'My first and last goals for Ipswich were both scored against Pat Jennings,' he remembered. Beattie's knees crumbled underneath him. 'I don't blame Bobby or anyone at Ipswich for the amount of cortisone which was pumped into me,' Beattie told me.

> I wanted to play. I could have said no to the shots, but I didn't. Now I can't walk more than a few yards without serious pain. Although the sense of relief when the needle went in was huge, cortisone was the curse of my generation of players. But I wouldn't swap winning at Wembley for anything.

In the years that followed, both Osborne and Beattie played for Colchester, and stayed in Suffolk. Beattie died in 2015, after years of ill health. Osborne, who lives in the same house he did as a player, became a lorry driver and later managed a local sports centre, where his signed Cruyff shirt took pride of place on a wall.

> Scoring the goal at Wembley didn't change my life. I'd done other jobs before I turned professional and knew I'd have to after I left the game. But I never get tired of people coming up to me and talking about '78. The only problem is they're getting greyer by the year...

17

THE SUPERSTARS

'Don Revie told me I'd made a bloody idiot of myself in that canoe.'
Stan Bowles, 2004

Aldershot army base, June 1976. After clocking a so-so time of 12.6 seconds in the 100-metre sprint and finishing fourth, impish Queens Park Rangers forward Stan Bowles is dreading the second event in the 1976 UK *Superstars* final – the 125-metre canoe race. The nervous long-haired luminary from Loftus Road informs BBC presenter David Vine, 'I don't really like the water.' As the race begins and boxer John Conteh, racing driver James Hunt and 400-metre hurdles Olympic champion David Hemery streak ahead, Bowles wobbles, cuts across the lanes and ploughs into Newcastle striker Malcolm Macdonald's boat. Both capsize. 'Supermac,' who'd cruised to victory in the opening event – the 100-metre sprint – is unimpressed and the incident does little to alleviate the tension between Bowles and Macdonald, who've never seen see eye to eye. Bowles finishes the overall competition with seven points, the lowest-ever UK score, reinforcing his reputation in the public eye as a hapless scallywag. But at least the two footballing superstars have one thing in common: their inability to win the confidence of England manager Don Revie.

David Vine had an important question for me. 'Can you hum the *Superstars* theme tune?' asked the presenter, whose crinkly hair, oversized glasses and kipper ties were omnipresent on BBC television sports shows like *Ski Sunday* in the '70s. 'I find it impossible. Most people do. You try.' As he wrapped his hands around a cup of coffee to stay warm on a chilly London morning in the early 2000s, I gave humming the tub-thumping theme tune, one of the '70s most memorable TV tracks, a go and failed miserably. Vine laughed, 'See, I told you it was difficult.' After suggesting to him that humming the *Ski Sunday* theme would likely be equally vexing, I was treated to the spectacle of Vine rapidly bobbing his head from side to side, da-da-da-ing Sam Fonteyn's snowy classic to me. 'I still reckon *Superstars* is trickier,' he opined. We moved on to discuss the show that Vine co-presented with athletics coach Ron Pickering. 'It sounds like a bad joke: "Did you hear the one about the judo star, the speed skater and the footballer?"' Vine said. 'Superstars worked because it brought out the competitive streak in the participants – with the exception of Stanley Bowles, obviously...' The first *Britain's Sporting Superstars* competition was held at Crystal Palace National Athletics Stadium in 1973, featuring seven competitors from seven different sports. England's World Cup-winning skipper Bobby Moore was the first footballer to feature, competing against the likes of golfer Tony Jacklin, boxer Joe Bugner and Welsh rugby star Barry John. From the off, Vine realised the concept of Superstars worked a treat:

It was a new challenge for these men to compete against stars from other sports. Roger Taylor – the tennis player – beat Bobby Moore in the 100-metre sprint. Bobby wasn't the quickest, but it was still a badge of honour for Roger, because Bobby was a bit of a hero of his.

Moore finished sixth out of the seven competitors, and the show's allure grew.

In the 1974 UK final, Southampton's Mick Channon and Manchester City's Colin Bell competed against one another. Channon finished in seventh place overall, but Bell eventually finished in third, coming in behind David Hemery and the winner John Conteh. As expected, both Channon and Bell were blisteringly quick in the 100 metres (Channon won and Bell, who slipped at the start, recovered to finish third) and in the 600-metre steeplechase the positions were reversed with Bell winning comfortably. Then there was Kevin Keegan's infamous tumble from his bike at a heat in Bracknell in 1976, when his front wheel clipped Belgian football captain Gilbert van Binst's back wheel as the pair raced to get a lead going into the first corner. Keegan crashed to the floor, skidding across the cinder track on his back, his arms and shoulders exposed by his vest red raw and burnt. 'I think some people thought Kevin had bloody died,' said a wincing Vine. 'It was horrific. Think of someone scraping their finger-nails down a blackboard and multiply it by 100. But Kevin refused medical help and won the rerun race, and the heat.' The whole incident cemented his reputation as a fighter in the eyes of the British public. On the way back from *Superstars*, Keegan passed out and woke up in Northampton General Hospital, where he stayed for three days on a drip. Wife Jean informed her husband that he would *not* be partaking in an international event in Florida later that year.

Out of all English footballers, Malcolm Macdonald made the biggest splash on *Superstars*. Macdonald had already taken full advantage of the commercial opportunities that proliferated by the early '70s for high-profile footballers. After completing his £180,000 transfer to Newcastle and securing a £100-per-week deal, *The Sun* offered him £250 per week to pen his own column. Factor in ownership of a Newcastle boutique (named Malcolm Macdonald: For The Exclusive Man) and his directorship of a Luton-based second-hand car showroom (GS Twigg), 'Supermac' was the very embodiment of the nouveau riche footballer, earning more outside the game than inside. Then came the opportunity to compete in the second *European Superstars* 1975 heat in Malmö.

With his explosive pace, the powerfully built Macdonald was firm favourite for the 100-metre sprint. Seven athletes lined up at the start, and Swedish table tennis player Kjell Johansson got out of the blocks significantly before the starter's gun and had a lead of several yards on the field. Macdonald blazed past the Swede to win in a record time of 11.0 seconds. However, the show's technical adviser Ron Pickering claimed that the false start invalidated the race and a rerun was ordered. This time Macdonald was even faster, clocking 10.5 seconds, a new *Superstars* record: 'Ron Pickering beckoned to me. "It's the second quickest time in Europe this year. If I coached you I could help you shave half a second of that time," he said.' Macdonald won the pistol shooting and weightlifting events, and after finishing a creditable third in the steeplechase, he won his heat.

'The *Superstars* competitors weren't insured – which would be unthinkable these days,' said Macdonald, 'but Newcastle boss Joe Harvey reckoned it would be good publicity for the club if I competed.' He scooped £2,500 in prize money, and an elaborately carved painted elephant. 'In European *Superstars*, they awarded all the competitors something unique to the locality – not that there are too many elephants roaming around in Sweden,' he laughed.

The fella who finished last got this tiny 1.5in. elephant. As the presentation ceremony went on, in ascending order with the elephants getting heftier and heftier, I got handed a 2ft-high elephant which weighed a bloody ton. At the airport, Giacomo Agostini, the Italian motorcyclist – looked at me struggling and said, 'To win something that large takes great stupidity.'

By now, *Superstars* regularly pulled in TV audiences of over 10 million. Palitoy Parker released the bestselling *Superstars* boardgame in time for Christmas, with Macdonald's face and signature on the front of the box, tucked between John Conteh and David Hemery. Like Leicester hairdresser Bill 'Mr Mastermind' Woodward, who, along with model Cecilia Fung, appeared on the box of the Mastermind boardgame, which sold an estimated 35 million copies worldwide, Macdonald made nothing in royalties from the game. 'Image rights weren't really a thing back then,' he explained. Macdonald, with an eye-catching £333,333 move to Arsenal in the offing, readily accepted the invitation to compete in the 1976 UK *Superstars* final, blissfully unaware that Stan Bowles was about to steal the show.

Dressed in a dapper suit, with his grey hair brushing his shoulders, Bowles was in fine fettle when I met him at a pub near Brentford's Griffin Park in the mid-2000s. In his playing days, the prodigiously gifted Bowles's most infamous scam was to pocket £200 from football boot manufacturers Gola (to whom he was contracted) and also trouser £250 when an adidas representative, touting for business, convinced Bowles to represent them. For England's match against Wales in 1974, Bowles circumnavigated the rules by wearing a boot from either company on his left and right foot.

A quarter of a century later, he was still side hustling. He'd recently received a ticking off from publishers Orion because, instead of saving his 'exclusive' stories for his forthcoming autobiography, he was also peddling them in his *FourFourTwo* magazine column. He was also getting phone calls from London Weekend Television.

Bowles had been one of the subjects in the *After They Were Famous* show and had led the show's producers to believe that he owned a successful tile shop: 'I convinced a mate of mine – who was happy about the free advertising – to make it look like I owned the shop on the show. LWT tried to reclaim the £300 fee they'd paid me. I told them it had vanished at the dog track.' Bowles's antics incurred the wrath of former QPR teammate Dave Thomas. In *FourFourTwo*, and in his autobiography, Bowles claimed that, when he was renting a house from Rangers chairman Jim Gregory, he sold a greenhouse to gardening fanatic Thomas for £100, pocketed the money and that Gregory never noticed. Thomas strongly denied Bowles's claim. But, aside from the fallout from his occasionally too-tall stories, retired life wasn't too bad for Bowles. His wife was helping him get his gambling under control (Bowles claimed to have lost around £250,000 over the years) and after-dinner speaking opportunities were popping up. In conversation, he alternated between confessional and wisecracking:

> Those evenings are like comfort food for fans from that era, but it wasn't always a picnic. A lot of '70s footballers were functioning alcoholics and gambling addicts. Still are. Useless husbands and fathers we were. Selfish. We were the first generation of footballers to have some disposable cash. Some of us disposed of the whole bloody lot...

Bowles lapsed into one of his long silences that occasionally punctuated our interview, his blue eyes looking into the distance, but his mood brightened considerably when the conversation turned to Queens Park Rangers and *Superstars*.

In the 1975–76 campaign, QPR enjoyed their best-ever season. The tone was set at Loftus Road on the opening day when Dave Sexton's team defeated eventual champions Liverpool 2–0. Captain

Gerry Francis scored a superb opening goal, following a sublime flick from Bowles and a one–two with forward Don Givens. Sexton, a keen observer of Dutch football, built a team which played fast, fluid football. 'He'd take off on a Sunday and watch all these teams in Holland,' Bowles explained. 'It was when they were playing total football, and it made an impression on Dave. At that time Rangers and Manchester United were the purest football sides around. Everyone else just kicked the shit out of each other.' Rangers remained unbeaten at Loftus Road all season. 'Playing football that year was a bloody joy,' Bowles explained. 'We just went out and played naturally, with no shits given.' Agonisingly, QPR lost out on the title by a single point. They ended the campaign by beating Leeds and were a point ahead of Liverpool, but Bob Paisley's side had one more game to play – away at Wolves, but not until ten days later because they were in the UEFA Cup final. 'We got herded into a TV studio to watch it, and they won 3–1. I went on the piss for three days solid.' But Bowles – in his oversized hooped shirt – was the most compelling sight in Division One that season. The catalyst for the majority of Rangers' attacks, Bowles waxed lyrical about 'the telepathic relationship on the pitch which I had with Gerry Francis'.

A goal from Stanley Bowles was always an *objet d'art*. In April 1976, with Rangers (seemingly) on the cusp of winning the title, Bowles ambled into the Middlesbrough box, feinted to curl the ball into the far corner of Jim Platt's net, before rifling it at the near post in a 4–0 win. 'I loved to trick goalkeepers, give them the eyes, and do the opposite of what they expected,' he reminisced. With Rangers at their counter-attacking best against Sunderland in October 1976, the insouciant Bowles seized a long Dave Thomas pass, shaped to curl the ball in with his favoured left foot, slipped it onto his right and fired the ball home. It was a perfect fusion of grace and precision finishing. 'I was always comfortable using either foot,' he recalled. 'The best players are.' Like several of his contemporaries,

I discovered that Bowles was a huge *Porridge* fan. 'I loved Fletch [played by Ronnie Barker] because he was always trying to get one over the screws, and he often beat the system. I identified with him.' Bowles got a couple of mentions on the back page of Fletch's copy of *The Sun*, which he said 'thrilled me to bits'. One read, 'Bowles in Flare Up'. 'That was when I had a set to with Alan Ball when we played Arsenal. Always snapping at my bloody heels, he was.'

In the 1976 close season, Bowles, after refusing to go on tour to Israel (he didn't like flying) received the offer to participate in *Superstars*. As usual, his agreement was driven by a need to get his hands on ready cash, as he was having 'issues with bailiffs at the time'. However, Bowles's track record with high-profile media stunts had been appalling – posing with topless model Jenny Clarke in the *Mirror* earlier that year had convinced his first wife to leave him. He lost a small fortune when he invested in a greyhound that he ended up promptly selling after he discovered he 'could run faster than the dog'. But *Superstars* was his most infamous public own goal.

The BBC forwarded him a £500 appearance fee, and he trousered another £500 from QPR after convincing chairman Jim Gregory that the BBC money hadn't been forthcoming. With his friend and teammate Don Shanks in tow, Bowles drank heavily at the competitors' hotel the night before filming began: 'When James Hunt – who liked the high life – headed off to bed at 9.30 for an early night, I should have followed suit, but I was my own worst enemy.' Bowles was looking forward to taking on Malcolm Macdonald, who had been in equally fine form for Newcastle. In February 1976, during an explosive FA Cup fifth-round tie against Bolton at Burnden Park, which ended 3–3, he netted arguably his best ever televised goal. From a Tommy Craig throw, Macdonald swivelled and shot in one movement after the ball bounced, volleying home from 35 yards. 'It was one of the most incredible things I ever saw on a football pitch,' explained commentator Barry Davies. 'A goal of power and beauty. Pure Macdonald. It almost broke the back of the net.' But Macdonald and Bowles didn't hit it off during *Superstars*. 'All that Supermac stuff, what a load of crap,' Bowles said. I pointed out to Bowles that the Supermac moniker was one that Macdonald never much cared for, in fact. 'Hmmm,' he harrumphed, 'well, he was always shouting his mouth off, anyway.' When QPR played Newcastle in April 1976, Bowles scored a last-minute winner and promptly ran over to Macdonald, shouting, 'How do you like that?' in his rival's face. 'He'd said in the press that Newcastle would derail our title challenge. So I let him have it.' Bowles claimed.

Bowles admitted that he was 'too weedy and pasty to be a Superstar', and that he'd displayed poor judgement by agreeing to appear in the first place. After the debacle in his canoe, when the floundering Bowles torpedoed Macdonald's chances in the race, he pulled a back muscle in the third event, which was weightlifting, and lost to squash champion Jonah Barrington in the first round of the tennis. In the pistol shooting he accidentally shot a hole in the table his gun was resting on, much to the hilarity of his fellow contestants. 'For a split second, I thought I'd shot my bloody foot off,' Bowles described. 'I'd heard that as a lad in Manchester, Stan hung around with the notorious Quality Street gang running errands for them – but it seems they never taught him to handle a gun properly,' David Vine laughed. Vine remembered that at the end of the first day of the tournament, one of the other competitors produced a football and, after throwing it to Bowles, 'they were treated to an astonishing juggling display as Stan showed off all his skills and tricks. It was like he came alive with a ball at his feet.' But not, alas, in any of the other events on *Superstars*. Bowles held off the challenge of

Welsh rugby star J. P. R. Williams to finish third (out of four athletes) in the swimming – thereby nabbing four points – ducked
out of the gym test (which included parallel bars dips and squat
thrusts) and had the satisfaction of beating Malcolm Macdonald
in the steeplechase. Finishing second-last in the race failed to grab
Bowles any more points, and so he ended on a historic low of seven
points.

A few weeks later, Macdonald signed for Arsenal, informing the
gathered journalists that he'd score thirty goals for the Gunners
that season. He was almost as good as his word, netting twenty-nine times. As Arsenal prepared to face QPR in October 1976 at
Highbury, *SHOOT!* brought Bowles and Macdonald together for a
'Cross Talk' piece. The mood was tense. 'Frankly, in the skill stakes,
I believe you are one of the most talented footballers in the game.
But I question your consistency,' Macdonald said. 'By the same
token, I've never denied you are a first-rate goal scorer. Your record
speaks for itself. But I question your level of ball skills,' Bowles responded. Ironically, Don Revie had long since harboured similar
doubts about the relative merits of both players.

———

As a public relations exercise at least, Don Revie's decision to invite
seventy-nine current and potential England players to an overnight
get-together at the Manchester Piccadilly Hotel in September 1974
had been a shrewd one. By 'reaching out' to such a large talent pool,
the ex-Leeds boss showed that whoever they played for, they were
all part of his grand design. Revie wished to set out his vision for
the future and delivered a call-to-arms speech to his new charges.
Stan Bowles was unimpressed by what he saw: 'I didn't recognise
some of the players there. At best, there were on average a couple of
international-quality players at each club.' Not all in the press pack

were pleased to see Bowles invited to the gathering. Four months previously, Bowles walked out of the England camp when caretaker manager Joe Mercer substituted him at half-time during a Home Internationals match with Northern Ireland; Bowles headed straight to White City dog track. In his *Sunday People* column, Mike Langley insisted that 'peevish, petulant' Bowles 'symbolised nearly everything that mature spectators regard as wrong with the modern game'.

Revie insisted that when it came to Bowles and England, he would let bygones be bygones, but, at that initial gathering, the QPR star did what he did best: he engaged his mouth before his brain. Revie informed the players that although the basic fee for an England appearance would remain at £100, they would now also receive £100 for a draw and £200 for a win. Liverpool defender Emlyn Hughes piped up, 'I don't need money to play for my country, Mr Revie.' There was an uncomfortable silence in the room, until Bowles chimed, 'If you don't want it, Emlyn, I'll happily take it off your hands.' As the room dissolved into fits of schoolboy sniggering, Bowles described how Revie looked 'daggers' both at him and Hughes, 'In our different ways, we'd pissed on his parade.' As Hughes recalled, 'I should have kept my mouth shut. Revie looked at me as if to say: "You little shit stirrer." And although he played me at first, he left me out for eighteen months when I was playing my best football for Liverpool.'

Following victory over Czechoslovakia in his opening game, and a draw against Portugal in his second (both European Championships qualifiers), Revie set his sights on the prestige international friendly against World Cup winners West Germany at Wembley in March 1975. Although Revie didn't include Bowles in his squad, he selected Macdonald – who'd made his England bow under Alf Ramsey – for the first time. When Macdonald reported to the team hotel in Hertfordshire, he walked into the lobby and spotted a stern-looking Revie sat in armchair. 'No injuries to report, boss,' smiled Macdonald. Revie glared back and informed Super-mac, 'You'll be playing against the Germans, but the only reason is because the press want you in the team. I don't. Fail to score and I won't pick you again.' Macdonald believed the source of Revie's frosty reception may have stemmed from the winning goal that he'd scored for Newcastle against Leeds in April 1972, which ultimately cost Leeds the title.

Macdonald scored with a close-range header in the 2–0 win over West Germany, but Revie pointedly refused to shake his hand afterwards. Informing Macdonald that he would play in the European Championships qualifier against Cyprus, Revie remarked, 'Well, I can't drop you now, can I?', but he also repeated that if Macdonald failed to find the net he would never again be picked for England. Macdonald plundered all five goals in a 5–0 victory over the Cypriots, with Alan Ball instructing teammates to tee-up the forward whenever possible. 'Congratulations – Supermac 5 Cyprus 0' read the electronic scoreboard. After the match, Macdonald detected that the journalists were a little frosty when they interviewed him, despite him breaking the record. He later discovered that Revie had demanded £200 in notes from Fleet Street's finest for access to Macdonald and pocketed the money. Revie remained unconvinced that Macdonald was international class, informing Newcastle manager Joe Harvey (although not the player himself) that his ability to bring teammates into play was limited. At the hub of England's midfield against West Germany was Colin Bell, Alan Ball and Stoke City's Alan Hudson, winning his first cap. An uncharacteristically effusive Revie even suggested that the trio 'could operate at the hub of England's midfield at the 1978 World Cup'. By some distance, Hudson was the standout performer on the night. Bell had scored a scrappy opener, but for different reasons, this was the only occasion upon which the three played together.

Prior to the 1975 Home International tournament, Revie had told his 22-man squad that he'd got the appearance fee increased from £100 to £200. Ball, the last of the boys of '66, spoke out against the need for the extra renumeration: 'I told him that playing for England was purely about the three lions on the shirt, not an extra £100. Revie wasn't impressed. Me and Emlyn Hughes, eh? The two mouthy falsettos,' said Ball. 'Revie looked utterly deflated. To be put in his place by the only survivor from '66 was humiliating,' explained Malcolm Macdonald, who looked on as Ball spoke out. By May 1975, Ball was cast out permanently by Revie, and Macdonald jettisoned soon afterwards. Six months later, Colin Bell's knee was wrecked in a tackle by Manchester United defender Martin Buchan in a League Cup clash, and, despite his Herculean attempts to regain fitness, he never played for England again. 'Colin Bell's injury was a tragedy – both for him and for England,' recalled Alan Ball. 'He was the complete midfielder and suddenly he was no longer on the scene.' Hudson played against Cyprus before being, like Ball, frozen out. 'I wasn't his kind of player or his kind of man,' Hudson explained. Through a combination of his own stubbornness and pure bad luck, Revie's midfield options were seriously depleted. The lack of variety, pace and big-game experience in the centre of the park proved to be his undoing, and, after a crucial European Championships qualifier loss to eventual tournament winners Czechoslovakia in Bratislava, England failed to reach the 1976 finals.

———

With only the group winners granted passage to the 1978 World Cup finals, Revie acknowledged that chalking up goals in England's opening two group fixtures (the other group members were Italy and Luxembourg) against the part-timers from Finland might eventually prove crucial. His side ran out easy 4–1 winners in Helsinki but almost choked at Wembley, scrambling home 2–1.

England headed to Rome in November 1976 for the crunch match with Italy. It was a match England simply couldn't afford to lose, but, from the outset, the presence in midfield of defenders Brian Greenhoff and Trevor Cherry was never going to be sufficient to prise open the Italian defence. Revie brought Stan Bowles in from the cold, hoping that the QPR man's impish skills would disrupt Enzo Bearzot's side's intimidating backline. Bowles – who played alongside Kevin Keegan and Mick Channon up front, recalled, 'Revie was shaking before the game and was sweating – literally sweating – with nerves. By the time he'd given the squad his encyclopaedic knowledge of the Italian players' strengths, he'd built them up to be superheroes.' Bearzot and his coaching staff had done their homework and selected Claudio Gentile to follow Bowles around the park and mark him out of the game. 'I never got a kick,' Bowles admitted. 'Gentile used all the tricks – elbows, sly kicks, you name it – to snuff me out, but he was also a fantastic player with a marvellous first touch.' Goals from Giancarlo Antognoni and Roberto Bettega consigned Revie's men to a 2–0 defeat.

After the Rome clash, the press was largely sympathetic towards Bowles, though not towards Revie or the general state of English football. In the *Sunday Times*, Brian Glanville wrote, 'The most alarming feature of the English defeat was that this was probably the best, or the least bad, team that Revie could have put out. This meant, inevitably, that Stan Bowles had to be integrated within ninety minutes into a team which knew him not.' In mitigation, Bowles had little interest in integrating himself into Revie's way of doing things. The forensic dossiers prepared by Revie's coaching staff, which analysed the strengths and weaknesses of the opposition, ended up being used as score cards during card games, and, like many of his teammates, Bowles detested carpet bowls and bingo. 'Stan wasn't one for team bonding,' Kevin Keegan noted in his autobiography. Liverpool team mate Emlyn Hughes, who was recalled for the Italy game after an eighteen-month absence, took a harsh view on Bowles, telling me,

> Stan had more skill in his little finger than I had in my whole body. But if you want to win, you've got to work hard, apply yourself and be professional. Stan had his chances for England and didn't deliver. So perhaps, for all his bravado, he wasn't as good as he thought he was.

Bowles was given one more chance in an England shirt when he played in a 1977 friendly against Holland at Wembley. At half-time England were 2–0 down to a brace of Jan Peters goals, and Revie implored his troops, 'For God's sake – you're at Wembley. Show some passion.' But England's stodgy approach work against the World Cup runners-up – in marked contrast with the fluent passing of Johan Cruyff, Johan Neeskens and co. – showed what they'd become under Revie: second-rate. Bowles was perhaps the most accomplished England performer that night, but that was cold comfort.

Ultimately, England missed out on qualification for the 1978 World Cup on goal difference, and failure to put more than two goals past Luxembourg cost them dear. They defeated Italy 2–0 at Wembley, but it was too late, and, by then, caretaker manager Ron Greenwood was in charge of the team, following Revie's shock resignation in July 1977. Revie had prevaricated about which tactical system to deploy for England and threw caps around like confetti as he searched in vain for the right blend. But he was clear on one thing at least. At an England get-together in spring 1977, he pulled Frank Worthington, Alan Hudson, Stan Bowles and Tony Currie aside, informing them brusquely that they would no longer be considered for selection. Quite simply, the long-haired loafers weren't to Revie's taste. 'He only picked us because he felt pressured into doing so. It wasn't a surprise,' said Bowles. Derby County's Charlie George, enjoying a new lease of life at the Baseball Ground, wasn't at the gathering at all. After playing the right-footed George on the left side of midfield in a friendly against Ireland for his international debut, and substituting him on the hour, Revie shook George by the hand and asked if he wanted to sit on the bench or have a bath. 'Fuck you,' came George's measured response. No further olive branches were offered. The system had won, even if Revie's England hadn't. England's rebellious entertainers had always taken delight in rejecting authority but now, in no uncertain terms, football's ultimate authority figure had rejected them. As Macdonald reflected on Revie's time as England coach, 'At Leeds, he'd known many of the players since they were teenagers, and [he] was able to be the father figure. With England, he saw the players more rarely. They weren't his sons. The dynamics and the relationships were different.'

Following his move to Arsenal, Macdonald plundered goals aplenty in N5 until knee injuries ended his career in 1979, but despite several London-based newspaper campaigns, he never featured again for his country. He appeared on *Superstars* once again in 1977, but never received the £500 that Bowles owed him after the pair struck a bet before the 1976–77 season for who would score most league goals. Despite Macdonald being comfortably in the lead, when Bowles broke his ankle in April 1977 and was laid off for the rest of the season, the QPR man declared the bet null and void.

For Bowles, there was to be no second bite of the *Superstars* cherry. As he packed up to leave the competitors' hotel in 1976, he recalled, 'I said to the bird who was overseeing the event that I'd try to do better next time. She looked me sternly in the eye and said, "There won't be a next time, Mr Bowles."'

I look back on the afternoon I spent with Bowles with a mixture of fondness and sadness. The once gregarious Stan the Man, whose tales of the unexpected are tightly woven into the fabric of English football, now lives in full-time care, having suffered from dementia for several years. His memories have slipped away, and his once piercing gaze is now just a thousand-yard stare. I'm thankful that I got to meet him at his bullish best.

Preparing to take his leave of me and our pub on a chilly London night, he put on his coat and shook his head: 'I try not to dwell on things, but I still don't understand why Revie disliked me so much.' Perhaps, I ventured, it had something to do with his dislike of dossiers, curfews and carpet bowls? 'Boring, boring, boring. No wonder England during that era were so crap,' he remarked as he screwed up his face.

At least *Superstars* provided some light relief.

18

THE HOOLIGANS

'To travel to and from matches is to run the gauntlet with these packs
of marauding fiends as they terrorise the community at large.'
The Times, 1 September 1975

Anfield, 25 February 1978. Almost 50,000 supporters cram inside
Anfield to watch the latest instalment of the Liverpool v. Manchester United soap opera. On all four sides of the ground, fans are
behind the red steel cages that were erected during the close
season. Around 6,000 travelling United fans are wedged into the
left-hand corner of the Anfield Road terrace. Red Devils supporter
Peter Brookes – then seventeen – remembered the atmosphere well:
'Toxic, as always. Police would herd United fans to Anfield from the
station or the coach. Outside the ground, women pushing prams
would flick their Vs at you. There was all kinds of verbal abuse
and threats.' Early in the first half, objects start flying over into the
United section: golf balls, coins and stones. Something hits Brookes
on the nose. 'At first I thought it was a coin,' he recalled. 'But then I
noticed that my vision was partly obscured because – as I realised
– a dart had embedded itself in my nose and was sticking across
it.' Brookes makes his way down to the first-aiders, who look at him
aghast. With his arms around the shoulders of an ambulanceman

and a policeman, Brookes is carried away and a *Mail* photographer snaps the stricken United fan, with the caged supporters as a backdrop. It remains the most shocking of all '70s football images. The photograph features prominently in most of the Sunday papers, and creates waves abroad. *L'Equipe* prints it, asking 'English football – how has it come to this?' Despite the best efforts of sociologists, journalists, politicians, documentary-makers and key figures within the game, there are no clear answers.

———

For want of a better word, the '70s are often seen as the 'heyday' of hooliganism, thanks in part to copious numbers of veteran troublemakers' memoirs, which continue to fly off the shelves in huge numbers. The 'kick lit' churned out by – amongst others – Chelsea fan Martin King (*Hoolifan*) and Arsenal supporter Colin Ward (*Steaming In*) paint a brutal picture of football in the era. Increasingly ramshackle stadia resembled war zones. The streets surrounding the grounds and the 'football specials', which criss-crossed the country and ferried supporters to games, teemed with hooligans running amok. It was often suggested that much of the violence was tribal and territorial, and that the participants did it of their own volition. That's rather wide of the mark. When the likes of Leeds United and Manchester United headed to town, terrified locals battened down the hatches, boarding up shops, businesses and pubs, and sought sanctuary indoors as if a typhoon were about to blast through town.

A raft of innocent bystanders – like Peter Brookes – were caught in the crossfire.

After I was taken to the ambulance, I saw a Liverpool fan who'd been hit by a brick. He was covered in blood and was in a far worse state than me. At the hospital, a doctor tried to pull out the dart but my head kept moving with it. In the end, four people had to heave it out. Two held my head and two other pulled the dart out. It was one of those '70s pub darts with a long tip and it went through the cartilage on both sides of my nose. I never found out who threw it. There might have been some toing and froing with it between both sets of fans. When people first saw the photo, I think many thought it had gone into my eye, but there wasn't any lasting damage to my nose.

For roughly a fortnight, Brookes became a celebrity, receiving a sack full of fan mail, including around £100 in cash, a marriage proposal and countless letters of sympathy – some from Liverpool fans.

On the Sunday morning, my photo was on the front of most newspapers. I did an interview for *Today* on Radio 4 and still got royalty cheques for £12 a few years later. I got a letter from a lady in Oldham who sent me £20. We even exchanged Christmas cards and, years later, her daughter asked if I could meet her mum as she was terminally ill in hospital. I went with my dad and it was a very moving experience, although the hero-worship element was a little odd. Once a year, or more, I get interviewed about what happened. Last year, it was by Norwegian TV. The image still resonates.

Although hooliganism moved to another level entirely in the '70s, its roots were planted firmly in the previous decade. Sports Minister Denis Howell commissioned British psychiatrist John Harrington to complete a 1968 report into hooliganism, in what amounted to the first serious attempt to probe the issue. Data was collected from clubs (only nine out the twenty-two First Division clubs responded), the police, transport officers and supporters

– the opinion of whom was obtained via the unlikely medium of *The Sun*. The Harrington Report honed in on the 'immaturity' and 'loss of control' of groups of fans, ignoring wider social issues. A year later, a working party chaired by Sir John Lang, vice-chairman of the Sports Council, recommended 'offenders having to report on subsequent match days at a place and time away from the ground' and advocated 'extra seating in stadia to improve crowd behaviour'. The Lang Report was the first to seek solutions to a problem which, at that time, wasn't even clearly defined. But its conclusions lacked depth. One part stated, 'There can be no doubt that the consumption of alcohol is an important factor in crowd misbehaviour', without any evidence being provided about the extent of drinking behaviour amongst crowds.

The notorious 'Battle of Flitwick' in August 1969 gave a clear insight into the nature of the growing problem. After watching their team suffer a 5–0 shellacking at the hands of Derby County, around 500 Tottenham fans went berserk on the train bringing them home, smashing toilets, ripping up seats and, most dangerously of all, pulling the communication cord repeatedly. The driver brought the train to a juddering halt in the quaint Bedfordshire village of Flitwick and, after the police turfed them off the train, the hooligans rampaged through the village, whilst locals, many of whom had been enjoying a cheese and wine evening in the local village hall, sought refuge. 'It was like the bloody Vikings had arrived', explained local MP Stephen Hastings. Cheap fares on the 'football specials' meant that an increasing number of away fans travelled to matches in large groups. Outbursts of violence at grounds saw segregation become more rigorous after the FA advised clubs to introduced fenced 'pens'. A 'them and us' atmosphere at football proliferated. The ante was well and truly upped. As the '70s dawned, the battle lines were drawn.

Since the mid-1960s, Manchester United's hooligan problems had worsened. In February 1971, during a home match with Newcastle, United fans threw various objects at opposing fans, including a knife. As a punishment, United were forced to play their opening two matches of the 1971–72 season at neutral venues: Anfield and Stoke City's Victoria Ground. On a truly jarring Friday night in August, United fans twirled their scarves around their heads, sang 'United!' at top volume and stood on the Anfield Kop to watch the 'home' team take on reigning champions Arsenal. Designed to be a deterrent for hooliganism, the match inadvertently provided a blueprint for much of the trouble that blighted the '70s. Outside Anfield, *The Times* reported that 'a mob of 600 Liverpool skinheads' – keen to protect their territory – confronted United fans and police with dogs had to disperse them, before they 'rampaged' through nearby streets.

As United and Arsenal prepared to kick off, *The Times* reported how 'thousands of stupid young United supporters' charged across the pitch, sweeping past police and officials, in an attempt to get to the Arsenal fans at the other end. It was an early sign that, for some, the purpose of travelling away was as much about taking an opponent's end as watching one's team go on the road and potentially grab two points, which United did courtesy of goals from Alan Gowling, Bobby Charlton and Brian Kidd in a 3–1 'home' win. Although some United fans were ejected, none were arrested and they quickly retreated back to the Kop for the start of the game.

As a result of events at Elland Road on 13 April 1971, Leeds United were also forced to play the first four home matches of the 1971–72 campaign outside the city. Referee Ray Tinkler's decision to allow West Bromwich Albion striker Jeff Astle's controversial goal to stand saw irate supporters pour onto the pitch to protest at the injustice and furious Leeds players surround Tinkler. Police came onto the pitch to help restore order. Afterwards, chairman Percy Woodward excused the scenes, claiming there was 'every justification' for the anger. His comments didn't go down well with the local police: 'The problem of keeping soccer violence in check is difficult enough without the impression being given that crowds have a right in protesting violently against an unpopular decision.' Leeds were fined £500 by the FA and Woodward censured for his comments. On top of that, attendances at those four matches away from Leeds were significantly below what they would have been had they been played at Elland Road, which left Leeds significantly out of pocket. They also had to recompense Wolves, Tottenham, Newcastle and Crystal Palace due to the loss of their share of the gate. Manchester United had to do likewise to Arsenal and West Brom because the respective 27,649 and 23,146 gates were significantly down on the Old Trafford average of 47,000. 'A stigma is now attached to our club,' mourned United general manager Matt Busby, whilst Don Revie accepted that being exiled from Elland Road 'reflect[ed] poorly on Leeds'. But if either Revie or Busby believed that being temporarily evicted from their grounds would curb their clubs' growing hooligan problems, they were gravely mistaken.

Following the United v. Arsenal clash at Anfield, the FA's Andrew Stephen noted, 'We have tried to find an answer to this problem and I must admit that we are baffled to know what else we can do.' Tabloids poured fuel on the fire. In a misguided attempt to shame hooligans they published photographs of fans being dragged away by the police at the United v. Arsenal clash at Anfield. These scenes would be repeated multiple times throughout the decade. The *Daily Mirror* introduced a 'League of Violence', ranking cases of hooliganism by club (by May 1974 United were in top spot, named as 'the team whose visit is most dreaded') and the *Daily Mail* followed suit with the 'Thugs' League'. The 'firms' revelled in the exposure.

The problems at Manchester United worsened. Fans swarmed onto the Old Trafford pitch after Denis Law scored the winner for Manchester City in May 1974, the day on which United's relegation to Division Two was confirmed. Players were taken off the field, temporarily, but after a mass invasion three minutes before the final whistle, the match was abandoned. Reaction was mixed. United chairman Louis Edwards defended his fans. 'This was not a riot,' he insisted. 'There was a 57,000 crowd and a lot of noise with everyone whistling for the end of the game. It was a matter of excitable youngsters rather than malicious thugs.' Tabloids disagreed, with the *Mirror* screaming, 'FENCE IN THE LOUTS!' By the start of the 1974–75 campaign, United fans watched matches on the Stretford End from behind a high metal fence. The 'animals' – as they were often described – were caged in. The travelling United fans, frequently outnumbering home supporters, laid waste to Bristol and Cardiff city centres as they followed Tommy Docherty's exciting young team around the country. 'What followed over the next nine months ... was probably the greatest period of off the field anarchy in the history of any football club,' author Richard Kurt wrote in his *The Red Army Years: Manchester United in the 1970s*.

By the mid-1970s, new depths were plumbed with depressing regularity. Seventeen-year-old Kevin Olsson became the first victim of hooliganism inside a stadium when he was fatally stabbed during clashes between Blackpool and Bolton fans in August 1974 at Bloomfield Road. An ashen-faced Sports Minister Dennis Howell visited the scene of the murder during the following week and mooted the possibility of the government introducing identity cards for all football supporters. Blackpool introduced segregation for fans on their Kop and fenced them in with immediate effect.

A plaque was unveiled by the Blackpool Supporters' Association in 2009 at the part of the rebuilt ground that replaced the former Spion Kop where Kevin Olsson was killed. A few months earlier, as Tottenham travelled to Rotterdam for the second leg of the UEFA Cup final against Feyenoord, twenty-one English fans were arrested for looting a clothes shop and an off-licence, and, over the stadium's public address system, Spurs director Sidney Wale pleaded for order inside the ground: 'You hooligans are a disgrace to Tottenham and England. This is a football game not a war.' But a riot ensued for twenty minutes, with 100 Dutch police needed to quell the chaos. 'This is the saddest day of my life. It makes you wonder if it is all worth it when you see people behaving like animals,' manager Bill Nicholson lamented afterwards. The year after, Leeds United reached the European Cup final, playing Bayern Munich at the Parc des Princes in Paris. Leeds fans, enraged by the referee's questionable decisions, ripped up their seats and threw them at the riot police. UEFA banned Jimmy Armfield's team from all European competitions for four years, although this was later reduced to two. 'We are feeling quite depressed,' Armfield explained. 'It's all been made much worse by the behaviour of some of our supporters. We want nothing to do with them and wish they would stay away from the club and football.' His words fell on deaf ears.

When London clubs travelled north and Leeds, Manchester United or Liverpool headed south, it cost somewhere between £4 to £5 for the 'privilege' of bagging a return journey on one of the football specials laid on by British Rail. The names of various 'firms' originated from the trains they caught to get to games. Portsmouth's 6.57 Crew was named after the time the train left Portsmouth and Southsea station for London on matchday and West Ham's Inter City firm and the Leeds United Service Crew also associated themselves with the trains they laid waste to. Virtually without exception, football specials were the worst rolling stock that British Rail had to offer and travelling on them became a rite of passage for '70s fans.

The conditions on many of the trains were usually squalid. 'The toilets were always blocked or overflowing, which meant that the whole carriage stunk of piss,' explained Liverpool fan Pete Jessop.

It was pretty easy to smuggle on booze, although it was officially banned. You'd normally piss in cans or bottles if you couldn't access the toilet. Or out of the window. Seats got set fire to or thrown out of windows. Windows got smashed, either from inside the train or because rival supporters lay in wait as you approached the station and pelted the carriages with stones. You had to hit the floor sometimes. It was like something out of a bad Western. I never got why fans on the train would smash windows on the way up, because usually the same train would take you home. But people did it because they could. Who was going to stop them? The police left it to the guards on the train, and they left it to us to self-police. It was a bastion of lawlessness.

In an attempt to attract more upwardly mobile supporters to matches – and trains – a joint venture between the Football League and British Rail saw a hefty £250,000 spent on the League Liner, which made its maiden voyage in January 1973. For £1,000 a pop, clubs could hire the train (the press soon dubbed it the 'Rock and Roll Special'), which whisked fans and players to games in '70s opulence. 'It is packed with things to occupy the high-flying supporter,' wrote Alastair Wilson in the *Daily Express*. 'A 63ft-long discotheque with disc jockey studio at one end. A closed circuit television coach at the front. Two music coaches equipped with headphones. And for those who like it cool, nine first-class coaches with card tables.' Football League Secretary Alan Hardaker believed that the luxurious League Liner represented the future of football travel. 'If you treat football supporters like human beings, they will behave like human beings,' he argued. 'The added touch of luxury provided ... will encourage fans to bring their wives and families with them.'

The feedback was overwhelmingly positive, and even hard-bitten media hacks revelled in the experience. On the liner's maiden voyage, *Times* journalist Norman Fox travelled back to Lancashire with Burnley fans, who'd seen their top-of-the-table team beaten at Loftus Road by Queens Park Rangers. 'Their supporters took defeat really well,' Fox wrote. 'The League Liner waited to give them a jolly journey home, and they had dined on chicken and chips. It all cost £3.50 and two points which they could well afford.' But with the train grinding its way around the country, the plush interior soon faded, the service became blighted by delays and the gizmos and gadgets cost a fortune to maintain. Cash-strapped clubs decided it was a luxury they could ill afford, and by 1976 the League Liner had completed its final voyage.

———

Travelling to matches by train became pricier because, by September 1975, British Rail – desperate to rebuild their reputation as a modern transport provider – abruptly withdrew all cheap day return tickets on long-distance journeys that began before 3 p.m. on a Saturday. The railway's reputation had taken a real battering, and the last thing they wanted was hooligans smashing up their trains every weekend. The decision came in the wake of 200 people being arrested on the last Saturday of August at grounds (after Chelsea fans rioted at Luton Town's Kenilworth Road, during which the Hatters' goalkeeper was punched to the ground). A furious Denis Howell labelled football fans as 'madmen' and police reported that there had been more trouble on the trains that weekend than they'd experienced in the whole of the previous campaign. A week later, when British Rail fares went up, only two supporters were arrested, for fighting at Manchester's Navigation Road Station. 'It looks as though the action taken had a remarkably good effect. It's very promising for the future,' explained a British Rail official. The era of wanton destruction on the football specials may have been over, but fighting inside the grounds and in the surrounding streets carried on unabated.

In August 1976, with Britain enduring its driest summer in 200 years, Sports Minister Denis Howell – in his second spell in the post – saw his portfolio expanded when he was also appointed Minister for Drought by new Prime Minister James Callaghan. His brief was simple: to encourage the nation to save water, and to make it rain. Howell demurred from performing a rain dance, which Callaghan half-jokingly suggested he perform on behalf of the nation, but after taking questions from the press (he told them that he and wife Brenda shared baths to cut down on water use), the politician explained, 'It might be an easier job to make it rain again than end the scourge of football hooliganism.' Howell was right. In early September, the heavens finally opened (Howell was quickly appointed Minister of Floods) but the terrace tear-ups rumbled on.

Howell set up a committee in 1977, which met weekly in his office, including the principal officers of the Football Association and Football League: Sir Harold Thompson, Denis Follows, Lord Westwood and Alan Hardaker, together with the police, British Rail and coach operators. Clubs were instructed to 'prevent supporters from trespassing on to the playing area', which meant the erection of metal fences. Alcohol was banned on official supporters' club coaches, stops at pubs en route were banned and fans on those journeys were not allowed to arrive at grounds more than one hour before kick-off. Howell insisted that Manchester United and Chelsea away matches were made all-ticket in a bid to prevent rogue troublemakers rocking up to grounds on the day.

For some, Howell's measures didn't go far enough. Labour MP John Evans urged 'more fences and a ban on the sale of alcoholic drinks in or around grounds'. Conservative MP Michael Brotherton called for the use of corporal punishment on young offenders, a measure which had been endorsed by Manchester United boss Tommy Docherty. After crowd trouble erupted at Carrow Road during his side's loss to Norwich City in April 1977, Docherty attempted to calm the United supporters but was almost maimed as a roof tile, thrown by a member of the crowd, frisbeed its way past his head. When pressed on what he'd like done to football hooligans, he argued, 'I'd like to try the birch, and take it from there, but the authorities are afraid to do this.'

Michael Butterfield, chief executive of the National Association of Youth Clubs, despaired, arguing there was 'little hope of combating football hooliganism if all we can think of is punitive measures'. More enlightened solutions were thin on the ground, although, in his Birmingham Small Heath constituency, Denis Howell piloted a scheme where misbehaving fans who'd been turfed out of Birmingham City's St Andrews spent Saturday afternoons 'making good' and litter picking or volunteering in old people's homes. The carrot was that if they worked hard, they could earn their ticket back to St Andrews.

The period between June 1977 and April 1978 saw the media spotlight on hooliganism intensify. At the tail end of the 1976–77 season, Ally MacLeod's rejuvenated Scotland team journeyed south to Wembley and crushed the Auld Enemy 2–1 in a Home Internationals clash. Afterwards, thousands of kilt-clad Scots (including Rod Stewart, who was carried shoulder-high by Scottish fans) swarmed across Wembley's pitch, ripped out chunks of turf and snapped the crossbar.

In September 1977, Manchester United were turfed out of Europe following crowd trouble before, during and after their 1–1 draw away at French Cup winners Saint-Étienne. Following a mercy mission by director Matt Busby, United were reinstated, but the club was ordered to play the return leg at Plymouth Argyle's Home Park. 'We don't want these hooligans,' Busby said. 'I wish that we could fine them and throw them in the river.' Four months after Busby's eleventh-hour intervention for United, near neighbours Manchester City travelled to Elland Road for an FA Cup third-round clash. Midway through the second half, and with the home team 2–0 down, a pitch invasion by Leeds fans saw the players led off by referee Colin Seel, and mounted police enter the fray to cajole the Leeds fans back onto the terraces. 'This match will not be abandoned. I repeat. It will NOT be abandoned,' announced Seel over the loudspeaker. With the crowd quelled, City ran out 2–1 winners.

On the evening of 14 November 1977, the BBC broadcast a revelatory *Panorama* documentary called *F-Troop, Treatment & the Half-Way Line* about Millwall's three hierarchical hooligan firms. The Den – situated amidst scrapyards and tunnels and with tower blocks looming in the distance – was the perfect foreboding backdrop for an exposé on hooliganism. Millwall played in a part of London that had been heavily bombed and then rebuilt following the Second World War and the area had been repopulated by several waves of immigration. 'The area had been through the ringer – blown up, torn up and roughly put back together,' explained Millwall boss Gordon Jago. Millwall fans had a reputation both for loyalty and abrasiveness in equal measure. Four months after *Panorama*, it would be temporarily shut by the Football Association after Millwall supporters invaded the pitch during an FA Cup quarter-final game with Ipswich.

Broadcast at 8.10, following an episode of *Are You Being Served?*, the documentary contained a warning about 'language you don't usually hear on television'. Viewers may have tittered about the double entendres flying around the ladies' and gentlemen's clothing department at Grace Brothers, but there was nothing equivocal about the uncensored stories of terrace battles recounted by hardened Millwall hooligans in the programme. 'A good game of football, a good punch-up and a good piss-up. That's all about Millwall,' boasted Harry the Dog. Harry was the top boy with Millwall's F-Troop, whom reporter David Taylor described as 'the real nutters'. Then there was Treatment, who wore surgical masks on the terraces. They didn't pick fights, 'but are always there when they happen', Taylor informed viewers. The Half-Way Line (named after their favourite spot at the Den) 'imitate their elders'.

The hooligans' monikers were cartoonish, and their '70s clobber and haircuts now afford the documentary an 'otherworldly' status. As well as Harry the Dog, characters with names such as Mad Pat, Bobby the Wolf and Winkle all featured. Some elements of the documentary were tragi-comic. Mick Harris, a 27-year-old caretaker at an experimental playgroup, explained that he jilted his fiancée Lorraine (a Chelsea fan) so he could go rucking for Millwall, and F-Troop's coach broke down on the way to a match at Bristol Rovers, meaning that top boys like Harry the Dog had to hitchhike the rest of the way there. But there was nothing remotely amusing about Bobby the Wolf remarking, 'I won't take it from a northerner … I'm not going away for some dirty northern ponce to spit all over me. If he spits over me, I'll put a fucking pint glass in his head.' Harry the Dog insisted, 'If I wasn't a Millwall fan I wouldn't go down the Den. They're fucking mad. Everyone carries a tool.' These were real-life hoodlums, revelling in their notoriety.

The most insightful segments in the documentary were David Taylor's conversations with the frizzy-haired, bespectacled 21-year-old Billy Plummer. Plummer left school at thirteen, made ends meet by doing odd jobs (for example, painting houses in Deptford), referred to a violent father and a stepfather who was in prison, and was honest about his limited horizons. 'I've never had a chance to fulfil my ambitions. If I have any ambitions, I don't know what they are.' Plummer argued that he'd been brought up on 'street fighting', and that fighting for Millwall gave him a purpose in life: 'Just as long as I've got enough money to go and see Millwall, that does me.' Plummer was open about the fact he owed £300 in fines for hooliganism and that he was 'happy to do time' to avoid paying them. Denis Howell was incensed about the *Panorama* documentary, describing it as 'glorifying violence', but later admitted that it was 'certainly eye-opening.' In fact, Plummer's soundbites, encompassing a raft of subjects including territorialism, regionalism, urban decay, a lack of male role models in young men's lives and an increasingly disenfranchised working class cocking a snook at 'outsiders', were a composite of the explanations that were made for football hooliganism by social scientists.

Plummer later regretted his contributions to *Panorama*, insisting that it 'was edited to make us look like knuckle scrapers'. Millwall FC took umbrage, arguing that the documentary overlooked 'the positive ways in which Millwall contribute to the local community', which included open days for fans and Sunday markets outside the ground. The tail end of the programme showed some of Millwall's hooligans meeting manager Gordon Jago on one of the open days, who told them that the fans' reputation was costing the club thousands of pounds because away supporters were reluctant to travel to the Den. Billy Plummer insisted that the TV exposure upped the ante at matches even further. 'Some revelled in it. It created faces. It sent out the message that you could get famous – or infamous – from hooliganism. It became its own little industry from that point on. Some "faces" from the '70s have made a living from books and films, but not Millwall fans,' he told me. Several of Millwall's main protagonists in the documentary became targets for rival fans and suffered severe beatings as a result. Both Billy Plummer and Harry the Dog subsequently died in tragic circumstances – albeit unrelated to football violence.

Rightly or wrongly, the dystopian *F-Troop, Treatment & the Half-Way Line* – acted out on the grim and windswept terraces of the era – shaped Millwall's reputation for violence in the public consciousness during the decades that followed. The stark *Panorama* exposé remains a disturbing period piece. It pushed the issue of football hooliganism into the open and made football authorities confront it. But the 'English disease' – as it would come to be known in the 1980s – would only become more virulent.

19

THE BLACK PIONEERS

THE 'STYLISTICS'

=====

'We'd had all the abuse and everything else you can imagine thrown
at us at non-league level, so why not at least get paid for it?'
Phil Walker

Thames Television Studios, October 1975. 'The arrival of Phil
Walker and Trevor Lee at Third Division Millwall is further evidence
that the sight of coloured players in London football is becoming
more common,' explains *Today* presenter Bill Grundy in jarring,
archetypal '70s language. The fact that Lee – alongside manager Gordon Jago – is signing for Millwall in front of TV cameras
demonstrates just how newsworthy the pair's signing is. Receiving
treatment for an injury, Walker is indisposed, so it's left to Lee, a
pacey right-winger, to cite West Ham's Bermudian star Clyde Best
as his role model and vow to 'give it everything I've got at Millwall'.
For a combined £40,000 fee, Lee and Walker have joined from
Surrey side Epsom & Ewell, who had enjoyed a stellar 1974–75
campaign, even reaching the inaugural FA Vase Final at Wembley,
where they lost to Hoddesdon Town. Lee, who'd received only travel
expenses from Epsom & Ewell, earned £150 per week labouring

on London's building sites and is 'delighted' with his princely £50 per week at Millwall. Walker was fired from his job as an electrician after his boss discovered that rather than turn up at work he'd been playing in the FA Vase final. He is grateful for the regular paycheque. At twenty-one, the lifelong friends – Londoners born and bred – are delighted to get a crack at professional football. By the end of the 1975–76 season, their impact will be so seismic, with the club gaining promotion to the Second Division, that influential black political activist Darcus Howe – editor of *Race Today* – pens an article labelling them the 'Stylistics of Millwall'.

⸻

By the mid-1970s, a smattering of black footballers were plying their trade in the capital. Brendon Batson made a handful of appearances for Arsenal before departing to Cambridge United, Ade Coker, Clive Charles and striker Clyde Best – who scored forty-six goals in an eight-year spell at Upton Park – played for West Ham and Bobby Fisher and Laurie Cunningham played for Orient. Apart from facing one other during matches, meetings between London's black players usually came about only by coincidence. Brendon Batson – still with Arsenal at that point – recalled sitting next to Clyde Best quite by chance at Brisbane Road to watch Laurie Cunningham turn out for Orient. 'Laurie was like a young matador,' Batson explained to me, 'beckoning defenders to tackle him as he stood on the touchline. He had such quick feet. Clyde and I loved his swagger and impudence.' As for the prejudice black players encountered, they faced it alone. 'It was our business,' said Trevor Lee. In 1970, Clyde Best received a letter warning him that acid would be thrown in his face as he left the tunnel for his next away game and the police took the threat seriously enough to form a cordon around him when he ran out of the tunnel. In December 1974 at the Den, various objects, including bananas and a carving knife, were thrown at Bobby Fisher and Laurie Cunningham during a Millwall v. Orient clash. At the final whistle, the pair made black power gestures at the barrackers. Paddington-born Dave Busby reassured a concerned newsagent, 'I've come to buy a newspaper, not to rob you,' when he played for Barrow, a town of few black faces, in the late '70s. Such stories weren't recorded at the time. The Best incident only came to light in his 2016 autobiography *The Acid Test*, and Busby spoke to authors Bill Hern and David Gleave in 2020 for their excellent *Football's Black Pioneers* book. Phil Walker and Trevor Lee were unaware of the altercation between Millwall fans and Fisher and Cunningham as they embarked on their professional careers at the Den.

Making their debuts against Mansfield in October 1975 at the Den, Walker scored the winner and Lee provided the assist. 'We were pitched straight in. Sink or swim. The winning debut helped us enormously,' Trevor Lee told me. By the time Lee netted his first goal against Rotherham later that month, Walker was injured once more, and, as he watched the team from the sidelines, he heard at close quarters how the language directed at Lee rapidly changed. Playing out wide as the team's creative foil, Lee was likely to incur the wrath of the notoriously vocal and demanding Millwall supporters if he didn't perform to the required standards. 'The crowd was encouraging, but you had to win them over. At first, they used the racial slang of the '70s to describe Trevor,' Phil Walker explained. 'But, very quickly, it was a case of "Give it to Lee!" "Go on Lee!" "Lee – do him!" Then it was just: "Give it to Trevor Lee!" Because he played so well, the supporters now called him by his full name. "Trevor Lee!" It was a sign of respect.'

The racist slang of the time that Walker was referring to was reinforced on popular TV sitcoms. On Thames Television's *Love Thy Neighbour*, which often drew 10 million-plus audiences, a West Indian couple – Bill and Barbie Reynolds – moved in next to a white working-class couple – Eddie and Joan Booth. Although the wives got on well, the two men took an instant dislike to one another, and threw racial insults one another's way. Football fans amplified the language that appeared in such shows.

In the early '70s, around 1 million Caribbean, Indian and Pakistani immigrants lived in Britain. More than half resided in London, and a high concentration of Caribbean immigrants, who'd responded to the British government's clarion call to fill employment vacancies, travelled across from the West Indies in the 1950s on vessels, such as HMT *Empire Windrush* and settled in the East End. In the midst of an economic downturn, there were protests from dockers and meat packers about keeping jobs 'white'. Housing associations teemed with racial tension, with some white tenants furious that lodgings were being 'taken' from them. The National Front was highly active in the East End, and the *Panorama* documentary *F-Troop, Treatment & the Halfway Line* showed a number of Millwall supporters bragging that they'd gone on National Front marches. The party's co-leader Martin Webster told presenter David Taylor, 'I think there's a lot you can do with the soccer hooligan … we feel that the very, very fanatical adulation by supporters for their particular clubs is a sort of sublimated patriotism.' 'So it's a case of Millwall today and National Front tomorrow?' asked Taylor. 'We hope so,' Webster responded. 'The club used to be called the Dockers, but the docks were closing. There were fewer jobs for the white working classes. Some blamed immigrants. People look for scapegoats in those circumstances,' Millwall fan Billy Plummer explained. I asked Plummer whether he believed Millwall fans in the '70s were – on the whole – racist. 'Some were. But I never saw them give any grief to [Trevor] Lee or [Phil] Walker. That would be ridiculous. If you're Millwall, you're Millwall. We look after our own.'

When he arrived at the ground for one of his first home matches, Trevor Lee was 'a little surprised' to have a National Front leaflet thrust into his hand. 'I couldn't work out what the fella's game was. Was he winding me up? I ripped up the leaflet in front of him and walked off,' he described. Phil Walker got a taste of the double standards that Millwall fans would sometimes apply. During a match at the Den, Walker chased Stoke City striker Garth Crooks to the byline:

> 'Phil, kick the black bastard,' the fans shouted. 'Phil, sort out the black bastard. Phil, break the darkie's fucking leg...' I couldn't be-lieve it – Garth Crooks was a 'black bastard', but I was still 'Phil'. It showed me that Millwall supporters would say anything to put opponents off their game.

Tactically, Lee and Walker were a perfect fit for Millwall, enabling Gordon Jago to inject some much-needed verve into the mix. Lee, whose blistering turn of speed and ability to swerve past his marker added flair to Millwall's attack, and the deep-lying Phil Walker's ability to pick out teammates with precision passes, earned them the immediate respect of their teammates. On top of that, they played a key role in Gordon Jago's attempts to give the club a much-needed makeover. Blocked in his attempt to rename the intimidating sounding Cold Blow Lane as the more exotic Montego Bay, Jago encouraged players to mix with the supporters as much as possible and foster an atmosphere of togetherness. On train trips home after away matches, Lee and Walker vacated their first-class carriage and – along with their teammates – mingled with supporters, often playing cards in second-class compartments. 'I think we met all of the high-profile supporters who appeared on *Panorama*: Harry the Dog and Billy Plummer too. I remember them,' recalled Trevor Lee.

> If you played your heart out, and didn't have airs and graces, they had your back. They may well have hated everything and

everyone outside Millwall, and given all kinds of abuse to visiting players, but on a personal level they were no different from many of the blokes whom I'd worked with on building sites ... plain speaking. Part of me wondered whether they were just playing up to the cameras on *Panorama*.

It was on those away trips that Walker and Lee discovered that being black and British in the '70s made them a target for some vicious abuse. 'We played away at Newcastle United in the League Cup in an evening game, and it was pretty bad,' Lee explained. 'Throughout the game, it was constant – the monkey chanting.' Was Lee ever tempted to respond, I asked him.

No. From an early age, my mum – she arrived from Jamaica in England in 1952 on the *De Grasse*, and was part of the Windrush generation – she told me never to respond to that kind of thing, not to dignify them with a response. I grew a pair of *cojones*, and took it with a pinch of salt.

'I ignored it. That's how we did things,' Phil Walker concurred. Not that Walker and Lee could have done much in any case. Although the Race Relations Act 1976 had been passed – which outlawed discrimination on the basis of 'colour, race, nationality or ethnic or national origins', a blind eye and a deaf ear was turned by the authorities and the media when it came to the racist abuse of black footballers. 'There was no support network. Teammates had our backs, but really, what could they do?' Trevor Lee reflected.

Millwall entered a rich vein of form after Christmas 1975, and stormed to promotion. Trevor Lee scored a stupendous overhead kick in a crucial 3–1 victory over Brighton to help nudge his team closer to promotion. Lee's spectacular goal was due, in part at least, to the intervention of TV hypnotist Romark – real name Ronald

Markham. After falling out with flamboyant Crystal Palace manager Malcolm Allison over the alleged non-payment of fees, Romark, who'd urged Palace players to live by the mantra of 'positive thinking', upped sticks, accepting Gordon Jago's offer to work with Millwall instead. 'So, Romark told me to visualise scoring a fantastic goal. He was a quirky character – shall we say,' recalled Lee, 'but I concentrated and visualised myself scoring a brilliant overhead kick. Then, in the Brighton game I actually went and did it. They had to stop Romark from invading the pitch, he was so excited.'

The media interest in Lee and Walker continued apace. 'It was crazy,' Lee explained. 'Barry Kitchener was a club legend, played over 500 games for Millwall, and never appeared on the *SHOOT!* Focus page – but there I am, declaring my love of Kojak, *Monty Python* and James Coburn!' The May 1976 Darcus Howe article in *Race Today* remains a testament to the impression the pair made – not just in the Third Division but on the wider community. Formerly known as Leighton Radford, Howe first came to national prominence in 1970 when, following repeated police raids on the Mangrove restaurant in Notting Hill, he was arrested along with eight others, accused of attempting to incite a riot. At the Mangrove Nine trial, a white jury acquitted all nine of the most serious charge. It was one of the first trials to acknowledge that the behaviour of the Metropolitan Police was motivated (in this case) by racial hatred rather than legitimate crowd control. Howe became editor of the influential and radical *Race Today* in 1973. In his piece on Lee and Walker, he wrote how they came from a community that had been 'severed from its roots in the Caribbean, without quite yet establishing the new. In these circumstances, adventure and creativity are given full rein.' Howe also wrote that individualism – in the Millwall duo's case – 'need not express itself at the expense of the collective'. The major impact that Walker and Lee made on the club 'represent[ed] a new dimension to our play', as teammate

Tony Hazell said, without which Millwall would not have achieved promotion.

The derivation of the 'Stylistics' nickname (after the Philadelphia soul band who'd charted hits on both sides of the Atlantic), which Howe claimed Millwall fans gave Lee and Walker during the 1975–76 season – is more unclear. Neither player has any recollection of being afforded the sobriquet by supporters. 'Darcus Howe coined it. Not the fans. It was a good title for the article, though', argued Trevor Lee, 'and it reflects the fact we'd brought something new and exciting to Millwall.'

Howe initially tried to make the article a little more hard-hitting. In a 2000 *New Statesman* piece, he wrote that as soon as he arrived at the Den to watch Walker and Lee, 'there were mumblings of "that fucking darkie", even from the better-behaved section of the crowd … a glimpse of cold steel, until I convinced a police officer to rescue me,' but he didn't refer to this episode in his *Race Today* piece. When Howe – who at the turn of this century argued that black players should walk off the pitch in protest if they suffered racist abuse from the crowd or fellow players – attempted to push Trevor Lee a little too forcefully during the interview with regards to racial politics, Lee's mother gave him short shrift. 'My mother told Darcus Howe that he wouldn't be using me to further his political career, and that he should leave,' Lee explained.

Despite efforts by Millwall down the years, the club's relationship with racism remains decidedly complex; but Phil Walker, who now runs a coaching school in south-east London, insisted, 'Whenever I go back to Millwall, I feel like I'm going home.' As Trevor Lee argued, 'The club and our teammates welcomed us with open arms. We enjoyed ourselves there.' Decades later, the pair remain crowd pleasers whenever they're guests on matchdays. Despite the fact that Trevor Lee emphasised to me that that they were 'just footballers', given that the pair thrived during such a fraught period in

English cultural history, and in such an unforgiving environment, they were rather more than that.

THE THREE DEGREES

'I thought that when I joined Cyrille and Laurie and West Brom that there would be safety in numbers. But the sight of three black men in the same team was too much for some. The volume of abuse only increased.'

Brendon Batson

After an unbeaten run of ten league games, West Bromwich Albion's virtuoso performance at Old Trafford during their 5–3 win on 3 December 1978 is extraordinary. A perfect fusion of pace, power, ingenuity and clinical finishing. But that's not the only reason the game will live long in the memory. The white noise emanating from the stands and terraces reaches a jeering crescendo whenever one of West Brom's three black players – Laurie Cunningham, Cyrille Regis and Brendon Batson – touch the ball. With Albion a goal down early on, winger Cunningham, lithe and alert, receives the ball on the left, darts infield, slips a pass through to Tony 'Bomber' Brown and the veteran forward fires home to equalise. The racist din that accompanies Cunningham's artistry is deafening. A minute later, Cunningham – booed mercilessly once more – leaves Manchester United's Steve Coppell and David McCreery for dead, slots a ball to Cyrille Regis and Regis's perfectly weighted backheel is fired home superbly by midfielder Len Cantello.

With the scores tied at 3–3, Cunningham latches on to a header from Regis, scorches through United's backline and slams the ball past goalkeeper Gary Bailey: 4–3. The catcallers are now sullen and silent. In the dying minutes, with dynamic midfielder Bryan

Robson controlling the middle of the park, Regis drills home Alistair Brown's sublime flick to give his side a dramatic 5–3 victory after another sumptuous Albion move. 'It was peak West Brom, and peak Laurie Cunningham,' insisted Cyrille Regis years later. More than any other football match in that era, it perfectly encapsulates the zeitgeist of the late '70s.

<hr />

Against a backdrop of rubbish-strewn streets, widespread disruption to food and petrol supplies and a raft of public-sector workers' strikes, Britain appeared to be in a state of near-paralysis. Power shortages, as frequent in the '70s as star-studded Hollywood disaster movies, were back with a vengeance. England's friendly at Wembley against Czechoslovakia in November 1978 appeared to be in serious doubt in the hours leading up to the game when the floodlights cut out, but the game went ahead, allowing Viv Anderson to become the first black player to represent England. Prime Minister James Callaghan, keen to avoid inflation, had refused to agree to the pay rises proposed by the unions, and the 'Winter of Discontent' – as the 1978–79 winter soon became known – held the country in its icy grip. Yet, somehow, with football clubs around the country in an increasingly glaciated state, West Brom's stirring brand of football was at its most fluid and fresh. 'We were at our very best that winter, and couldn't wait for the next match,' explained Brendon Batson during our 2021 interview. In February 1978, the Cambridge United right-back had joined the newly installed Albion manager (and Batson's former boss at Abbey Stadium) Ron Atkinson at the Hawthorns for £28,000. Batson – whom Atkinson nicknamed 'Batman' – linked up with burly striker Cyrille Regis, signed from non-league Hayes five months earlier, and the smooth winger Laurie Cunningham, whom player-manager Johnny Giles signed from Orient in 1977. Under Giles, Albion finished a creditable seventh in the 1976–77 season, a position which Atkinson bettered the following campaign. A sixth-place finish was enough to secure a UEFA Cup berth, and Albion also reached the FA Cup semi-final, where they were defeated by eventual winners Ipswich Town. The ultra-confident, perma-tanned Atkinson vowed that Albion would 'make people sit up and take notice in the 1978–79 campaign'.

'Many forget that Laurie, Cyrille and me were only teammates for fifteen months,' Brendon Batson explained. 'During that period, we never lost a match when the three of us played together.' The trio forged a close bond on their 1978 preseason tour of China, which featured on an episode of BBC's *The World About Us*. Thanks to Albion chairman and arch-football diplomat Bert Millichip pulling the strings behind the scenes, Atkinson's team was offered a rare glimpse inside a communist country. 'The sheer greyness of the place sticks with me,' explained Cyrille Regis. 'The buildings were grey, the skies were grey and the work clothes were grey. The stadiums that we played in had huge crowds but they were almost silent.' The tour is perhaps best remembered for an incident at the Great Wall of China, with young midfielder John Trewick telling a reporter, 'When you've seen one wall, you've seen them all.' 'It was meant as a deadpan joke, and John had a very dry sense of humour, but it didn't come across too well in print...' Brendon Batson argued. Batson, Cunningham and Regis got on famously. 'It was a gruelling tour and a little different from the usual golf and beer end-of-season bash in Spain,' said Regis. 'I think that Laurie, Brendon and I were perhaps open to different cultural experiences, given our different backgrounds.'

The 1978–79 Albion side was a superbly balanced outfit, fusing defensive acumen with attacking flair. Old warhorses like captain John Wile and goalscoring midfielder Tony Brown lent Albion much-needed know-how and Bryan Robson offered bite and industry in midfield. Up front, the power and sorcery from Regis and Cunningham gave Albion the sharpest of cutting edges. 'Each week, my players seem to reach new heights,' said a delighted Atkinson after watching his side thrash Coventry City 7–1 in October. Off the pitch, Albion created cultural waves which travelled well beyond the Midlands. Subbuteo makers produced a West Brom team that included three black figurines, and such was the attention to detail that one of these was given a moustache like Batson. Laurie Cunningham was interviewed by the *New Musical Express*. On the subject of the malevolent presence of the National Front at games, he argued, 'Those people have probably never met a black, you know.' Journalist Monty Smith wrote that although Cunningham was 'one of an exciting crop of black players currently rejuvenating our game', he was 'shy' and 'nervous' throughout the interview. Cunningham preferred to show his more expansive side in dance competitions (he won plenty in London nightclubs when he played for Orient), his fashion sense (with his penchant for hitting the town in 1920s-style double-breasted suits) and out on the football pitch.

From the outset, the prospect of the trio becoming venerated by the local community appeared remote. Attacks on Pakistani and Caribbean immigrants increased in the area and West Bromwich became increasingly dilapidated in the mid-1970s as factories closed and unemployment rose to around 20 per cent. In the May 1973 West Bromwich by-election, the National Front registered 16 per cent of the vote, with candidate Martin Webster promising to 'send back the coloured immigrants' if he won. Nearby, the Black Country constituency of Smethwick had, in 1964, sent Conservative Peter Griffiths to Westminster with Griffiths refusing to distance himself from the neo-Nazi British Movement's slogan, 'If you want a n****r for a neighbour, vote Labour.' Early on in their Albion careers, Cunningham showed Regis some racist graffiti scrawled on a wall near the Hawthorns. It read, 'Laurie Cunningham is a black cunt.' 'That graffiti was there for months and months,' Regis told me. 'No one made any effort to remove it.' I met with Regis in London in 2017. En route to deliver a speech on behalf of Kick It Out, football's equality and inclusion organisation, he argued, 'The battle against racism in football is still there to be fought. Perhaps the mass booing of black players has gone – in England anyway – but individuals still do it at matches, and the abuse has gone online. Trolling. It's so insidious and cowardly.'

As a youngster, Brendon Batson was used to racist abuse being hurled at him in the street and in park football. At school, he was advised that cricket or athletics might be more his thing, given his Caribbean background. Following his mother's advice, he tried not to respond to the ignorance and abuse. 'My mum was from the West Indies. She told me to look the world in the eye, and be the best advert I could for my community,' he explained. 'I also did my best to adhere to Bertie Mee's advice at Arsenal to "remember who you are, what you are and where you come from".' On two occasions at Cambridge United, the provocation became too much. Batson was sent off twice for reacting to – on both occasions – racist abuse from opponent Tony Coleman. Batson saw the vitriol from crowds intensify in the First Division with Albion: 'We ran the full gauntlet. We got abusive letters through the post. At away games you'd see National Front leaflets being distributed. We'd get spat at, have things thrown at us, all the chants. Everything. The volume was incredible. You name it, it came our way.' Regis concurred:

It was the time that *Roots* – the Alex Haley story about the black slave – had been syndicated on British TV. I remember a whole section of Middlesbrough fans chanting 'Kunta Kinte' [the name of the slave at the heart of the story] at me during the second half of one game. Me and Laurie said afterwards that at least they were watching something decent on telly. I never responded to that type of provocation. I normalised the abuse early in my career.

━━━━

At Old Trafford on 30 December 1978, the 45,091 hardy souls who braved the chill were instructed by the stadium announcer to vacate the ground as soon as possible after the final whistle, in order that the floodlights could be switched off promptly due to the power shortages. But there was no shortage of electricity flowing through the West Bromwich Albion team, clad in their classic late '70s Umbro navy blue and white striped shirts. 'On that day everything we tried came off,' Regis told me. Albion's joyful performance on the pitch was in marked contrast with the depressing backdrop from the terraces. The fact the match was televised magnified events that afternoon. Breaking with convention, commentator Gerald Sinstadt called out the hecklers. As Cunningham set up Tony Brown for the opening goal amidst a cacophony of abuse, Sinstadt began with, 'The booing of the black players...' before being abruptly interrupted as Brown scored '...paid off there, or repaid by Tony Brown.' In the second half, Sinstadt once more described the booing as 'unsavoury, which says nothing for their [the hecklers'] sportsmanship at all'. It was the first time on British TV that a commentator had specifically referred to racism in football.

'Beforehand, racist chanting had always been the elephant in the room which commentators never mentioned. Now, at least Gerald Sinstadt had drawn attention to it,' explained Batson. Cyrille Regis's sheer joy at scoring his blistering goal for Albion was palpable, as he stood there with a beaming smile, arms outstretched. 'Scoring goals, and goals like that, was my only riposte,' he declared. He also made a point of playing in short sleeves at Old Trafford, due to comments made to him by a Fleet Street doyen:

> This writer suggested: 'You boys might start to struggle in the cold.' I asked him, 'Do you mean the whole team, or just Laurie, Brendon and me?' 'The three of you,' he said. I told him that I'd lived in London since I was four years old, that Laurie was born here, that Brendon had arrived from the West Indies when he was nine and that we were used to chilly weather. I wore those short sleeves.

After blizzards blew in on New Year's Eve, there was widespread disruption across all four divisions of the Football League. Over 100 league matches were postponed, dozens abandoned and of the matches that did go ahead attendances were severely hit due to the problems with road and rail services. A 50-mile stretch of the M6 between Birmingham and Walsall was shut for several days due to a blanket of snow, but Albion's match against Bristol City at The Hawthorns on New Year's Day – watched by a shivering 35,768 crowd – was given the go-ahead, despite the pitch being virtually unplayable due to snow. Ron Atkinson ordered his in-form team to wear multi-pimpled Astroturf boots, which had the appearance and feel of trainers, and which he'd purchased whilst the club was on tour in West Germany. As the Bristol City players slipped and slithered in their old boots, Albion's stars kept their feet and composure, winning 3–1. Atkinson's willingness to innovate was clear, but the team's title push was curtailed by the brutal weather. By mid-February, Liverpool were storming clear in an uneven, higgledy-piggledy Division One table with forty-one points from twenty-five games, five points ahead of Arsenal who'd played twenty-seven games. After the win against Bristol City,

Albion failed to win throughout the rest of January and February (though they only played four league matches) tailing off to secure third place, with their thin squad unable to cope with the inevitable backlog of fixtures in April.

Not that Ron Atkinson appeared concerned. 'I think this team has made everyone sit up and take notice. I'm always seeking new ways for West Bromwich Albion to catch the eye,' he enthused. Cunningham, Regis and Batson were about to be thrust directly into the limelight in March 1979 when, in training, Atkinson beckoned to them and said, 'Right, the Three Degrees, over here.'

The Philadelphia soul group were no strangers to English football. In 1974, the trio of Sheila Ferguson, Fayette Pinkney and Valerie Holiday (all clad in hooped shirts) were photographed with bemused QPR boss Gordon Jago as they publicised their forthcoming *Take Good Care of Yourself* album at Loftus Road. Five years later, with Helen Scott replacing Pinkney, the Three Degrees were on a British tour and due to appear at Birmingham's Big Night Out club. After accepting Atkinson's invitation (he told the press, 'I've got my own Three Degrees') to visit the Hawthorns and meet Batson, Cunningham and Regis, photographers snapped all six with the group wearing West Brom tops and the players sporting fur coats. The following month, the Three Degrees visited the Hawthorns for a home match against Everton, greeted the players as they ran onto the pitch (Albion won 1–0 thanks to a Tony Brown goal) and invited the players to meet up with them at Holy City Zoo, a popular Birmingham club, that evening. Batson declined to join them, insisting, 'I did the photograph, but wasn't especially comfortable with the whole thing because it was a little contrived, a bit of a distraction.' Despite pranging his car en route to the nightclub, Regis made the rendezvous and even dated Sheila Ferguson for a short while. He looked back on that period with a sense of wry amusement: 'At the time, it was great fun. The Three Degrees label came with good intentions. It's definitely of its era – shall we say,' Regis said. Batson reflected, 'I objected more to the names the press gave us – like "Black Flash" and "Black Pearl". I never had an issue with the Three Degrees nickname at the time.'

The Three Degrees weren't the only pop stars to be closely linked to Albion in the late '70s. Former Yardbirds member Eric Clapton – whose cover version of 'I Shot the Sheriff' helped bring Bob Marley's music to a white audience – declared himself to be a Baggies fan and, to show his allegiance, presented every member of the Albion team with a gold disc of his *Slowhand* album, inscribed with a plate which read, 'To WBA on the occasion of their appearance in the UEFA Cup – September 1978.' Some suggested that Clapton's zoning-in on Albion – and his declaration of 'adoration' for the three black players – was his attempt to atone for his racist tirade at the Birmingham Odeon back in 1976. When the *NME* interviewed Laurie Cunningham at his Edgbaston flat in May 1979, he was asked if he was aware of Clapton's diatribe where he declared that Britain 'was turning into a black colony. We need to make clear to them that they are not welcome. England is for white people.' Cunningham insisted that he wasn't and that, in any case, 'Everyone's entitled to their opinions.' He joked that he might have to 'burn it now' (the gold disc that was on the wall of his flat). In the interview, Cunningham also expressed doubt that the proposed blacks v. whites match for Albion veteran Len Cantello would happen that summer. But, in the end, it did.

In training, during five-a-side matches, Atkinson began pitting, as Regis described it, 'Jocks and blacks against the whites. It was what we did in training to break things up and was a bit of fun.' In June 1979, for Cantello's testimonial match, a black XI took on a white XI at the Hawthorns, in front of a 15,000 crowd. Despite being played in the era of apartheid, 'No one, including Laurie, Cyrille and me batted an eyelid, because it was an extension of what we did in training, and it was innocent and quite progressive, because we weren't in a minority any more. We were our own team playing – ironically – in all-white shirts,' Batson recalled. A raft of other well-known black footballers from that era joined them, including Stoke City's Garth Crooks and Wolves defender George Berry, but it marked the break-up of Albion's 'Three Degrees' – as Cunningham headed to Spain that summer after Real Madrid's £950,000 offer was accepted by Albion. Atkinson's team remained a fine side over the next few seasons, but lost its lustre after Cunningham's departure. 'We were never quite the same again,' Batson admitted.

━━━━

As the decades passed, the trio became interwoven with the fabric of British cultural history. In 2017, Laurie Cunningham's statue was unveiled outside his former club Leyton Orient's Brisbane Road ground and, twelve months previously, English Heritage affixed a blue plaque to the house where Cunningham – who died in a car crash in Spain in 1989 – lived as a child in Lancaster Road, Haringey. In 2011, sculptor Graham Ibbeson drew up plans for a statue called 'The Celebration' depicting the three players embracing after a goal. Speaking in 2017, Cyrille Regis said of the plans, 'It's a tremendous honour. I think we showed that black people could succeed if they were talented and creative, in an era when there was considerable resistance towards multiculturalism.' What would Laurie Cunningham – I asked Regis – have made of the fact that the players' experiences were now the subject of books, documentaries and Black History Month lessons and school assemblies across the country? 'He'd have found it hilarious,' Regis smiled, 'but he'd have been annoyed that he's always wearing his football kit. He'd rather have been in one of his Gatsby suits. He wanted to be a fashion designer after his football career.'

By the time 'The Celebration' statue was unveiled in West Bromwich town centre in 2019, and a play about Cunningham called *Getting the Third Degree* began a nationwide tour, Regis had also passed away. Batson is reluctant to dwell on the fact that he is the only surviving member of West Brom's pioneering trio. 'Cyrille's death was a great shock, but I don't want to be sad. I've got plenty of living to do,' he reflected. After retiring from the game, Batson spent two decades as deputy chief executive of the Professional Footballers' Association, and was awarded an OBE in 2015.

> What we achieved at West Brom didn't solve the issue of racism
> in football or in society. There were still good young black foot-
> ballers put off pursuing a career in the game because of the abuse
> they saw us get. But we showed the second wave of black foot-
> ballers in the '80s that they could make it.

As for the Graham Ibbeson statue, Batson said, 'It captures Laurie perfectly. When I look at it, he's always the young star I remember.'

Batson, Regis and Cunningham made their mark at the Hawthorns when West Brom – as the *NME* put it – were briefly English football's 'in thing'. More than that, the trio became role models and left an indelible mark on the history of the game at a time when turning the other cheek often appeared to be the only option available to black players in England.

20

THE CONTINENTALS

THE OTHER WORLD CUP WINNER

———

'By the end, Alberto was a lost soul in an alien land.'
Jim Smith

St Andrews, November 1978. Birmingham City's World Cup winner Alberto Tarantini is finally delivering a performance to justify his hefty £297,000 transfer fee. From beneath his famous mop of curls, the roving former Boca Juniors left-back is prising open Dave Sexton's Manchester United. With the Blues 3–1 up at half-time thanks to a goal from Kevin Dillon and two from Alan Buckley, Tarantini marauds further forwards in the second half. His free kicks set up Buckley's first goal and Jimmy Calderwood's late strike which sees Jim Smith's men – rock-bottom of Division One and without a win since April – run out 5–1 winners. Yet, after the game, Smith faces a barrage of enquiries regarding the second-half clash between Tarantini and Brian Greenhoff, during which the United midfielder was knocked unconscious and stretchered off. Tarantini also squared up to United striker Joe Jordan, who'd given United an early lead, and assistant manager Tommy Cavanagh in the ensuing rumpus. 'Alberto has quite wrongly been labelled as some sort of hatchet man,' Smith insists. Tarantini's assertion that Greenhoff simply 'fell asleep' does little to quell the media storm.

———

The tale of Alberto Tarantini's ill-fated 23-game spell at Birmingham City became the blueprint for subsequent signings of foreign players that went wrong. In comparison to the hullaballoo that surrounded fellow Argentinians Ricky Villa and Ossie Ardiles when they joined Tottenham, Tarantini likened himself to 'the third man on the moon. No one remembers his name.' Ironically, the feisty Charles 'Pete' Conrad, who headed up the Apollo 12 mission (often dubbed the 'forgotten' mission in the US) in November 1969, and who stepped onto the lunar surface four months after Neil Armstrong and Buzz Aldrin, had the personal mantra 'When you can't be good, be colourful'. Rightly or wrongly, that was how Tarantini came to be seen during his Birmingham career.

Tarantini's was the edgy B-side ballad to Ossie Ardiles and Ricky Villa's smash hit at Tottenham, which saw both Argentinian internationals become part of White Hart Lane folklore following their country's 1978 World Cup win. Just a fortnight after the hosts beat Holland 3–1 in the final, bearded wide man Villa and playmaker Ardiles signed on the dotted line for newly promoted Tottenham in a combined £750,000 deal. 'SPURS SCOOP THE WORLD' yelled the *Daily Express*. The pair were greeted like pop stars at Heathrow airport when they jetted into the UK on 11 July 1978 and there was a tickertape-strewn welcome for them at White Hart Lane. Vendors outside White Hart Lane sold false Villa-style droopy moustaches and fake gaucho gear. On top of the World Cup triumph, the opening of the Andrew Lloyd Webber musical *Evita* in the West End in June 1978 meant that interest in Argentinian history and culture had never been greater.

The pair's arrival marked the end of a joint 1931 Ministry of Labour/Football Association ruling which declared that players who weren't British-born could only play for English teams if they'd been living in the country for at least two years. Chilean striker George Robledo (Newcastle United) and German goalkeeper Bert Trautmann (Manchester City) – who'd spent time in a Lancashire prisoner-of-war camp at the end of the Second World War – made their names in English football, but they were notable exceptions to the rule. In February 1978, the European Community ruled that the football associations of its member states could no longer deny access to players based on nationality, and, that summer, the Football League lifted the 47-year-old ban, although it capped the number of foreigners at any one club to two players. When Ardiles and Villa were unveiled to the press, there were cautionary words from PFA representatives. 'It could spread like wildfire,' complained secretary Cliff Lloyd. 'Every foreign player of standing in our league represents a denial to a UK player of a place in the team.' Such was the publicity surrounding Tottenham's double heist that the issue even reached the House of Commons, with John Cartwright MP asking Employment Secretary John Grant 'what inquiries are to be undertaken; and when a decision is likely to be made' regarding work permits.

The move was facilitated by Sheffield United manager Harry Haslam, who'd been in Argentina for the World Cup finals. He'd attempted to persuade his board of directors at Bramall Lane to grant him £400,000 to sign seventeen-year-old Diego Maradona, who'd failed to make Argentina's final 22-man squad. The Blades' board baulked at the asking price and the Argentinian Football Association steadfastly refused to allow its prized young bull to leave the country in any case. Whilst still out in Argentina, Haslam contacted Tottenham manager Keith Burkinshaw about Spurs possibly signing Huracán's Ardiles. Burkinshaw flew out to Buenos Aires and the deal was done, with Ardiles also suggesting to Burkinshaw that Spurs also sign Racing Club's Ricky Villa.

The Tarantini deal came about differently, with Jim Smith approached by a Spanish agent about whether he'd be interested in taking the Argentinian to St Andrews. Intrigued, Smith confirmed that he was keen and Tarantini quickly gave a verbal assurance that he would sign on the dotted line. Given the 22-year-old's consistent displays for Argentina in the finals, the fact he was present and correct in every match and that as a Boca Juniors player he revelled in the Buenos Aires nightlife, it seems bizarre that he was keen to come to Birmingham, who'd finished eleventh in Division One in the 1977–78 season, at all. The reason, Tarantini told me, was because he 'had to leave Argentina very quickly'. When I interviewed Tarantini in 2009 for *Death or Glory: The Dark History of the World Cup* on a sunny Buenos Aires morning, he seemed mildly surprised that I was even aware of his sojourn in the Midlands. Now greying, his hair was cut short, and he smiled a lot as he sipped his coffee. My translator told me that, compared to most Argentinian footballers of that era, he'd aged well, which Tarantini heartily agreed with. But the joviality faded when our conversation turned to the country's politics in the '70s.

In 1976, a right-wing military junta, headed by General Jorge Videla, ousted President Isabel Perón (the third wife of former President Juan Perón) and commenced its policy of state terrorism against those even suspected of opposing Videla's dictatorship. The 'Dirty War', as it became known, led to the illegal arrest, torture and murder of tens of thousands of Argentinians. The exact number of deaths has never been ascertained, although estimates suggest it could be up to 30,000. These people became known as 'the disappeared'. In Buenos Aries, Tarantini's circle of friends included several Perónistas and left-leaning university students, who fell foul of the new regime. Shortly before the 1978 World Cup began, the footballer enquired as to what happened to them. 'I was met with a wall of silence,' Tarantini told me. It was a risky thing to do but, for now, Tarantini was protected because the Videla regime saw huge advantages to Argentina prospering at their World Cup, in terms of alleviating some of the gloom at home and improving the regime's status abroad. Argentina's chain-smoking coach, César Luis Menotti, urged his team to win for the oppressed population, not the military. 'Our aim was to bring some relief to the people, and I believe we did just that,' Tarantini said. As the tournament progressed, Argentina's approach encompassed the graceful movement, energy and passion that was known as *La Nuestra* (Our Way). The passion of the crowds, reflected in the tickertape storms that greeted the team whenever they entered the field of play, added a sense of theatre and drama to proceedings. '*La Nuestra* was a very Argentinian way of playing football. Menotti told us to stick to our roles within the team, but to also express ourselves when we had the chance. It was what the crowds wanted to see,' Tarantini said.

In 1978, successful sides needed to progress through two group stages to reach the World Cup final. In what became arguably the World Cup's most notorious match, Argentina, needing to win by three clear goals to reach the final ahead of South American rivals Brazil, defeated Peru 6–0 in their final group match. Argentina's group games took place not in the capital but in provincial Rosario, where a wall was built alongside the main road into the city to hide the slums lying behind it. Painted with colourful houses, it quickly became known as 'the misery wall'. The hosts annihilated the Peruvians, with leading striker Mario Kempes (his long hair and swashbuckling approach saw him being nicknamed '*El Matador*') scoring twice, and Tarantini (dubbed '*Conejo*', 'the rabbit', due to his prominent front teeth) heading in his country's second goal from a corner. Peru's abject second-half collapse spawned numerous conspiracy theories in the years that followed. In 1986, a *Sunday Times* article alleged that bribes had been paid and deals done between Argentine and Peruvian generals to fix the match.

Following the game, Videla visited the Argentinian dressing room to congratulate the players as they showered. Tarantini decided that now was the time to make a stand:

> I bet Daniel Passarella [the captain] $1,000 that if Videla came over to me, I'd rub soap all over my bollocks and then shake his hand. Passarella said, 'You're on.' Sure enough, Videla came across so I soaped myself down there and offered him my soapy hand. All the photographers were there and Videla made a face as if to say 'yuck!' I don't regret what I did, but I had to play abroad after the World Cup for my own safety, and let things cool off.

Teammates have suggested that the story may not be completely waterproof, and, perhaps tellingly, Tarantini said that Passarella never paid up. What is true is that when Tarantini scored against Peru, he tore across the pitch, screaming obscenities. 'To the Military Junta, to the three of them. I shouted, "Go fuck yourselves, you can all die, sons of bitches!"' he told journalist Diego Borinsky. In the final, Tarantini put in an accomplished performance in Argentina's 3–1 victory and, when the final whistle blew, knelt down and embraced goalkeeper Ubaldo Fillol. 'A boy with no arms ran towards us and threw himself on top of us,' Tarantini explained. The iconic image became known in Argentina as 'the hug of the soul'. Half a mile away from the celebrations in the River Plate Stadium, there was a detention and torture centre at the Argentine Navy Mechanical School. Prisoners, chained up and with hoods over their heads, heard the goals from the stadium and cheered as Argentina won the World Cup. 'That leaves an incredibly eerie feeling,' Tarantini said, 'I hope they were able to draw some strength from our victory.'

But now, rather than revel in the victory, it was time for Tarantini to leave the tumult and controversy of the 1978 World Cup behind and head for England.

━━━━━

Throughout a managerial career that lasted nearly forty years, Jim Smith coached over a dozen clubs and bought and sold hundreds of players, of whom a fair few came from abroad. Not too much fazed the 'Bald Eagle', but even he took a sharp intake of breath when I mentioned Tarantini's name. 'Few if any had the baggage that Berto [Tarantini] carried, but it only came to light after he'd arrived in the Midlands,' Smith told me when we met in 2004. The Birmingham manager believed that Tarantini, who was equally comfortable playing down the left or in central defence, would be an asset for his team. But there was a hitch with his paperwork. 'Only later did Berto tell me about the incident with the leader [Videla] and that the Argentine FA wanted to make life difficult for him.' Tarantini came to the UK with girlfriend Patricia 'Pata' Villanueva. At the time, the actress/model was in dispute with her former husband about custody of their child. 'I liked her a great deal,' said Smith, 'but there was a lot going on back at home. It was difficult for her and Berto.' By the time he finally made his debut against Tottenham on 14 October, the Blues were already toiling in the relegation zone. Star player Trevor Francis was ruled out with an injury and Tarantini's flamboyant style was out of kilter with Birmingham's. 'We never gave him the platform he deserved,' Smith told me. 'He liked to push forward, which led people to think that he was undisciplined. He wasn't, but we couldn't adapt our style to his style. Not at that time.'

Tarantini's face lit up when I mentioned Jim Smith's name. 'He was a kind and generous man, who looked after me well,' he said.

In 2018, the details of Tarantini's Birmingham contract came to light when sports memorabilia specialist Tim Beddow put it up for auction on eBay. On a basic wage of £363 (around £1,800 in today's money) per week, Tarantini also received transport costs and the club paid the rent on his house in Henley-in-Arden. It was more than double what his colleagues earned, and made him one of English football's highest earners. The whole package meant that Tarantini earned the equivalent of £120,000 that season.

But as was the case with Ardiles and Villa, Tarantini's more-than-adequate renumeration couldn't solve his general sense of discombobulation living 11,000 miles from home. Nor did it reduce the bafflement he felt when he witnessed the drinking habits of the British players. 'They drank many pints of beer,' Tarantini said. 'In Argentina, it was a cold bottle. Maybe two after a game.' Tarantini expressed bemusement with his teammates' love of baked beans and fried bread as they tucked into their cooked breakfasts before training. 'Greasy bread? Why?' he asked. He was open-mouthed when he opened his curtains in December and saw a blanket of snow outside, which didn't disappear for several weeks, but less than impressed when he was told to train it. At least the defender was able to phone home to Buenos Aires on a semi-regular basis, unlike Ricky Villa, whose parents didn't have a phone line on their farm and whose father had to travel three hours to the nearest village to pick up his son's call. Tarantini didn't begrudge Ardiles's and Villa's eventual success at Tottenham, but admitted, 'It was a little easier for them because the team [Spurs] was better and they had one another for support, like the Dutchmen at Ipswich [Thijssen and Mühren].' Jim Smith had considered whether to sign Tarantini's international teammate René Houseman but baulked at the asking price.

For English footballers who'd watched that summer's World Cup, they knew that Argentinian players weren't shrinking violets when it came to the physical side of the game. Tottenham skipper Steve

Perryman tipped off teammates prior to a five-a-side match in training that Ricky Villa 'was a nasty bastard'. Perryman's comment came off the back of Villa's high tackle on Brazil's Roberto Rivellino a few weeks before. In fact, Villa was not a player who particularly relished the combative aspects of the game, whereas the lithe Ardiles was more than capable of looking after himself. Tarantini certainly had a low boiling point. 'Opposition players tried to annoy me, to get a reaction. They'd jab or kick me or swear at me. They weren't saying "Welcome to England." Or if they did, they didn't mean it. It was hard not to react.' On that infamous clash with Brian Greenhoff, Tarantini claimed, 'It was an accidental clash. The blond United midfielder [Greenhoff] was okay after a while.' Greenhoff claimed that Tarantini 'targeted me with his elbow when the ball was nowhere near us'.

On the little footage in existence of the Argentinian playing for Birmingham, it's sometimes hard to tell the difference between Tarantini and teammate Tony Towers – also rocking a gigantic frizzy hairdo. But highlights of a match at St Andrews against Leeds in early February speak volumes. Tarantini, clearly struggling in the icy conditions, shanked a clearance out for a corner, appeared to be caught in two minds about whether to defend or attack, and cut an increasingly forlorn figure as Birmingham sank to a 1–0 defeat. By the spring, with Trevor Francis sold to Nottingham Forest for £1 million, twitchy directors indicated to Jim Smith that, with relegation almost an inevitability, Tarantini would need to be sold too. Although Smith argued against it, suggesting that the Argentinian could spearhead the Blues' promotion push from Division Two, the decision was taken out of his hands when Tarantini, after being barracked by a section of Birmingham fans during yet another depressing loss, had an 'altercation' with a supporter after wading into the crowd to remonstrate. Fists flew. 'By then they [the fans] were angry with the situation, and I was very angry with how things were going at Birmingham,' the defender said. A parting of ways was inevitable and, when Tallares de Córdoba offered to recoup Birmingham's initial outlay, Tarantini went home, insisting that 'the situation [with the military junta] had now cooled down'. There was virtually no mention of his low-key departure – not a 'DON'T CRY FOR ME ARGENTINA' headline in sight.

Jim Smith bumped into Tarantini – by this time with River Plate – when Argentina visited London for an international friendly against England in 1980. After exchanging greetings, Tarantini shrugged, 'Boss, with me you have a crap side. Without me, you have a good side.' Smith steered Birmingham to promotion – and an immediate return to Division One – the season after. He kept his place in Argentina's 1982 World Cup squad, after which his career petered out in France with Toulouse. Tarantini still believed that his move to England 'was the right thing to do, but Birmingham were a struggling team'. Although Tarantini was certainly no angel, there is a more nuanced and compelling story behind his troubled Birmingham City spell than online 'Top ten worst foreign signings' and 'Biggest wastes of money in football' articles suggest. And, if Tarantini's Videla story is even half true, it's doubtful that any international signing since has had a more pressing reason to leave their native country and ply their trade in England.

THE ORANJE REVOLUTION

'They caress it and they address it and they pass it and they distribute it in such a way that it's a joy to watch.'
Bobby Robson

Portman Road, 30 December 1978. On a chilly Suffolk afternoon, young defender Russell Osman puts Bobby Robson's side into the lead against Chelsea with a clever header and midfielder John Wark drills home superbly from just outside the box to put Ipswich almost out of sight. Either side of Wark's goal, Dutch midfielder Arnold Mühren, whose exquisite free kick set up Osman's goal, fires home two crackers with his beguiling left foot and England striker Paul Mariner makes it 5–1 to Ipswich. After the match, journalists besiege Robson about Mühren, who, after an uncertain start in England, has come good during the bleak midwinter. 'He's a bloody marvel,' enthuses Robson. In fact, so impressed is Robson with the former Twente Enschede midfielder, and the impact he's having on his band of FA Cup winners, that he asks Mühren if he knows of any other Dutch stars who might be interested in joining Ipswich. Mühren looks long and hard at Robson. 'I do know of one, yes. Frans Thijssen. He plays for Twente, and he's a far better player than me,' he says modestly. 'I doubt that,' Robson smiles, 'but perhaps you could call him and sound him out.' Mühren agrees. Soon the English press, who've labelled Mühren as the 'Dutch Master' will adapt their headlines to 'Double Dutch'.

On the hop across from Holland, the private plane carrying Mühren, his wife Geerie and Bobby Robson flew over what geologists call the once fertile 'Doggerland'. Tectonically speaking at least, the fact that Suffolk and Holland were once joined at the hip ('Doggerland' slipped under the North Sea thousands of years ago) perhaps explains why Arnold Mühren and Frans Thijssen eventually slotted in so well at Ipswich. Once they'd flown over the harbour, Robson told the Mührens to look out for Portman Road. After they spotted Ipswich's compact ground down below, Robson instructed them to keep watching. 'As the plane buzzed over it, we could clearly make out a dozen or more Ipswich players waving enthusiastically to us from the training pitch,' Mühren explained during our 2021 interview. When the plane landed at the airfield a few minutes later, the clamour from Ipswich fans took Mühren's breath away. 'I felt like one of the Beatles. I hadn't even joined Ipswich yet. I thought that perhaps the crowd had been told that the plane carried Johan Cruyff.' Given the technical excellence of Dutch players at the 1974 and 1978 World Cups, where they'd finished runners-up on both occasions, it was little wonder that there was a frisson of excitement when Mühren touched down. Or perhaps Ipswich fans had heard of Mühren's minor rock-star status in Holland. Alongside his brother Gerrie, Arnold had recorded the 1974 single '*Ajax is de Koning van de Mat*' ('Ajax is the King of the Pitch') which made it into Holland's top forty.

Robson turned up in Arnold and Geerie Mühren's kitchen in their Volendam house the day before the flight to try to convince Mühren to join Ipswich. At twenty-seven, Mühren was in his prime but had been enduring a difficult few months. Although his Twente Enschede contract had expired, they'd reneged on a verbal agreement that he could rejoin Ajax for 400,000 guilders (clubs could still demand a fee for a player even though their contract had expired), doubling the asking price to 800,000, due to Mühren's fine form. As a result, a furious Mühren returned to his home town of Volendam, a picturesque port which had spawned musicians, poets and artists galore down the centuries, and trained with the local club (where he began his career) during the summer, determined never to play for Twente again. He'd narrowly missed the cut for Holland's 1978 World Cup squad, despite being in the original 26-man party. 'So, when Mr Robson made us feel so welcome, it was like a breath of fresh air,' Mühren explained. Robson had long been a fan of Dutch football, and Ipswich played several friendlies against Dutch sides throughout the '70s, which is where Robson first clapped eyes on Mühren. It was love at first sight. 'We couldn't get the ball off him. He treated the ball as a friend. I never forgot him,' Robson explained.

On 17 August 1978, Mühren put pen to paper at Amsterdam's Schiphol airport, signing a two-and-a-half-year contract. He wasn't the first Dutch footballer to ply his trade in England. Goalkeeper Nico Schröder had briefly turned out for Swansea City in 1976 and, back in the 1930s, another goalkeeper, Gerrit Keizer, had kept goal for Arsenal on Saturdays before flying home to play for Ajax on Sundays. But Mühren became the first full-time Dutch professional in England. The initial training sessions were eye-opening. The defenders, a blend of seasoned internationals like Kevin Beattie, Mick Mills, George Burley and Allan Hunter and emerging stars like Terry Butcher and Russell Osman, favoured lofting long balls forward, which meant that Mühren spent much of his time 'looking to the skies', as he put it. Whenever Mühren did get hold of the ball, though, his quality shone through. 'The first thing I remember him doing was clipping this lovely ball to me from 30 yards away,' recalled former Town striker Paul Mariner. 'I'm embarrassed to say that I mis-controlled it and it ran out of play...'

Mühren was pitched in at the deep end against European Cup winners Liverpool at Portman Road in the season's second game. 'Keep an eye on Terry McDermott,' Robson told him. 'Lose track of him and we could be in trouble.' Mühren's debut was disappointing. Liverpool ran out 3–0 winners with goals from Graeme Souness and a brace from Kenny Dalglish, and the Dutchman barely got a kick. 'I think I touched the ball three times,' he told me. 'Once at the kick-off, once for a throw-in and once to hand the ball back to the referee at the end of the match.' Holed up in Ipswich's Copdock Hotel, Mühren joined the Liverpool players (also staying there before journeying back up north) in the bar afterwards and offloaded on McDermott: 'I think I might have made a mistake in coming here. I have barely touched the ball,' he shrugged. McDermott sympathised, but his response was a little unhelpful: 'Welcome to English football, Arnold!' he laughed.

After another match spent studying cloud formations and vapour trails, Mühren sought out his manager and laid his cards on the table:

'Mr Robson,' I said to him. 'If, from now on, I am expected to play as I did against Liverpool, then you don't have to put me in the starting line-up. Anyone who's fit can run up and down and block the opponent's way. The kitman, for example. If you want to enable me to put my qualities to good use, you need to ensure that the ball is played to me more often. This is where my strength lies and is the reason you signed me, I think.'

A receptive listener, if hardly a groundbreaking tactician, Robson responded, 'OK, we'll discuss it later.'

'I felt a little guilty, because I'd only just arrived at the club,' Mühren explained, 'but I think that what I said to Mr Robson was good for all of us in the long term.' At the next training session, Robson instructed his Ipswich players to ensure that Mühren received the ball more often. They nodded enthusiastically in agreement. 'Suddenly, they passed to me too much!' Mühren laughed. The evolution of Ipswich's style was evident in the third game of the season against Manchester United. With Kevin Beattie restored to the starting line-up, Ipswich defenders began passing from the back with growing confidence, and their new teammate saw more of the ball. Mühren conducted the orchestra in midfield and two Paul Mariner goals and a strike from Brian Talbot saw Ipswich run out 3–0 winners. The Oranje revolution had begun in earnest – instigated not from above, but from below by the unassuming, yet quietly determined, Mühren.

In many ways, Mühren's formative years weren't so very different from those of the other Ipswich players. He honed his skills on the *achterstraat* (backstreet) right behind his parents' house with his elder brother Gerrie and other local kids. Rather than use jumpers for goalposts, the Mühren brothers played *paaltjesvoetbal*, where each player had to defend an upright brick. From the age of eleven, Mühren, like all promising young footballers, was schooled in the art of the 4–3–3 formation, with Dutch sides generally playing with two wingers and a lone striker. After making his professional debut for Volendam, Arnold made the move to Ajax, where he often played second fiddle to his brother and Johan Cruyff. Moves were built from the back, originating from ball-playing defenders, whereas at Ipswich, Paul Mariner held the ball up and brought teammates into play. Mühren was struck by their adaptability. 'Mick Mills and George Burley were quick, overlapping full-backs and John Wark, Eric Gates and Alan Brazil could play any style.' Mühren said. 'By Christmas of '78, Terry Butcher and Russell Osman, who were very young, were already far more comfortable bringing the ball out of defence.'

In January 1979, with the £450,000 sale of midfielder Brian Talbot to Arsenal confirmed, Bobby Robson reinvested £200,000 in Frans Thijssen. It was a symbolic exchange. Talbot was a typically industrious English midfielder. Thijssen offered something different. Mühren had told him on the phone, 'You're ideally suited for Ipswich. You specialise in twisting and turning and I think that skill of yours will catch on very well here.' During his four-year spell at Portman Road, there simply wasn't a finer dribbler or feinter in the country. Thijssen – once a right-winger – described to me how he'd leave a trail of dizzied defenders trailing in his wake, 'I'd pretend to turn to one side, but then I twisted with the ball the other way,' he said. 'Or I'd act as if I was about to pass, but then twist the ball behind my standing leg. My opponent would often keep running a few metres and that would buy me time and space.' During his early years at NEC Nijmegen, Thijssen was coached by the highly influential Dutch coach Wiel Coerver, dubbed the 'Albert Einstein of football' in his native Holland. Coerver brought a highly academic approach to coaching and expected his players to study training materials between sessions. He quickly recognised Thijssen's prodigious gifts. When Thijssen was just eighteen, Coerver asked him to demonstrate his skills at turning and shielding the ball to established NEC stars like Miel Pijs and Cas Janssens, Thijssen's childhood heroes. 'It was all about technique, and I feel fortunate that Coerver schooled me,' Thijssen explained.

Quite naturally, the Dutchmen (and their respective families) gravitated towards one another after Thijssen's arrival. Together, they navigated their way through the peculiarities of English football in the late '70s, and the fog of cigarette smoke emanating from Kevin Beattie in the dressing room. 'What are you doing in here?' Ipswich's physiotherapist Tommy Eggleston asked Mühren, when he appeared in the treatment room prior to a match. 'I have tight calf muscles and need a massage,' Mühren replied. 'No, no, just go and run around outside for ten minutes. That will help loosen them up,' came the response. 'I was a bit taken aback, and I don't think I went in there again,' Mühren laughed. Instead, he went to the spacious exercise room upstairs and devised his own stretching routine prior to matches. Over the coming weeks and months, his teammates, who'd previously taken warm baths prior to matches, joined him.

On hearing a kerfuffle in the players' room one Saturday lunchtime, Mühren opened the door, saw the TV in the corner blaring out a horse race and Alan Brazil, Eric Gates and Paul Cooper, who'd placed bets on the race, galloping across the room on turned around chairs, pretending to be jockeys. The Dutchmen listened open-mouthed to some of Kevin Beattie's stories, like the time when, on the way to an England under-23 international, he decided instead to alight in Carlisle and go on a mammoth drinking session with his father and missed the match. A tabloid photographer snapped him, and only Bobby Robson's intervention saved Beattie's international career. En route back to Suffolk after away games, the card school commenced and players got stuck into the copious amounts of beer that had been loaded onto the coach by the kitman/driver Trevor 'Wheels' Kirton. Once the bottles had been drained by the players they'd be lobbed into the stairwell, and Wheels dutifully cleared up the detritus at Portman Road, once it all cascaded out and smashed on the concrete, to enormous cheers. 'Win or lose, we're on the booze,' was Terry Butcher's mantra. But the Dutch pair never felt pressured to match their colleagues' drinking exploits. 'When I socialised,' Mühren explained, 'I was happy to stick to one lager and lime, and the others respected that.' Thijssen enjoyed playing snooker and darts, and he and Paul Mariner befriended the gigantic Canadian snooker player Bill Werbeniuk, who'd moved to England as the snooker revolution began in the late '70s, even presenting him with an official Ipswich club tie, which Werbeniuk sometimes wore during televised events. 'Mr Robson created a family atmosphere at the club. He was always asking if Arnold and I were OK and checking that our kids were fine in their schools,' Thijssen recounted. Thijssen was given the nickname 'Sam' by Kevin Beattie, who believed that because of his features and his moustache, he bore a close resemblance to detective Sam McCloud, played by Dennis Weaver. No nickname was forthcoming for Mühren, although, perhaps inevitably, whenever there was a televised Ipswich match in the Midlands, commentator Hugh Johns liked to call him 'Arnie'. 'The size of Ipswich suited us,' Arnold Mühren explained. 'It had a similar feel to Twente Enschede. We played at Portman Road and trained there, so it was intimate, and we got to know everyone at the club.' That included the groundsman, Stan Prendergast, who maintained arguably the finest playing surface in the country.

Tactically, the Dutch duo dovetailed perfectly with John Wark on the billiard-table surface. Wark loved pushing forwards to grab a goal or two, and the two Dutchmen were content to sit deep and shore up midfield when the moustachioed Scot surged forward. Wark returned the compliment whenever Thijssen or Mühren moved up the pitch. Thijssen endeared himself to the Portman Road faithful when he scored the decisive goal against Norwich City in April 1979 and, by the end of the campaign, Ipswich finished in sixth place, a huge improvement on their eighteenth-place finish in 1977–78. After a fine start to the 1979–80 campaign, Ipswich faced Norwich City in another frenetic East-Anglian derby on Boxing Day 1979 at Carrow Road, which Ipswich ended up drawing 3–3 after conceding a late Keith Robson goal. One moment of real quality shone through. With the visitors trailing 2–1, Frans Thijssen, twisting and turning this way and that, left a string of bewildered Norwich City defenders trailing in his wake. Several teammates called for the ball, but Thijssen, biding his time, slipped the ball to his right and Arnold Mühren placed a shot perfectly into the top corner of the net from just outside the box. Despite his annoyance at letting two points slip, Bobby Robson predicted that the Dutchmen's 'technical influence will help us push for trophies and make a name in Europe'. Never was a truer word spoken...

21

THE WHOLE WORLD
IN THEIR HANDS

'We all agree, Nottingham Forest are magic, are magic, are magic...'
Nottingham Forest fan chant, 1978

The City Ground, September 1978. Title winners Nottingham Forest put reigning European champions Liverpool under constant pressure in the first leg of their European Cup clash. In the first half Garry Birtles, signed from Long Eaton for just £2,000, gives Liverpool defender Phil Thompson a torrid time, dummying him and forcing a superb save from Ray Clemence. Minutes later, Tony Woodcock slips the ball sideways to his teammate and Birtles, in only his third Forest appearance, gives Brian Clough's side the lead. In a high-intensity match, with both sides at their flowing best, Forest can't extend their lead. Phil Thompson tells the Forest players that a slender one-goal lead won't be enough to take to Anfield for the second leg. With minutes to go, Brian Clough urges his team to avoid doing anything rash and allowing Liverpool to nick an away goal. Despite his manager's orders, full-back Colin Barrett rampages forwards to see if he can grab another goal. 'What the fuck is Barrett doing up there?' Clough rants at his substitutes in the dugout. Peter Taylor puts his head in his hands. Seconds later, Barrett volleys home superbly from a Woodcock flick-on. At home, Barrett's expensive new JVC video records the highlights and he'll enjoy watching his goal from time to time – that is, until his wife Sue records the 'Who Shot J. R.?' episode of *Dallas* over the top of it two years later. Barrett's teammates enquire of Phil Thompson whether a two-goal cushion might suffice. Clough punches the air in delight. 'Great goal, son!' he yells. 'We always tell our full-backs to go on the attack,' a beaming Taylor tells journalists. Asked whether Forest, undefeated on five consecutive occasions against Bob Paisley's side, could be classed as Liverpool's 'bogey-team', Taylor responds, 'These days, Nottingham Forest are *everyone's* bogey team.'

n his interview with David Frost in November 1974, Brian Clough explained how he was taking a few months out of management to reassess and reflect upon the events of the last year following his departure from Leeds. In the interview, Clough spoke of how, despite the enormous pay-off he'd received, 'money is never sufficient for anything'. He spoke of the pain of rejection and raised doubts about whether he'd reach the heights he'd scaled at Derby again. Clough briefly pondered whether to stand as a Labour MP in the Midlands and even considered going into teaching. Finally, a concrete offer to return to football management came his way in February 1975 from Nottingham Forest. Once known as the 'gentleman's club', former England manager Walter Winterbottom described it as 'the club everyone wants to manage'. Forest had a democratically elected committee rather than a board of directors, and refused to permit advertising at the City Ground. The club had won the FA Cup back in 1959, and finished Division One runners-up to Manchester United as recently as 1967, but success didn't appear to be a requisite for City Ground managers. However, from the moment

Brian Clough parked up in his new Mercedes, which he'd kept as part of his Leeds pay-off, everything began to change.

For the first fifteen months at the City Ground, Clough was a one-man band, with Peter Taylor still going it alone down on the south coast with Brighton. Forest finished a lamentable sixteenth in 1974–75. What made it worse was that Derby County won the First Division under Clough's successor Dave Mackay. Mackay had signed the likes of Bruce Rioch and Francis Lee, drawing praise from Clough at the end of the season. Yet, he still believed Clough was omnipresent, saying, 'The Bring Back Clough campaign still rumbled on.' The knives eventually came out for Mackay after a poor start to the 1976–77 campaign, and he went on to reinvigorate his managerial career in the Middle East. When Mackay watched *Porridge* in the years that followed, he was reminded of his sacking by the 'MACKAY OUT' cutting which Fletcher kept on his cell wall, to annoy prison officer Mr Mackay. 'It's a permanent reminder of what happened at Derby, but I eventually came to see the cutting as a badge of honour,' Dave Mackay told me.

Meanwhile, Clough pondered how to move Forest forwards. Within a month of taking over, he summoned trainer Jimmy Gordon, who'd coached him at Middlesbrough, and had been with Clough during the highs at Derby and the lows at Leeds. A robust wing-half for Newcastle and Middlesbrough, he'd lost his best playing years to the Second World War, but his spell in the army gave him a military demeanour that served him well during his coaching career. On the face of it, Gordon was just a physical training instructor but, to Clough and his players, he was much more than that. Gordon also had an infectious enthusiasm for football. In all weathers, he'd be out on the training pitch in short sleeves, telling everyone how wonderful it was to be alive. Gordon's zest for life was utilised well by Clough, who later admitted that he couldn't have survived those tricky early months at Forest without Gordon by his side. Gordon warned Forest players when Clough was on the warpath, advising those who were late to training to change in the toilets to avoid the coach's wrath. Next to arrive at the City Ground were John McGovern ('I'd have walked the length and breadth of the country to play for him again,' he said to me) and John O'Hare. 'I'd hoped he'd come in for me, but I took a 50 per cent pay cut to go there and sold my house to make ends meet,' O'Hare explained. To O'Hare's trained eye, some of Clough's bluster and confidence had gone. 'He wasn't complete without Peter Taylor. He needed Pete to make him whole again.'

After an eighth-place finish in 1975–76, Clough made his move, heading off to Cala Millor where Taylor was holidaying to convince him that it was time to resume their partnership. Taylor quickly agreed, saying later, 'We both knew we were banging our heads against a brick wall on our own. Together we could do any job.' Like other '70s double acts, the one simply couldn't function effectively without the other. Asked if he'd ever considered solo projects away from his comedy partner Ernie Wise, Eric Morecambe responded that, when he met with a TV producer to discuss a solo project, he 'broke out in cold sweats and went home'. Actor Richard Briers, narrator of '70s kids' TV cartoon *Roobarb*, focusing on the adventures of an energetic green dog, reckoned it was 'only right and proper' when the title of the second series was changed to *Roobarb and Custard* to acknowledge the crucial role played by the smirking, purple cat who lived next door. 'They get on each other's nerves, but where would one be without the other?' Briers asked. That was the reality facing Clough and Taylor, with Clough acknowledging that whilst he was 'the front of the shop, Taylor was the goods at the back'. Taylor immediately lightened the mood at Forest, making Clough and the players laugh with his daft impressions. Crucially, Taylor was also now in charge of buying and selling, and assessing which of Forest's current stock was worth salvaging. The club's fortunes were about to improve dramatically.

For three years, Clough and Taylor's buying and selling policy was perfectly executed. In fairness to Clough, he'd kick-started the initial bargain-basement hunt for players by nabbing 31-year-old Frank Clark in 1975, who'd just been given a free transfer by Newcastle and was poised to move to Fourth Division Doncaster Rovers. Clough believed that Clark's defensive acumen would serve Forest well for a season or two, but he was typically abrasive when he met the defender, telling him, 'I want you because no one else wants to play left-back at the club, and because you're cheap.' As was the case at Derby, Taylor was a master of ferreting around for under-achievers, lost souls and awkward customers whom he believed could add value at the City Ground. When questioned by a journalist why he rarely hunted outside the Midlands, Taylor's dead-pan response was that he was he 'loved the area's beaches and sunny weather'. Taylor suggested to Clough that although battering-ram Birmingham City striker Peter Withe was the forward Forest needed in order to add some muscle up front, he also had a gift for holding up the ball for teammates, which could be nurtured and encouraged. Clough agreed that the 25-year-old Toxteth-born forward, who'd rejuvenated his career in South Africa and the United States, would be a good fit for Forest.

In came Larry Lloyd, the lumbering centre-half whom Liverpool had sold to Coventry for £240,000. Tactically, Bob Paisley had written off Lloyd, whom he believed was unable to adapt to a more enlightened passing game. Taylor reckoned Lloyd would flourish at the City Ground, particularly if he was partnered with a central defender who was comfortable bringing the ball forward. Clough

had doubts, as Lloyd's spell at Coventry had been little short of disastrous, due to a back injury and because, as Lloyd admitted, 'I was
behaving like a big-time Charlie there.' There was no chance of that
happening at the City Ground. Lloyd arrived in October 1976, initially on loan, before signing permanently for £60,000. In transfer
negotiations, Lloyd haggled for more. Clough asked him whether
he had a washing machine, to which Lloyd answered in the negative. The next morning, a washing machine was delivered to his
house, with water dripping from the pipes at the back. At training
that day, Lloyd was berated by Forest's laundry ladies, who had no
way of washing the team kit because 'Mr Clough' had taken their
machine. 'My relationship with him was never smooth,' Lloyd admitted in an interview with journalist Tony Francis. 'In his eyes, I
was the big "shithouse", and I thought he was a big-headed bastard.
And we told each other so. But him and Peter Taylor got the best
out of me.'

As for those already at the City Ground, Taylor completed the
evaluation process that Clough had begun. On his first day as manager, Clough burst into the treatment room, glared at the injured
Ian Bowyer and snapped, 'So, this is where the sick, the lame and
the lazy hang out.' Bowyer went on to make more appearances
under Clough than any other Forest player, but it was an early sign
that his new boss had lost none of his raging intolerance for injured players. Clough's reaction to the racist abuse that emerging
right-back Viv Anderson received from the terraces was typically
unconventional. Anderson told the *Daily Mail* that as he warmed
up at Carlisle in the mid-1970s, the home fans hurled all kinds of
fruit at the Forest player and he retreated to the comparative safety
of the dugout. 'I thought I told you to warm up,' said Clough. 'I
have done, boss,' replied Anderson, 'but they're throwing fruit at
me.' Clough stared at him for a second or two, before responding,
'Get your fucking arse back out there then and fetch me two pears

and a banana.' Later, Clough pulled Anderson to one side and told him, 'If you let people like that dictate to you, I'm going to pick somebody else because you're going to be worrying about what the fans are going to say'. It was very much a 'turn the other cheek' response, although by the late '70s, Clough encouraged the Anti-Nazi League to advertise for free in the Nottingham Forest programme. Anderson quickly became a firm fixture, with midfielder Martin O'Neill instructed to get the ball to the roving right-back to launch Forest's attacks.

Midfielder John Robertson, whom Clough later described as 'a deeply unattractive young man; I look like Errol Flynn when I sit next to him', made Clough despair. But after observing Robertson in training, Taylor detected hidden qualities and decided he was worth persevering with. However, first, Taylor gave him a sandblasting. 'You're a disgrace to the game,' Taylor informed him, 'smoking and drinking and living out of a frying pan. Shape up or ship out.' Robertson listened and, following some 'conversion therapy', became arguably the most effective winger in European football in the late '70s. The problem-solving strategies Clough and Taylor deployed when moving players around in the team says much about their forensic eye for detail. When Clough arrived, Ian Bowyer was playing as a striker, but with Barry Butlin also at the club, and forward John O'Hare incoming, he told the striker that he was shifting him to the centre of the park 'because you're better equipped to play in midfield'. Despite his initial reservations, Bowyer adapted quickly. Robertson's conversion into a wide man came about due to an injury to Terry Curran, a pacey, orthodox winger whom Clough had signed from Doncaster for £50,000. Ian Bowyer recalled that the upbeat Curran was 'a forgotten catalyst in Forest's revival'. With Forest pushing hard for promotion in 1976–77, 'Terence' – as Clough called him – got injured and Clough was forced to move John Robertson out wide on the left. Robertson wasn't quick, but his crossing was unerringly accurate. Curran lost his place, and the technically outstanding Robertson took to his new position like a duck to water. Clough kept a close eye on him, analysing the finer points of his performances with him. 'I didn't give Robertson any of his extraordinary abilities,' Clough said, 'all I did was offer him the chance to use them.'

Events followed a similar pattern to those at Derby earlier in the decade. As with Alan Hinton at the Baseball Ground, the majority of Forest's attacks were channelled through Robertson on the left wing. And, just as Derby had lifted the Watney Cup at the beginning of the '70s, Forest won the much-derided Anglo-Scottish Cup in 1976. 'We travelled to places like Ayr and Kilmarnock. It was an adventure – a break from the routine. Our philosophy was that we'd rather play games than train, and Brian understood that. It also helped the promotion season fly by,' Ian Bowyer told me. Early in the campaign, an injury crisis created an opportunity for John McGovern. 'Here,' said Clough, throwing the ball at him, 'seeing as no other bugger wants the job, if you can catch this, you can be captain.' McGovern caught it. 'Congratulations, skipper,' came the response. McGovern replaced local favourite Sammy Chapman, and any dissenters were silenced as Forest ran out 6–1 winners against Sheffield United in his first game in the role.

Forest didn't exactly gallop towards promotion, but with Tony Woodcock – previously on loan at Doncaster and Lincoln – now up front alongside Peter Withe, they looked a far more polished unit. They won their final game of the campaign against Millwall, and as the Forest team flew to Mallorca for their post-season bash, Second Division champions Wolves beat Bolton 1–0 to confirm Forest's promotion. Just as Wolves had beaten Leeds in 1972 to confirm Derby as champions, the men from Molineux now helped Clough get over the line by the finest of margins once more. And, on both occasions, Clough's players were in Spain when they discovered the result. The players were jubilant, but realistic. Forest had lost nearly a third of their matches in going up. During their Cala Millor break, Clough and Taylor spent much of their time on the phone to England, honing in on the transfer targets that they hoped would take Forest to hitherto unscaled heights.

Of all the signings Clough and Taylor made, the capture of Birmingham City striker Kenny Burns was the most brilliantly counter-intuitive. Burns's combative approach on the pitch, and his reputation for drinking and gambling to excess off it, initially prompted Clough to tell Taylor that he 'didn't want an ugly bastard like Burns littering up my club', or so he said in his autobiography. The Glaswegian had arrived in Birmingham as a defender, before being instructed to play up front following Bob Latchford's departure to Everton in 1974. Taylor had him trailed to Perry Barr dog track, where he spent much of his time. The feedback was that Burns was only a small-time flutterer, and his drinking wasn't out of control either. Clough acquiesced and Burns was converted back into a sweeper to play alongside Larry Lloyd and clear up anything Lloyd couldn't deal with. On the day the deal was sealed, Clough took 'Kenneth' to a sweet pea show, which he was judging, noting that the car which Burns drove didn't have a car tax disc on show in the window. Clough noted in his autobiography that Burns was a 'young man of low standards,' and vowed to help him raise them.

The capture of Stoke City goalkeeper Peter Shilton represented a sea change for Clough and Taylor. An established England international who was on a £400-a-week index-linked wage (handy with the rampant inflation rates in the late 70s), Shilton was the highest paid footballer in the country, and he had a team of 'advisers' urging their client to push for as much money as he could. Clough loathed such figures, and to show his distaste at having to deal with them, hid behind a door as Jon Holmes and Jeff Pointon walked in and tripped them both up with his squash racquet. During negotiations, Clough sat tapping the racquet against his leg. Eventually he left, after saying they were getting nowhere, but a few days later Clough met Shilton privately and agreed on a £20,000 annual wage, with the keeper moving to the City Ground for £250,000. 'I knew that with Shilton at the club,' Taylor said, 'we had every chance of winning the title.' Although Shilton was hardly 'damaged goods', in the same way that Lloyd and Burns were, Clough and Taylor sensed his frustration at the lack of silverware he'd won during his career. That was about to change. Forest also 'stole' – as Clough put it – Archie Gemmill from Derby for just £25,000 in September 1977. Finally, all of the pieces of the jigsaw were in place.

Forest took the top flight by storm. Even though Frank Clark remembered that 'the noise from the home fans at Goodison Park almost knocked us off our feet', they won their opening game against Everton 3–1. For the first twenty minutes, the home side piled on the pressure. Then, from Forest's first chance, Peter Withe scored from a corner and the mood changed. 'We played our normal passing game, and, as we'd done in the Second Division, hit Everton on the break,' Clark told me in our 2021 interview. After the final whistle, with the players in great spirits, Bill Shankly popped into the dressing room to congratulate them on their performance. 'Shankly said that we shouldn't sell ourselves short, and that we could be a genuine force in Division One,' Ian Bowyer recalled. The Forest bubble never burst. They followed up the win at Everton with victories over Bristol City and Derby and, despite a 3–0 hammering at Arsenal, their form never really wavered. By the time Forest faced Villa on 17 September, Shilton was in goal and John Middleton was out, following shaky displays against Arsenal and then at Wolves, a match which Forest won 3–2. After the Arsenal match, Clough warned Middleton, 'I'll kick you in the bollocks if you play like that again.' The ruthless side of the Clough/Taylor partnership was shown as Middleton, once tipped to play for England, went to the Baseball Ground as part of the Gemmill deal. 'I knew it was curtains for me when Peter Shilton arrived,' Middleton told me, 'but Peter Taylor's explanation went beyond blunt. "Shilton will win us games. You'll lose us a few," he told me. And that was that.' Tellingly, Shilton kept two clean sheets in wins against Aston Villa and Leicester City. Forest cruised onwards.

Clough and Taylor rarely if ever referred to the opposition in their team meetings. Ian Bowyer recalled Clough once telling the team before playing Norwich, 'If I see Martin Peters in space, believe me you'll hear my voice above the crowd,' but, Peters aside, other opposition players went unmentioned. 'On a Friday, we'd have a team meeting where we'd discuss what we'd do,' McGovern explained to me. 'It was all about our game. Because we were winning, Clough and Taylor trusted us to carry out our roles. It bred confidence and kept things simple.' On matchdays, fifteen minutes before kick-off, Clough strode into the dressing room and instructed a reserve to fetch him a whisky and Taylor a cigar. He'd yell at McGovern, 'Is the team ready, skipper?' When McGovern answered in the affirmative, Clough barked, 'Get them out there, then.' And out they'd trot. The confidence radiating from Clough and Taylor was infectious, and this was never better illustrated than when Forest hammered Manchester United 4–0 at Old Trafford a week before Christmas.

With Archie Gemmill the dynamo in Forest's lightning-quick breakaways, Clough's team dismantled the Red Devils. Brian Greenhoff unluckily turned Tony Woodcock's shot into his own net, and then Woodcock doubled Forest's lead with a thumping finish from 10 yards out. In the second half, with Forest repeatedly hitting United on the break, Robertson and Woodcock completed the rout. Afterwards, as the Forest players travelled back to Nottingham, the joyful Clough serenaded his players with his rendition of the Frank Sinatra/Dean Martin classic 'You've Either Got or You Haven't Got Style' and, the following day, with a gruelling Christmas schedule looming, the Forest players flew out to Spain for a spot of winter sun. 'Clough was a pioneer in that he knew players needed a change of scene and routine in 42-game league seasons,' explained Frank Clark. On Boxing Day, Forest held firm, as champions Liverpool came to the City Ground. The 1–1 draw was played in front of 47,218 – the ground's biggest crowd of the season by some distance. In the three years he'd been at the City Ground, Clough had frequently expressed his annoyance at the comparatively low turnouts. Back in the autumn, he'd complained that the stadium was too quiet. 'It's about time they willed us to victory,' Clough said.

The lukewarm attitude of Nottingham fans wasn't the only thing that occupied Clough's thinking in 1977. At Forest, Clough had mostly reined in the barbed comments about rival mangers that had dominated his time at Derby, but when his old nemesis Don Revie resigned from the England job in the summer of 1977 and accepted a lucrative offer to manage the United Arab Emirates, he didn't hold back. 'He has left us wearing a black armband for football,' Clough wrote in the *Sunday Mirror*. 'He has sold football short.' In a *Daily Mail* exclusive, Revie explained that, following losses to Italy, Holland and Scotland, he woke up one day and felt the job 'simply wasn't worth it'. After Revie broke the news of his resignation in the *Mail*, he was banned for ten years for bringing the game into disrepute, and although the ban was subsequently overturned by the courts, the FA remained furious at Revie's treachery and he never managed in England again when his Middle East tenure ended.

His departure from the England post created a vacancy at

Lancaster Gate. Former West Ham manager Ron Greenwood took temporary control of the team, narrowly failing to steer them to the 1978 World Cup, but, in December, the FA interviewed Greenwood, Lawrie McMenemy, Jack Charlton, Dave Sexton and Brian Clough for the role. Despite once again being 'the people's favourite' for the job, and by all accounts giving a great interview, Clough was never going to be appointed. Especially not after he labelled FA chairman Sir Harold Thompson 'a stroppy, know-all bugger'. Greenwood got the post, and so Clough became, as the sections of the media labelled him, 'the best manager England never had'. If Clough had been offered and taken the England job, it's entirely possible that he'd have ended his managerial career with just one trophy – the league championship he'd won at Derby. As it was, Forest's trophy cabinet was about to burst.

———

Forest's grip on the top spot did not loosen in the new year, and, after a 1–0 defeat at Elland Road (of all places) on 19 November, they did not lose a league game. Archie Gemmill's lung-bursting goal in a 2–0 win over Arsenal in January typified Forest's fluid approach. The tough little Scot sprang an Arsenal attack on the edge of the Forest box, passed the ball to Peter Withe, bombed forward and finished off the move himself. Later that month, Nottingham group Paper Lace approached the club with their proposal to release a singalong version of the biblical 'He's Got the Whole World in His Hands', reworked to encompass Forest's ever-broadening horizons. The song's rabble-rousing chorus may have helped the song break into the top twenty, but it didn't sit entirely comfortably with Brian Clough, who warned that, although his team had played well up to that point, 'we don't literally have the world in our hands because we haven't actually won anything yet.'

That changed in March when Forest reached the League Cup final. In the lead-up to the match, Peter Taylor took the team on a daytrip to Scarborough, where Forest players doubled up as removal men to help Taylor move furniture into his new seaside flat. After a goalless draw with Liverpool at Wembley, Forest won the League Cup in an Old Trafford replay, despite Liverpool claims (confirmed on TV replays) that defender Phil Thompson had initially fouled John Robertson outside the box, so Robertson's 52nd-minute penalty should have been a free kick. Clough spoke excitedly of the confidence which the League Cup win would give his side on the run-in. A 2–0 reverse against Ron Atkinson's emerging West Bromwich Albion in the FA Cup sixth round at the Hawthorns ended hopes of a domestic treble. Clough had given John McGovern and Archie Gemmill short shrift before the match when they told him they were struggling with injuries. 'What's wrong with you, McGovern?' he asked his captain when he saw him in the treatment room. 'I explained that I had a pelvic problem, and that I just couldn't run,' recounted Clough's former captain to me. 'You never could run. You're playing tomorrow,' Clough told him. His tack with Gemmill was slightly different after the Scot told him he was only 50 per cent fit. 'But you're twice as quick as the opposition so you're playing tomorrow too,' Clough replied. After the 2–0 defeat, Clough was merciless towards the struggling duo, telling a journalist, 'We had one midfielder [O'Neill] playing today. It's a shame the other two didn't bother to join in.'

Peter Shilton's superb reflex saves were crucial in Forest maintaining their form in the spring, with Clough expressing admiration for Shilton's broad shoulders, long arms and zealous training regime. His save at Highfield Road, on the day Forest won the title following a goalless draw with Coventry, was the most stupendous of all. Following a lofted cross from Ian Wallace, the Sky Blues' Mick Ferguson headed the ball from five yards out and Shilton

THE WHOLE WORLD IN THEIR HANDS

miraculously deflected the ball over the crossbar. Ferguson fell to his knees in disbelief. 'To finish seven points clear of Liverpool, given that only three years ago many of these players were playing in the Second Division, is nothing short of unbelievable,' exalted Clough. To have steered one provincial team – Derby County – to promotion from the Second Division and then the title was achievement enough, but to do it twice was utterly extraordinary. With Forest qualifying for the European Cup, Clough had a chance to partly banish the raging sense of injustice which festered within him following Derby's exit in the same competition at the hands of Juventus and scoop the European Cup. For the Forest players who'd played in the Anglo-Scottish Cup two years earlier, the team spirit affirming road-trips they'd enjoyed were firmly back on the menu.

Even as Forest landed silverware, Peter Taylor's withering gaze never lost its intensity, and he continued to look for signs of complacency and battle fatigue amongst the players. In 1978, striker Peter Withe had endured several barren spells in front of goal, and Taylor reckoned Withe had gone off the boil. After one game of the 1978–79 season, where Forest drew at home to Tottenham, Withe was sold to Newcastle United for £225,000, which replenished the coffers, but left Forest short up front. The reigning champions drew their first four games of the league season, scoring only a solitary goal in the process. Critics suggested that Withe had been jettisoned prematurely, particularly as Liverpool won their first four matches, opening up a commanding gap from the chasing pack. Although Forest had conceded vital ground to Liverpool, the introduction of striker Garry Birtles, who'd thought long and hard about returning to his job as a carpet fitter after initially failing to break into the first team, proved timely when it came to the European Cup first-round double-header against Bob Paisley's side. Birtles's all-round game was a revelation in Forest's 2–0 first-leg win. Clough sensing that the players were tense before the away leg, the team headed off to Scarborough once again, where they washed down their lunch with a glass or two of Chablis and proceeded to squeeze the life out of Liverpool at Anfield, grabbing a 0–0 draw to steer them safely into the next round in late September.

The era of English football's 'million-pound madness' – as tabloids later described it – was ushered in by Clough, in front of a gaggle of TV crews and cameramen on 9 February 1979 at the City Ground. The irascible Forest boss, wearing his firebird-red sports jacket, glanced at his new million-pound man – forward Trevor Francis – picked up his squash racquet and semi-joked, 'I've brought this along in case he [Francis] makes a balls of it [signing the contract] and then I'll whack him with it.' It was typical of Clough's non-conformist approach that at such a seismic moment for Forest and English football, he chose to lark about. Concerned that Forest were treading water in the league, Clough made his move for Birmingham City's jet-heeled forward Francis. 'Trevor is star quality,' explained Clough's assistant Peter Taylor, 'and he'll add flair to the team.' Oddly, the only rival bid came from mid-table Coventry City, whose chairman, Jimmy Hill, was also co owner of NASL side Detroit Express, for whom Francis had played the previous summer. 'We'd have bettered the wage which Forest paid him,' Jimmy Hill told me, 'but Forest could offer him European Cup football, which we couldn't.'

There remains some conjecture over Francis's fee, with Clough claiming he paid £999,999 because he didn't want Francis saddled with being the first million-pound footballer, but by the time VAT and other fees were factored in, the price rose to around £1.18 million. Clough believed in an egalitarian policy for all his players. Asked by a journalist at the press conference where and when

Francis would play in the team (he was cup-tied for the early rounds in Europe and the domestic cups), Clough responded bluntly, 'He'll play when I select him.' And so it proved. Francis, banned from bringing in his own soap and towel ('You'll use the same gear as all the others, young man,' Clough warned him), was instructed to pour the tea for his teammates in games he wasn't playing. Like all clubs, Forest had suffered during the bitter winter, and had only played two league games since Boxing Day. Clough was distinctly unimpressed when Arsenal knocked Forest out of the FA Cup at a slowly thawing City Ground in late February, courtesy of Frank Stapleton's towering header and, a week later, lambasted his new million-pound man at half-time in an away match at Ipswich. Francis punched a cross into the net, and the referee ticked him off after spotting the infringement. 'We are Nottingham Forest. Don't ever do that again while you are playing for this football club,' a furious Clough barked. Without cup-tied Francis, Forest retained the League Cup, defeating Southampton 3–2 with two goals from Garry Birtles, and there were also the latter stages of the European Cup to look forward to.

After beating Liverpool in the first round, in October, Forest had travelled to play AEK Athens in the European Cup and, despite a hostile reception by the Greek fans, acquitted themselves well, winning 2–1 thanks to goals from McGovern and Birtles. Forest hammered AEK 5–1 at the City Ground, and swatted Grasshopper Zürich aside 5–2 on aggregate in the quarter-final. 'Clough and Taylor treated European football as an adventure,' explained Ian Bowyer, 'and the 1978–79 season flew by because we played so many matches.' Some of the swagger had gone from Forest's game, with Clough and Taylor reasoning that keeping both the ball and clean sheets were the keys to European success. The semi-final against FC Köln was tense. On a sodden pitch, reminiscent of the Baseball Ground's surface, the West German champions ran Forest ragged at the City Ground. 'We were a little surprised,' Ian Bowyer told me, 'not because Köln weren't a very a good side, but because we thought they'd sit back. Instead they came at us.' Belgian forward Roger Van Gool put Köln into the lead and then set up a second for German international Dieter Müller. Birtles pulled a goal back before half-time, and then Bowyer blasted home from 10 yards out like the striker he once was, before Robertson headed home to give Forest a 3–2 lead. In the dying seconds, Yasuhiko Okudera – the first Japanese footballer to play professionally in Europe – grabbed a dramatic equaliser for Köln. In Germany, Burns and Lloyd soaked up all the punishment that Köln meted out before Bowyer headed home a flick from John Robertson's corner in the second half. 'When you achieve what we went on to achieve, you look back at certain key moments, and this is my abiding memory of the European Cup run, for obvious reasons.' Forest, 4–3 winners on aggregate, had made it into the European Cup final where they would face Swedish champions Malmö.

Englishman Bobby Houghton worked a miracle with Malmö, a club which only turned full-time in 1977. This was despite a recession in Sweden that saw Kockums shipyard, Malmö's major employers, fall into terminal decline. At Halmstadts, Roy Hodgson also ushered in an era of success, and, to Swedish football fans, the influential 'Bob 'n' Roy', as they became known, tripped off the tongue as easily as ABBA's 'Benny 'n' Björn'. Houghton's home-grown teams were utilitarian and played a strict 4–4–2 formation, with zonal marking at the heart of their success. Malmö sides were hardly easy on the eye, and the report which Clough and Taylor received on Houghton's side suggested they were ordinary, at best. But they were ultra-fit and tactically astute. En route to the final, they'd defeated Monaco, Dynamo Kyiv, Wisła Kraków and Austria Wien. Goals were at a premium, but the Swedes were generally watertight at the back. Malmö were struck by ill fortune in the lead-up to the final. Talismanic striker-turned-sweeper Bo Larsson injured ligaments against Kraków and Roy Andersson, recently named Swedish Player of the Year, was also ruled out of the final in Munich. Captain Staffan Tapper broke a bone in his foot in training the night before and, although he started the match, he was substituted in the first half.

Houghton described the 6:1 odds against his team as 'insulting', and set the scene for a cagey final by arguing, 'Our duty is not to football as a spectacle, but to our club.' Brian Clough picked Trevor Francis, who was by this time eligible to play in the European Cup, although when he found out that Francis was offered a £1,000 deal to wear new boots for the match he threatened to drop him. 'You'll wear the same pair you've worn all bloody season,' he scowled. Clough also picked Frank Clark, who'd missed much of the season with injury, over Archie Gemmill and Martin O'Neill, who'd only recently recovered from injury.

In a stultifying first half, punctuated only by referee Erich Linemayr peeping his whistle each time Birtles or Woodcock became ensnared in Malmö's well-marshalled offside trap, Forest failed to show anything like the panache they'd demonstrated under Clough and Taylor over the past three years. Although the game was lent a futuristic backdrop by the Olympiastadion's undulating roof of acrylic transparent glass canopies, Forest resorted to a tried and tested formula to unlock Malmö's obdurate defence. As the Austrian official checked his watch at the end of the half, Ian Bowyer pinged the ball out left to find John Robertson. The Swedish champions had tasked two players – Roland Andersson and Robert Prytz – with closing down Forest's main playmaker. For forty-five minutes, they stuck to their job manfully, but in the forty-sixth,

Robertson, described as the 'fat man' by Clough to journalists earlier that day, sauntered down the touchline, gave his markers the slip and dispatched a perfect cross. It was headed home by Clough's million-pound player, Trevor Francis, whose momentum from the header sent him tumbling into the ground's shot-put circle. 'Well that's what I *wanted* to see Robertson do,' exclaimed a relieved Barry Davies, commentating on the match for the BBC. It proved to be the winning goal, although, in the second half, Robertson came close to doubling Forest's lead when he hit the post. Forest, with their disparate band of players, many of whom had been dismissed as has-beens and lost causes, now ruled Europe.

Frank Clark, originally bought by Clough to help Forest climb out of Division Two, played his final match that night. 'There are worse ways to bow out,' he told me in our 2021 interview, before describing the 'sense of incredulity' at what Forest had accomplished. 'It was such a rapid rise to become European champions, and it was all done without a huge investor bankrolling the whole thing.' For captain John McGovern, lifting the silver pot with the big ears 'was, apart from holding my children for the first time, the greatest feeling of my life'. And substitute John O'Hare, the 33-year-old striker-turned-defender, reflected upon the fact that 'we'd won medals which most of us couldn't possibly have conceived we would less than two years before'. By moulding Kenny Burns and Larry Lloyd, both fully paid-up members of the awkward squad, into arguably the most effective central defensive pairing in Europe, Clough and Taylor proved they were footballing alchemists. And Clough had now finally trumped his bête noire Don Revie, who'd never won the European Cup with Leeds.

The goal provider and goal scorer spoke volumes for the new approach that Clough and Taylor adopted to managing the club. Robertson had been practically bullied (particularly in the early days) into becoming a top player at Forest, whereas Francis had been feted as a stellar talent since he made his debut for Birmingham at sixteen. Despite the different backgrounds, they were now both European Cup winners, playing football the Clough and Taylor way.

The 1979 European Cup final between Nottingham Forest and Malmö neatly encapsulated the fact that the 1970s was an era when provincial clubs (both at home and abroad) enjoyed their heyday. It was of its time. In the latter part of the decade, a clutch of provincial clubs made it to European Cup finals, including Saint-Étienne, Borussia Mönchengladbach and Bruges, but they all failed to win. Now, Forest (with a metropolitan population of just 470,000) had overcome Malmö (with a population of 600,000) to become kings of Europe, and Forest were the ultimate provincial success stories. 'I'd like this feeling to go on for ever,' Brian Clough said after the 1979 European Cup victory. But nothing stays the same. Forest directors were already looking to the future. When the club signed Trevor Francis back in January, Peter Taylor had said that 'Trevor's signing will help us pack our brand-new grandstand'. Despite concerns over City Ground attendances, the Forest board made the decision to spend £2.5 million on an 8,000 double-decker stand, complete with executive boxes. The board believed they would recoup the cost of the stand if the team qualified for Europe each year and superstar players like Francis helped entice the crowds to matches. Chairman Stuart Dryden insisted that the scheme wouldn't affect transfer spending and that the loan for the stand would be paid off in five years. As it turned out, he was wrong on both counts. In the short term, the purchase of Francis appeared to vindicate the buoyant confidence surrounding the club, but by shelling out £1 million on Francis, Clough had released the genie from the bottle. In Munich, Francis had delivered on the grand stage, but, given Forest's size, there could be no margin for error when it came to making major transfers work: Justin Fashanu's million-pound move to the City Ground from Norwich City in the summer of 1980 proved disastrous for himself, for Forest and for the Clough–Taylor partnership.

In the May 1979 general election, as Margaret Thatcher defeated James Callaghan at the polls, New Right economic thinking won out over socialism, and, throughout the 1980s, furrow-browed directors attempted to balance the books and pondered how to maximise their clubs' revenue streams in testing economic times. Liverpool announced a 'commercial relationship' with Japanese company Hitachi that commenced at the start of the 1979–80 season. The two-year £100,000 agreement with the Japanese conglomerate allowed the club to flash the brand in any league games that weren't televised. Manchester United's board of directors discussed the possibility of selling club shares to raise extra capital. Larger clubs wanted, and quickly received, a larger slice of the footballing pie. The free market, falling attendances and spiralling transfer fees had alarming consequences for several of English football's bigger names in the '80s. On the European stage, clubs from larger industrial cities like Liverpool, Turin and Milan quickly reasserted themselves, effectively ending the era of the provincial club.

Against a bewildering backdrop of violence and tragedy, football entered its own brave new world of million-pound transfer madness, sponsorship deals, more lucrative TV contracts and an elite of increasingly moneyed stars.

ACKNOWLEDGEMENTS

This book wouldn't have been possible without the cooperation, kindness and good humour of so many people over the past twenty-five years. I'd firstly like to thank Barry Davies, who for me will always be the stirring and evocative voice of '70s football, for writing the foreword for the book.

Secondly, my huge thanks to the '70s footballers who spoke to me, giving their time freely and generously, several of whom have sadly passed away in the intervening period. Gentlemen, it was an absolute pleasure to speak to you all, either face-to-face in pre-pandemic times or via the various miracles of modern technology more recently. I've done my best to ensure that your distinctive voices ring loud and clear throughout the book: Colin Addison, Alan Ball, Brendon Batson, Kevin Beattie, George Best, Stan Bowles, Ian Bowyer, Ian Callaghan, Jack Charlton ('Just get on and write the bloody thing'), Trevor Cherry, Frank Clark, Ray Clemence, Ray Crawford, Terry Curran, Tommy Docherty, Alan Durban, Dick Graham, Les Green, Brian Greenhoff, Ron Guthrie, Gordon Hill, Alan Hudson, Emlyn Hughes, Norman Hunter, Chris Kelly, Ray Kennedy, Brian Labone, Trevor Lee, Malcolm Macdonald, Roy McFarland, Peter McGillicuddy, John McGovern, Dave Mackay, Rodney Marsh, Billy Meadows, Jim Montgomery, Arnold Mühren,

John O'Hare, Roger Osborne, Peter Osgood, Ronnie Radford, Cyrille Regis, Alan Shoulder, Jim Smith, Tommy Smith, Alberto Tarantini, Frans Thijssen, Dennis Tueart, Phil Walker, Frank Worthington.

Thanks also to the impresarios, designers, agents, commentators, officials and pipe smokers I spoke to, whose voices and designs lent the period its distinctive flavour. Your candour was much appreciated: Barry Davies, Gordon Hill (referee), Jimmy Hill, Lindsay Jelley, Hugh Johns, Brian Moore, Bert Patrick, Ken Stanley, Jack Taylor, Paul Trevillion, David Vine, Malcolm Wagner.

And finally, to the following supporters for their time and memories: Peter Brookes (Manchester United), Pete Jessop (Liverpool), Billy Plummer (Millwall), Chris Richards (Hereford United).

I'm also grateful to the following for opening their contact books – both virtual and real – and helping me gain access to some of my interviewees: Danny Taylor, Leo Moynihan, Anton Rippon, Nigel Gordon, Tom van Hulsen, John Devlin, Lance Hardy and Matt Healey. And to Veronica Lake, the Blyth Spirit website, former Millwall photographer Jim Standen and Dennis Tueart for access to photos. To Dave Poulter and Jim Standen for supplying me with the retro magazines. And to the sorely missed Lance Hardy, who put me in touch with Barry Davies.

Also to my schoolmates Barry and Phil, for their friendship and football chat over the past forty years (and counting!), and to Seb and Brummie for the hours spent watching football videos like *101 Great Goals* at Keele when we should have been working. And to William and Sharn for the lockdown walks and the '70s football nattering; chaps, you have no idea how your encouraging words helped as the project took shape during such bizarre times.

I'm hugely grateful to James Stephens and Olivia Beattie at Biteback for commissioning the book, and to James Lilford for his boundless enthusiasm, encouragement, fact-checking and diligent editing of the manuscript. It's been a pleasure and a truly immersive experience. Thank you.

And finally, to my wife Helen, for helping me choose the book's title during a long traffic jam on the M4, and my lovely girls, Phoebe and Lacie, who unceasingly rolled their eyes at me each time I blasted out 'Get It On' (or 'Turn It Off' – as it became known) when I'd finished writing each chapter xx

BIBLIOGRAPHY

Barrett, Norman, *The Daily Telegraph Football Chronicle* (London: Stanley Paul, 1993).

Bidmead, Steve, *Bowles* (London: Virgin, 2002).

Bolton, Stuart and Paul Collier, *Trailing George Best: The Manchester Haunts of United's Greatest* (Hove: Pitch Publishing, 2018).

Bowles, Stan, *Stan Bowles: The Autobiography* (London: Orion Publishing, 2004).

Burtenshaw, Norman, *Whose Side are You on, Ref?* (London: Barker, 1973).

Clough, Brian, *The Autobiography* (London: Corgi, 1994).

Crooks, Richard, *Grandad, What was Football Like in the 1970s?* (Hove: Pitch Publishing, 2017).

Davies, Hunter, *Glory Game* (Edinburgh: Mainstream, 1972).

Dawson, Jeff, *Back Home: England and the 1970 World Cup* (London: Orion, 2001).

Denton, Graham, *Me and My Big Mouth: When Cloughie Sounded Off in the TV Times* (Hove: Pitch Publishing, 2019).

Dunphy, Eamon, *Only A Game? The Diary of a Professional Footballer* (Harmondsworth: Penguin Books, 1987).

Francis, Tony, *Clough: A Biography* (London: Stanley Paul, 1989).

Hardy, Lance, *Stokoe, Sunderland and '73: The Story of the Greatest FA Cup Final Shock of All Time* (London: Orion, 2009).

Herbert, Ian, *Quiet Genius: Bob Paisley, British Football's Greatest Manager* (London: Bloomsbury, 2017).

Hern, Bill and David Gleave, *Football's Black Pioneers: The Stories of the First Black Players to Represent the 92 League Clubs* (London: Conker Publishing, 2020).

Hewitt, Paolo and Mark Baxter, *The Fashion of Football* (Edinburgh: Mainstream, 2004).

Hey, Stan, *Liverpool's Dream Team* (Edinburgh: Mainstream, 1997).

Hill, Gordon and Jason Tomas, *Give a Little Whistle: The Recollections of a Remarkable Referee* (London: Souvenir Press, 1975).

Hill, Jimmy, *The Jimmy Hill Story* (London: Hodder, 1998).

Hornby, Nick, *Fever Pitch: A Fan's Life* (London: Victor Gollancz, 1992).

Howell, Denis, *Made in Birmingham: The Memoirs of Denis Howell* (London: Queen Anne, 1990).

Hudson, Alan, *The Working Man's Ballet* (London: Robson Books, 1997).

Inglis, Simon, *The Football Grounds of England and Wales* (London: Willow, 1983).

Kavanagh, Dermot, *Different Class: Football, Fashion and Funk – The Story of Laurie Cunningham* (London: Unbound, 2019).

Keegan, Kevin, *My Life in Football: The Autobiography* (London: Macmillan, 2018).

Keith, John, *The Essential Shankly* (London: Robson Books, 2001).

Kelly, Stephen, *Back Page Football: A Century of Newspaper Coverage* (London: Queen Anne, 1988).

Kelly, Stephen, *Bill Shankly, It's Much More Important Than That: The Biography* (London: Virgin, 1997).

Kuper, Simon and Stefan Szymanski, *Why England Lose & Other Curious Football Phenomena Explained* (London: HarperCollins, 2009).

Kurt, Richard, *The Red Army Years: Manchester United in the 1970s* (London: Headline, 1997).

Kurt, Richard, *Red Devils: A History of Man United's Rogues and Villains* (London: Prion Books, 1998).

Lovejoy, Joe, *Bestie: A Portrait of a Legend* (London: Pan, 1998).

Macdonald, Malcolm, *Supermac: My Autobiography* (Newbury: Highdown, 2003).

McKinstry, Leo, *Sir Alf: A Major Reappraisal of the Life and Times of England's Greatest Football Manager* (London: HarperSport, 2006).

Marsh, Rodney, *I Was Born a Loose Cannon* (Altrincham: Optimum Publishing, 2010).

Morris, Desmond, *The Soccer Tribe* (London: Cape, 1981).

Mourant, Andrew, *Don Revie: Portrait of a Footballing Enigma* (London: Mainstream, 2003).

Osgood, Peter, *King of Stamford Bridge* (London: Mainstream, 2002).

Parkinson, Michael, *Best: An Intimate Biography* (London: Hutchinson, 1975).

Parkinson, Michael, *George Best: A Memoir* (London: Hodder & Stoughton, 2018).

Partridge, Pat, *Oh Ref!* (London: Souvenir Press, 1979).

Peace, David, *The Damned Utd* (London: Faber and Faber, 2006).

Rees, Paul, *The Three Degrees, The Men Who Changed British Football Forever* (London: Constable, 2014)

Richards, Steve, *The Prime Ministers: Reflections on Leadership From Wilson to Johnson* (London: Atlantic Books, 2019).

Ronay, Barney, *The Manager: The Absurd Ascent of the Most Important Man in Football* (London: Sphere, 2010).

Sandbrook, Dominic, *State Of Emergency: The Way We Were: Britain 1970–1974* (London: Penguin, 2010).

Sandbrook, Dominic, *Seasons in the Sun: The Battle for Britain, 1974–1979* (London: Penguin, 2012).

Spurling, Jon, *Rebels For the Cause: The Alternative History of Arsenal Football Club* (London: Mainstream, 2003).

Steen, Rob, *The Mavericks: English Football When Flair Wore Flares* (Edinburgh: Mainstream, 1994).

Taylor, Rogan and Andrew Ward, *Kicking and Screaming: An Oral History of Football in England* (London: Robson Books, 1995).

Tesser, Greg, *Chelsea FC In The Swinging '60s: Football's First Rock 'n' Roll Club* (Stroud: The History Press, 2013).

Thomas, Clive, *By the Book* (London: Willow, 1984).

Ticher, Mike (ed.), *FOUL: Best of Football's Alternative Paper, 1972–1976* (London: Simon & Schuster, 1987).

Tossell, David, *Big Mal: The High Life and Hard Times of Malcolm Allison, Football Legend* (Edinburgh: Mainstream, 2008).

Tossell, David, *Tommy Doc: The Controversial and Colourful Life of One of Football's Most Dominant Personalities* (Edinburgh: Mainstream, 2013).

Van Hulsen, Tom, *Game Changers: The Remarkable Story of Dutch Masters Arnold Mühren And Frans Thijssen* (London: Portman Road Products, 2016).

Wagner, Malcolm and Tom Page, *George Best & Me: Waggy's Tale* (London: Empire Publishing, 2010).

White, Jim, *The Manchester United Dream Team* (Edinburgh: Mainstream, 1998).

Williams, John, *Red Men: Liverpool Football Club: The Biography* (London: Mainstream, 2010).

Wilson, Jonathan, *The Anatomy of England: A History in Ten Matches* (London: Orion, 2010).

Wilson, Jonathan, *Brian Clough: Nobody Ever Says Thank You* (London: Orion, 2011).

Wilson, Jonathan, *The Anatomy of Liverpool: A History in Ten Matches* (London: Orion, 2013).

Winner, David, *Brilliant Orange: The Neurotic Genius of Dutch Football* (London: Bloomsbury, 2000).

ABOUT THE AUTHOR

Author photo © Helen Spurling

A history and politics teacher by day, Jon Spurling has written articles and interviewed footballers for numerous publications at home and abroad, including *FourFourTwo*, *When Saturday Comes*, *The Blizzard*, *Nutmeg*, *11 Freunde* and the official Arsenal programme. He has authored six previous books, including the bestselling *Highbury: The Story of Arsenal in N.5* and *Death or Glory – The Dark History of the World Cup*. A child of the '70s, he is currently writing an '80s follow-up to *Get It On* and lives in Canterbury with his wife and two daughters. He tweets from @JonSpurling1.

INDEX

379

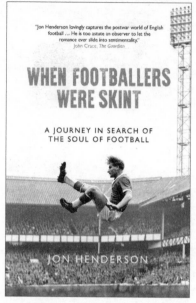